T0291192

Managing Interpartner Cooperation in Strategic Alliances

A volume in
Research in Strategic Alliances
T. K. Das, *Series Editor*

Research in Strategic Alliances

T. K. Das, Series Editor

Published

Researching Strategic Alliances: Emerging Perspectives (2010)
  Edited by T. K. Das

Strategic Alliances in a Globalizing World (2011)
  Edited by T. K. Das

Behavioral Perspectives on Strategic Alliances (2011)
  Edited by T. K. Das

Strategic Alliances for Value Creation (2012)
  Edited by T. K. Das

Management Dynamics in Strategic Alliance (2012)
  Edited by T. K. Das

Managing Knowledge in Strategic Alliances (2013)
  Edited by T. K. Das

Interpartner Dynamics in Strategic Alliances (2013)
  Edited by T. K. Das

Managing Public-Private Strategic Alliances (2014)
  Edited by T. K. Das

Strategic Alliances for Innovation and R&D (2014)
  Edited by T. K. Das

Managing Multipartner Strategic Alliances (2015)
  Edited by T. K. Das

Strategic Alliances for SME Development (2015)
  Edited by T. K. Das

Governance Issues in Strategic Alliances (2016)
  Edited by T. K. Das

Managing Alliance Portfolios and Networks (2017)
  Edited by T. K. Das

Managing Trust in Strategic Alliances (2018)
  Edited by T. K. Das

Managing Interpartner Risks in Strategic Alliances (2019)
  Edited by T. K. Das

Managing the Partners in Strategic Alliances (2021)
  Edited by T. K. Das

Managing Interpartner Cooperation in Strategic Alliances (2022)
  Edited by T. K. Das

In Development

Managing International Strategic Alliances
  Edited by T. K. Das

Managing Interpartner Cooperation in Strategic Alliances

edited by

T. K. Das
City University of New York

INFORMATION AGE PUBLISHING, INC.
Charlotte, NC • www.infoagepub.com

Library of Congress Cataloging-in-Publication Data

CIP record for this book is available from the Library of Congress
http://www.loc.gov

ISBNs: 978-1-64802-960-8 (Paperback)

978-1-64802-961-5 (Hardcover)

978-1-64802-962-2 (ebook)

CONTENTS

Foreword to the Book Series
Michael A. Hitt .... *vii*

About the Book Series
T. K. Das .... *ix*

1. The Legitimation Process of a New Multipartner Alliance
    Renate Taubeneder, Jens K. Roehrich, and Brian Squire *1*

2. Embracing the Competition-Cooperation Angst: Individual
    Ambivalence as a Driver of Strategic Alliance Performance
    Hilary Schloemer, Kristie Rogers, and Laura Poppo *33*

3. The Imbrication of Internal and External Coopetition in
    Strategic Alliances
    Kaouther Ben Jamaa-Boubaya, Olivier Furrer, Foued Cheriet,
    Laure Dikmen, and Mouhoub Hani *63*

4. Institutional Differences and the Value of Identity Bridging
    Role of Trust in Cross-Border Alliances
    Rekha Krishnan and Preet S. Aulakh *91*

5. A Contingent View of Interfirm Cooperation: The Role of
    Firm Similarity in the Linkages Between Trust and Contract
    Steven S. Lui, James Robins, and Hang-yue Ngo *129*

6. Affiliated or Aligned? Orchestration Modes for Multipartner
    Innovation Among Incumbent Firms and New Ventures
    Pia Kerstin Neudert and Markus Kreutzer *155*

7. R&D Collaboration and Multimarket Contact:
How Overlap and Asymmetry Influence Partner Selection
Ha Hoang 201

8. The Effect of Knowledge Flows on the Decision to
Cooperate: Differences for Sector and Firm Size
*Eva-María Mora-Valentín, Marta Ortiz-de-Urbina-Criado, and
Ángeles Montoro-Sánchez* 225

9. A Network Approach to Open Innovation and
Strategic Alliances
Amalya L. Oliver and Gordon Müller-Seitz 247

10. Social Technology and Stability/Transformation of Alliance
Networks: Dilemmas and Paradoxes of Cooperation
Sof Thrane and Jan Mouritsen 275

11. How Much Does Partner Diversity Matter for Alliance
Performance, Really? A Meta-Analysis
Giulio Ferrigno and Angelo M. Solarino 305

12. To Cooperate or Not to Cooperate? The Dilemma Faced by
Inexperienced Firms in R&D Consortia
Isabel Estrada, Natalia Martin-Cruz, and Victor M. Martin-Pérez..... 329

About the Contributors 355

Index 367

FOREWORD TO THE BOOK SERIES

Relationships have been important to commercial activity and economic transactions for thousands of years. Yet, the development of a global competitive landscape has substantially enhanced the importance of partnerships between economic entities. These partnerships, referred to as strategic alliances, provide access to resources and capabilities that allow firms to gain economies of scope and to increase their productivity and innovation. The economies, productivity and innovations are necessary to at least maintain competitive parity and especially to achieve a competitive advantage in the often highly competitive global markets. Strategic alliances have also become a prominent means of entering new markets, especially foreign markets. Therefore, alliances and the networks of firms of which they are a part have become essential for the conduct of business for all types of firms, large, small, established, and new. Because of their growing importance, research on strategic alliances has increased markedly in the last two decades. Yet, there is need for an authoritative compendium of strategic alliance research and knowledge. This book series on *Research in Strategic Alliances* fills this critically important gap in our field. It provides a thorough examination of significant topics that provide complete and up-to-date knowledge on strategic alliances. This book series will serve as a catalyst for more effective management of strategic alliances and will guide future research on them. I commend it to you.

—Michael A. Hitt
Distinguished Professor and Joe B. Foster Chair in Business Leadership at Texas A&M University, and Past President of the Academy of Management and the Strategic Management Society.

Managing Interpartner Cooperation in Strategic Alliances, pp. vii–vii
Copyright © 2022 by Information Age Publishing
www.infoagepub.com
All rights of reproduction in any form reserved.

ABOUT THE BOOK SERIES

The globalization of markets has led to increased interdependence among business firms, leading to an explosion in the number of strategic alliances. Strategic alliances, briefly, are cooperative arrangements aimed at achieving the strategic objectives of two or more partner firms. These interfirm arrangements can range from joint R&D to equity-based joint ventures. However, the scholarship relating to strategic alliances remains largely dispersed in the literatures of traditional academic disciplines such as strategic management, marketing, economics, and sociology.

This book series on strategic alliances will cover the essential progress made thus far in the literature and elaborate upon fruitful streams of scholarship. More importantly, the book series will focus on providing a robust and comprehensive forum for new scholarship in the field of strategic alliances. In particular, the books in the series will cover new views of interdisciplinary theoretical frameworks and models (dealing with resources, risk, trust, control, cooperation, learning, opportunism, governance, developmental stages, performance, etc.), significant practical problems of alliance organization and management (such as alliance capability, interpartner conflict, internal tensions, use of information technology), and emerging areas of inquiry. The series will also include comprehensive empirical studies of selected segments of business, economic, industrial, government, and non-profit activities with wide prevalence of strategic alliances. Through the ongoing release of focused topical titles, this book series will seek to disseminate theoretical insights and practical management information that will enable interested professionals to gain a rigorous and comprehensive understanding of the field of strategic alliances.

—T. K. Das
City University of New York

Series Editor
Research in Strategic Alliances

Managing Interpartner Cooperation in Strategic Alliances, pp. ix–ix
Copyright © 2022 by Information Age Publishing
www.infoagepub.com

CHAPTER 1

THE LEGITIMATION PROCESS OF A NEW MULTIPARTNER ALLIANCE

Renate Taubeneder, Jens K. Roehrich, and Brian Squire

ABSTRACT

This chapter explores the process of legitimizing a new multipartner alliance (MPA) between one buyer and five suppliers. The buyer-supplier MPA is distinct insofar as it is governed by two contracts (a vertical contract between the buyer and the suppliers, and a horizontal contract between the suppliers), and therefore introduces dynamics that would not be present when studying either dyadic vertical buyer-supplier relationships, or horizontal strategic alliances alone. Our in-depth, longitudinal case study, drawing on observations, interviews, site visits, board papers, and archival data, reveals how the formation of a new buyer-supplier MPA was initiated through a mechanism referred to as theorization: The buyer starts by problematizing conventional dyadic contracts, and introduces the buyer-supplier MPA as a novel and superior solution. The subsequent legitimation process was an interactive negotiation that occurred across both the vertical and horizontal relationships, and addressed dimensions of moral and pragmatic legitimacy. The longitudinal nature of our study enabled us to show that the legitimation process is characterized by episodes of legitimacy build up, break down, and repair, but that both types of legitimacy are needed before contract signature. We further found distinct drivers that support the build-up of each type of legitimacy.

Managing Interpartner Cooperation in Strategic Alliances, pp. 1–32
Copyright © 2022 by Information Age Publishing
www.infoagepub.com
1

INTRODUCTION

Strategic alliances are cooperative arrangements between two or more firms that aim to pursue mutual strategic objectives (Das & Teng, 2000). Establishing strategic alliances has become a central strategy to many firms as it can enable them to enter new markets quickly, to gain new competencies or resources, to share risks, or to develop new technologies (Eisenhardt & Schoonhoven, 1996). Multipartner alliances (MPAs), defined as interorganizational arrangements involving three or more firms (Lavie, Lechner, & Singh, 2007), and sometimes both vertical and horizontal partners (Lazzarini, Claro, & Mesquita, 2008), have become an increasingly popular choice for buying organizations seeking to consolidate formerly discrete dyadic relationships with suppliers to deliver large interorganizational projects. These cooperative buyer-supplier MPAs are distinctly different from R&D consortia, supplier networks, or (multipartner) joint ventures, which focus primarily on technical innovation (Lavie et al., 2007; Li, Eden, Hitt, Ireland, & Garrett, 2012; Mishra, Chandrasekaran, & Maccormack, 2015), as they involve both vertical buyer-supplier and horizontal supplier-supplier relationships (Lazzarini et al., 2008). Their purpose is often the delivery of services rather than the development and provision of goods (Aaltonen & Turkulainen, 2018; Suprapto, Bakker, Mooi, & Hertogh, 2016).

Prior strategy literature has argued that strategic alliances require inter-partner legitimacy (Kumar & Das, 2007), also sometimes called internal legitimacy. Interpartner legitimacy refers to the acceptance and support of an alliance by its member firms, and has been found vital to the formation and survival of new organizational structures (Paquin & Howard-Grenville, 2013; Persson, Lundberg, & Andresen, 2011; Zimmerman & Zeitz, 2002). The acceptance of and commitment to the alliance itself by its constituent parties, but also of each of the partners by the other partner(s), is essential to the formation and survival of a new alliance (Kumar & Das, 2007). In other words, this chapter does not investigate external legitimacy (the acceptance of an actor by the broader societal environment (Suchman, 1995), but the concept of "interpartner legitimacy" relating to legitimacy questions that "are found within such multi-partner entities (or alliances), whereby the legitimacy of each partner firm is at issue, have not been addressed by the current theories" (Kumar & Das, 2007, p. 1426). Building on the seminal work by Kumar and Das (2007), we argue that an initial focus (i.e., during alliance formation) on internal legitimacy (before turning to external legitimacy) may be an effective strategy in the long-term (in terms of impacting operation and performance processes). Legitimacy implies a congruency of values; hence, if a firm perceives its values to be aligned with the values of partnering firms, it will accept the decisions and behaviors of the other as their own (e.g., Brenner & Ambos, 2013; Kostova

& Roth, 2002). Interpartner legitimacy is vital to the formation of buyer-supplier MPAs, yet more difficult to establish due to the increased number of firms involved, when compared to dyadic alliances, and the unique structure consisting of horizontal and vertical ties (Hietajärvi & Aaltonen, 2018).

First, most MPAs, often described as horizontal agreements, are found in high-technology industries, and are referred to as strategic alliances or joint ventures in which firms decide to collaborate on R&D or new product development (NPD) activities (e.g., Fonti, Maoret, & Whitbred, 2017; Mishra et al., 2015). In contrast to MPAs, buyer-supplier MPAs are initiated by a large buyer that wants to contract the coordinated services delivered by multiple suppliers (Suprapto et al., 2016). Often these suppliers have no prior history of working together, or are competing for similar types of work within or outside the project (Hietajärvi & Aaltonen, 2018; Lloyd-Walker, Mills, & Walker, 2014). These often competing interests mean that it is difficult for the buyer to legitimate the buyer-supplier MPA and achieve high levels of commitment from suppliers (Hietajärvi & Aaltonen, 2018; Lloyd-Walker et al., 2014). Hence, the buyer has to legitimate the MPA with suppliers, who are otherwise opposed to this shared working arrangement.

Second, extant MPA research has shown that exchanges between multiple parties imply indirect reciprocity (Das & Teng, 2002), which make these arrangements more vulnerable to opportunism and free-riding behaviors than dyadic exchanges (Fonti et al., 2017; Zeng & Chen, 2003). Social exchanges in dyadic relationships are based on direct reciprocity as expectations and obligations are established between two parties (Das & Teng, 2002). In a MPA, reciprocity becomes more indirect as buyer and suppliers feed their resources into a common pool with often ill-defined boundaries of who does what and when (Das & Teng, 2002; Fonti et al., 2017). This encourages social dilemma situations in which firms evaluate how much effort they should allocate to the MPA (Zeng & Chen, 2003). To maximize the utility of their own limited resources, firms may choose to free-ride on other partners' efforts while reducing their own (Fonti et al., 2017). The increased number of parties and resulting complexity make it more challenging to develop contracts that are explicit enough to monitor and safeguard the MPA from such opportunism (Lavie et al., 2007; Li et al., 2012). Hence, to safeguard their interests and to be able to commit to it, suppliers may take an active stance in shaping the terms and conditions of the buyer-suppliers MPA. However, prior (interpartner) legitimacy research has predominantly focused on the actions of the legitimacy seeker without acknowledging the work or the legitimacy audience. This is an important omission given that the success of a MPA depends on the commitment of all parties involved.

Our research question, therefore, is: How does a buyer and its suppliers shape the interpartner legitimation of a novel buyer-supplier MPA?

To answer this question, we conducted a longitudinal case study on the formation of a new MPA between one buyer and five suppliers, delivering complex services at a nuclear construction site in the UK. We analyzed rich data sets comprised of both primary and secondary data in the form of observations, interviews, and archival data (including board papers) to answer our research question.

Our findings illustrate the interpartner legitimation processes underlying the formation of a new buyer-supplier MPA. In doing so, our study offers several contributions. First, we show the importance of theorization to initiate the legitimation process (Tolbert & Zucker, 1996). Second, our longitudinal study illustrates that the interpartner legitimation process is shaped by both the buyer and suppliers equally, which creates episodes of interpartner legitimacy build up, break down, and repair as parties negotiate the legitimacy of the MPA. Third, our analysis highlights the drivers for moral and pragmatic legitimacy for the buyer and suppliers during the legitimation process.

THEORETICAL BACKGROUND

Legitimacy and the Process of Legitimation

Institutional theorists understand legitimacy as the perception or assumption that the actions of an entity are desirable, proper, or appropriate within some socially constructed system of norms, values, beliefs, and definitions (Suchman, 1995). In other words, legitimacy is social approval, which enables the formation and survival of new structures (Zimmerman & Zeitz, 2002), and provides stability to institutions (Suchman, 1995). Early scholarly work on legitimacy focused on how an organization legitimizes itself within its broader external or societal environment (DiMaggio & Powell, 1983; Meyer & Rowan, 1977; Zucker, 1987). Legitimacy was found to be the driving force behind organizational strategies and structures as a firm's survival is dependent upon the support and acceptance of relevant stakeholders (Baum & Oliver, 1992; Dacin, 1997; Ruef & Scott, 1998). While this line of research often sees legitimacy as a static property, created in exchange with external audiences, more recent work focuses on legitimation as a process (e.g., Suddaby, Bitektine, & Haack, 2017), and the legitimation provided by internal audiences (Brown & Toyoki, 2013). In the case of buyer-supplier MPAs, internal legitimacy refers to the acceptance of the MPA as a viable form of organizing by all of the firms involved (Kumar & Das, 2007).

Processual work on legitimacy has defined legitimation as the "process that brings the unaccepted into accord with accepted norms, values, beliefs, practices, and procedures" (Zelditch, 2001, p. 9). Legitimation arises from the congruency and acceptance between the legitimacy seeker and its audience and, therefore, by definition, depends on consensus as a necessary precondition (Bitektine, 2011; Dowling & Pfeffer, 1975). Prior studies found that the attainment of legitimacy is an ongoing process of negotiation between multiple participants that each have a high degree of individual agency (Human & Provan, 2000; Suddaby et al., 2017).

A primary method of achieving legitimation is through a process of theorization (Greenwood, Suddaby, & Hinings, 2002; Suddaby et al., 2017), which consists of two dimensions: (i) the problematization of the status quo; and (ii) the "justification of a particular formal structural arrangement as a solution to the problem on logical or empirical grounds" (Tolbert & Zucker, 1996, p. 183). For example, Greenwood et al. (2002) examined the role of professional bodies and theorization in the major changes in the accounting profession over a 20-year period. They found that the justification of the change was predominantly based on moral values while pragmatic legitimacy played a lesser role.

Prior work on legitimation lacks an investigation of how the legitimation process is shaped by all parties involved, and not just one "institutional entrepreneur" that single-handily legitimizes a new venture or firm toward to an external audience (e.g., David, Sine, & Haveman, 2013; Sine, David, & Mitsuhashi, 2007). Hence, scholars have criticized prior work for artificially dividing the social world into legitimacy champions and their passive audience (Suddaby et al., 2017). It is therefore important to investigate the influential role of a buyer and its suppliers during the legitimation process to better understand how consensus between the values of the buyer and those of suppliers is achieved. Generally, theorization can be relevant to the legitimation of a new buyer-supplier MPA if firms problematize the previous dyadic organizational structures and convincingly confer the benefits of the MPA as a solution to these problems based on moral and pragmatic reasoning. The following section unpacks two types of legitimacy—moral and pragmatic—in more detail and discusses the potential implications for the legitimation process.

Pragmatic Legitimacy

Pragmatic legitimacy "rests on the self-interested calculations of an organization's most immediate audiences" (Suchman, 1995, p. 578). In Greenwood et al.'s (2002) study, pragmatic legitimacy depended on members seeing the functional superiority of the new organizational structure over the previous, problematized one. Kumar and Das (2007, p. 1434) reasoned that in the development process of strategic alliances, pragmatic legitimacy depended on members "see[ing] their involvement and contribution as furthering their own interests and the interests of the (larger) alliance." In the justification of a new MPA, this implies that the buyer and suppliers consider their involvement in and contribution to the MPA as advancing their own economic interests.

Pragmatic legitimacy is particularly important during alliance formation as it is here where partnering firms are most uncertain about the value they can expect from joining an alliance (Human & Provan, 2000; Kumar & Das, 2007; Paquin & Howard-Grenville, 2013). This uncertainty stems from two areas: (i) whether the anticipated alliance will generate the desired strategic value; and (ii) whether the partnering firms can and will contribute their fair share to support the undertaking (Kumar & Das, 2007). Hence, prior research suggested that to justify the MPA as the preferred solution, it is important that the buyer reduces uncertainty and communicates the expected value convincingly (Kumar & Das, 2007). However, in order for suppliers to accept the MPA as a preferred solution over a familiar (such as a dyadic) structure, the expected value might have to succeed the previous value given the additional horizontal threats inherent to MPAs due to indirect reciprocity (Fonti et al., 2017; Zeng & Chen, 2003). This may be unsustainable for the buyer, who sees the MPA as an opportunity to reduce costs. While prior studies have suggested that legitimation contains trade-offs between involved parties (Lee, Hiatt, & Lounsbury, 2017), these studies offer a limited understanding of how competing pragmatic interests shape the internal legitimation process.

Moral Legitimacy

The second type of legitimacy necessary in the legitimation process has been termed "moral legitimacy," and depends on judgments about whether the specific organizational structure is "the right thing to do" in terms of aligning with prevailing values and norms (Suchman, 1995, p. 579). It is important to note that despite its altruistic grounding, this legitimacy type is not entirely interest-free but reflects a pro-social logic, which differs deeply from narrow self-interest (Suchman, 1995). For instance, prior work showed that successful legitimation efforts require new organizational structures to appeal to the greater good, and the display of normative dignity by legitimacy seeking firms, such as by placing the legitimacy audiences interests above one's own, and thus openly rejecting narrow self-interests (e.g., David et al., 2013).

Greenwood et al. (2002) found that moral legitimacy was obtained by appealing to the traditional values inherent to the legitimacy audience's professional identity and demonstrating congruency with the proposed changes. Kumar and Das (2007) theoretically positioned that during the formation of alliances, moral legitimacy depends on whether partners behave properly, and moral legitimacy would be harmed by the violation of justice norms, the use of inappropriate negotiation tactics, as well as opportunistic behaviors or a lack of cooperation.

Persson et al. (2011) uncovered that low levels of moral legitimacy in the formation of a network improved once uncooperative firms were removed, which also impacted on pragmatic legitimacy as firms found it easier to agree on the strategic goals of the network. Of course, this option may not always be available within buyer-supplier MPAs, particularly where there is a lack of possible substitutes. Further, limited knowledge exists about how the MPA as a preferred solution is morally justified by both the buyer and suppliers. For instance, it may be difficult for the buyer to establish a narrative of how the MPA serves a greater good when it is abundantly clear that it does, in fact, provide much better commercial value to the buyer. Hence, this study fills this gap in prior studies to better understand the role of pragmatic and moral legitimacy during the formation of a new buyer-supplier MPA, and how buyer and suppliers influence the legitimation process.

METHODS

Research Setting and Case Selection

To study a MPA's legitimation process, we selected a MPA between one large project buyer (hereafter referred to as LPB) and five suppliers (Table 1.1) delivering complex services at a large nuclear construction project in the UK. LPB was established in 2008 to coordinate the design, construction, and commissioning of a new nuclear power plant in the UK. The timeframe for this study is from December 2017, when LPB approached suppliers with the intention of changing the siloed contracting approach, until June 2019, when the MPA contract was signed.

Our case selection was based on the following key criteria, which made it a logical candidate for sampling (Shah & Corley, 2006). First, for over 200 years it has been a common practice in the construction sector in the UK to employ suppliers on a dyadic "master-servant" basis. The shift toward more collaborative relationships such as MPAs has only occurred in recent years (Caldwell, Roehrich, & Davies, 2009; Hartmann et al., 2014; Roehrich & Lewis, 2014). This means that firms are often not used to this novel organizational structure whose success is still questioned. Hence, the formation of a MPA to replace more traditional dyadic arrangements requires legitimation among parties involved, who may have different expectations what a MPA should look like and what it can deliver.

Second, scholars as well as practitioners stress that the success of a MPA strongly relies on trust between the buyer and suppliers (Hietajärvi &

Table 1.1

Overview Suppliers and Buyer Organizations

	Electrical-CoA	Electrical-CoB	Mechanical Co	HVAC-Co	Support Co	LPB (buyer)
Ownership	Subsidiary of a UK public limited company	Family-owned for over 100 years	Subsidiary of a UK public limited company	UK subsidiary of a South Korean conglomerate	UK subsidiary of a French privately owned MNC	UK subsidiary of French MNC
Revenue (parent, in 2019; circa)	$10bn	$700m	$6bn	$16bn	$4bn	$87bn
Number of employees (Parent in 2020; circa)	20,000	3,000	30,000	40,000	40,000	165,000
Scope of work	Installation of electrical components		Installation of mechanical equipment	Installation of HVAC components	Scaffolding and other support services	Managing the construction of a new nuclear power station

Aaltonen, 2018). However, trust "is unlikely to exist at the outset" due to a lack of prior relationship experience or competition, and instead firms are required to "make an initial leap of faith" (Hietajärvi & Aaltonen, 2018). This leap of faith is particularly difficult given the traditionally adversarial nature prevalent in the construction sector (Zheng, Roehrich, & Lewis, 2008). Hence, parties rely on legitimizing of the MPA with all firms involved to gain commitment to the new organizational structure.

Data Collection and Sources

Our study combined primary data (observations, interviews, and site visits), secondary data (board papers, emails, personal meeting notes, presentation slides, government, and industry reports) sources, which we collected both live and retrospectively between 2017 and 2020 (Table 1.2). We collected data in three stages.

At first, in November 2017, two researchers attended a supplier event organized by LPB's parent company. At the event, we networked with several individuals working in LPB's supply chain and commercial teams, to help us build up an initial understanding of the supply chain and contracting processes at the project. In August 2018, we were invited for a conversation with LPB's commercial director, who informed us about LPB's plans to establish a MPA with five suppliers. During this meeting, we obtained confidential presentation slides and board papers, summarizing LPB's intentions and strategy with regards to the MPA formation.

Table 1.2

Overview of Data Sources and Use in Analysis

Data sources	Amount and sources	Use in analysis
Secondary data (414 pages)	6 LPB board papers (86 pages) 10 Presentations (166 slides) 2 Contract manuals and implementation plan (63 pages) 7 Emails Meeting notes (1st MPA supplier workshop; 7 pages) 3 policy reports (85 pages)	Familiarization with LPB language, vision, and strategy for the MPA, storyline of formation process including changes in strategy between board papers. Understanding project's industry and political background and resulting pressures on LPB.
Observations (167 hours)	2 site visits (8h) 159 meeting hours between October 2018–June 2019	Gathering data on the legitimation of the MPA during the MPA formation
Interviews (26 hours ~ 298 pages verbatim)	**First round (Sep. 2018–June 2019)** 11 semi- and unstructured interviews with LPB and supplier informants all involved in the formation process of the MPA including solicitors, commercial managers, and supplier project directors.	Clarification about the ongoing negotiation process including the emergence of formal and informal governance, and their impact on vertical and horizontal relationships as well as vertical and horizontal cooperation and competition.
	Second round (Dec. 2019–Oct. 2020) 16 semi-structured interviews with LPB and supplier informants including solicitors, engineers, commercial managers, and supplier project directors.	Triangulation of initial findings, gathering of further information to address any lack of clarity in the data on the MPA formation

Second, after carefully studying the obtained materials, the lead researcher was embedded at LPB to observe the formation of the MPA in real time. She conducted non-participant observations of internal LPB meetings, meetings between LPB and suppliers, as well as internal supplier meetings between October 2018 and June 2019 (marking the formation phase of the MPA). During this time, she also collected supporting secondary data, to complement the observational data and to triangulate possible findings. She further conducted interviews to clarify open questions, and to gather any additional information about the MPA formation. Third, after MPA contracts were signed, the lead researcher conducted semi-structured interviews to corroborate and refine emerging findings with informants from the field. To ensure the reliability and objectivity of findings (Aben, van der Valk, Roehrich, & Selviaridis, 2021; Gibbert & Ruigrok, 2010), she interviewed both supplier's and buyers' informants from different functional roles and hierarchical roles.

Data Analysis

We followed the principles of open-ended, inductive theory-building, iterating between data and theoretical constructs (Corbin & Strauss, 2008). We imported all data into NVivo, a qualitative data analysis software, to create an integrated and chronological database, consisting of observations, interview transcripts, and archival documents. We first coded the board papers, presentation slides, supplier notes, and any other materials relating to the problematization of the previous organizational structure. We then coded the observations and secondary data for moral and pragmatic legitimacy. For pragmatic legitimacy, we coded segments that illustrated financial interests of firms or saw the MPA as a superior organizational structure based on prior literature. For moral legitimacy, we coded behavioral values that saw the MPA as the right thing to do beyond self-interested motivations as well as cooperative behaviors. The initial findings informed our interviews with key informants from the field to verify accuracy and gather additional information, such as the events occurring before the fieldwork started. In the second round of coding, we coded the interviews, and subsequently developed a longitudinal process consisting of seven episodes that marked phases of legitimacy build up, break down, or repair. In defining the episodes, we followed Ring and Van De Ven's (1994, p. 112) suggestion of "critical incidents when parties engage in actions related to the development of their relationship." The lead author coded each data source individually before discussing it with the other two authors.

FINDINGS

Our analysis discerned three distinct types of episodes occurring in the legitimation process of an MPA: (1) episodes in which legitimacy was built (episodes 1 and 2); (ii) episodes in which legitimacy was harmed (episodes 3, 5, and 6); and (iii) episodes in which legitimacy was repaired (episode 4 and 7). Table 1.3 provides an overview of episode 1 in which the buyer first problematized the current dyadic structure, and episode 2 in which the buyer justified the new MPA structure based on moral and pragmatic legitimacy. Table 1.4 provides detail of the episodes that followed subsequently in the legitimation process. Both tables contain empirical evidence from the data, which is referred to in the text via numbering (e.g., [3]).

Table 1.3

Problematization of Dyadic Structure and Justification of New Solution

Episode 1: Supplier workshop (December 2017)	
PROBLEMATIZATION	**Data extract**
Buyer highlights challenges within current approach	[1] *"Poorly coordinated planning and sequencing of execution fails system transition requirements"* (LPB workshop slides, p. 6).
	[2] *"Resource duplication exists across the MPA cope. Delivery of a contract scope does not translate into a functional system. [...] Arrangements for site works bulk commodities and core manufacturing are not optimized. Unacceptable overall risk provisions"* (LPB workshop slides, p. 5).
Buyer highlights implications if no change happens	[3] *"The business case imposes some challenging objectives with average installation rates assumed at 5% whereas the best achieved at Flamanville (FA3) was between 1% & 2% (not sure what the measure is but the difference represents a 250% to 500% improvement!) [...] It was agreed by all that the application of the current approach and the use of the current delivery model would result in failure"* (Supplier workshop notes).
	[4] *"The Project will not successfully deliver the Installation Phase on Schedule in this current context and so a fundamental change in delivery approach is required"* (LPB workshop slides, p. 5).

(Table continued on next page)

Table 1.3 (Continued)

Problematization of Dyadic Structure and Justification of New Solution

JUSTIFICATION

Moral legitimacy	Data extract	Pragmatic legitimacy	Data extract
Establish power symmetry	[5] *"There needs to be to be a heavy focus on values [...] to achieve the commercial operating date in 2025: Collaboration, Camaraderie and Partnership [have] to be adopted"* (Supplier notes from meeting). [6] *"Any agreed solution to the [MPA] proposal needs to work for all parties"* (Supplier notes from meeting). [7] *"[LPB] has an idea of where it wishes to go and how it anticipates getting there but wants to engage with, and hear from, the key members of the [MPA] group"* (Supplier notes from meeting).	Superior functionality of MPA	[8] *"We brought a guy [...] who formed an alliance arrangement which, essentially, ended up rescuing the North Sea oil platform fleet"* (engineering manager, LPB) [9] *"It seem[ed] like a good idea, it takes away all of the difficulties that we might have, in terms of getting this project to the best solution it can be"* (Project Director, ElectricalCoA).
Focus on benefits for the project	[10] *"The **PROJECT** has to be the focus of all parties"* (Supplier notes from meeting). [12] *"There was not a heavy sell from [LPB]. There was a room of people talking about the best way to deliver the biggest project in Europe and I guess we came up with the conclusion that this was how it should be"* (Project Director, ElectricalCoA).	Highlight economic benefits of new solution	[13] *"Key strategic benefits: [...] organizational efficiencies and economies of scale; commercial rationalization, value generation and risk reduction"* (LPB workshop slides, p.16).

Table 1.4

Legitimation Process

Moral legitimacy	Data extract	Pragmatic legitimacy	Data extract
Episode 2: Contract discussions (January– June 2018)			
Equal development of solution (power symmetry)	[1] *"All of the businesses worked with the customer to look at how we might be able to take that forward"* (Project Director, MechanicalACo). [2] *"[LPB and] our commercial director, they came up with an outline plan and it developed in discussion fairly openly collaboratively really [...] in this true spirit of alliancing"* (Project Director, ElectricalCoA).	Improved supplier financial returns as compared to previous model	[5] *"What was the trigger for the suppliers is, once they recognized that they could earn collectively more money, better returns [...] they did not think this was possible. In the early days the [suppliers] did not think it was possible, and we slowly changed them"* (Commercial Director, LPB). [6] *"We did not know how difficult this was going to be, it seemed like a great idea. There was the potential of unloading very significant amounts of revenue into our businesses"* (Project Director, ElectricalCoA).
Collaborative negotiation tactics (power symmetry)	[3] *"We were not going to be aggressive [...] we would say what [are] your concerns? What are you really concerned about, so we understand where you are coming from"* (legal manager, LPB). [4] *"Often a main meeting will be followed by several sub meetings [...] It is about taking the issue and trying to re-understand it, reshape it"* (Project Director, Supplier D)	Minimize supplier risk exposure and liability	[7] *"If those commercial obligations and financial obligations to our shareholders are achieved just in the contract, then we do not need to work hard on that, we just invest more of our people in making the project go well rather than the legal and commercial aspects"* (Project Director, ElectricalCoA). [8] *"The traditional construction contracts were all target cost with pain, with liquidated damages, with all of those nasty things that contractors get but the [MPA] contract, none of that existed. None. There were only carrots, no sticks"* (Legal Manager, LPB).

(Table continued on next page)

Table 1.4 (Continued)

Legitimation Process

Moral legitimacy	Data extract	Pragmatic legitimacy	Data extract
Episode 3: Disagreement and postponed contract signature (June–August 2018)			
Equality	[9] "*[We] went out to China and had very lengthy sessions over in China. [...] It was all around how you get [everyone] on board and get them to buy in. [We also] went out to France and met with all the seniors within France [...] There was a lot of toing and froing between what the [suppliers] were willing to accept and what [LPB] was willing to accept*" (Project Director, MechanicalCo).	Increase supplier risk exposure	[11] "*They [..] wanted us to take risk on all of our profit and that was a big challenge for us, and we thought we cannot do that*" (project director, ElectricalCoA). [12] "*[LPB] were pushing very, very hard to get as much risk transferred to the [suppliers] as possible. [...] That was not a position that any of the partners were willing to accept*" (Project Director, MechanicalCo).
Focus on benefits for the project	[10] "*The [mechanical, electrical, HVAC work ...] so far, in Taishan, Flamanville and in Finland has been a disaster. In Taishan they had to redo it and pull out all the cables and each of those projects had a silo contracts mentality [...] and it did not work, and it has never worked so [..] what is the lesson learnt*" (Legal Manager, LPB).	Highlight superior function-ality of MPA	[13] "*If you have got a single coordinated mind, multi-teams working in a single space, it will be safer. And you will get better quality. We [went] to Flamanville [..] and there is a lot of damaged equipment, because people have installed equipment, [...] the next trade has gone in bashed into it, and it gets damaged. So, [the MPA improves] safety, quality, time and cost*" (Commercial Manager, LPB).

(Table continued on next page)

Table 1.4 (Continued)

Legitimation Process

Moral legitimacy	Data extract	Pragmatic legitimacy	Data extract
Episode 4: Signature of memorandum of understanding and of supplier contracts (September–October 2018)			
Equal partners (power symmetry)	[14] *"The MoU [was] a pretty thing. The principles that were agreed then … I mean that was the right thing to do. It sent out a very important message about [us] being able to overcome some pretty thorny issues"* (Project Director, MechanicalCo). [15] *"I remember attending the MoU signing and everyone was patting themselves on the back. It was, you know, happy clappy so that was definitely a buzz for a while"* (Legal Manager, LPB).	Re-alignment on commercial concerns	[16] *"After long discussions we renamed part of the base fee, and called it overhead, and then the incentive[s] were termed part of the fee, and all of that is at risk. That satisfied their need to […] say, all the fee is at risk. All of the fee is, but the overhead is not so that is how we got around that, and that was a major sticking point for both sides"* (Project Director, ElectricalCoA). [17] *"There was a degree of constructive ambiguity in the wordings of the MoU to allow different positions to progress at that point in time"* (Project Director, MechanicalCo).
Episode 5: Changes to MoU principles and second contract signature delay (November–December 2018)			
Self-interested behaviors	[18] *"Some of the stuff [LPB] introduced, was just shockingly bad. […] It made it very hard under the proposed metrics and measures for us to make any money and for us to achieve any milestones. The implementation plan that got put together; it was just rubbish. None of our comments were accepted. So, all our feedback was ignored"* (Project Director, SupportCo).	Increase supplier risk exposure	[21] *"[LPB] wanted to renegotiate all of [the risk] whereas our view was, we have already negotiated this. We have already agreed it. That is put to bed […] we are not coming backwards to revisit something which is underpinning the whole contract"* (Project Director, SupportCo).

(Table continued on next page)

Table 1.4 (Continued)

Legitimation Process

Moral legitimacy	Data extract	Pragmatic legitimacy	Data extract
Episode 5: Changes to MoU principles and second contract signature delay (November–December 2018)				
Supplier conflict over power	[19] *"[LPB Manager] starts with an update: A meeting planned for Monday got cancelled [...] it seems that [suppliers are] not aligned at the moment [...] apparently there are a 'few cracks' and he needs to 'expose who is playing games'"* (observation Nov. 2018). [20] *"There was an awful lot of squabbling, and disagreements, within the [suppliers...] 'We're in charge now'... 'No, we're in charge'"* (Commercial Manager, LPB).	Doubts about supplier firms	[22] *"[MechanicalCo] should know they are much more expensive than the others. [LPB managers] say that this could potentially end in [MechanicalCo] having to leave the MPA [...] [Supplier representative] is not comfortable with HVAC-Co [... they are] the biggest risk and could sink productivity for all of them – [HVACCo] are doing something they have never done before [...]. [LPB Manager] adds they should also look at ElectricalCoA as they are sub-contracting a lot more than they originally said they would"* (observation, Dec. 2018).
Episode 6: Commercial alignment and shareholder approval (January–March 2019)				
Power asymmetry	[23] *"[ElectricalCoA] do not want to deviate from the MoU as a matter of principle [... they are] stirring and driving it and influence [the] others [... ElectricalCoA] has said several times [...] 'this is not the biggest job for us'"* (observation, Feb. 2019). [24] *"We have this term the five-headed beast now, you create this monster, they are stronger together"* (Commercial Manager, LPB).	Doubts about MPA	[27] *"Between MoU and signature of contract [we] had a very up and down life, on a number of issues [and] as it became more and more difficult [we] thought, do we really want to do this?"* (Project Director, ElectricalCoA). [28] *" [LPB Manager] thinks that [shareholders] will never vote for it [...Shareholder representative] has been whispering to him continuously that they would prefer the [siloed] contracts"* (observation, Feb. 2019).

(Table continued on next page)

Table 1.4 (Continued)

Legitimation Process

Moral legitimacy	Data extract	Pragmatic legitimacy	Data extract
Episode 6: Commercial alignment and shareholder approval (January–March 2019)			
Buyer-supplier conflict	[25] "*[EnergyCo] was under a lot of pressure to get it over the line […] Everyone wanted it signed but we had become quite polarized, and it was getting very emotive […they] called us, greedy contractors*" (Project Director, SupportCo). [26] "*[LPB Manager] explains that this is a big breach in trust for LPB. The [issue] was very important to LPB to convince its shareholders. […] This is a high-risk contract for LPB and its success will depend on the collaboration and trust between the parties […] Hence, incidents like this one are not good for building trust and confidence*" (observation, Feb. 2019).	Increase supplier risk exposure	[29] "*As LPB want fixed profits, depending on base scope, the discussion around this has become emotive because base scope is smaller than the original contract. Hence, if the original scope was £1.1 billion and the new scope is £800 million, the concluding % are a much smaller amount*" (observation, Feb. 2019). [30] "*I briefly chat with [Project Director, SupportCo] before the meeting, he mentions they are having tough discussions internally as well as with LPB, due to LPB wanting to have fixed profits now while at the same time they are realizing that scope might be bigger than expected, hence, discussions are very emotive at the moment*" (observation, Feb. 2019)
Episode 7: Third contract signature delay and scope alignment (April–June 2019)			
Removing contractual ambiguity	[31] "*If you get rid of all the uncertainty at that stage, its preferable to leaving unanswered questions which usually only ever raise themselves when there is conflict. […]And it would probably happen early in the alliance contract, before the teams are fully bonded together, and before everybody is fully on board with this, working to the best interests of the project*" (Project Director, ElectricalCoA).	Reduce buyer risk exposure	[34] "*For whatever reason, there was a number, which was something like 835 million. Now we know that if you took each of the delivery partner contracts […] you ended up with a bigger number than those numbers that we are referring to. So, we had to munch the scope*" (Project Director, ElectricalCoA).

(Table continued on next page)

Table 1.4 (Continued)

Legitimation Process

Moral legitimacy	Data extract	Pragmatic legitimacy	Data extract
Episode 7: Third contract signature delay and scope alignment (April–June 2019)			
Time	[32] *"The overall intention and the interest were just increasing as we progressed towards this, [...] There were lots of people who actually had invested in this thinking, 'It is the right thing to do'* (project director, ElectricalCoA) [33] *"The [supplier] team was quite fractious at the beginning because it was like an arranged marriage. We were all forced together. But having been on that journey for all that time, it brought us really close together"* (Project Director, SupportCo).	Certainty of scope	[35] *"From a company's perspective what was key is about clarity. So, when you've got all this uncertainty of scope, being clear about what is the basis of the scope [...] As a result, [...] we have now got a very clear position [...] Whereas before potentially we had a very amorphous position, and the customer going, 'No, no that was in the budget, No, that is no addition', which we had learned during our early works [...] The right thing to do [was] definitely getting clarity"* (Project Director, MechanicalCo).

Episode 1: Supplier Workshop (December 2017)

In December 2017, LPB invited four suppliers selected as preferred bidders for the work packages connected to the installation of electrical, mechanical, and HVAC (heating, ventilation, air-conditioning) equipment in the nuclear power plant. The installation work was expected to last over six years, and its estimated value was $2bn (value as of April 2018). The highly interdependent nature of the installation work, which required suppliers to install equipment across 4,000 rooms in 72 buildings, meant that large time and cost savings could be achieved if suppliers were able to deliver the work in parallel (Board Paper, Dec. 2017). However, the separation of the work based on the dyadic structure did not allow this, and instead required formal handovers between trades and meticulous planning work by the buyer to sequence the work of suppliers (Senior Manager, LPB). To overcome these anticipated issues, LPB wanted suppliers to deliver the work in a MPA to enable the benefits from parallel installation and joint planning (observation, Oct. 2018; Board Paper, Dec. 2017)

In the workshop with suppliers in December 2017, LPB first provided an overview of the current structure, which it then problematized by: (i) highlighting the challenges within this approach [Table 1.3: 1,2]; and (ii) the subsequent implications for project success if these challenges remained unaddressed and the dyadic structure was contained [3,4]. The problematic nature of the siloed, dyadic structure as portrayed by the buyer in the workshop was understood and supported by all suppliers [3].

LPB then presented a MPA structure as a possible solution to overcome these challenges. In legitimating the new organizational solution, LPB relied on both moral and pragmatic legitimacy. Relatively limited emphasis was placed on highlighting the economic benefits derived from a MPA [13], instead LPB sought to illustrate the organizational structure's superior functionality by inviting a guest speaker who had worked on a construction project that was successfully delivered once a MPA was formed [9]. LPB sought to establish moral legitimacy by stressing the importance of collaborative values and behaviors as key factors to ensure project success [5]. The external guest speaker cautioned that the MPA would only lead to successful outcomes if parties were able to elevate themselves from the antagonism inherent in traditional buyer-supplier relationships (workshop slides Dec. 2017; supplier pers. meeting notes Dec. 2017). This would require a "*quantum leap*" in behaviors (supplier notes from meeting Dec. 2017): The MPA would have to develop its own common identity; it would require the empowerment of suppliers moving from a buyer-led to a joint-led approach, in which decisions are made for the "*greater good*" of the project, but not for the interests of individual firms (workshop slides Dec. 2017). Hence, LPB addressed suppliers as partners in the workshop, emphasizing that the final solution would be a joint creation in which each partner had an equal say [6,7], thereby, encouraging suppliers to explore ways to deliver a solution that would work for every party involved and would be in the best interest of the project [10,11]. At the end of the workshop, all suppliers expressed an interest in continuing to explore the formation of a new MPA.

Episode 2: Contract Discussions (January–June 2018)

In January 2018, LPB invited another supplier, SupportCo, to join the monthly discussions related to the MPA formation. To ensure moral legitimacy, LPB continued to be clear that the final solution would be a "*collective model*" and that "*nobody had the monopoly on how this should work*" (Commercial Director, LPB). Hence, suppliers were asked to equally contribute their ideas. From January 2018 onward, LPB and suppliers developed several MPA options with different degrees of integration [Table 1.4: 1,2]. From April 2018, LPB and all suppliers started to develop the commercial model and contract that would govern the various relationships.

The discussions were shaped by each party involved as expressed by a supplier representative:

> It was not like [LPB] had an idea about how it was going to be done and said, "There it is. Take a look. Go away." There were numerous discussions going on where contractors were saying, "We have done this before, and it worked really well in these circumstances. Which bits of that could we absorb into the [MPA] to produce a model that would work." (Project Director, ElectricalCoA)

In cases of disagreement, LPB sought to ensure that diverging positions were explored jointly in more detail, rather than employing aggressive negotiation tactics [3, 4].

To create pragmatic legitimacy, LPB and suppliers developed a commercial structure—through a "*generous*" overhead and incentive structure—that would enable suppliers to have greater profits by committing to the MPA than they would have obtained within traditional dyads (legal manager, LPB) [5,6]. Additionally, LPB accepted carrying significantly more risks than suppliers for the MPA work by limiting suppliers' liability for work, and by employing a fully cost-reimbursable contract, LPB accepted that it would pay for all supplier costs [8]. While this provided additional financial incentives to suppliers, it also ensured that suppliers would be able to focus all resources on the achievement of the MPA works instead of protecting their individual firm's interests:

> [We were] trying to find a mechanism where we were not so heavily focused on managing the commercial tensions between our organizations that it created a huge cost [...] 120 [surveyors] for seven or eight years is a huge number, if we get rid of that, [...] you have that available either as a saving to the project or an incentive mechanism. (Project Director, ElectricalCoA)

With the removal of potential commercial tensions through a no-claims contract, firms also expected positive outcomes for the relationships between firms in the MPA, as each firm was able to only focus on delivering their work to the project instead of protecting individual interests [7]. Overall, the developed commercial structure was aligned with suppliers' commercial interests and therefore established pragmatic legitimacy with suppliers for the new MPA.

Episode 3: Disagreement and Postponed Contract Signature (June–August 2018)

In June 2018, LPB's Commercial Director presented the jointly developed MPA solution to LPB shareholders, who rejected the proposal, as they did not see any pragmatic legitimacy. The shareholders argued that LPB accepted too much risk and did not shift enough risk to suppliers (Senior Commercial Manager, LPB). Additionally, LPB shareholders expected the MPA to be an opportunity for the project to save time and costs, but due to the incentive and overhead structure promised by LPB, LPB's shareholders feared that impact on project costs would be negative. Shareholders also doubted whether suppliers had the necessary managerial expertise to be in control of the MPA's coordination. Consequently, LBP shareholders questioned whether LBP's Commercial Director was still representing the interests of LPB, and he was removed from the discussions with suppliers (observation, Oct. 2018). LPB was forced to revisit previously established agreements with suppliers to change the developed MPA. Throughout June 2018, suppliers could not agree to accept any changes, and the pragmatic legitimacy of the MPA was at a breaking point [11,12].

LPB's Managing Director stepped in and changed the focus of the discussions to the moral legitimacy of the MPA. Together with shareholder and supplier representatives, several visits to other nuclear construction projects in China and France were conducted [9]. This highlighted to senior personnel from all parties the importance of a MPA to the success of the project [13]. Hence, the legitimation process was moved away from purely focusing on firms' self-interests, and towards serving the best interests of the project by highlighting the general superior functionality of the MPA as opposed to the dyadic contracts [10,13]. This was done by referring to failures in previous nuclear projects, which could have been prevented through a MPA [10,13]. These discussions made parties more open to finding a common ground between each other's positions as expressed by a project director (HVACCo):

> It was a mixture of meeting[s], going to see the [Chinese nuclear power station] and other [nuclear] sites, and [was] a vehicle for five days of conversation between [our] MDs and LPB, it was very good and it firmly fixed [the MPA] as a proposition.

Episode 4: Signing the Memorandum of Understanding and the Supplier Contracts (September–October 2018)

The joint meetings between senior representatives of each of the firms, and the visits to other nuclear construction sites, facilitated a better understanding of why a MPA was needed and surfaced the concerns of each party. While the meetings fostered alignment on critical commercial issues that had hampered the build-up of pragmatic legitimacy of the MPA for shareholders [16], they also reinvigorated a sense of purpose for the MPA.

As it became clear to firms that the anticipated contract signature in September 2018 was not achievable, parties sought to sign a memorandum of understanding (MoU) to signal commitment toward each other, and to commit jointly to the further exploration of a MPA structure. The MoU summarized the key principles that parties had been able to agree on up to this time [17]. Yet, given the difficulty of aligning parties' key commercial concerns, the MoU remained a voluntary agreement, ambiguous in its wording, and had no legal consequences for any of the parties involved.

LPB and suppliers were still willing to celebrate the MoU signing as a success, and LPB's Managing Director used the formal occasion to address suppliers:

> We signed the MoU in the middle of 2018 and we had a celebration … he gets up and talks about it with such a passion … he says I will not speak to anybody about whether this project is possible to deliver, I will talk about probability all day but unless you believe that it is possible, I do not want you on this project. (Project Director, SupportCo)

All suppliers felt inspired by LPB's commitment to the MPA and the significance of the MPA to project success. Hence, suppliers perceived the MoU signature as what was required as it affirmed a commitment toward each other, and that they should not give up despite the given lack of pragmatic legitimacy of a MPA [14,15].

Episode 5: Changes to MoU Principles, and Second Contract Signature Delay (November–December 2018)

In November 2018, it became clear that LPB wanted to revisit some of the commercial principles agreed in the MoU, particularly in relation to suppliers' risk exposure [21]. More specifically, this action meant that, potentially, a higher percentage of suppliers' overhead would be at risk should the MPA fail to achieve performance milestones. Additionally, LPB wanted to move away from a cost-reimbursable contract and reintroduced a target-cost contract. However, suppliers did not want to deviate on the principles that had been agreed on in the MoU, and expressed that pragmatic legitimacy was at a breaking point should LPB enforce these changes:

> That was a real challenge and the point where we said, "We will not be signing the contract if you insist that we have to put all of our overhead and incentive profit at risk." … It seemed strange to have to restate something that was known at the signature of the MoU … nothing had really changed. (Project Director, ElectricalCoA)

Suppliers also started to observe a change in the relationship with LPB: In the work to develop the contract and operational structure of the MPA, LPB provided unhelpful comments or its suggestions were punitive. For instance, LPB suggested key performance indicators (KPIs) that would be very difficult to achieve for suppliers [18]. While in early episodes suppliers had been treated like partners, an asymmetry in power was now apparent, and suppliers felt that the relationship with the buyer moved closer to a "traditional master-servant relationship" instead of a partnership [18].

Doubts emerged at LPB about the suitability of the selected suppliers [22]. During a benchmarking exercise of suppliers' original cost proposals, it was found that MechanicalCo charged significantly more than other suppliers for a similar type of work. LPB managers were upset when MechanicalCo defended its approach on the basis that it had won the preferred bidder status. As a result, LPB threatened MechanicalCo's position in the MPA should they not align their rates with other suppliers. LPB also detected that ElectricalCoA had intended to subcontract a lot of the project work, which would enable them to potentially employ their resources for other projects. This fostered doubts in LPB about the moral legitimacy of suppliers. LPB expected suppliers to act in the best interest of the project instead of following narrow firm interests. Doubts also emerged between suppliers, who were concerned about HVACCo's capability to deliver their part of the work successfully, given that the required work was not a core capability of the firm. Hence, suppliers feared HVACCo would underperform, which would harm overall MPA performance and endanger the achievement of KPI incentives and, with this, the pragmatic legitimacy of the MPA.

Further to the emergent doubts, suppliers were arguing about the incentive share. The conflict exposed power asymmetries between suppliers, who were fighting for their status and decision-making power among each other [19,20]. Hence, supplier firms were narrowly focused on their individual interests instead of collaborating on the development of an equitable share mechanism. The conflict deepened already existent doubts about the MPA, and the unresolved moral and pragmatic concerns meant that the anticipated contract signature for December 2018 had to be delayed.

Episode 6: Commercial Alignment, and Shareholder Approval (January–March 2019)

In January 2019, LPB and supplier managers distilled several areas that damaged pragmatic legitimacy, and which stopped the parties from committing to the MPA. One key area of pragmatic legitimacy was that LPB wanted to ensure that the overall incentive scheme for suppliers was fixed at contract signature [29]. Suppliers were opposed to this proposal, worrying that it might lead to LPB asking suppliers to provide more work for the same incentive sum. In turn, LPB feared that if the incentive amount was not fixed but was instead subject to changes, LPB would end up paying even more to suppliers, on top of what was already perceived by LPB as a very generous incentive scheme. The overhead and incentive structure became a contested cornerstone of pragmatic legitimacy between LPB and suppliers [30].

In February 2019, ElectricalCoA changed their position on a key issue (reduced overhead for re-works) that was previously agreed between LPB and suppliers. For LPB, this change in agreement presented a breach in trust between LPB and the supplier [25,26] as LPB had in turn agreed to not fix the incentive sum and contain the generous overhead fee. LPB felt suppliers were "*greedy*" and that moving away from such a commercially important point could endanger the MPA formation [28].

In March 2019, the relationship between LPB and suppliers had become conflicted and polarized [25,26]. LPB felt that suppliers were acting opportunistically and taking advantage of their increasing bargaining power as expressed by their legal manager "*It was like they were already up eight-nil but they wanted to win ten-nil.*" LPB worried that suppliers would continue to act opportunistically in the future and take advantage of the cost-reimbursable contract model: "*[LPB manager] thinks the biggest issue for LPB is to get the suppliers in the right mindset [for the MPA], because until now it feels like they are just here to make money*" (informal conversation, Feb. 2019). In March 2019, LPB's shareholders approved the MPA, but requested LPB managers to reduce the overall budget for MPA work by 20 percent prior to contract signature (observation, Apr. 2019).

Episode 7: Third Contract Signature Delay, and Scope Alignment (April–June 2019)

In April 2018, LPB negotiated the new MPA budget to safeguard pragmatic legitimacy of the MPA with its shareholders. Suppliers did not feel confident in the revised budget proposed by LPB [34,35]. Due to this ongoing disagreement, planned contract signature for April 2018 was replaced with a "heads of terms agreement," which was legally binding, to show that progress had been made since the MoU and that parties were still committed to the MPA. However, suppliers wanted to develop a clear alignment between the new budget and the work scope of the MPA covered within the budget [35]. Suppliers thought this was important to ensure their pragmatic legitimacy of the MPA: A clear alignment of budget and work would prohibit future scope increases as the buyer could argue that these were part of the budget [34]. The alignment of budget and scope was also seen as important to the moral legitimacy of the MPA: Ambiguity could lead to future conflicts about what scope was or was not included in the budget [31].

Overall, in this final episode, suppliers found that moral legitimacy increased given the vast amount of time all parties had spent on forming the MPA [32]. Although the relationship with LPB was still described as "*polarized*" by suppliers, the relationships between suppliers had improved and were infused with values of equal partnership and a shared identity [33]. Despite this, suppliers were ready to abandon the MPA if LPB were to introduce changes unaccepted to them; as explained by a supplier representative:

> Absolutely at the final signature, there was the idea of going back to target cost [contract]. Everybody in one voice on the contractors' side said, "This is walk away for us, we just do not sign and we will not be coming back tomorrow." Then [LPB] made a phone call, came back, and said, "We have deleted that idea." (Project Director, ElectricalCoA)

The agreement to commercial terms created levels of pragmatic legitimacy for all parties that led to contract signature.

DISCUSSION AND IMPLICATIONS

We investigated how a buyer and its suppliers shape the legitimation process of a buyer-supplier MPA. We analyzed primary and secondary data sets from a longitudinal case study on the formation of a MPA. Our longitudinal study offers important implications for the formation and legitimization of MPAs and buyer-supplier MPAs more specifically.

First, our findings highlight the importance of theorization in initiating the legitimation process (Greenwood et al., 2002; Suddaby et al., 2017; Tolbert & Zucker, 1996). In the first step the buyer problematized the status quo. This was done by highlighting the negative impact the current dyadic contracts would have: (i) on the delivery of the work, and thus the direct negative impact on the work of suppliers; and (ii) for overall project success. In doing so, the buyer exhibited normative dignity in making the issue personal to suppliers: It wanted to smoothen the delivery process for suppliers and, second, to focus on the wider implications to the project. In the second step, the buyer proposed the MPA as a preferred solution to overcome these challenges, based on moral and pragmatic legitimacy. Pragmatic legitimacy stemmed from the superior functionality the MPA would provide to the delivery of the work. Moral legitimacy developed from several areas: First, the improved functionality of the MPA had wider benefits to project success, which was beyond firms' narrow self-interests, given the importance of the project to the country's infrastructure. Hence, the MPA was stylized as a "project savior": The project was doomed to fail without a MPA. Second, the MPA would be accompanied by a change in values that would elevate the position of suppliers: The traditional dyadic contracts were characterized by a master-servant culture; the MPA, however, would be characterized by an equal partnership between the buyer and suppliers. The goal of this equal partnership was to jointly develop a MPA solution that was in the best interest of the project.

Second, our study is one of the first to offer an in-depth examination of the internal legitimation process between the buyer as the legitimacy seeker on one side and suppliers as the legitimacy audience on the other as they developed legitimacy for the MPA. Prior work on legitimation has been criticized for artificially dividing the social world into creators of legitimation and a passively accepting audience, namely the suppliers in our study (Suddaby et al., 2017). Overall, we found that suppliers' agency was vital in shaping the legitimation process. We found that while the legitimation process of the new buyer-supplier MPA was time-consuming, it also required buy-in from all parties involved. More specifically, our longitudinal study revealed that the legitimation process of forming a MPA was cyclical and characterized by episodes of build-up, breakdown, and repair. Episodes of breakdown were initiated by a one-sided distribution of pragmatic legitimacy (e.g., cost-reimbursable versus target cost contract, where either solution presented pragmatic legitimacy to one party but not the other). Here, moral legitimacy became important in sustaining the legitimation process and initiating repair. This was done by widening participants' attention to the wider benefits of the MPA to the project, and because of this, parties were able to continue the formation process and work on a solution that would provide sufficient pragmatic legitimacy for all parties involved. To achieve contract signature and move to the operations phase, both types of legitimacy need to be present. Pragmatic legitimacy of the MPA was achieved for the buyer via the reduction of the overall MPA budget, while suppliers were able to preserve the cost-reimbursable contract and incentive structure. For the buyer, moral legitimacy was given by suppliers agreeing to the MPA. For suppliers, moral legitimacy was presented in the positive horizontal relationships with each other and the insistence on removing any contractual ambiguity, which could potentially create conflict with the buyer in the future.

Third, prior studies offer limited insights into the drivers of moral and pragmatic legitimacy during the formation stage of an alliance (Kumar & Das, 2007). We found that pragmatic legitimacy was closely linked to the commercial aspects of the MPA such as the incentive scheme, cost-reimbursable contract, or budget, which constituted the financial risk of the MPA for the parties involved. Here, the suppliers were able to align their interests toward low supplier risk, increased overall supplier profits, while the buyer focused on increasing supplier risk and decreasing supplier profits. Hence, pragmatic legitimacy became highly contested during the formation process, and caused episodes of legitimacy breakdown. We found that moral legitimacy came in various shapes and forms. While prior studies emphasized it stemming from the non-violation of behavioral values between partnering firms (Kumar & Das, 2007), others solely considered it as providing a pro-social logic to a new organizational structure (Paquin & Howard-Grenville, 2013). Our findings illustrate both facets of moral legitimacy. Having pro-social logic or reason for the MPA was particularly important during the initial theorization of the MPA and during episodes of pragmatic legitimacy breakdown, as it enabled parties to lift themselves from narrow self-interests and see the wider purpose of the MPA. The behavioral component of the MPA was particularly important to the horizontal relationship between suppliers to enable them to commit to contract signature.

Boundary Conditions and Further Research

While our study closely examined the legitimization of a MPA for the delivery of services to a project in the nuclear construction industry, we believe that our insights hold true in other settings. We adopted a single case study because we wanted to depict the legitimation process over time. However, the narrow focus on one MPA within a specific setting may limit the generalizability of our findings to other contexts. Hence, we encourage future research to test whether our findings persist under different circumstances, such as in different industries or countries. Future research should also compare our findings to other types of MPAs (e.g., different number and characteristics of suppliers; including public actors—Caldwell, Roehrich, & George, 2017; Roehrich & Kivleniece, 2022), in other industries (e.g., with different clock speed as this may impact how and why pragmatic and moral legitimacy is being developed—Howard, Roehrich, Lewis, & Squire, 2019; or different product/service solutions—Johnson, Roehrich, Chakkol, & Davies, 2021), or under other market and environmental conditions (e.g., Phillips, Roehrich, & Kapletia, 2022). A further interesting research area, which our study did not address, would be to investigate whether the legitimacy trade-offs parties agree to for the MPA to survive have an impact on the later operational stage of the MPA.

Implications for Practice

Our study provides implications for firms and managers seeking to motivate suppliers to form a new (buyer-supplier) MPA. To avoid a lengthy formation process, parties must be aware that it is not sufficient to high-light the challenges of the previous organizational structure and point out the benefits of the new MPA, but that all parties see sufficient moral and pragmatic legitimacy in the new MPA. Moral legitimacy is based on seeing the wider benefits of a MPA as well as trying to build a relationship based on power symmetry and equal partnership. This can be achieved by giv-ing suppliers an equal say in the formation process in relation to all key decisions. Pragmatic legitimacy rests on creating the right financial incen-tives for suppliers to join a MPA; if this is not attainable, the buyer can minimize suppliers' risks through a cost-reimbursable contract. Managers and firms need to be aware that each party is expected to make concessions to pragmatic legitimacy, and if parties focus too narrowly on their own self-interests, not only moral legitimacy is harmed through conflicts and struggles for dominance, but also the formation process is either prolonged or dissolved.

CONCLUSIONS

This chapter explored how a buyer and suppliers legitimate the forma-tion of a new MPA. We contribute to the alliance literature by studying a unique type of MPA between one buyer and several suppliers, which has become increasingly common in practice, but remains relatively unex-plored in the strategy and alliance literature. Our in-depth, longitudinal case study revealed how the formation of a new buyer-supplier MPA was initiated by the buyer by problematizing the current dyadic contracts, and by highlighting the benefits of a new MPA arrangement. The subsequent legitimation process consisted of episodes of legitimacy build-up, break-down, and repair. It required both moral and pragmatic legitimacy to be developed and nurtured, and it was shaped by the buyer and suppliers equally. Moral legitimacy was two-faceted: one focusing on the provision of a pro-social logic for the MPA, the other on the non-violation of behav-ioral values. Pragmatic legitimacy was built by: either (i) providing more financial incentives to suppliers in comparison to the dyadic contracts; or (ii) reducing supplier risk exposure. The pragmatic legitimation of the new MPA required all involved parties to make trade-offs. We further found that it is sufficient to have either moral or pragmatic legitimacy present to avoid the dissolution of the MPA formation, but for contract signature both had to be present. We hope that our findings encourage future research to augment our understanding of the legitimation of different organizational structures that include multiple firms.

ACKNOWLEDGMENT

The authors would like to thank all interviewees and organizations involved in this research study for their support. We would also like to thank our colleagues from the HPC Supply Chain Innovation Lab, especially Dr Jas Kalra, for their support and insights.

REFERENCES

Aaltonen, K., & Turkulainen, V. (2018). Creating relational capital through socialization in project alliances. *International Journal of Operations and Production Management*, *38*(6), 1387–1421.

Aben, T. A. E., van der Valk, W., Roehrich, J. K., & Selviaridis, K. (2021). Managing information asymmetry in public-private relationships undergoing a digital transformation: The role of contractual and relational governance. *International Journal of Operations & Production Management*, *41*(7), 1145–1191.

Baum, J. A. C., & Oliver, C. (1992). Institutional embeddedness and the dynamics of organizational populations. *American Sociological Review*, *57*(4), 540–559.

Bitektine, A. (2011). Toward a theory of social judgments of organizations: The case of legitimacy, reputation, and status. *Academy of Management Review*, *36*(1), 151–179.

Brenner, B., & Ambos, B. (2013). A question of legitimacy? A dynamic perspective on multinational firm control. *Organization Science*, *24*(3), 773–795.

Brown, A. D., & Toyoki, S. (2013). Identity work and legitimacy. *Organization Studies*, *34*(7), 875–896.

Caldwell, N. D., Roehrich, J. K., & Davies, A.C. (2009). Procuring complex performance in construction: London Heathrow Terminal 5 and a Private Finance Initiative Hospital. *Journal of Purchasing and Supply Management*, *15*(3), 178-186.

Caldwell, N., Roehrich, J. K., & George, G. (2017). Social value creation and relational coordination in public-private collaborations. *Journal of Management Studies*, *54*(6), 906–928.

Corbin, J., & Strauss, A. (2008). *Basics of qualitative research: Techniques and procedures for developing grounded theory.* Thousand Oaks, CA: SAGE.

Dacin, M. T. (1997). Isomorphism in context: The power and prescription of institutional norms. *Academy of Management Journal*, *40*(1), 46–81.

Das, T. K., & Teng, B. (2000). Instabilities of strategic alliances: An internal tensions perspective. *Organization Science*, *11*(1), 77–101.

Das, T. K., & Teng, B. (2002). Alliance constellations: A social exchange perspective. *Academy of Management Review*, *27*(3), 445–456.

David, R. J., Sine, W. D., & Haveman, H. A. (2013). Seizing opportunity in emerging fields: How institutional entrepreneurs legitimated the professional form of management consulting. *Organization Science*, *24*(2), 356–377.

DiMaggio, P. J., & Powell, W. W. (1983). The iron cage revisited: Institutional isomorphism and collective rationality in organizational fields. *American Sociological Review, 48*(2), 147–160.

Dowling, J., & Pfeffer, J. (1975). Organizational legitimacy: Social values and organizational behavior. *The Pacific Sociological Review, 18*(1), 122–136.

Eisenhardt, K. M., & Schoonhoven, C. B. (1996). Resource-based view of strategic alliance formation: Strategic and social effects in entrepreneurial firms. *Organization Science, 7*(2), 136–150.

Fonti, F., Maoret, M., & Whitbred, R. (2017). Free-riding in multi-party alliances: The role of perceived alliance effectiveness and peers' collaboration in a research consortium. *Strategic Management Journal, 38*(2), 363–383.

Gibbert, M., & Ruigrok, W. (2010). The "what" and "how" of case study rigor: Three strategies based on published work. *Organizational Research Methods, 13*(4), 710–737.

Greenwood, R., Suddaby, R., & Hinings, C. R. (2002). Theorizing change: The role of professional associations in the transformation of institutionalized fields. *Academy of Management Journal, 45*(1), 58–80.

Hartmann, A., Roehrich, J. K., Frederiksen, L., & Davies, A. (2014). Procuring complex performance: The transition process in public infrastructure. *International Journal of Operations & Production Management, 32*(2), 174-194.

Hietajärvi, A. M., & Aaltonen, K. (2018). The formation of a collaborative project identity in an infrastructure alliance project. *Construction Management and Economics, 36*(1), 1–21.

Howard, M. B., Roehrich, J. K., Lewis, M. A., & Squire, B. (2019). Converging and diverging governance mechanisms: The role of (dys) function in long-term inter-organizational relationships. *British Journal of Management, 30*(3), 624–644.

Human, S. E., & Provan, K. G. (2000). Legitimacy building in the evolution of small-firm multilateral networks: A comparative study of success and demise. *Administrative Science Quarterly, 45*(2), 327–365.

Johnson, M., Roehrich, J. K., Chakkol, M., & Davies, A. (2021). Reconciling and reconceptualising servitization research: Drawing on modularity, platforms, ecosystems, risk and governance to develop mid-range theory. *International Journal of Operations & Production Management, 41*(5), 465-493.

Kostova, T., & Roth, K. (2002). Adoption of an organizational practice by subsidiaries of multinational corporations: Institutional and relational effects. *Academy of Management Journal, 45*(1), 215–233.

Kumar, R., & Das, T. K. (2007). Interpartner legitimacy in the alliance development process. *Journal of Management Studies, 44*(8), 1425–1453.

Lavie, D., Lechner, C., & Singh, H. (2007). The performance implications of timing of entry and involvement in multipartner alliances. *Academy of Management Journal, 50*(3), 578–604.

Lazzarini, S. G., Claro, D. P., & Mesquita, L. F. (2008). Buyer-supplier and supplier-supplier alliances: Do they reinforce or undermine one another? *Journal of Management Studies, 45*(3), 561–584.

Lee, B. H., Hiatt, S. R., & Lounsbury, M. (2017). Market mediators and the trade-offs of legitimacy-seeking behaviors in a nascent category. *Organization Science*, *28*(3), 447–470.

Li, D., Eden, L., Hitt, M. A., Ireland, R. D., & Garrett, R. P. (2012). Governance in multilateral R&D alliances. *Organization Science*, *23*(4), 1191–1210.

Lloyd-Walker, B., Mills, A., & Walker, D. (2014). Enabling construction innovation: The role of a no-blame culture as a collaboration behavioural driver in project alliances. *Construction Management and Economics*, *32*(3), 229–245.

Meyer, J. W., & Rowan, B. (1977). Institutionalized organizations: Formal structure as myth and ceremony. *American Journal of Sociology*, *83*(2), 340–363.

Mishra, A., Chandrasekaran, A., & MacCormack, A. (2015). Collaboration in multi-partner R&D projects: The impact of partnering scale and scope. *Journal of Operations Management*, *33–34*, 1–14.

Paquin, R. L., & Howard-Grenville, J. (2013). Blind dates and arranged marriages: Longitudinal processes of network orchestration. *Organization Studies*, *34*(11), 1623–1653.

Persson, S. G., Lundberg, H., & Andresen, E. (2011). Interpartner legitimacy in regional strategic networks. *Industrial Marketing Management*, *40*(6), 1024–1031.

Phillips, W., Roehrich, J. K., & Kapletia, D. (2022). Responding to information asymmetry in crisis situations: Innovation in the time of the COVID-19 pandemic. *Public Management Review*. https://doi.org/10.1080/14719037.2021.1960737

Ring, P. S., & Van de Ven, A. H. (1994). Developmental processes of cooperative interorganizational relationships. *Academy of Management Review*, *19*(1), 90–118.

Roehrich, J. K., & Lewis, M. A. (2014). Procuring complex performance: Implications for exchange governance complexity. *International Journal of Operations & Production Management*, *32*(2), 221–241.

Roehrich, J. K., & Kivleniece, I. (2022). Creating and distributing sustainable value through public-private collaborative projects. In G. George, M. R. Hass, H. Joshi, A. McGahan, & P. Tracey (Eds.), *Handbook on the business of sustainability: The organization, implementation, and practice of sustainable growth* (pp. 473–499). Cheltenham, UK: Edward Elgar Publishing.

Ruef, M., & Scott, W. R. (1998). A multidimensional model of organizational legitimacy: Hospital survival in changing institutional environments. *Administrative Science Quarterly*, *43*(4), 877–904.

Shah, S. K., & Corley, K. G. (2006). Building better theory by bridging the quantitative-qualitative divide. *Journal of Management Studies*, *43*(8), 1821–1835.

Sine, W. D., David, R. J., & Mitsuhashi, H. (2007). From plan to plant: Effects of certification on operational start-up in the emergent independent power sector. *Organization Science*, *18*(4), 578–594.

Suchman, M. C. (1995). Managing legitimacy: Strategic and institutional approaches. *Academy of Management Review*, *20*(3), 571–610.

Suddaby, R., Bitektine, A., & Haack, P. (2017). Legitimacy. *Academy of Management Annals*, *11*(1), 451–478.

Suprapto, M., Bakker, H., Mooi, H., & Hertogh, M. (2016). How do contract types and incentives matter to project performance? *International Journal of Project Management*, *34*(6), 1071–1087.

Tolbert, P. S., & Zucker, L. G. (1996). Institutionalization of institutional theory. In S. R. Clegg, C. Hardy, & W. R. Nord (Eds.), *Handbook of organizational studies* (pp. 148–174). Thousand Oaks, CA: SAGE.

Zelditch, M. (2001). Processes of legitimation: Recent developments and new directions. *Social Psychology Quarterly*, *64*(1), 4–17.

Zeng, M., & Chen, X. (2003). Achieving cooperation in multiparty alliances: A social dilemma approach to partnership management. *Academy of Management Review*, *28*(4), 587–605.

Zheng, J., Roehrich, J. K., Lewis, M. A. (2008). The dynamics of contractual and relational governance: Evidence from long-term public-private procurement arrangements. *Journal of Purchasing and Supply Management*, *14*(1), 43–54

Zimmerman, M. A., & Zeitz, G. J. (2002). Beyond survival: Achieving new venture growth by building legitimacy. *Academy of Management Review*, *27*(3), 414–431.

Zucker, L. G. (1987). Institutional theories of organization. *Annual Review of Sociology*, *13*, 443–464.

CHAPTER 2

EMBRACING THE COMPETITION-COOPERATION ANGST

Individual Ambivalence as a Driver of Strategic Alliance Performance

Hilary Schloemer, Kristie M. Rogers, and Laura Poppo

ABSTRACT

Several decades of alliance research have examined management of the opposing competitive and cooperative tensions inherent to the alliance context. The firm-level mechanisms of relational governance, trust, and contracts are widely discussed, but far less attention is given to the individual members of the alliance team and their experience of the cooperation-competition tension. Similarly, alliance process research falls short of describing how managers effectively manage alliance team members so that competition does not erode alliance performance. This is an important gap, and if not managed, alliance team members can cognitively withdraw from the activities that enable benefits to their firm as well as the alliance: effective problem solving, knowledge sharing, and collaboration. Drawing upon the growing body of research on the advantages of ambivalence, "the simultaneous experience of opposing orientations toward an object or target" (Rothman, Pratt, Rees, & Vogus, 2017, p. 35), we show that when alliance team members embrace "holism"—both the competitive and cooperative orientations at the team and individual level—they can improve alliance outcomes as well as firm-

Managing Interpartner Cooperation in Strategic Alliances, pp. 33–61

level outcomes. Our theoretical model posits that harnessing ambivalence can enhance cognitive processing at the individual and team levels, promoting problem solving, perspective taking, and creativity. The psychological mechanisms of psychological safety and nested identities, along with dual compensation and knowledge sharing operational routines, are core to fully harnessing "ambivalence" to benefit both the firm and the alliance.

INTRODUCTION

The juxtaposition of competitive and cooperative forces represents a fundamental challenge to the management of alliances (e.g., Das & Teng, 2000). Over several decades, research has primarily centered on solving this challenge at the firm level, focusing on the use of contracts, equity, and authority to align firms' interests (e.g., Hennart, 1988; Makadok & Coff, 2009; Oxley, 1997), and relational mechanisms, including prior experience, inter-organizational trust, and relational governance, to minimize competitive tensions and encourage cooperation (e.g., Gulati, Lavie, & Singh, 2009; Inkpen & Currall, 2004; Madhok & Tallman, 1998; Poppo & Zenger, 2002). This firm-level focus has left the individual-level experience of this challenge and potential solutions largely unexamined. Instead, the prevailing firm-level logic suggests that if contractual safeguards and relational mechanisms are deployed, the alliance team and its members will operate in a space relatively free from the soils of competition while simultaneously fertile with seeds of cooperative relational mechanisms (Dyer & Singh, 1998; Madhok & Tallman, 1998).

A nascent literature, however, suggests that the individual-level experience of governance mechanisms is not necessarily consistent with the above description. In their case study of two exploratory alliances, Faems, Janssens, Madhok, and Van Looy (2008) show managerial sensemaking determines how governance choices are interpreted and thus (re)framed. If alliance managers as well as operational managers interpret contracts as rigid sanctioning devices, team functionality decreases, but if they interpret the same contract loosely, alliance team functionality and performance increases. Whereas Faems and colleagues (2008) argue that sensemaking alters the *ex ante* contractual frame, Weber and Mayer (2011) propose the alternative: that a direct relationship exists between contractually-specified goals and how individuals interpret the contract. Promotion-framed contractual goals direct positive emotion and energy toward the idealized goal; prevention-framed contractual goals induce vigilant behavior to avoid missing the goal. While these studies suggest that a focus on individuals is important to understand how to manage the dynamics of cooperation (i.e., relational mechanisms) and competition (i.e., formal contracts), their logic parallels that of the alliance literature: to allow cooperation, we void competition, either through contract design or sensemaking, unless rigid execution is desirable to achieve exchange goals.

We provide an alternative perspective to the alliance governance challenge of how to manage the juxtaposition of competition and cooperation. Rather than adopt the univalent lens that alliance performance occurs by minimizing competition (through formal contracts) and maximizing cooperation (through contractual reframing or relational mechanisms), we argue that embracing ambivalence (Ashforth, Rogers, Pratt, & Pradies, 2014) to sustain the juxtaposition of competition and cooperation could produce better performance than eliminating it, and ultimately contribute to firm and alliance performance. Because of their joint position, individual alliance team members must grapple with the motivation to further the interests of their parent firm (i.e., competition) and the alliance (i.e., cooperation). Opposing demands, such as these, are precisely what triggers the experience of ambivalence for individuals in organizations.

Ambivalence is a psychological state defined as "the simultaneous experience of opposing orientations toward an object or target" (Rothman et al., 2017, p. 35) which "occurs when cognitions clash, emotions clash, or cognitions and emotions clash" (Ashforth et al., 2014, p. 1454). Strong norms for managers and organizational leaders to resolve contradictions, tensions, and conflicting interests date back to some of the earliest management research (e.g., Barnard, 1968), building a perception that ambivalence is a fairly rare and negative occurrence in organizations. However, a body of research on ambivalence has flourished in recent years and suggests that experiencing ambivalence in organizations is likely more common than *not* experiencing ambivalence due to the complexity, contradiction, and competing demands faced daily by individuals at all levels of organizations, and "contrary to assumptions, when it comes to ambivalence, experiencing it rather than resolving it may be functional and beneficial" (Rothman et al., 2017, p. 35). Indeed, empirical research on ambivalence among CEOs reveals better strategic decision-making and action among ambivalent CEOs than those not experiencing ambivalence (Plambeck & Weber, 2009), and studies in organizational behavior link ambivalence to favorable outcomes such as creativity (Fong, 2006) and adaptability (Molinsky, 2013). When considered in the context of alliance team members, these ambivalence findings pose a stark contrast to the notion that alliance performance will be optimized if competition is minimized and cooperation is maximized, provocatively suggesting that maintaining the juxtaposition is a plausible, and potentially preferable, approach.

In this chapter, we theorize about the positive potential of ambivalence in the alliance context and propose a series of mechanisms to deliberately sustain the ambivalence experienced by alliance team members. First, we review the mechanisms in the alliance literature for managing competition and cooperation and detail boundary conditions of our theorizing. Next, we draw on ambivalence research in organizational and psychology literatures to propose a conceptual model of ambivalence driving functional outcomes in the alliance context. We propose that a nested team identity, alliance team routines that maintain the salience of ambivalence, members' perceptions of psychological safety, and a dualistic compensation scheme are levers that firms can use to encourage team members to embrace both the competition and cooperation motives. We further posit that the cognitive and behavioral elements supported by proactively managed ambivalence have the potential to support both alliance and firm performance. We conclude with implications for both theory and practice.

A REVIEW OF PERSPECTIVES AND PROCESSES FOR MANAGING COMPETITION AND COOPERATION IN STRATEGIC ALLIANCES

The dominant perspective in the governance of alliances—as well as buyer-supplier exchanges—advances the use of both formal controls and relational mechanisms to address the complex dynamics of competition and cooperation. Well-documented in this literature is the importance of crafting contractual safeguards to specify and protect firms' interests (Williamson, 1996; for reviews see Macher & Richman, 2008; Schepker, Oh, Martynov, & Poppo, 2014). The most complex and uncertain transactions require sophisticated contracts, in which expectations and terms are not only specified in detail but customized for the particular transaction. For these transactions, parties often specify ownership rights, including their intellectual property (Reuer & Ariño, 2007). In addition, the arrangment may also require shared equity and investments (e.g., bilateral credible commitments) to promote cooperation and incentives to maximize joint payoffs.

Relational mechanisms may also be used as they augment cooperation. For example, armed with trust, partners are more willing to work together over time and share knowledge (e.g., Gulati et al., 2009; Inkpen & Currall, 2004; Li, Poppo, & Zhou, 2010), and the development of a shared alliance team identity has the potential to promote cooperative problem-solving activities (Poppo, Schloemer, & Rogers, 2019). Another relational mechanism, relational governance, specifies the norms, values, and practices that define how parties work together: for example, joint communication, coordination, joint action, shared goals, and acknowledgement of latent organizational differences between partner organizations (e.g., Bercovitz, Jap, & Nickerson, 2006; Lavie, Haunschild, & Khanna, 2012; Poppo & Zenger, 2002; Schreiner, Kale, & Corsten, 2009). While meta-analytic reviews demonstrate that the combined use of formal controls and relational mechanisms positively impact business-to-business performance (Cao & Lumineau, 2015), their effectiveness varies as a function of the level of behavioral and environmental uncertainty (Krishnan, Geyskens, & Steenkamp, 2016). Thus, governance choices do not resolve the inherent tension of managing competition and cooperation at the individual level.

Our review of alliance process models indicates a similar opportunity for extensions and new perspectives. These works generally favor a process in which distinct stages evolve over time and alliance members are expected to oscillate between a cooperative or competitive focus depending on their location within this process (Ring & Van de Ven, 1994; Zajac & Olsen, 1993). For example, Zajac and Oslen's (1993) process consists of three stages: the initializing stage in which firms estimate the expected return of the alliance relationship, begin to learn about each other, and discuss joint interests and expectations; the processing stage in which they create relational norms, develop trust, and establish how the value created by the relationship will be distributed; and the reconfiguring stage, in which performance is evaluated and any performance gaps are assessed and used to redefine the exchange. A commonality shared among these models is that, despite the intent of oscillating stages, alliance members maintain a concern for self-interest (i.e., individualized value creation and capture) even when the alliance relationship is characterized by a high level of cooperation. An alternative process model uses an alliance management function to accumulate and share knowledge regarding how to manage alliances, commonly referred to as an alliance management capability (Schreiner et al., 2009). However, this work outlines, at an alliance management level, the kinds of activities that support value-creation within the alliance—it does not address our fundamental question of *how* individuals tasked with managing the alliance tensions productively manage and respond to the competing demands.

Consistent with the focus of this work on managerial- and firm-level action, alliance research, and strategy research more broadly, has yet to fully relate its phenomena to the psychological drivers at the individual and group level of analysis (Powell, Lovallo, & Fox, 2011), for it typically assumes that "a single entity takes on responsibility (e.g., an organization or an individual) when in fact decisions in organizations are often made by groups of individuals" (Argote & Greve, 2007, p. 344). By removing the alliance team members from the phenomenon, the existing alliance literature assumes that formal contracts, incentives, and relational mechanisms shield teams and members from managing the juxtaposition of competition and cooperation. We find this assumption problematic, as it is possible individuals at the operational level may operate in a manner which is inconsistent with the expectations that exist at the firm level

(Faems et al., 2008; Fan & Zietsma, 2017). For example, team members may share private knowledge, such as key interfaces or skill sets that underlie the performance of their process. Such "unintended" spillovers can occur at the individual level if alliance members prioritize the alliance over the goals of their parent firms. Alternatively, individuals who hold specific knowledge may hoard their private knowledge or use it as a ploy to direct alliance activity to benefit their firm, not the alliance—these dynamics impact knowledge sharing and integration, a critical facet underlying effective exploration in alliances.

In sum, the extensive literature on the management of strategic alliances tells us a great deal about governance, contracts, and relational mechanisms; however, there remains much to learn about the alliance management process at the individual level—those who grapple with the tensions inherent in an alliance scenario on a day-to-day basis. It is essential to examine how individual members of the alliance team can manage tension and contradiction in ways that are consistent with both the parent firm and alliance goals. According to our logic, described next, a key consideration of individual-level alliance management is the psychological experience of ambivalence. Drawing on psychological perspectives on organizational ambivalence (Ashforth et al., 2014; Rothman et al., 2017), we argue that, if managed ineffectively, responses to ambivalence undermine simultaneous competition and cooperation. We propose a set of firm- and alliance-level tactics to promote the harnessing of individual-level ambivalence, which promotes knowledge sharing, integration, and problem solving to enhance firm and alliance performance.

Boundary Conditions of Our Theorizing

It is useful to clarify several boundary conditions of our theorizing before introducing our theoretical model. First, throughout the chapter we reference the alliance team and individual alliance team members. We consider parent firm members whose role responsibilities are primarily tied to the alliance to be members of the alliance team, and we are especially focused on their cognitive processing of opposing demands (i.e., competitive forces to maximize value for their own firms; cooperative forces to maximize value creation in the alliance project). We refer to these members as individuals and theorize about the within-person, or intrapersonal, cognitive, and affective experience of ambivalence. We assume that these individuals have the discretion to share information and make decisions related to their ascribed role/job, such that their individual behaviors have an important impact on the performance of the alliance team as a whole.

Our theorizing is also specific to alliances with goals that are exploratory in nature, requiring complex problem solving and strategic combination of resources from each firm. Additionally, we consider alliance performance to be the key outcome of our theorizing, and view performance of the alliance as value creation for the alliance as a whole, which is related to but distinct from the performance of a single firm in the alliance.

Finally, our focus on ambivalence is related but distinct from the growing attention to paradox in the management literature (e.g., Stadtler & van Wassenhove, 2016; Waldman, Putnam, Miron-Spektor, & Siegel, 2019). We follow the delineation of the constructs developed by Ashforth and colleagues (2014) in the construction of their nomological network—a paradox is a situation external to the individual composed of "contradictory yet interrelated elements—elements that seem logical in isolation but absurd or irrational when appearing simultaneously" (Lewis, 2000, p. 760). Ambivalence, on the other hand, is the individual-level cognitive and emotional experience of tension produced by holding two or more contradictory orientations toward something (e.g., an object, task, or individual; Rothman et al., 2017). Thus, organizational members' experience of ambivalence may be triggered by the presence of a paradox, such as the competing goals of cooperation and competition.

AMBIVALENCE IN THE ALLIANCE CONTEXT

As noted, members of the alliance team face pressure to cooperate in ways that will create value for the alliance as a whole and to simultaneously maximize or claim value for their parent firm. These competing and prevalent demands of competition and cooperation constitute contradictory goals (Parkhe, 1993) and perhaps even a hybrid identity (i.e., what is core, distinctive, and more or less enduring about the group includes oppositional demands, like cooperation and competition), both of which are noted as significant organizational triggers of ambivalence (Ashforth et al., 2014). As suggested by traditional consistency theories (e.g., cognitive dissonance theory, Festinger, 1957), individuals often view these simultaneous oppositional demands as an aversive experience likely to produce negative reactions and behavioral outcomes. The way in which one cognitively responds to ambivalence is characterized by the extent to which he or she is focused on each orientation, ranging from nonconsciously avoiding both orientations to consciously and effortfully integrating both orientations in a holistic way (Ashforth et al., 2014). A range of outcomes has been documented, and the function or dysfunction for the organization appears to be dependent on the cognitive response and subsequent behaviors. Rothman and colleagues (2017) posit that these outcomes of ambivalence range along two continua, flexible-inflexible and engagement-disengagement, with inflexible/disengaged outcomes including resistance to change, avoiding advice from others, indecision, and one-sided judgments, and flexible/engaged outcomes including adaptability, collaboration, integrative problem solving, creativity, and openness to change.

Given the relevance of these outcomes to alliance performance, it seems that deliberately responding to ambivalence in ways that maintain the juxtaposition of competition and cooperation can have significant and positive performance implications. But why might alliance team members respond in a particular way? Our goal in this section is to propose a theoretical model detailing the individual-level experience of ambivalence in the alliance context, and how contextual features of the alliance and deliberate actions by their firms can prompt individuals to harness ambivalence in ways that produce flexible and engaged outcomes (see Figure 2.1). We begin by distinguishing between the dysfunctional and functional responses to ambivalence in the alliance context, discuss the alliance- and firm-level moderators of responses, and the impact on both the alliance and parent firms.

Ambivalence and Alliance Dysfunction

Organizational members' responses to ambivalence characterized by inflexibility (e.g., indecision, paralysis, resistance to change) and disengagement (e.g., reduced advice-taking, reduced commitment) are likely to be most dysfunctional (Rothman et al., 2017). We posit that such responses would be especially problematic in the alliance context, given the necessity for resourceful cooperation, adaptability, and complex problem solving to maximize performance (Gulati et al., 2009; Inkpen & Currall, 2004; Madhok & Tallman, 1998; Nickerson & Zenger, 2004).

But what would prompt alliance team members to respond to ambivalence in ways that lead to inflexible or disengaged outcomes? From the consistency theory perspective (e.g., Festinger, 1957) noted above, ambivalence produces psychological discomfort, which naturally drives individuals to employ coping mechanisms that will quickly minimize the discomfort (Cacioppo, Gardner, & Berntson, 1997; Cramer, 2006). This set of coping mechanisms serves to obviate the conscious processing and thoughtful consideration of opposing orientations, instead providing a quick fix for the ambivalence-induced discomfort, which can include decision-making shortcuts such as heuristics, schemas, assumptions, and other "sense-jumping processes" (Guarana & Hernandez, 2015, p. 59). Individuals experiencing ambivalence may also respond by avoiding both orientations all together, by allowing one orientation to supersede the other and become dominant

Figure 2.1

Multilevel Model of Ambivalence in Strategic Alliances

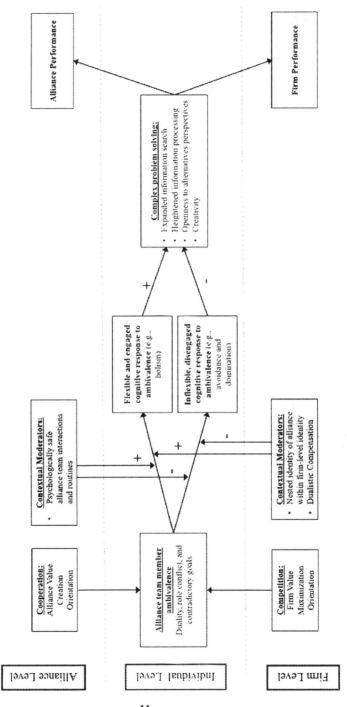

(see Ashforth et al., 2014 for a review), or by relying on someone else's expertise rather than one's own judgment (Guarana & Hernandez, 2015). Individuals who rely on these inflexible and disengaged responses, such as avoidance or allowing one orientation to dominate over the other, will make extreme or one-sided judgments (e.g., response amplification, Bell & Esses, 2002; Pratt & Doucet, 2000) or display rigid decision-making behaviors such as indecision or paralysis (Emmons & King, 1988; Lüscher & Lewis, 2008; Sincoff, 1990). We theorize that these responses are likely to be especially damaging in the alliance context because they discourage the flexible processing and thoughtful consideration of alternatives necessary for the successful complex problem-solving that optimizes alliance functioning (Paulus & Yang, 2000).

Ambivalence and Alliance Performance

Rothman and colleagues (2017) review of the ambivalence literature focuses on a recent body of ambivalence research that represents a shift in the consistency-focused thinking (e.g., Festinger, 1957) described above. Many studies over the past 10 years suggest that the experience of ambivalence cannot only be managed, but can be harnessed in ways that produce better outcomes than ambivalence managed in dysfunctional ways—and more provocatively—better outcomes than the absence of ambivalence (Rothman et al., 2017). Take for example Plambeck and Weber's (2009) study of CEO ambivalence and strategic action, where surveyed CEOs who reported ambivalence toward a change in the environment led organizational responses that were more action-oriented, novel, and of greater scope than those of CEOs who did not report ambivalence toward the change.

Ambivalence, when consciously and proactively managed in a way the preserves both orientations simultaneously (i.e., holism; Ashforth et al., 2014), can be a source of positive complex problem-solving behaviors and cognitions. According to the Rothman et al. (2017) framework described above, these outcomes are characterized by engagement and flexibility through wisdom, adaptability, collaboration, and integrative problem-solving, among other functional cognitive and behavioral responses. Because of the inherent complexity of the problem-solving setting in an alliance, both due to the complexity of the problem and the complexity of the associated social and firm dynamics, adaptive, collaborative and integrative problem-solving is especially important to alliance success.

Managing the opposing demands and the resulting ambivalence in engaged and flexible ways requires a great deal of cognitive complexity and effort (Brownstein, 2003; Conner & Armitage, 1998). In the alliance context, when members of the alliance team can be encouraged and supported to harness ambivalence by simultaneously pursuing the competition and cooperation motives, ambivalence is likely to cue more collaborative, adaptable, and creative approaches to problem-solving that, in turn, would support alliance performance. Consistent with prior conceptualizations, we consider complex problem solving as a process comprised of search, information processing, and solution generation (e.g., Posen, Keil, Kim, & Meissner, 2018). Additionally, we integrate conceptual work (e.g., Poppo & Schloemer, in press; Rindova & Martins, 2021) that advances the proposition that, for solutions to complex problems to create value, they must also be novel and useful (i.e., creative; Amabile, 1988). Building on these perspectives and following the structure outlined in Figure 2.1, we detail several specific ways that ambivalence can positively impact alliance performance.

Search Behaviors

One way in which ambivalence has been shown to support complex problem-solving is through a greater expansion of search behaviors. These search behaviors manifest at several different levels. First, individuals who are consciously aware of the ambivalence and its source(s) (i.e., "identified ambivalence," Guarana & Hernandez, 2016) exhibit greater contextual awareness, meaning they are more aware of the stimuli in their context and more motivated to include these stimuli within their search (Brown, Ryan, & Creswell, 2007; Nyanaponika, 1973). This increased contextual awareness also "enables them to deliberatively process contrasting relevant cues" (Guarana & Hernandez, 2016, p. 4), further supporting search behaviors that might turn up conflicting information. Because of the complexity present in an exploratory alliance and the paradoxical nature of pursuing opposing motives like competition and cooperation, conflicting information and cues are likely to be present and a broad array of relevant contextual stimuli are likely necessary for effective complex problem-solving.

Second, individuals consciously engaged in experiencing ambivalence are more likely to engage in relational search behaviors and seek advice from their peers (Rees, Rothman, Lehavy, & Sanchez-Burks, 2013). In a study of hotel managers who were friends with their competitors, Ingram and Roberts (2000) found that the relational ambivalence encouraged both relational search behaviors and the actual sharing of information, facilitating collaboration and improving the performance of the studied firms. These findings suggest that ambivalence can be used to encourage alliance team members to engage in the help seeking, help giving, mutual inspiring, and reframing (Hargadaon & Bechky, 2006) necessary to engage in knowledge work and complex problem-solving, which, in the context of alliances, would support performance goals.

Another way in which ambivalence would be expected to encourage search behaviors is through the introduction of doubt. Rothman and Wiesenfeld (2007) theorize that group members introduce doubt and uncertainty into group decision-making processes when they demonstrate ambivalence. This doubt and uncertainty, in turn, reduces group conformity, encouraging higher levels of cognitive complexity and additional informational search. With the introduction of ambivalence into a group setting, members are motivated to draw their own conclusions based on their own understanding of information they have gathered rather than relying merely on group consensus. In an alliance context, such motivation would encourage team members to engage in broad search behaviors that uncover and draw on information external to the group (and thus, potentially, less fraught with ownership conflicts), allowing them to make more informed decisions that balance their opposing cooperative and competitive demands when approaching complex problem solving and improving alliance performance (see Figure 2.1).

Information Processing

While increased search behaviors are beneficial to complex problem-solving attempts, it is necessary for individuals to suitably process the high levels of information that result from these searches to gain this benefit. Ambivalence also has the potential to motivate more thoughtful and systematic processing of information. Ambivalence has been theorized to increase cognitive flexibility (Firfiray & Gomez-Mejia, 2021; Guarana & Hernandez, 2015) and, in direct opposition to the effects of unmanaged ambivalence, has been shown to reduce decision-makers' vulnerability to cognitive biases when the source of the ambivalence is identified and salient (Guarana & Hernandez, 2016). Because ambivalence serves as a cue that uncertainty and complexity in a situation are high, it encourages a more systematic approach to information processing that would manage uncertainty and complexity, resulting in increased cognitive activity (Jonas, Diehl, & Brömer, 1997; Maio, Bell, & Esses, 1996).

Thus, when alliance team members experience ambivalence as a result of harnessing both the competition and cooperation orientations, the inherent effort, complexity, and uncertainty would motivate them to engage in more thorough, unbiased processing of the broad array of information they gained through increased search behaviors, supporting complex problem-solving and improving the performance of the alliance.

Openness to Alternatives

The increased search behaviors and more systematic information processing motivated by feelings of ambivalence are further amplified by an increased openness to conflicting or alternative perspectives and information. Ambivalence encourages individuals to question assumptions and to consider the viability of perspectives that diverge from their own (Guarana & Hernandez, 2015; Rees et al., 2013; Rothman & Melwani, 2017). This allows individuals to "both expand their cognitive interpretative boundaries by remaining open to a broad set of interrelated alternatives and deepen their cognitive evaluations by having to ultimately resolve their contrasting evaluative orientations to reach a conclusion" (Guarana & Hernandez, 2015, p. 51), increasing the quality of their complex problem-solving.

These expanded interpretative boundaries encourage individuals to engage in "broad thinking" (Vogus, Rothman, Sutcliffe, & Weick, 2014, p. 592) and result in increased receptivity to alternative perspectives (Rees et al., 2013; Rothman & Melwani, 2017). Ambivalence promotes double-loop learning in which underlying assumptions and framing are questioned (Usher & Bryant, 1989), allowing individuals to think more deeply. In alliances, this openness to alternative perspectives and questioning of underlying assumptions is especially important as the alliance team members are faced with potentially competing parent firm goals and frames that introduce conflicting viewpoints and considerations they must engage with cooperatively to accomplish alliance work. This style of thinking would focus members' on new information gathered and the goals of the team and their parent firm, increasing error detection (Guarana & Hernandez, 2015) and the potential for deep change as they broadly consider alternatives and question existing practices.

The effects of a greater openness to alternatives in terms of receptivity, balanced consideration, and questioning of assumptions brought on by the conscious experience of the tension between the competitive and cooperative orientations would allow alliance team members to better solve complex problems, improving the performance of the alliance.

Creativity

Others have conceptualized creativity as an essential process underlying the development of solutions to complex problems (e.g., Poppo & Schloemer, in press; Rindova & Martins, 2021). Thus, a final way that ambivalence supports alliance performance and the associated solving of complex problems is by serving as a creativity prompt. Using the affect-as-information model (Schwarz & Clore, 1983), Fong (2006) found that the atypicality of the emotional ambivalence experience cues individuals to look for other atypical elements in their environment: to "process stimuli in this environment in a flexible, multifaceted way, and to be on the watch for new associations" (p. 1019). The discomfort and disequilibrium produced by this atypical experience has also been theorized to encourage an adoption of more adaptive cognitive frames (Pratt & Barnett, 1997). Additionally, Miron-Spektor and colleagues (2011) found that the conflict arising from a paradoxical frame (i.e., ambivalence) increased "exploration, sensitivity to unusual associations, and generation of new associations between seemingly contradictory elements" (p. 238) which are important elements in creative idea generation and complex problem solving. If the alliance team members feel that the ambivalence created by their experience of the competition-cooperation tension is unusual and a source of conflict they will be more likely to adapt and recognize other "unusual" (i.e., novel) relationships between ideas and gathered information. This connection of disparate ideas and concepts is essential to the generation of the creative (i.e., novel and useful, Amabile, 1988) ideas often necessary to solve complex problems (Poppo & Schloemer, in press; Rindova & Martins, 2021), particularly in ways that benefit both parties in an exploratory alliance.

Contextual Factors Promoting the Deliberate Harnessing of Ambivalence

As ambivalence can have both positive and negative effects, it is essential that alliance managers seek to manage ambivalence in a way that promotes its benefits for complex problem-solving and mitigates negative consequences to protect and support alliance performance. However, current research tells us very little about what organizations can actually do to impact the way ambivalence is managed (Rothman et al., 2017). In this section we build on existing literature to propose several mechanisms that can be used in an alliance team context, encouraging team members to actively grapple with the ambivalence inherent in their roles and support the benefits of ambivalence outlined in the previous section.

Ongoing Salience of the Alliance Team and Parent Firm

An individual experiencing intense ambivalence is likely to experience it as salient, such that "the actor is consciously aware of the opposing orientations" (Ashforth et al., 2014. p. 1460). As noted, the positive outcomes of ambivalence are generally associated with a flexible and engaged or deliberate management of the tension. But how might one consciously maintain the cooperation-competition juxtaposition over time, particularly when previous work suggests there is a natural inclination toward adopting an avoidant or univalent stance rather than maintaining an engaged experience of ambivalence? We posit that members of an alliance team are likely to experience intense ambivalence and struggle to balance the competitive orientation associated with their connections to/interactions with the parent firm and the simultaneous cooperative orientation associated with their connections to/interactions with the alliance team. Thus, a consistent connection to both the parent firm and the alliance team represents an important element of maintaining members' ambivalence. This would ensure the salience of ambivalence, which, for organizational members more broadly, is important to deliberately and flexibly harnessing it, and allow team members to avoid less-functional coping mechanisms in which the cooperation or competition orientation overwhelms the other, the integrity of each is compromised, or both are avoided all together (Ashforth et al., 2014).

The nested nature of identities in the organizational context provides a cognitive frame for viewing the simultaneous salience of parent firm-focused competition and alliance-team-focused cooperation. An identity, or that which is central, distinctive, and enduring about a collective (Albert & Whetten, 1985), is considered nested within a wider collective (e.g., organization) when it is embedded, such as a department identity being embedded in a wider divisional or organizational identity (Ashforth & Johnson, 2001). An alliance team identity is uniquely nested, as it overlaps with each alliance partner. An important function of identity at the organizational level is to differentiate the organization from others in the industry in order to make competition salient in the minds of organizational members (Livengood & Reger, 2010).

At the alliance team level, an important function of identity is to unify alliance members in ways that promote collaboration and the pursuit of a common goal (Poppo et al., 2019). Opposing orientations of nested identities, such as these, are referred to as a between-level identity foil, such that together the identities support the firm-level and alliance-level goals by "providing checks and balances" or "jointly constituting a holistic approach" (Ashforth et al., 2011, p. 1151). For alliance team members, this suggests that a nested identity provides a cognitive frame to regularly remind members of both the team-level and parent firm-level identities, preserving, and potentially embracing, the ambivalence of alliance team members in beneficial ways (Stadtler & Van Wassenhove, 2016).

The salience of the competition and cooperation orientations prompted by the between-level identity foil may also serve the purpose of helping alliance team members identify the source of their ambivalence, which prior work has noted as an important precursor to effective utilization of ambivalence (Guarana & Hernandez, 2016). If the discomfort and uncertainty associated with ambivalence is misattributed, the deliberate harnessing of ambivalence outlined above is diminished (e.g., systematic information processing; Nordgren, van Harreveld, & van der Pligt, 2006) and coping mechanisms associated with the misattributed source of discomfort would be employed instead, resulting in poorer quality problem-solving processes and outcomes.

In the context of these nested identities, it is necessary that alliance team members feel empowered in their role as boundary spanners (Guarana & Hernandez, 2015) and not feel forced to choose between the competitive and cooperative orientations (Stadtler & Van Wassenhove, 2016). In circumstances where ambivalent individuals feel disempowered and forced to choose between one side or the other, the unpleasant aspects of ambivalence (e.g., stress, disequilibrium, uncertainty) are highlighted, encouraging dysfunctional coping and decision-making (Bereti & Simpson, 2021; van Harreveld, Nohlen, & Schneider, 2015; van Harreveld, van der Pligt & de Liver, 2009).

By contrast, in situations where ambivalent individuals do not feel forced to choose sides, ambivalence is not a significant source of stress, reducing the motivation to employ dysfunctional coping mechanisms (van Harreveld, Rutjens, Rotteveels, Nordgren & van der Pligt, 2009). We posit that, to the extent that members of the alliance team understand the complementary nature of the alliance team and parent firm identities (Stadtler & Van Wassenhove, 2016) and view their nesting as an implicit endorsement of one another's identity content, they will be unlikely to feel pressure to declare an allegiance to one identity over the other, ultimately diffusing the pressure to choose just one orientation. Thus, the seemingly dysfunctional opposition between the alliance team-level identity and the parent firm-level identity can serve an important ambivalence-related function: maintain the salience of the opposing orientations in ways that facilitate ongoing functional harnessing of ambivalence among alliance team members.

Psychologically Safe Reflection and Negotiation Routines

The development of flexibly regulated routines is a powerful mechanism to help individuals engage in managing opposing goals (Salvato & Rerup, 2018), such as those posed by the paradoxical competitive and cooperative directives. In their study of work integration social enterprises, which must balance oppositional commercial and social goals, Battilana and colleagues (2015) found that one successful way of managing oppositional goals was through the creation of "spaces of negotiation"—mandatory meetings to assess progress on goals and manage coordination issues between the groups tasked with each set of goals—that were supported by a common understanding of the superordinate goal and by an emphasized mutual dependency to achieve that goal. Similar meetings with rituals to maintain opposing ideologies were observed by Ashforth and Reingen (2014) in their study of a natural food cooperative, and Guarana and Hernandez (2015) suggest that "formal debriefing routines" should be used to emphasize ambivalence and "cultivate counterfactual thinking" (p. 97).

Taken together, these findings and suggestions indicate that formal alliance team meetings that allow for dialogue about the competition-cooperation tensions would enable alliance team members to reflect upon their experiences and engage in the negotiation within themselves and between members. This reflection and negotiation would allow for a coenactment of the competitive and cooperative orientations and discourage team members from pursuing the "dogmatic and one-sided strategies or identities" (Plambeck & Weber, 2010, p. 705) that would result in dysfunctional coping mechanisms. These reflection and negotiation routines would serve as a "safety valve [to keep] contradiction alive" (Ashcraft, 2001, p. 1315) and encourage a positive embracing of ambivalence while also creating routinized opportunities for group-oriented search behaviors, information-sharing, help-giving, help-seeking, and reflective-reframing (Guarana & Hernandez, 2016; Hargadon & Bechkey, 2006) which, as discussed previously, support group complex problem-solving.

A key component of developing and maintaining an effective dialogue about the competitive-cooperative tension is the presence of psychological safety in the alliance team. A social setting characterized by psychological safety is one where the consequences of taking "interpersonal risks" are low (Edmondson & Lei, 2014, p. 24). Members should feel that alliance team interactions represent safe spaces to share ideas and emotions and that, despite the continued salience of a competitive orientation, they will not be unduly criticized or exploited for cooperative behaviors. This sense of safety is especially important when considering findings that expressed ambivalence can be perceived as a sign of weakness and invites domination by decision or negotiation partners (Rothman, 2011; Rothman & Northcraft, 2015), such as the members of the opposing parent firm on an alliance team. Additionally, low levels of psychological safety are associated with feelings of embarrassment and fear which would erode the emotionally and cognitively open conversations needed for reflection and negotiation and promote the use of dysfunctional coping mechanisms, like the domination of one orientation. In order to avoid such perceptions and the creation of a tempting competition-domination scenario, alliance team leaders should carefully monitor and guide the alliance team norms and routines to promote "safe" ambivalence conversations that support growth and complex learning (Pratt & Barnett, 1997, p. 65) and maintains the salience of both motivations.

Additionally, maintaining high levels of psychological safety within an alliance team would serve to reinforce positive team interactions broadly and thus the overall efficacy of team complex problem-solving (Edmondson, 1999). Psychological safety is also considered an important antecedent to creative idea generation, as such perceptions are thought to enable group processes such as curiosity (Harrison & Rouse, 2014) and as individuals need to feel safe to express ideas that are novel and represent image and performance risks (Kanter, 1988; Yuan & Woodman, 2010). Because psychological safety promotes the maintenance of competing motivations, positive group interaction, and creativity, it would likely promote the positive harnessing of ambivalence toward successful group complex problem-solving.

Dualistic Compensation

Compensation acts as both a reward and informational mechanism, directing attention and effort towards incentivized goals (Ocasio, 1997). Thus, when developing a compensation structure in a setting with multiple and/or multilevel goals, it is important to ensure that the incentives target the appropriate goal(s) to motivate the desired performance. Previous study of multilevel compensation systems has shown that systems addressing two levels (e.g., individual and team) increase the prevalence of behaviors that contribute to the attainment of both goals simultaneously (e.g., Zander & Wolfe, 1964); however, systems that address only a single level reduce performance at the unaddressed level (e.g., Hackman, 1998) and the nature of motivated behaviors varies based on the compensation-targeted level (Beersma et al., 2003). In an intra-firm innovation context, Smith and Tushman (2005) suggest managing the tension created by competition and cooperation goals between teams by offering rewards at the product-level and at the organization-level to encourage competition between managers overseeing various products as they jockey for the resources that enable innovation but also to encourage the information-sharing and help-giving necessary to further organization-level goals.

Alliance team members are similarly exposed to competing, multilevel demands stemming from both competitive and cooperative orientations. By offering dualistic rewards contingent upon the performance of both the alliance and the parent firm, management signals that both outcomes are important and merit attention, and alliance team members can be motivated to attend to and pursue goals related to both competition and cooperation simultaneously and, where possible, pursue mutually beneficial courses of action. Additionally, such a compensation scheme acknowledges that the alliance and parent firm performance have the potential to be closely interrelated when parent firms can mutually capture the benefits of alliance performance. By supporting the ambivalence associated with the alliance team member role and motivating dualistic performance in this role, a dualistic compensation scheme would support complex problem-solving and, thus, alliance performance.

Alliance- and Firm-Level Performance

We posit that when alliance team members manage the ambivalence they experience in response to the competing cooperation and competition demands of their role with flexible and engaged cognitive responses (e.g., holism; Ashforth et al., 2014), they will be better able and motivated to engage in expanded information search, process information, remain open to alternative perspectives and ideas, and be creative. As these behaviors support complex problem solving by the alliance team members, the performance of the alliance itself will benefit from the behaviors induced by such harnessed ambivalence.

Additionally, alliance team members' responses to ambivalence have the potential to affect firm performance. One of the incentives for firms to engage in alliances in the first place is learning—firms can acquire knowledge through knowledge spillovers or joint knowledge creation activities, and that knowledge can be applied to improve firm operational effectiveness (Faems et al., 2008; Gulati et al., 2009). As discussed previously, previous approaches to managing the cooperation-competition tension in alliances typically subvert competition at the alliance team level through the use of relational mechanisms or contracts or delegate competitive concerns to managers who are not part of the alliance team, preventing alliance team members from attending to firm-beneficial knowledge development or spill overs.

However, when alliance team members embrace a holistic approach to ambivalence, they maintain a competitive orientation alongside a cooperative one. This encourages them to remain vigilant to the ways in which knowledge developed (or spilled over) in the alliance context can benefit firm performance. Thus, the same problem-solving behaviors motivated by a flexible and engaged response to ambivalence (i.e., information search and processing, openness to alternatives, and creativity), can support both alliance- and firm-level performance, enabling value creation at both levels.

DISCUSSION AND FUTURE DIRECTIONS

For several decades, scholars have described how the tension of competition and cooperation defines interorganizational collaboration (Das & Teng, 2000; Ring & Van de Ven, 1994; Williamson, 1996; Zajac & Olsen, 1993), yet we know very little about the cognitive experience of individuals charged with navigating these tensions in the alliance context (cf. Stadtler & Van Wassenhove, 2016). As others have noted (Argote & Greve, 2007; Powell et al., 2011), strategy research has struggled to relate phenomena to the individual and group levels of analysis. In keeping with this observation, much of the alliance research focuses on the use of firm-level mechanisms to reconcile the competition-cooperation tension, endorsing the complementary use of formal structures and relational mechanisms (e.g., Gulati et al., 2009; Inkpen & Currall, 2004; Oxley, 1997; Poppo & Zenger, 2002).

We extend this literature by examining this tension at the alliance team member-level, drawing upon a growing body of literature on the experience and outcomes of ambivalence. Unlike previously articulated approaches to the competition-cooperation tension that focus on reducing competitive orientations while bolstering cooperation, we suggest a deliberate management of this ambivalence such that the competitive and cooperative orientations are preserved. Examining evidence in the ambivalence literature, we argue that harnessing ambivalence in engaged and flexible ways motivates the search, information processing, openness to alternatives, and creativity that are key to successfully solving complex problems and bolstering alliance and firm performance.

Building upon this, we articulate several mechanisms that managers in an alliance can employ to deliberately shape individual members' responses to ambivalence. The facilitation of a nested alliance team identity and alliance team interaction routines highlights and maintains the salience of the ambivalence and provide psychologically norms for alliance team members to negotiate their dual roles. A dualistic compensation scheme further highlights the salience of the ambivalence and motivates team members to continue to grapple with the competition-cooperation duality. These mechanisms provide both recommendations for present action and targets for future testing, extending the alliance literature by outlining a novel alliance management tactic.

Additionally, identifying the contextual levers firms can employ to shape individual responses to ambivalence represents an important extension of the ambivalence literature for, as Rothman and colleagues (2017) observe, the ambivalence literature has left largely unspecified the conditions that influence individuals' experience of and reaction to ambivalence in organizations. We further extend the ambivalence literature by contextualizing the experience of ambivalence to a specific organizational setting—exploratory alliances. By applying the construct of ambivalence to a specific setting with articulated boundary conditions and dynamics, we present a model of ambivalence that is amenable to testing and application and encourages extension into other specific settings. Also, the selected alliance context is one in which the flexibility-inflexibility and engagement-disengagement outcome framework proposed by Rothman and colleagues (2017) is particularly evident and has a strong influence on alliance and firm performance. The prominence of these elements in this context would allow for empirical examination of their validity and efficacy.

Practical Implications

In the quest for competitive advantage, managers often seek alliances when they cannot integrate through acquisition or through internal development related but distinct resources and capabilities necessary to compete in a given product market. The Nissan-Renault alliance, for example, enabled both companies to benefit from scale economies in purchasing shared components and exploiting shared platforms, which created an opportunity for learning that allowed both companies to upgrade their design and manufacturing capabilities. Similarly, Microsoft and Intel worked "hand in hand" for several decades developing software and hardware that propelled their products into "virtually every home and business" (Tilley, 2017, para 1). Yet, on the other side of the spectrum, managers report that alliances often fail to realize expected goals, with failure rate estimates of roughly 50% (Park & Ungson, 2001). The obvious managerial dilemma is how to structure an alliance to improve the odds of success as well as further explore the factors that underlie very successful alliances.

While the prior literature emphasizes mutual dependency, partner selection, formal contracts, incentives, controls, relational mechanisms and alliance oversight through a dedicated alliance management function, there is little theorizing as to how alliance managers and operational managers should relate the joint tensions of cooperation and competition to team members. Most often advised is an additional management structure embracing a balanced scorecard approach in which an advisory board tracks progress and conflicts (Kaplan, Norton, & Rugelsjoen, 2010). We advance that alliance and operational managers need to deliberately manage the experience of ambivalence. We posit that managers can harness the positive potential of ambivalence by promoting the formation and maintaining the salience of a nested alliance team identity, establishing interaction routines and norms of psychological safety within the team, and employing a dualistic compensation scheme that motivates activities to bolster alliance and firm performance. We argue that this type of structure will help overcome the negative experience associated with ambivalence through greater cognitive processing of the key issues and conflicts inherent in integrating and upgrading each firm's resource and capability base.

Managers of strategic alliances can employ our model to encourage members of the alliance team to actively evaluate the environment and grapple with the competition-cooperation tension. This facilitates real-time strategic positioning to occur within the alliance, to maintain the alignment of firm and alliance interests where possible and, where not possible, to safeguard firm interests with minimized compromising of the alliance interests. In essence, this real-time, alliance team-level positioning allows those with the most immediate and most contextualized knowledge to make quick decisions to balance competition and cooperation rather than relying on centralized decision-making which lacks this tacit knowledge and contextualization. The flexibility and responsiveness afforded by this mechanism may also broaden the scope of appealing potential alliances to include those in which environmental uncertainty is prominent and discouraging of contractual alliance management solutions.

Future Research Directions

As discussed, the typical approach to alliance management in the literature has been to advocate firm-level tactics that reduce competitive concerns and either clear the way for or motivate cooperation. Our model represents a significant departure from this approach by advocating for the active management and embracing of the competition-cooperation juxtaposition at the individual alliance team member level of analysis. Thus, one avenue for future research is to examine the potential boundary condition that we highlight: the nature of the alliance purpose. Because of the complex problem-solving supported by deliberately managed ambivalence, this alliance management tactic may be more appropriate for alliances pursuing exploration-oriented goals than exploitation.

An additional important avenue for future research is an examination of potential methods to help individuals, like those on the alliance team, deal with the cognitive burdens represented by significant information search and consideration. In a paradoxical setting, the potential for overload is high, which is why many individuals elect to manage the resulting ambivalence with simplifying coping mechanisms (Brownstein, 2003; Conner & Armitage, 1998). The ambivalence-harnessing mechanisms we identify are intended to discourage the use of these coping mechanisms, but they do not offer a complete mechanism for managing the resulting cognitive load. The use of regular interaction routines in which alliance team members actively negotiate their ambivalence may help reduce this cognitive load, but further research is needed to provide and test additional solutions to the cognitive capacity issues surrounding sustained ambivalence.

Finally, a potentially fruitful focus of future research is on the empirical extension of the specific mechanisms that allow for the emergence of individual-level cognitions and behaviors to team-, alliance-, and firm-level performance. While there is some understanding of how the individual-level cognitions and behaviors encouraged by deliberately managed ambivalence would contribute to the performance of higher-order levels, empirical work in this area is nascent and needed. One potential direction for this work is to examine how an ambivalence-based alliance management tactic affects firms' abilities to capture returns from jointly created knowledge compared to previously proposed alliance management mechanisms.

CONCLUSION

In conclusion, decades of research on alliances and alliance management have produced significant understanding of the ways in which the competition-cooperation tension can be managed at the firm level. We propose a model to direct attention to the individual alliance team member-level by suggesting an alliance management approach that focuses on the individual experience of this tension and provide mechanisms for harnessing its innovative potential. It is our hope that our contributions spur future research that extend the theoretical and practical understanding of optimal alliance management across the individual, alliance, and firm levels of analysis.

REFERENCES

Albert, S., & Whetten, D. A. (1985). Organizational identity. *Research in Organizational Behavior*, 7, 263–295.

Amabile, T. M. (1988). A model of creativity and innovation in organizations. *Research in Organizational Behavior*, 10(1), 123–167.

Argote, L., & Greve, H. R. (2007). A behavioral theory of the firm—40 years and counting: Introduction and impact. *Organization Science*, 18(3), 337–349.

Ashcraft, K. L. (2001). Organized dissonance: Feminist bureaucracy as hybrid form. *Academy of Management Journal*, 44(6), 1301–1322.

Ashforth, B. E., & Johnson, S. A. (2001). Which hat to wear. In M. A. Hogg & D. J. Terry (Eds.), *Social identity processes in organizational contexts* (pp. 32–48). New York, NY: Psychology Press.

Ashforth, B. E., Rogers, K. M., & Corley, K. G. (2011). Identity in organizations: Exploring cross-level dynamics. *Organization Science*, 22(5), 1144–1156.

Ashforth, B. E., & Reingen, P. H. (2014). Functions of dysfunction: Managing the dynamics of an organizational duality in a natural food cooperative. *Administrative Science Quarterly*, *59*(3), 474–516.

Ashforth, B. E., Rogers, K. M., Pratt, M. G., & Pradies, C. (2014). Ambivalence in organizations: A multilevel approach. *Organization Science*, *25*(5), 1453–1478.

Barnard, C. (1968). *The functions of the executive* (2nd ed.). Cambridge, MA: Harvard University Press.

Battilana, J., Sengul, M., Pache, A-C., & Model, J. (2015). Harnessing productive tensions in hybrid organizations: The case of work integration social enterprises. *Academy of Management Journal*, *58*(6), 1658–1685.

Beersma, B., Hollenbeck, J. R., Humphrey, S. E., Moon, H., Conlon, D. E., & Ilgen, D. R. (2003). Cooperation, competition, and team performance: Toward a contingency approach. *Academy of Management Journal*, *46*(5), 572–590.

Bell, D. W., & Esses, V. M. (2002). Ambivalence and response amplification: A motivational perspective. *Personality and Social Psychology Bulletin*, *28*(8), 1143–1152.

Bercovitz, B., Jap, S., & Nickerson, J. (2006). The antecedents and performance implications of cooperative exchange norms. *Organization Science*, *17*(6), 724–742.

Bereti, M., & Simpson, A. V. (2021). The dark side of organizational paradoxes: The dynamics of disempowerment. *Academy of Management Review*, *46*(2), 252–274.

Brown, K. W., Ryan, R. M., & Creswell, J. D. (2007). Mindfulness: Theoretical foundations and evidence for its salutary effects. *Psychological Inquiry*, *18*(4), 211–237.

Brownstein, A. L. (2003). Biased predecision processing. *Psychological Bulletin*, *129*(4), 545–568.

Cacioppo, J. T., Gardner, W. L., & Berntson, G. G. (1997). Beyond bipolar conceptualizations and measures: The case of attitudes and evaluative space. *Personality and Social Psychology Review*, *1*(1), 3–25.

Cao, Z., & Lumineau, F. (2015). Revisiting the interplay between contractual and relational governance: A qualitative and meta-analytic investigation. *Journal of Operations Management*, *33–34*, 15–42.

Conner, M., & Armitage, C. J. (1998). Extending the theory of planned behavior: A review and avenues for further research. *Journal of Applied Social Psychology*, *28*(15), 1429–1464.

Cramer, P. (2006). *Protecting the self: Defense mechanisms in action*. New York, NY: Guilford Press.

Das, T. K., & Teng, B. (2000). Instabilities of strategic alliances: An internal tensions perspective. *Organization Science*, *11*(1), 77–101.

Dyer, J. H., & Singh, H. (1998). The relational view: Cooperative strategy and sources of interorganizational competitive advantage. *Academy of Management Review*, *23*(4), 660–679.

Edmondson, A. (1999). Psychological safety and learning behavior in work teams. *Administrative Science Quarterly*, *44*(2), 350–383.

Edmondson, A. C., & Lei, Z. (2014). Psychological safety: The history, renaissance, and future of an interpersonal construct. *Annual Review of Organizational Psychology & Organizational Behavior, 1*(1), 23–43.

Emmons, R., & King, L. (1988). Conflict among personal strivings: Immediate and long-term implications for psychological and physical well-being. *Journal of Personality and Social Psychology, 54*(6), 1040–1048.

Faems, D., Janssens, M., Madhok, A., & Van Looy, B. (2008). Toward an integrative perspective on alliance governance: Connecting contract design, trust dynamics, and contract application. *Academy of Management Journal, 51*(6), 1053–1078.

Fan, G. H., & Zietsma, C. (2017). Constructing a shared governance logic: The role of emotions in enabling dually embedded agency. *Academy of Management Journal, 60*(6), 2321–2351.

Festinger, L. (1957). *A theory of cognitive dissonance*. Stanford, CA: Stanford University Press.

Firfiray, S., & Gomez-Mejia, L. R. (2021). When is ambivalence good for family firms? Understanding the impact of family managers' emotional ambivalence on decision making. *Entrepreneurship Research Journal, 11*(3), 177–189.

Fong, C. T. (2006). The effects of emotional ambivalence on creativity. *Academy of Management Journal, 49*(5), 1016–1030.

Guarana, C. L., & Hernandez, M. (2015). Building sense out of situational complexity: The role of ambivalence in creating functional leadership processes. *Organizational Psychology Review, 5*(1), 50–73.

Guarana, C. L., & Hernandez, H. (2016). Identified ambivalence: When cognitive conflicts can help individuals overcome cognitive traps. *Journal of Applied Psychology, 101*(7), 1013–1029.

Gulati, R., Lavie, D., & Singh, H. (2009). The nature of partnering experience and the gains from alliances. *Strategic Management Journal, 30*(11), 1213–1233.

Hackman, J. R. (1998). Why teams don't work. In S. R. Tindale & L. Heath (Eds.), *Theory and research on small groups* (pp. 245–265). New York, NY: Plenum.

Hargadon, A. B. & Bechky, B. A. (2006). When collections of creatives become creative collectives: A field study of problem solving at work. *Organization Science, 17*(4), 484–500.

Harrison, S. H., & Rouse, E. D. (2014). Let's dance! Elastic coordination in creative group work: A qualitative study of modern dancers. *Academy of Management Journal, 57*(5), 1256–1283.

Hennart, J. F. (1988). A transaction costs theory of equity joint ventures. *Strategic Management Journal, 9*(4), 361–374.

Ingram, P., & Roberts, P. W. (2000). Friendships among competitors in the Sydney hotel industry. *American Journal of Sociology, 106*(2), 387–423.

Inkpen, A. C. & Currall, S. C. (2004). The coevolution of trust, control, and learning in joint ventures. *Organization Science, 15*(5), 586–599.

Jonas, K., Diehl, M., & Brömer, P. (1997). Effects of attitudinal ambivalence on information processing and attitude-intention consistency. *Journal of Experimental Social Psychology, 33*(2), 190–210.

Kanter, R. M. (1988). Three tiers for innovation research. *Communication Research, 15*(5), 509–523.

Kaplan, R. S., Norton, D. P., & Rugelsjoen, B. (2010). Managing alliances with the balanced scorecard. *Harvard Business Review*, *88*(1), 114–120.

Krishnan, R., Geyskens, I., & Steenkamp, J.-B. E. M. (2016). The effectiveness of contractual and trust-based governance in strategic alliances under behavioral and environmental uncertainty. *Strategic Management Journal*, *37*(12), 2521–2542.

Lavie, D., Haunschild, P. R., & Khanna, P. (2012). Organizational differences, relational mechanisms, and alliance performance. *Strategic Management Journal*, *33*(13), 1453–1479.

Lüscher, L. S., & Lewis, M. W. (2008). Organizational change and managerial sensemaking: Working through paradox. *Academy of Management Journal*, *51*(2), 221–240.

Lewis, M. W. (2000). Exploring paradox: Toward a more comprehensive guide. *Academy of Management Review*, *25*(4), 760–776.

Li, J. J., Poppo, L., & Zhou, K. Z. (2010). Relational mechanisms, formal contracts, and local knowledge acquisition by international subsidiaries. *Strategic Management Journal*, *31*(4), 349–370.

Livengood, R. S., & Reger, R. K. (2010). That's our turf! Identity domains and competitive dynamics. *Academy of Management Review*, *35*(1), 48–66.

Macher, J. T., & Richman, B. D. (2008). Transaction cost economics: An assessment of empirical research in the social sciences. *Business and Politics*, *10*(1), 1–63.

Madhok, A., & Tallman, S. B. (1998). Resources, transactions, and rents: Managing value through interfirm collaborative relationships. *Organization Science*, *9*(3), 326–339.

Maio, G. R., Bell, D. W., & Esses, V. M. (1996). Ambivalence and persuasion: The processing of messages about immigrant groups. *Journal of Experimental Social Psychology*, *32*(6), 513–536.

Makadok, R., & Coff, R. (2009). Both market and hierarchy: An incentive-system theory of hybrid governance forms. *Academy of Management Review*, *34*(2), 297–320.

Miron-Spektor, E., Gino, F., & Argote, L. (2011). Paradoxical frames and creative sparks: Enhancing individual creativity through conflict and integration. *Organizational Behavior and Human Decision Processes*, *116*(2), 229–240.

Molinsky, A. L. (2013). The psychological processes of cultural retooling. *Academy of Management Journal*, *56*(3), 683–710.

Nickerson, J. A., & Zenger T. R. (2004). A knowledge-based theory of the firm-the problem-solving perspective. *Organization Science*, *15*(6), 617–632.

Nordgren, L. F., van Harreveld, F., & van der Pligt, J. (2006). Ambivalence, discomfort, and motivated information processing. *Journal of Experimental Social Psychology*, *42*(2), 252–258.

Nyanaponika, T. (1973). *The heart of Buddhist meditation: Satipatthna: A handbook of mental training based on the Buddha's way of mindfulness*. Newburyport, MA: Weiser Books.

Ocasio, W. (1997). Towards an attention-based view of the firm. *Strategic Management Journal*, *18*(S1), 187–206.

Oxley, J. E. (1997). Appropriability hazards and governance in strategic alliances: A transaction cost approach. *Journal of Law, Economics, and Organization*, *13*(2), 387–409.

Park, S. H., & Ungson, G. R. (2001). Interfirm rivalry and managerial complexity: A conceptual framework of alliance failure. *Organization Science*, *12*(1), 37–53.

Parkhe, A. (1993). Strategic alliance structuring: A game theoretic and transaction cost examination of interfirm cooperation. *Academy of Management Journal*, *36*(4), 794–829.

Paulus, P. B., & Yang, H. (2000). Idea generation in groups: A basis for creativity in organizations. *Organizational Behavior and Human Decision Processes*, *82*(1), 76–87.

Plambeck, N., & Weber, K. (2009). CEO ambivalence and responses to strategic issues. *Organization Science*, *20*(6), 993–1010.

Plambeck, N., & Weber, K. (2010). When the glass is half full and half empty: CEOs' ambivalent interpretations of strategic issues. *Strategic Management Journal*, *31*(7), 689–710.

Poppo, L., & Zenger, T. (2002). Do formal contracts and relational governance function as substitutes or complements? *Strategic Management Journal*, *23*(8), 707–725.

Poppo, L., & Schloemer, H. (in press). Problem solving through the lenses of identity, identification, and work groups: A socio-cognitive theory of the firm. *Strategic Management Review*.

Poppo, L., Schloemer, H., & Rogers, K. M. (2019). Social psychological foundations of alliance cooperation: The role of identity and identification in shared alliance interest. In F. J. Contractor & J. J. Reuer (Eds.), *Frontiers of strategic alliance research* (pp. 152–168). Cambridge, UK: Cambridge University Press.

Posen, H. E., Keil, T., Kim, S., & Meissner, F. D. (2018). Renewing research on problemistic search—A review and research agenda. *Academy of Management Annals*, *12*(1), 208–251.

Powell, T. C., Lovallo, D., & Fox, C. R. (2011). Behavioral strategy. *Strategic Management Journal*, *32*(13), 1369–1386.

Pratt, M. G., & Barnett, C. K. (1997). Emotions and unlearning in Amway recruiting techniques: Promoting change through "safe" ambivalence. *Management Learning*, *28*(1), 65–88.

Pratt, M. G., & Doucet, L. (2000). Ambivalent feelings in organizational relationships. In S. Fineman (Ed.), *Emotion in organizations (2nd ed.)* (pp. 204–226). London, UK: SAGE.

Rees, L., Rothman, N. B., Lehavy, R., & Sanchez-Burks, J. (2013). The ambivalent mind can be a wise mind: Emotional ambivalence increases judgment accuracy. *Journal of Experimental Social Psychology*, *49*(3), 360–367.

Reuer, J. J., & Ariño, A. (2007). Strategic alliance contracts: Dimensions and determinants of contractual complexity. *Strategic Management Journal*, *28*(3), 313–330.

Rindova, V. P., & Martins, L. L. (2021). Futurescapes: Imagination and temporal reorganization in the design of strategic narratives. *Strategic Organization*, *20*(1), 200–224.

Ring, P., & Van De Ven, A. (1994). Developmental processes of cooperative inter-organizational relationships. *Academy of Management Review*, *19*(1), 90–118.

Rothman, N. B. (2011). Steering sheep: How expressed emotional ambivalence elicits dominance in interdependent decision-making contexts. *Organizational Behavior and Human Decision Processes*, *116*(1), 66–82.

Rothman, N. B., & Melwani, S. (2017). Feeling mixed, ambivalent, and in flux: The social functions of emotional complexity for leaders. *Academy of Management Review*, *42*(2), 259–282.

Rothman, N. B., & Northcraft, G. B. (2015). Unlocking integrative potential: Expressed emotional ambivalence and negotiation outcomes. *Organizational Behavior and Human Decision Processes*, *126*, 65–76.

Rothman, N. B., Pratt, M. G., Rees, L., & Vogus, T. J. (2017). Understanding the dual nature of ambivalence: Why and when ambivalence leads to good and bad outcomes. *Academy of Management Annals*, *11*(1), 33–72.

Rothman, N. B., & Wiesenfeld, B. M. (2007). The social consequences of expressing emotional ambivalence in groups and teams. In E. A. Mannix, M. A. Neale, & C. P. Anderson (Eds.), *Affect and groups (Research on managing groups and teams, Vol. 10)* (pp. 275–308). Bingley, UK: Emerald Publishing Group.

Salvato, C., & Rerup, C. (2018). Routine regulation: Balancing conflicting goals in organizational routines. *Administrative Science Quarterly*, *63*(1), 170–209.

Schepker, D. J., Oh, W. Y., Martynov, A., & Poppo, L. (2014). The many futures of contracts: Moving beyond structure and safeguarding to coordination and adaptation. *Journal of Management*, *40*(1), 193–225.

Schreiner, M., Kale, P., & Corsten, D. (2009). What really is alliance management capability and how does it impact alliance outcomes and success? *Strategic Management Journal*, *30*(13), 1395–1419.

Schwarz, N., & Clore, G. L. (1983). Mood, misattribution, and judgments of well-being: Informative and directive functions of affective states. *Journal of Personality and Social Psychology*, *45*(3), 513–523.

Sincoff, J. (1990). The psychological characteristics of ambivalent people. *Clinical Psychology Review*, *10*(1), 43–68.

Smith, W. K., & Tushman, M. L. (2005). Managing strategic contradictions: A top management model for managing innovation streams. *Organization Science*, *16*(5), 522–536.

Stadtler, L., & Van Wassenhove, L. N. (2016). Coopetition as a paradox: Integrative approaches in a multi-company, cross-sector partnership. *Organization Studies*, *37*(5), 655–685.

Tilley, A. (2017, March 10). The end of Wintel: How the most powerful alliance in tech history is falling apart. *Forbes*. https://www.forbes.com/sites/aarontilley/2017/03/10/microsoft-intel-divorce

Usher, R., & Bryant, I. (1989). *Adult education as theory, practice and research*. London, UK: Routledge.

van Harreveld, F., Nohlen, H. U., & Schneider, I. K. (2015). The ABC of ambivalence: Affective, behavioral, and cognitive consequences of attitudinal conflict. *Advances in Experimental Social Psychology*, *52*, 285–324.

van Harreveld, F., Rutjens, B., Rotteveel, M., Nordgren, L., & van der Pligt, J. (2009). Ambivalence and decisional conflict as a cause of psychological discomfort: Feeling tense before jumping off the fence. *Journal of Experimental Social Psychology, 45*(1), 167–173.

van Harreveld, F., van der Pligt, J., & de Liver, Y. 2009). The agony of ambivalence and ways to resolve it: Introducing the MAID model. *Personality and Social Psychology Review, 13*(1), 45–61.

Vogus, T., Rothman, N. B., Sutcliffe, K., & Weick, K. (2014). The affective foundations of high reliability organizing. *Journal of Organizational Behavior, 35*(4), 592–596.

Waldman, D. A., Putnam, L. L., Miron-Spektor, E., & Siegel, D. (2019). The role of paradox theory in decision making and management research. *Organizational Behavior and Human Decision Processes, 155*, 1–6.

Weber, L., & Mayer, K. J. (2011). Designing effective contracts: Exploring the influence of framing and expectations. *Academy of Management Review, 36*(1), 53–75.

Williamson, O. E. (1996). *The mechanisms of governance*. New York, NY: Oxford University Press.

Yuan, F., & Woodman, R. W. (2010). Innovative behavior in the workplace: The role of performance and image outcome expectations. *Academy of Management Journal, 53*(2), 323–342.

Zajac, E. J. & Olsen, C. P. (1993). From transaction cost to transactional value analysis: Implications for the study of interorganizational strategies. *Journal of Management Studies, 30*(1), 131–145.

Zander, A., & Wolfe, D. (1964). Administrative rewards and coordination among committee members. *Administrative Science Quarterly, 9*(1), 50–69.

CHAPTER 3

THE IMBRICATION OF INTERNAL AND EXTERNAL COOPETITION IN STRATEGIC ALLIANCES

Kaouther Ben Jamaa-Boubaya, Olivier Furrer, Foued Cheriet, Laure Dikmen, and Mouhoub Hani

ABSTRACT

Research on strategic alliances and coopetition has generated numerous contributions on the sources of paradoxical tensions and on the mechanisms for managing these tensions. These academic contributions have largely examined the dynamics of inter-organizational relations. However, despite the scientific interest in better understanding the evolution and management of internal and external coopetitive tensions, the question of understanding these interactions by examining the intertwining of competitive and cooperative, internal, and external tensions remains little explored to date. Based on a case study of a strategic alliance in the technology sector over the analysis period 2015–2017, this study aims to answer the question of how internal and external coopetition influence each other. To do this, we propose a conceptualization of the intertwining, or imbrication, of internal and external coopetition by highlighting the objects of imbrication, the forms in which it is revealed, and the mechanisms for managing it. This study provides an understanding of the concepts involved, aims to generate a fruitful dialogue, and feeds into future studies on the paradoxes of internal and external coopetition and the resulting tensions.

Managing Interpartner Cooperation in Strategic Alliances, pp. 63–90
Copyright © 2022 by Information Age Publishing
www.infoagepub.com
All rights of reproduction in any form reserved.

63

INTRODUCTION

Strategic alliances are long-term contractual or equity agreements between two or more firms to share resources in order to achieve common goals, while remaining independent outside the scope of the alliance (Das &Teng, 1998, 2000a). These relationships are accompanied by coopetitive dynamics (i.e., simultaneous cooperation and competition between partners, Brandenburger & Nalebuff, 1996), which generate internal and external tensions. Although cooperation is necessary if alliance partners are to achieve common goals, competition often emerges when the partners also seek to achieve individual goals (Bengtsson & Kock, 2000; Hamel, 1991). Similarly, within a firm, although managers of different business units need to cooperate to achieve common corporate goals, competition may also emerge when it comes to obtaining funding and other scarce corporate resources (Furrer, 2016).

There appears to be a consensus in the coopetition literature regarding the need to analyze internal and external coopetition and their interrelationships (Bengtsson, Raza-Ullah, & Vanyushyn, 2016; Chiambaretto & Dumez, 2016; Czakon, Srivastava, Le Roy & Gnyawali, 2020; Gernsheimer, Kanbach, & Gast, 2021; Raza-Ullah, Bengtsson, & Kock, 2014; Tidström & Rajala, 2016). However, several scholars have pointed out the scarcity of studies on internal coopetition (relative to those on external coopetition). For example, out of 142 studies on coopetition published between 1996 and 2014, only 5% concern the intra-organizational relationship, compared to 47% relating to the inter-organizational level (Bengtsson & Raza-Ullah, 2016). These results highlight how the tensions related to external coopetition between alliance partners have been more widely studied than the tensions inherent in internal coopetition between strategic units within the same firm.

Moreover, external and internal coopetition have been studied separately, despite the critically of studying their intertwining, or imbrication. The way they influence each other remains little explored in the strategic management literature (Thelisson, 2021). The extant literature also lacks insight into the interrelationships between internal and external coopetition (Raza-Ullah et al., 2014). Employees sometimes have a negative attitude toward external knowledge (Katz & Allen, 1982), which can be problematic when the knowledge source is a competitor (Raza-Ullah et al., 2014). As Mariani (2018) points out, the unit of analysis in internal coopetition studies is often firm-level. Yet, external relationships can influence internal coopetitive behaviors (Bengtsson & Raza-Ullah, 2016). The analysis of internal coopetition might provide promising insights to better understand the interactions between cooperation and competition inside and outside the firm (Gernsheimer et al., 2021; Song, Lee, & Khanna, 2016).

In order to explore the factors that generate internal coopetitive tensions and their interaction with coopetitive tensions with external strategic alliance partners, we conducted a case study based on semi-structured interviews with alliance managers and directors of three strategic alliances with the same focal firm. In addition to identifying the different sources of internal tensions and the relationships with external coopetitive tensions, we highlight the mechanisms used by alliance managers to manage the relationships between internal and external coopetition.

The remainder of this chapter is structured as follows. First, we review the relevant literature of the concepts of internal and external coopetition in order to develop a conceptual framework of the imbrication between internal and external coopetitive relationships. Second, we present in detail the case-based methodology used in this study. Finally, we present the main findings of our analysis before discussing them and outlining avenues for future research.

LITERATURE REVIEW

Coopetition refers to an inter-organizational situation characterized by the simultaneous presence of cooperation and competition (Gnyawali & Ryan Charleton, 2018). In recent years, coopetition in strategic alliances has attracted increasing attention of strategic management scholars (Hani & Dagnino, 2021). Several studies have examined the paradox of coopetition and the tensions that arise from it (Bengtsson & Kock, 2014; Chiambaretto, Mass'e, & Mirc, 2019; Fernandez, Le Roy, & Gnyawali, 2014; Raza Ullah et al., 2014). This stream of research has mostly focused on coopetition in the context of strategic alliances and inter-organizational relationships—i.e., external coopetition (e.g., Bengtsson & Kock, 2000). More recent studies, however, have begun to examine coopetition at the intra-organizational level—that is, internal coopetition (e.g., Chiambaretto et al., 2019), and to discuss the interrelationships between various internal tensions and their impacts on the management of strategic alliances with external partners (Das & Teng, 2000b).

External Coopetition

In coopetitive relationships, companies simultaneously compete and cooperate to improve financial performance and/or innovation (Brandenburger & Nalebuff, 1996; Gnyawali & Ryan Charleton, 2018). Traditionally, coopetition studies have sought to understand coopetition experiences that give rise to multifaceted relationships and that occur at different interorganizational levels: from the dyad to the firms. This growing literature has progressively produced a set of contributions that have identified the simultaneous coexistence of cooperation and competition, requiring specific management mechanisms for dealing with the resulting coopetitive tensions. These studies found that managing coopetition, often equated with managing paradoxical tensions (Chiambaretto et al., 2019), and requires three key elements: (i) establishing and maintaining a balance between competition and cooperation, (ii) the dynamics that occur during a coopetitive relationship, and (iii) mechanisms for managing tensions and conflicts (Dorn, Schweiger, & Albers, 2016).

This latter aspect has attracted increasing attention from coopetition scholars, leading them to identify several sources of tensions, such as the divergence of coopetitors' strategic goals and their historical experiences (Tidström, 2009); shared knowledge used to pursue common interests and to obtain private gains (Santos, 2021); the ambivalence of emotions within organizations (Raza Ullah et al., 2014); power, dependency, and opportunistic situations (Tidström, 2014); relational and contextual factors (Bengtsson & Kock, 2014); the experience of competitors interacting with each other (Dahl, 2014); the dilemma of joint value creation and its individual appropriation; and finally the risk of knowledge leakage (Fernandez et al., 2014).

These coopetitive tensions, mostly studied in the context of strategic alliances (Tidström, 2014; Wilhelm, 2011; Wilhelm & Sydow, 2018), differ from the organizational paradoxes identified in the management literature (e.g., Poole & Van de Ven, 1989; Smith & Lewis, 2011). Among the main mechanisms for managing coopetitive tensions identified in this literature, there are the principles of separation and integration, especially for information and learning management (Fernandez & Chiambaretto, 2016; Fernandez et al., 2014; Le Roy & Fernandez, 2015), or the creation of dedicated structures and teams (Bengtsson & Raza-Ullah, 2016). Fernandez (2014) and her colleagues (p. 222) suggest that "an organization based on a mix of separation and integration of competition and cooperation is useful for understanding and effectively managing coopetitive tensions."

Internal Coopetition: Manifestations and Management Mechanisms

Internal coopetition refers to a situation characterized by the simultaneous presence of cooperative and competitive actions within a company's organizational boundaries (Chiambaretto et al., 2019). Internal coopetition can occur at the management leadership level (Furrer, 2016) as well as at the team level (Tidström & Rajala, 2016). It is characterized by diverse interactions: between managers of different business units of the same firm, between members of the same team, between managers of a team and other organizational actors, and between different teams or support functions of the firm (Chiambaretto et al., 2019). The main causes of internal coopetition are the ambiguity of individual and team roles; emotional ambivalence; the search for a position in intra-organizational networks; conflict risk management; different and sometimes contradictory managerial expectations; and tensions between sharing and protecting learning, and between common and private benefits (Bengtsson & Raza-Ulah, 2016; Furrer, 2016).

Internal coopetition results in tensions between cooperation and competition within the organization through the management, in particular, of learning (its creation and dissemination and the degree of centralization and autonomy of the process) (Chiambaretto et al., 2019). Thus, internal coopetitive situations relating to sharing the value of created knowledge, competition for budgets, and races during new product launches clash with the need for organizational synergies and the need to federate R&D efforts between teams. In this internal coopetitive paradox, tensions can arise between the protection and dissemination of learning, between the objectives of the teams and the global strategy of the company, or between current and future projects (Luo, Slotegraaf, & Pan, 2006; Seran, Pellegrin-Boucher, & Gurau, 2016; Tsai, 2002). These internal tensions can constitute a risk for organizations and hinder learning.

Studies on internal coopetition has also investigated the mechanisms for managing coopetition (Bengtsson & Raza-Ulah, 2016; Tidström & Rajala, 2016). This literature has identified several mechanisms pertaining to coopetitive capabilities, learning management, and replications of previous coopetitive managerial experiences (Chiambaretto et al., 2019; Dahl, Kock, & Henriksson, 2016; Dahl, 2014). It should be noted that some of these mechanisms are developed internally, while others are derived from the firm's external coopetitive experience with strategic alliance partners (Bengtsson et al., 2016). For Tidström and Rajala (2016), managing internal coopetition involves implementing communication procedures between and within teams, establishing organizational routines, and reflecting at a company level on the replication of certain coopetitive patterns. Bengtsson and Raza-Ulah (2016), on the other hand, insist on establishing an adapted governance structure, clarifying roles and expectations through contractual management within teams, and developing internal coopetitive skills. This requires learning how to manage these coopetitive tensions and sometimes involves creating dedicated teams or implementing a specific governance mode.

Relationship Between Internal and External Coopetition

To the best of our knowledge, only few studies have analyzed the imbrication of internal and external coopetition: Bengtsson and his colleagues (2016) showed that managers in a coopetitive context face both internal and external tensions and therefore have to be even more ambidextrous than when facing only one type of tension. Bouncken, Fredrich, and Kraus (2020) examined how the strength of the paradoxical tensions inherent in coopetition can lead to external coopetitive tensions, which can then lead to internal coopetition. Chen, Yao, Zan, and Carayannis (2020) found that when a firm faces both a high intensity of external coopetition and a high level of internal coopetition, external knowledge integration is diminished. Finally, Klimas, Czakon, and Fredrich (2022) examined the interconnections between the external and internal factors of coopetition as perceived by coopetition managers.

Beyond this handful of studies highlighting the existence of interrelationships between external and internal coopetition, other studies have examined the effects that the management mechanisms of one might have on the manifestations of the other. For example, Dahl and his colleagues (2016) have shown that managing external coopetitive tensions requires organizational changes that provide greater flexibility and managerial autonomy to teams (Dahl et al., 2016) or the establishment of rules for internal coopetition. Similarly, Bengtsson and Raza-Ulah (2016) recommend using the managerial knowledge gained from managing external coopetition to manage internal coopetition by replicating and transferring it to internal coopetition situations.

Additionally, the managerial literature offers some anecdotal examples of the existence of interrelationships between internal and external coopetition. For example, Song, Lee, and Khanna (2016) present the case of Samsung's internal coopetition, which helped the company catch up with Apple. In 2013, by working closely with internal and external suppliers, Samsung was able to meet divergent customer needs by launching 50 different smartphone models, compared to Apple's two. Song and his colleagues (2016) explain that Samsung was thus able to build a dual sourcing system in which it purchased components both externally and internally and strongly encouraged component manufacturing partners to simultaneously sell their products outside the group. This dual sourcing policy allowed it to constantly detect and adopt new technologies, ensure stable supply by securing second sources, and keep costs down by letting internal and external suppliers compete fiercely. Because of this system, Samsung's divisions competed intensely with their external rivals, while internally, Samsung's rigorous evaluation standards encouraged divisions to compete with each other. This example provides evidence of the existence of intra- and inter-organizational coopetitive relationship linkages.

However, the scarcity of studies on the relationships between external and internal coopetition demonstrates the urgent need to conceptualize the relationships between these two types of coopetition (Depeyre & Dumez, 2010).

CONCEPTUAL FRAMEWORK

To further explore the relationships between internal and external coopetition and to develop a conceptual model that could help us interpret our empirical data, we propose an approach based on the semiotic square (Greimas, 2015). The semiotic square, which is derived from Aristotle's logical square, can be used to formalize relationships between opposing concepts. It involves representing concepts that are at the basis of a structure, such as internal and external coopetition, in pairs of opposite and complementary terms, such as cooperation and competition. The semiotic square has been used as an analytical tool in the field of marketing, advertising, and communication (Oswald, 2015; Signori & Flint, 2020). In strategic alliance research, Furrer, Tjemkes, Boymans, and Ubachs (2013) used Kiesler's (1983) interpersonal circle, an analytical tool similar to the semiotic square, to study the dynamics of partner behavior in strategic alliances.

Our adaptation of the semiotic square in Figure 3.1 identifies three types of relationships between internal and external coopetition: (1) horizontal relationships are oppositional relationships between internal cooperation and internal competition and between external cooperation and external competition; (2) vertical relationships are isomorphic relationships between internal cooperation and external cooperation and between internal competition and external competition; and (3) diagonal relationships are complementary relationships between internal cooperation and external competition and between internal competition and external cooperation.

As discussed in the above literature review, studies on coopetition have, until now, mostly focused on the oppositional relationships between cooperation and competition, separately from internal and external coopetition. In general, these studies have shown that the oppositional relationships are characterized by a relative decoupling that can generate paradoxical tensions (Czakon et al., 2020). In other words, while one would expect to find oppositional relationships between cooperation and competition (where one is strong and the other is weak), coopetitive situations are most often characterized by a simultaneously high level of cooperation and competition (Bengtsson & Kock, 2000; Gnyawali, He, & Madhavan, 2006; Ketchen,

Figure 3.1

Conceptual Framework: The Semiotic Square of Coopetition

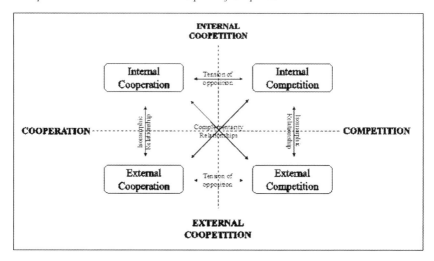

Snow, & Hoover, 2004). Isomorphic and complementary relationships, on the other hand, have not yet, to our knowledge, been studied in depth in studies of internal and external coopetition.

These isomorphic and complementary relationships are, however, crucial to understanding how internal and external coopetition interact. The existence of isomorphic relationships indicates a similarity between internal and external coopetition. If there are strong isomorphic relationships, a firm that has developed high cooperative (or competitive) competencies can use these competencies to manage both internal and external coopetitive tensions. Conversely, the existence of complementary relationships indicates that a firm manages internal and external coopetitive tensions in a complementary way. In other words, strong internal cooperation will allow the firm to control the risks of external competition; or, conversely, strong internal competition, to be effective, requires strong external cooperation. To understand how to manage coopetitive tensions effectively and to better understand how internal and external coopetition affect each other, we need to identify which of the isomorphic and complementary relationships are dominant.

Indeed, the decoupling of oppositional relationships raises the question of the relative importance of isomorphic and complementary relationships. In other words, does strong external cooperation, for example, call for strong internal cooperation (isomorphic relationship) or strong internal competition (complementary relationship)? Which of these two types of relationship is dominant? Similarly, does strong external competition call for strong internal competition (isomorphic relationship) or strong internal cooperation (complementary relationship)? In other words, is there a mirror effect between internal and external coopetition (i.e., internally cooperative behaviors lead to externally cooperative behaviors and internally competitive behaviors lead to externally competitive behaviors or vice versa)? Or, on the contrary, is there a substitution effect between internal and external coopetition (i.e., internally cooperative behaviors complementarily lead to externally competitive behaviors and internally competitive behaviors complementarily lead to externally cooperative behaviors or vice versa)? The key question is therefore: Are the relationships between internal and external coopetition isomorphic (mirror effect) or complementary (substitution effect)?

Answering this question has important theoretical and managerial implications. If internal and external coopetition have isomorphic relationships, we can expect that learning from the mechanisms of managing external coopetition can be transferred to the management of internal coopetition and *vice versa*. Conversely, if internal and external coopetition have complementary relationships, each of the two types of coopetition may require its own management mechanisms.

We define internal coopetition as competition and cooperation between internal teams within the same firm and external coopetition as competition and cooperation between independent and competing firms and nested coopetition as the interrelationships between internal and external coopetition (see Figure 3.2).

METHOD

Case Study of an Enterprise Resource Planning Giant: Alpha

Alpha (not the real name; it is used to preserve the firm's anonymity) operates in the Enterprise Resource Planning (ERP) sector. Its main activity is to develop software that helps to manage firms' operating processes via a single repository, which involves creating information systems using client server technology composed of several modular applications that share single databases. Alpha provides the database software necessary for firms' operating systems, intervening in the installation and the parameterization of the system. Alpha, which was founded in 1977, is a giant in the database software market. The focus of our case analysis is on how Alpha responds to calls for tenders for database software with the help multiple strategic alliance partners (see Tables 3.1 and 3.2).

Figure 3.2

Nested Coopetition of the Interrelationships Between Internal and External Coopetition

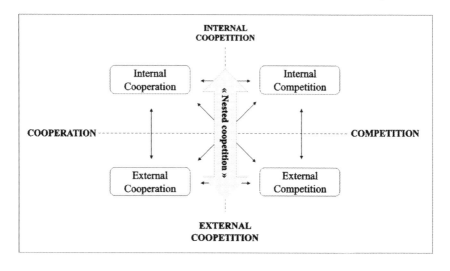

Table 3.1

Characteristics of Alpha

Interviews	• 17 semi-structured interviews • The interviews lasted between 55 min and 1 hr 33 min • The average interview length is estimated at 1 hr 16 min • The final corpus represents a total duration of 19 hr 53 min • Raw material of 128 pages of transcripts
Profile of respondents	• Alliance Managers • Partnerships Director • Alliances and Partnerships Director
Time period	• Between 2015 and 2017
Country of origin	• United States
Industry	• ERP
Nature of strategic alliances	• R&D Partnerships • R&D Coopetition
Strategic partners	• Beta. Operating system editor
	• Gamma. ERP Editor
	• Delta. Service companies
Date of creation	• 1977

Table 3.2

Characteristics of Strategic Partners

Partners	Description of the alliance
Alpha – Beta (an operating system editor)	Database software partners. Alpha provides Beta with 80% of the databases it needs to publish its ERPs. At the same time, Alpha is Beta's competitor in the ERP market. Alpha contributes to Beta's success by providing the database software that Beta's customers require. In return, Beta is Alpha's primary source of business, as each ERP sale by Beta brings Alpha a new order for database software. The two companies have been leaders in the ERP market since 1995.
Alpha – Gamma (an ERP editor)	Partnership in the early 1990s. This allowed Alpha to benefit from a sufficiently large structure to distribute its products by exploiting the enormous potential of its competitors in terms of manpower and distribution infrastructure.
Alpha – Delta (a service company)	This partnership began in the mid-1990s, when Delta offered Alpha database software.

Historical analysis of the industry shows that the phase of coopetition between companies started in the 1990s and became more pronounced from 1995 onwards. Since then, the industry has continued to grow, as the intensity of rivalry between incumbent firms. At the same time, numbers of strategic alliances were created between these competing firms. Alpha's main competitors are operating system vendors, such as Beta; ERP companies, such as Gamma; and service companies, such as Delta. Very powerful client solutions have been developed in recent years through coopetitive relationships between these competing companies. Intense rivalry between competitors has thus been moderated by cooperative strategic alliances. To manager its strategic alliances with Beta, Delta, and Gamma, Alpha use internal teams that are, to some extent, in competition with each other, fostering internal coopetition.

To study the interrelationships between internal and external coopetition, we adopted a qualitative research methodology approach and conducted a case study of strategic alliances between Alpha and three of its partners: Beta, Delta, and Gamma. As advocated by Yin (2013), we opted for a single case study approach because it is deemed appropriate to focus on focal firm to understand the interrelationships between internal and external coopetition, controlling for firm effects. The case was selected because it offers a framework of internal and external coopetition. The Alpha case is exemplary because it fulfills all the necessary conditions required to test, challenge, or extend the proposed conceptual framework for relationships between internal and external coopetition. The empirical study is based on 17 semi-structured interviews with individuals involved in the management of internal and external coopetition relationships between 2015 and 2017. Secondary data, such as press articles on Alpha's various strategic alliances, were also collected and analyzed to triangulate the interview data. The interviews lasted between 55 minutes and 1 hour and 33 minutes (see Appendix). The final corpus represents a total duration of 19 hours and 53 minutes of interviews, i.e., raw material of 148 pages of transcripts (see Table 3.1). All interviews were recorded and transcribed in full (Miles, Huberman, & Saldaña, 2018). The data collected were processed with thematic analysis (Miles et al., 2018), using NVivo software to preserve the integrity of the transcripts' meaning (Langley, 1999).

Analysis and Interpretation of the Data

The interpretation of the data follows Tesch's (2013) recommendations in that our theoretical corpus has been "decontextualized" into three themes: (i) internal coopetitive tensions, (ii) the manifestation of internal and/or external coopetition, and (iii) the management mechanisms of external and/or internal cooperation/competition, which were then "recontextualized" into external and/or internal coopetition (see Table 3.3). The content analysis of the primary data enabled us to study the representations of the actors involved in these relationships and to better understand the underlying logic of the coopetitive situation.

Table 3.3

Data Coding Process

Step 1: Body of Research	Step 2: Decontextualizing the corpus	Step 3: Recontextualizing the corpus
17 interviews	• Theme 1: Coopetitive tensions • Theme 2: Manifestation of internal and/or external coopetition (cooperation/ internal and/or external competition) • Theme 3: Management mechanisms for external and/or internal cooperation/ competition	External and/or internal coopetition Management of external and/ or internal coopetition

FINDINGS

Relationships Between Internal and External Coopetition

Coopetition not only relates to the collaborative relationship between competing partners in the same industry (i.e., external coopetition), our data also highlight that coopetition also operate, within firms, between business units, leading to internal coopetition. The business units in our case are teams formed to respond to calls for tender. To respond to these calls for tender, these business units collaborate with different external partners within a framework of strategic alliances. These alliances are formed with direct competitors and have the objective of winning the tenders. Alpha uses these strategic alliances to multiply its responses (with different partners) to call for tenders in order to maximize its chances winning them.

Although these teams belong to the same firm, they are also competitors because their objectives are not aligned. Each team try to win the call for tender against the others. This creates a situation of internal coopetition between teams. These teams work on the same project, using the same resources of the same firm but are attempting to achieve individual objectives as highlighted in the following quote:

> When Alpha responds to a brief with Beta, if I am in charge of the alliance with Gamma, I will make sure that Gamma has all the elements to be able to respond correctly and win the tender. Bearing in mind that Alpha will respond with Delta as well. So, there are situations of internal competition. (Alliance manager P1-BU1)

The local alliance manager of the alliance with Gamma (P1-BU3) adds,

> the difficulty ... is that we are always in a competitive environment internally. Sometimes we work together, and sometimes we are competing.... Our firm responds to calls for tender by cooperating with several external companies. If we can submit three responses, thcen to respond to this call for tender, the company will put three alliance managers in competition. (Alliance manager P1-BU2)

Sources of Tensions

The analysis of the data highlights the different sources of coopetitive tensions. These tensions are about sharing resources, difficulties related to the management of objectives, and opportunism of the partners.

Sharing of Resources

In a situation of nested coopetition, in which internal coopetition is intertwined with external coopetition, each business unit is responsible for a strategic alliance with a different external partner and thus promotes the interest of the relationship with its own partner in order to win the tender and become the "star" of the firm. It is therefore a intricated situation, where internal colleagues may sometimes cooperate with each other regarding information and internal resources common to the firm. While, at other times, competition among them may dominate their relationships, requiring discretion and the retention of the information and the resources necessary to develop a response to the call for tenders.

> In the framework of the call for tenders, we are obliged, internally, to alternate cooperation with competition. Sometimes we share certain things. Our offices are on the same floor. We are colleagues within the same company. We used to be, perhaps, even friends. But that doesn't mean that we are going to collaborate together to respond to the tender or share our knowledge and skills internally. (Alliance manager P1-BU3)

> Internally, and in relation to responding to calls for tender, we have noticed behavior where information isn't shared, behavior where we are waiting for information to be able to continue our work. People wait, follow up once, twice, three times, it takes a certain amount of time and they don't get an answer. Then, when you start to really push and you start to get annoyed ... the reason is that business unit X is withholding information for themselves and their team. (Partnership manager P1)

This is a typical conflict-of-interest situation linked to the need to share technical, human, and/or logistical resources relate to the response to the call for tenders. This internal coopetitive situation is a source of tensions and frustrations because the business units are faced with a difficulty in managing the relationships with colleagues from the same firm. Each team tries to obtain, from the corporate headquarters, the resources they need to develop a winning response to the call for tenders while protecting strategic information from the other teams. Indeed, sharing the corporate resources might be a problem for teams if they result in the dissemination of team-specific confidential information to the other competing teams. Therefore, although corporate resources are usually shared, at times, when they are insufficient to satisfy the needs of all of the teams, competition between team develops. In our data, we can find several occurrences of a shift from sharing resources to competing for resource between internal teams. Extreme vigilance is therefore required. This situation generates disagreements and misunderstandings and can even lead to conflicts that impede the progress of responding to the call for tenders.

> We have reached the point, internally, where we can no longer agree on the sharing of resources and information and resolve the issue.... These are very dangerous situations ... it isn't easy and it's a real difficulty.... People can appear to be a bit deaf; they can even put a spoke in the wheel. (Alliance manager P1-BU1)

In terms of resource sharing, our informants indicate that it is easier to manage external coopetition than internal coopetition because the agreements in the former are more explicit and often formalized in the alliance contract, as the following quote shows:

> The first thing to do when you start answering calls for tenders with an external alliance partner, you have to put together a team, assign an alliance manager or a business unit, and select the support services. The legal department is systematically involved. You need to assign a lawyer to the file. Then, a team will be set up with the different functions that are needed for the alliance. There might be an industrial supply of products. Since alliances are more research-oriented, we also need specialists in research and development.... So, the first thing is to dispatch the resources internally in multiple teams in order to bring the different alliances to life.... We expect the same from our partners. (Partnership Director – P1)

Once the resources to be exchanged have been clearly specified and the areas of collaboration clarified, external alliance counterparts may become closer than internal colleagues from competing teams, as indicated by the alliance manager P1-BU3: "With the partner I understood clearly how to manage our relationship, but on the other hand, I had difficulties managing the alliance relationship internally." Such a relationship is indicative of a complementarity relationship between internal and external coopetition.

Management of Objectives

The imbrication of internal and external coopetition highlights specific managerial difficulties in relation to the definition of the objectives of the internal and external relationships. The internal teams are supposed to defend the interests of their firm against external alliance partners, which are also competitors. However, at the same time, they should also defend the interests of their alliances with external partners against their internal competitors in order to win the call for tenders. The internal teams are therefore torn by contradictory objectives which should sometimes be shared and sometimes are in conflict with at their internal and external partners. A P1-BU2 alliance manager indicates that "the difficulty [is] that we are always in a competitive environment internally and externally. Sometimes we work together and sometimes we are in competition."

Internally, the business units compete with each other in responding to calls for tenders, but they have a common objective, which is to win the call for their firm. On the one hand, on the external side, there have rival objectives that are inherent to the competitive situation and the desire to win contract and improve corporate performance and reputation. On the other hand, the common objective with their external alliance partner is the desire to win the tender and improve the performance and the reputation of their unit with the firm. In line with this, the P1 alliances director acknowledge that "my teams must sometimes serve common objectives, but sometimes they need to beware of contradictory objectives, both internally and externally." It should be noted that the desire to win the tender often brings the external partner closer and distances the internal colleague, which is again indicating of the presence of a complementarity relationship between internal and external coopetition. The P1-BU2 alliance manager indicates that "the desire to win the tender brings me closer to my external counterpart and distances me from my internal colleagues."

Internal and External Opportunism Between Partners

There are two types of opportunism: one, which is external, when it comes from external partners and one, which is internal, when it is generated by the behavior of internal partners. In this respect, our data indicate that in the context of the call for tenders, opportunism is more likely to stem from internal partners due to the existence of competing objectives, rather the external partners. This is because, external partners are more likely to act cooperatively to avoid jeopardizing the chances to win the call or their reputation as a trusted partners in future alliances.

> Opportunism exists in alliances but not on the side of the partner's people, because for these people, alliances have to be successful, and to be successful in the short term and in the long term, you should not jeopardize an alliance for opportunistic tactical objectives. (Partnership and Alliances Director – P1)

In addition, competing business units may attempt to retrieve strategic data in order to use key information from a team's bid response as noted by a P1-BU1 alliance manager: "I won't share the specific resources needed to successfully respond to a bid even if a colleague wants to take it and tries every means possible; and I have briefed every member of my team about this."

Internal teams may also hide important information from each other or try to protect the access to information from members of other teams. "Internal competitors can take advantage of an opportunity, making an opportunistic decision.... Hiding information that should normally be shared with everyone" (Alliance manager P1-BU3). This situation leads to disagreements and misunderstandings, which are likely to trigger conflicts that are difficult for the firm to manage.

> We have reached the point where we no longer feel confident internally ... these are very dangerous situations ... it isn't easy. The fear of disclosing information internally becomes a handicap.... You have to be very English in this kind of situation, in other words, you have to be firm and strong against people's constant opportunism. (Alliance manager P1-BU2)

In sum, in situations where internal and external coopetition are interrelated, internal opportunism is likely to be exacerbated and external opportunism reduced, which is consistent with a complementarity relationship between internal and external coopetition.

Mechanisms to Manage Nested Coopetition

Our data also highlight several mechanisms for managing nested coopetition: separating teams, setting up a system for selecting information, or even establishing a team dedicated to the interface between levels and teams. These mechanisms are sometimes mobilized simultaneously to better regulate the interrelationships between internal and external coopetition. These mechanisms are generally put in place in order to reduce the occurrence of the negative consequences of internal competition (e.g., internal opportunism), without endangering external cooperation, which means to reenforce isomorphic relationships between internal and external coopetition.

Separation of Teams

In order to manage a situation of nested coopetition, firms can build fences between the teams that are managing external strategic alliances with different partners. The alliance department that manages the different external alliance relationships should plan regular meetings with each team and prevent collective meetings between competing teams in order to avoid conflicts and information theft. This should help to reduce internal competition without reducing external cooperation (i.e., reenforcing isomorphic relationships between internal and external coopetition).

> Private meetings are used to avoid giving internal partners information they are not supposed to have. It is important to remain prudent within the scope of the call for tenders and to be careful not to copy and paste data between teams. (Partnership director P1)

Another informant reveals that,

> In private meetings, our manager tells us, "Well this, this, and this is for you ... this, this, and this belongs to the other team ... this, this, and this, don't give it to them, even if the colleague wants to take it." And we have regular meetings. (Alliance manager P1-BU2)

During these regular meetings, the teams are able to discuss difficulties they have with the opportunistic behavior of certain of their internal colleagues. The partnership management thus sought compromise solutions between the teams, as highlighted in the following quote:

> Facing problems that we try to solve through meetings and encounters ... What we do is sit down around a table, we debrief, we see whether or not there is an inappropriate attitude. If the attitude is really inappropriate, we really question the people. Remind people that we are colleagues, competitors at times but friends forever. Remind them that we must collaborate internally. (Local alliance manager P1-BU3)

Creation of a "Coopetition Management Team"

A *"coopetition management team"* acting as a *"filter"* could be used to manage the coopetitive tensions between the teams internally and to allocate resources across these teams in ways that do not affect their relationships with their external partners. As the global alliance manager P1-BU2 noted:

> It is important to have a team that can act as a filter. The separation between teams is mandatory. You have to establish a dedicated team that manages internal collaboration and the sharing of resources. This team will set the rules of competition between the other teams.

This filtering of information and resources is especially important with respect to incoming information from external partners. All incoming information from external partners is received by the coopetition management team before being dispatched to the various business units. It is therefore necessary to verify that the information is correctly directed to the relevant business unit concerned by the information.

> We have to filter the incoming information on the internet portal. I check
> who I have to share it with on the intranet.... This information concerns
> one team but not another.... The alliance team must check that we are not
> disseminating information that should not be disseminated. (Partnership
> director P1)

Accordingly, for example, the coopetition management team often
advises the use of BU-specific team emails in order to avoid information
leaks to competing internal teams, as indicated by one of our informants:
"I only use my personal email for my multiple exchanges with my external
counterpart. This is recommended in my company. And it minimizes the
risk of leakage of strategic information relating to our offer" (Global alliance manager BU2).

The coopetition management team can also warn competing teams
about the potential opportunism of external partners. In the case of Alpha,
the team is composed of two divisions in order to manage external coopetition: a competitive division that deals with real competition on the market
with the alliance partner and a cooperative division that deals with aspects
relating to the cooperation and strategic alliance relationship with the alliance partner. The organization thus separates the teams that manage these
two paradoxical aspects of coopetition.

> We are shown the areas of exchange between the partners. We have to be
> careful not to give the partner information that it is not supposed to have.
> We stay within the scope of the alliance. That's why it's important to have
> an alliance team that can act as a filter. We have dedicated a team for col-
> laboration and a team for competition. (Local alliance manager P1-BU3)

In sum, the objective of the creation of such a *"coopetition management
team"* is to increase internal cooperation in ways that do not trigger external
competition (i.e., reenforcing isomorphic relationships between internal
and external coopetition).

Selection of Information to Be Disseminated

Our data show that it is difficult to partner with your competitor even
if your competitor is an internal colleague. Strategic information must be
compartmentalized, and it must be clearly explained to the competing
teams which type of information could be shared and which one should
be kept secret, hence the need for good communication. The right selection of information to be disseminated internally and externally helps to
reduce internal competition as much as external competition (i.e., to foster
isomorphic relationships between internal and external coopetition).

> We have to protect our internal strategic knowledge.... We won't give it away, even if internal colleagues want to take it. And we have regular meetings.... In the same way, with regard to competing partners, I remind my teams what our intellectual property is and what should not be transferred. (Alliance manager P1-BU1)

This filtering of information creates a climate of extreme vigilance with regard to the information to be communicated internally and externally. Informants stated that they are usually less vigilant and reticent when cooperating with an external partner than when cooperating between different internal business units responding to the same call for tenders (i.e., a complementary relationship between internal and external coopetition), as explained by the alliance director P1: "We have to filter at the level of the internet and intranet portal.... The alliance team must check that specific and secret information is not being distributed to teams that are not concerned." Similarly, a P1-BU3 global alliance manager added, "Strategic internal information risks being revealed, ... there is a risk ..., the confidentiality of information is difficult to guarantee."

Therefore, clear rules about which information could be disseminated internally or externally is likely to help to reduce internal competition as much as external competition (i.e., to foster isomorphic relationships between internal and external coopetition).

Training and Coaching to Facilitate Learning

Within the framework of this intertwined internal and external coopetition and in order to cope with the resulting coopetitive tensions, regular coaching sessions are scheduled to develop isomorphic relationship between internal and external cooperation and reduce isomorphic relationships between internal and external competition. At Alpha, training schedules covering management of stressful situations and tensions are organized to help internal colleagues acquire new skills that will facilitate the management of the internal and external coopetition relationship. These training sessions should lead to fruitful exchanges between the teams and between the teams and their external partners. Informants mentioned that these session help alliance managers to realize that they could become the victims of a kind of "Stockholm syndrome," a feeling generated by the paradoxical situations imposed by the interrelationships between internal and external coopetition. The coaching sessions might recommend that the teams develop empathy with their internal and external partners when dealing with these situations. "The coaching explains that in the face of this Stockholm syndrome, which we are victims of because of this coopetition....

You must be able to put yourself in the shoes of your counterpart. You need to have empathy" (Partnership manager P1).

As a P1-BU1 alliance manager points out,

> This training was very useful, it made our lives easier. It clarified things. It reminded us that we are colleagues. That it is the best who wins, but that it's for the benefit of our common company Alpha.... It's true that at times, we forgot that we work for the same company.... That even if we lose the tender with Gamma and we lose the bonus allocated to the star who wins, we increase our skills, knowledge, and mastery of different techniques.

Training courses could also address issues with external coopetition. They could emphasize the multiple exchanges and coordination efforts between partners and consolidate the feeling of belonging to a group and reinforce learning between the partners. Courses could also encourage the exchange of good practices related to responding to call for tenders with external partners.

> The different techniques learned and presented in the training courses teach us how to be more fluid and tolerant with our external partner, encourage us to acquire their good habits and working methods, and help us to master the software used in the collaboration. (Global alliance manager P4)

Alliance Management Capabilities.

Our data show that both Alpha and its partners have had together previous strategic alliances and developed partner-specific alliance management capabilities. These capabilities developed from previous alliance experiences with the same partners facilitate the external coopetition learning process. Because the firms know each other and are used to working together, responding to calls for tenders can start quickly and most effectively. In addition, these capabilities allow partners to develop a collaborative relationship. An alliance manager P2 specifies that, "We are buddies, so things are much easier than if the partner is an unknown company. Our past common experiences make the work much easier." These capacities developed from external coopetitive relationships are likely to be useful to manage internal coopetitive relationship. Internal teams could transpose management tools developed with external colleagues to manage their relations with internal colleagues. A director of alliances and partnerships P1 agree with this: "We are inspired by past experiences with our external partners to establish logical arrangement of tasks and achieve coordination of the parties in order to move forward on the responses to the call for tenders and maximize learning."

In sum, data analysis highlighted: (i) the relationship between external coopetition and internal coopetition, (ii) the main sources of coopetitive tensions, namely the sharing of resources, the difficulties related to objectives and the manifestation of internal and external opportunism, and (iii) the mechanisms for managing nested coopetition and in particular the separation of teams, selection of information to be disseminated, training and coaching to facilitate learning and the alliance management capabilities (see Figure 3.3).

Figure 3.3

Tensions and Management Mechanisms in Nested Coopetition

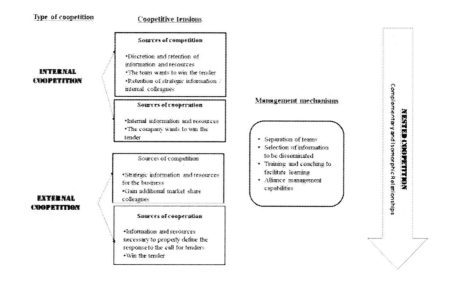

DISCUSSION AND CONCLUSION

Our study explores the imbrication between internal and external coopetitive tensions in strategic alliances. This imbrication is reflected in the intersection of several types of relationships (between cooperation and competition on the one hand, and internal and external relationships on the other, and the relationships between the two). This nested coopetition is revealed in inter- and intra-organizational tensions and their interrelationships and shows the need for management mechanisms that integrate cooperative management tools and the necessities of external competition management. Cooperative behaviors of firms transcend their own organizational boundaries, while learning becomes a means of transferring strategic practices and developing experiences. The conceptual model of nested cooperation translates in this sense a "holistic" view of coopetition.

Despite the abundance of recent studies on coopetition, the coopetitive tensions that emanate from the intertwining of internal and external coopetition remain insufficiently studied. Some studies have begun to explore internal coopetitive tensions, highlighting the simultaneous presence of competition and cooperation between business units that are part of the same organization. This emerging literature on internal coopetition within organizations has identified several sources of tensions and several mechanisms for managing them. Our study contributes to this literature by analyzing the imbrication of internal and external coopetition. Our findings show that internal and external coopetition are interrelated and that complementarity relationships dominate. This is, internal coopetition is generally dominated by a high level of internal competition, which triggers external cooperation, as a dominant aspect of external coopetition. Our findings also highlight several mechanisms or managerial tools reduce the intensity of these complementarity relationships and develop isomorphic relationships in the forms of increased internal and external cooperation and decreased internal and external competition. Identified examples of such mechanisms for managing coopetitive relationships are the establishment of a kind of "filter" team as a neutral interface between internal teams and external partners, greater vigilance in the dissemination of information, and finally a temporary or permanent separation of the teams.

These findings are partly consistent with those obtained by Chiambaretto et al. (2019) regarding the development of specific capabilities (or even dedicated functions) for information management at both the internal and external levels. It also seems that in the case studied, the establishment of a filter team reflects a tool developed in an *ad hoc* manner to fit the specific context of nested coopetition, as previously suggested by Dahl (2014) and Dahl et al. (2016). Moreover, these coopetitive relationships give rise to coopetitive learning (Bengtsson & Raza-Ulah, 2016). In the case studied, this relates to transferring the management of external competition, thereby facilitating the preparation of responses to calls for tender at the internal level. To some extent, our results also differ from those of previous studies by taking into account the whole cooperative process, beyond the sole question of appropriation and diffusion of learning. Moreover, they show the cross-fertilization of internal and external competitive and cooperative levels.

Our findings possess several managerial implications: First, managers can learn from their strategic alliances by replicating certain mechanisms to manage coopetitive tensions internally. Second, our findings indicate that mechanisms dedicated to the management of nested coopetition can be put in place, especially in terms of information management. Finally, these management tools, which can be developed temporarily, must be flexible and adapted to the observed coopetitive situations, leading to the transfer of learning and experience across internal and external coopetitive relationships.

Our study has made it possible to highlight the existing relationships between internal and external coopetition, to propose a conceptual framework of analysis to study these relationships, and to empirically explore the usefulness of this conceptual framework in the case of a company and the strategic alliances it has set up with some of its competitors. As with any research, our study has a number of limitations that relate primarily to its exploratory nature. Our study is based on a single case and is studied qualitatively on the basis of interviews with key players. The case of Alpha was chosen for its exemplary nature, but it is not necessarily representative of all companies in a situation of internal and external coopetition. Quantitative studies on the basis of representative samples could contribute to the validity of our conceptual framework. In addition, our study is specific to the technology industry (ERP). Thus, other studies could be carried out to validate our results in other sectors of activity. Being qualitative in nature, our study may have been influenced by subjectivity biases on the part of respondents. Although we took all necessary measures (e.g., triangulation) to minimize the impact of this bias, it may still arise when respondents are asked to recall and justify their behaviors and decisions. Larger-scale studies using secondary databases could be conducted to confirm our results.

Despite these limitations, our work opens up several perspectives for analyzing the relationships between internal and external coopetition. First, a deeper examination of the imbrication of internal and external coopetition and of cooperation-competition through other case studies would be useful. Second, a more in-depth examination of nested coopetition in innovation projects or in technological sectors could shed additional light on the issue of information management within and between allies. Finally, the issue of the management information should not obscure the questions of sharing resources and the value created on the one hand, and the issue of coopetitive learning on the other. Longitudinal studies would allow for a more in-depth understanding of these two coopetitive issues.

REFERENCES

Bengtsson, M., & Kock, S. (2000). Coopetition in business networks—To cooperate and compete simultaneously. *Industrial Marketing Management*, *29*(5), 411–426.

Bengtsson, M., & Kock, S. (2014). Coopetition-quo vadis? Past accomplishments and future challenges. *Industrial Marketing Management*, *43*(2), 180–188.

Bengtsson, M., & Raza-Ullah, T. (2016). A systematic review of research on coopetition: Toward a multilevel understanding. *Industrial Marketing Management*, *57*(1), 23–39.

Bengtsson, M., Raza-Ullah, T., & Vanyushyn, V. (2016). The coopetition paradox and tension: The moderating role of coopetition capability. *Industrial Marketing Management*, *53*(1), 19–30.

Bouncken, R. B., Fredrich, V., & Kraus, S. (2020). Configurations of firm-level value capture in coopetition. *Long Range Planning*, *53*(1), 1–14.

Brandenburger, A. M., & Nalebuff, B. J. (1996). *Coopetition*. New York, NY: Currency Doubleday.

Chen, H., Yao, Y., Zan, A., & Carayannis, E. G. (2020). How does coopetition affect radical innovation? The roles of internal knowledge structure and external knowledge integration. *Journal of Business & Industrial Marketing*, *36*(11), 1975–1987.

Chiambaretto, P., & Dumez, H. (2016). Toward a typology of coopetition: A multi-level approach. *International Studies of Management & Organization*, *46*(2–3), 110–129.

Chiambaretto, P., Mass'e, D., & Mirc, N. (2019). "All for One and One for All?"—Knowledge broker roles in managing tensions of internal coopetition: The Ubisoft case. *Research Policy*, 48(3), 584–600.

Czakon, W., Srivastava, M. K., Le Roy, F., & Gnyawali, D. (2020). Coopetition strategies: Critical issues and research directions. *Long Range Planning*, *53*(1), 1019–1048.

Dahl, J., (2014), Conceptualizing coopetition as a process: An outline of change in cooperative and competitive interactions, *Industrial Marketing Management*, *43*(2), 272–279.

Dahl, J., Kock, S., & Lundgren-Henriksson, E. L. (2016). Conceptualizing coopetition strategy as practice: A multilevel interpretative framework. *International Studies of Management and Organization*, *46*(2/3), 94–109.

Das, T. K., & Teng, B. (1998). Between trust and control: Developing confidence in partner cooperation in alliances. *Academy of Management Review*, *23*(3), 491–512.

Das, T. K., & Teng, B. (2000a). A resource-based theory of strategic alliances. *Journal of Management*, *26*(1), 31–61.

Das, T. K., & Teng, B. (2000b). Instabilities of strategic alliances: An internal tensions perspective. *Organization Science*, *11*(1), 77–101.

Depeyre, C., & Dumez, H. (2010). The role of architectural players in coopetition: The case of the US defense industry. In S. Yami & F. Le Roy (Eds.), *Coopetition: Winning strategies for the 21st Century* (pp. 124–141). Cheltenham, UK: Edward Elgar.

Dorn, S., Schweiger, B., & Albers, S. (2016). Levels, phases and themes of coopetition: A systematic literature review and research agenda. *European Management Journal*, *34*(5), 484–500.

Fernandez, A. S., & Chiambaretto, P. (2016). Managing tensions related to information in coopetition. *Industrial Marketing Management*, *53*(1), 66–76.

Fernandez, A. S., Le Roy, F., & Gnyawali, D. R. (2014). Sources and management of tension in coopetition case evidence from telecommunications satellites manufacturing in Europe. *Industrial Marketing Management, 43*(2), 222–235.

Furrer, O. (2016). *Corporate level strategy: Theory and applications.* London, UK: Routledge.

Furrer, O., Tjemkes, B., Boymans, C., & Ubachs, M. (2013). A circumplex model of interpartner dynamics in strategic alliances. In T. K. Das (Ed.), *Interpartner dynamics in strategic alliances* (pp. 97–130). Charlotte, NC: Information Age.

Gernsheimer, O., Kanbach, D. K., & Gast, J. (2021). Coopetition research-A systematic literature review on recent accomplishments and trajectories. *Industrial Marketing Management, 96*(1), 113–134.

Gnyawali, D. R., & Ryan Charleton, T. (2018). Nuances in the interplay of competition and cooperation: Towards a theory of coopetition. *Journal of Management, 44*(7), 2511–2534.

Gnyawali, D. R., He, J., & Madhavan, R. (2006). Impact of co-opetition on firm competitive behavior: An empirical examination. *Journal of Management, 32*(4), 507–530.

Greimas, A. J. (2015). *Sémantique structurale: recherche de méthode [Structural Semantics: Methodological Research].* Paris, France: Presses Universitaires de France.

Hamel, G. (1991). Competition for competence and interpartner learning within international strategic alliances. *Strategic Management Journal, 12*(S1), 83–103.

Hani, M., & Dagnino, G. B. (2021). Global network coopetition, firm innovation and value creation. *Journal of Business & Industrial Marketing, 36*(11), 1962–1974.

Katz, R., & Allen, T. J. (1982). Investigating the Not Invented Here (NIH) syndrome: A look at the performance, tenure, and communication patterns of 50 R&D Project Groups. *R&D Management, 12*(1), 7–20.

Ketchen, D. J., Jr., Snow, C. C., & Hoover, V. L. (2004). Research on competitive dynamics: Recent accomplishments and future challenges. *Journal of Management, 30*(6), 779–804.

Kiesler, D. J. (1983). The 1982 interpersonal circle: A taxonomy for complementarity in human transactions. *Psychological Review, 90*(3), 185–214.

Klimas, P., Czakon, W., & Fredrich, V. (2022). Strategy frames in coopetition: An examination of coopetition entry factors in high-tech firms. *European Management Journal.*

Langley A. (1999). Strategies for theorizing from process data. *Academy of Management Review, 36*(4), 691–710.

Le Roy, F., & Fernandez, A. S. (2015). Managing coopetitive tensions at the working-group level: The rise of the coopetitive project team. *British Journal of Management, 26*(4), 671–688.

Luo, X., Slotegraaf, R. J., & Pan, X. (2006). Cross-functional "coopetition": The simultaneous role of cooperation and competition within firms. *Journal of Marketing, 70*(2), 67–80.

Mariani, M. (2018). The role of policy makers and regulators in coopetition. In A. S. Fernandez, P. Chiambaretto, F. Le Roy, & W. Czakon (Eds.), *The Routledge companion to coopetition strategies* (pp. 105-116). Abingdon, UK: Routledge.

Miles, M. B., Huberman, A. M., & Saldaña, J. (2018). Qualitative data analysis: A methods sourcebook (4th ed.). Thousand Oaks, CA: SAGE.

Oswald, L. R. (2015). The structural semiotics paradigm for marketing research: Theory, methodology, and case analysis. *Semiotica*, *2015*(205), 115–148.

Poole, M. S., & Van de Ven, A. H. (1989). Using paradox to build management and organization theories. *Academy of Management Review*, *14*(4), 562–578.

Raza-Ullah, T., Bengtsson, M., & Kock, S. (2014). The coopetition paradox and tension in coopetition at multiple levels. *Industrial Marketing Management*, *43*(2), 189–198.

Santos, J. N. (2021). Linking joint value creation to the interplay of competition and cooperation: a fuzzy set approach, *Industrial Marketing Management*, *92*(1), 45–54.

Seran, T., Pellegrin-Boucher, E., & Gurau, C. (2016). The management of coopetitive tensions within multi-unit organizations. *Industrial Marketing Management*, *53*(1), 31–41.

Signori, P., & Flint, D. J. (2020). Revealing the unique blend of meanings in corporate identity: An application of the semiotic square. *Journal of Marketing Theory and Practice*, *28*(1), 26–42.

Smith, W. K., & Lewis, M. W. (2011). Toward a theory of paradox: A dynamic equilibrium model of organizing. *Academy of Management Review*, *36*(2), 381–403

Song, J., Lee, K., & Khanna, T. (2016). Dynamic capabilities at Samsung: Optimizing internal co-opetition. *California Management Review*, *58*(4), 118–140.

Tesch, R. (2013). *Qualitative research: Analysis types and software*. London, UK: Routledge.

Thelisson, A. S. (2021). Coopetition in a merger process: Regulators and management of coopetitive tensions. *International Review of Administrative Sciences*.

Tidström, A. (2009). Causes of conflict in intercompetitor cooperation. *Journal of Business & Industrial Marketing*, *24*(7), 506–518.

Tidström, A. (2014). Managing tensions in coopetition. *Industrial Marketing Management*, *43*(3), 261–271.

Tidström, A., & Rajala, A. (2016). Coopetition strategy as interrelated praxis and practices on multiple levels. *Industrial Marketing Management*, *58*(1), 35–44.

Tsai, W. (2002). Social structure of "coopetition" within a multiunit organization: Coordination, competition, and intraorganizational knowledge sharing. *Organization Science*, *13*(2), 179–190.

Wilhelm, M. (2011). Managing coopetition through horizontal supply chain relations: Linking dyadic and network levels of analysis, *Journal of Operations Management*, *29*(7), 663–676.

Wilhelm, M., & Sydow, J. (2018). Managing coopetition in supplier networks—A paradox perspective, *Journal of Supply Chain Management*, *54*(3), 1–42.

Yin, R. K. (2013). *Case study research: Design and methods*. Thousand Oaks, CA: SAGE.

APPENDIX: DESCRIPTION OF INTERVIEWS

Alliances	Respondents' Profile and Firm (P1-Alpha); (P2-Beta); (P3-Gamma); (P4-Delta)		Date of Interview	Duration of Interview (min)
All three alliances	1.	World alliances director (P1)	2015	55
	2.	Director of alliances and partnerships (P1)	2015	79
Business Unit 1 (BU1)-Beta (P2)	3.	Alliance manager (P2)	2017	58
	4.	Global alliance manager (P1)	2017	52
	5.	Local alliance manager (P2)	2017	63
	6.	Commercial alliance manager (P1)	2015	59
Business Unit 2 (BU2)-Gamma (P3)	1.	Alliance director (P3)	2015	67
	2.	Alliance manager (P1)	2015	64
	3.	Alliance manager (P1)	2015	61
	4.	Alliance manager (P1)	2017	59
	5.	Partnership manager (P3)	2017	55
	6.	Partnership manager (P3)	2015	88
Business Unit 3 (BU3)-Delta (P4)	1.	Alliance director (P4)	2015	89
	2.	Global alliance manager (P1)	2019	91
	3.	Global alliance manager (P4)	2013	76
	4.	Local alliance manager (P1)	2013	93
	5.	Local alliance manager (P4)	2019	84

INSTITUTIONAL DIFFERENCES AND THE VALUE OF IDENTITY BRIDGING ROLE OF TRUST IN CROSS-BORDER ALLIANCES

Rekha Krishnan and Preet S. Aulakh

ABSTRACT

Prior research has highlighted the importance of trust in facilitating mutual identification between alliance partners which is generally agreed to be beneficial. Yet, there might be conditions under which this quality of trust does not yield the expected benefits. We hypothesize that in alliances between emerging economy and developed country firms, although mutual identification fostered by trust allows alliance partners to overcome organizational institutional differences at the micro level that otherwise would hamper alliance functioning, the very same quality of trust can be a liability under regulatory institutional differences at the macro level that would require each alliance partner to maintain their independent identities. Our findings, based on a survey sample of 167 international strategic alliances of firms in Latin America, confirm that whereas trust benefits alliance performance under organizational institutional differences, it hinders performance under regulatory institutional differences.

Managing Interpartner Cooperation in Strategic Alliances, pp. 91–127
Copyright © 2022 by Information Age Publishing
www.infoagepub.com

INTRODUCTION

Strategic alliances blur firm boundaries and create mutual dependence between partners with distinct identities of their own (Lane, Salk, & Lyles, 2001; McEvily, Zaheer, & Perrone, 2003). Past research has highlighted the importance of trust in facilitating mutual identification between alliance partners (Lewicki & Bunker, 1996; McEvily et al., 2003). It is generally agreed that such shared identity fostered by trust is beneficial in inter-organizational relationships as it helps reduce interpartner conflict and allows the partners to channel their attention towards obtaining synergistic benefits (McEvily et al., 2003; Zaheer, McEvily, & Perrone, 1998). However, there might be conditions under which this quality of trust may not be as beneficial as portrayed. In particular, research is yet to consider situations where alliance partners might have to maintain distinct identities and mutual identification is not very desirable.

The mutual identification that trust brings about is highly relevant in alliances between partners embedded in disparate institutional frameworks, as identities of these partners are shaped by different beliefs, norms, rules (Scott, 2008) that remain imprinted on to the partners' structures, policies, and practices (Kostova & Roth, 2002) and form "the basis of how they understand and interpret different situations and environments" (Abdi & Aulakh, 2012, p. 479). We argue that in alliances between emerging economy and developed country firms, where distinct identities of partners is more salient, although mutual identification fostered by trust allows partnering firms to overcome organizational institutional differences at the micro level, the very same quality of trust is a liability under regulatory institutional differences at the macro level as it requires each alliance partner to maintain their independent identities.

Specifically, at the micro level, organizational institutional differences introduce challenges in devising compatible interpartner routines as values and beliefs of many emerging economy firms are shaped by narrow range of learning experience compared to their developed country partners (Hitt, Dacin, Levitas, Arregle, & Borza, 2000). For instance, although various emerging economies have made the transition from import substitution to export orientation regimes, some firms may remain imprinted with routines designed for the old regime (Kriauciunas & Kale, 2006). They may naturally tend to remain imitators and struggle to innovate (Bortagaray & Tiffin, 2005). Under such conditions, by allowing partners to identify with and internalize each other's core values and goals, trust encourages the local partner to respect the foreign partner's knowledge boundaries, and the foreign partner to earnestly assist the local partner in acquiring the necessary skills.

This very same quality of trust can, however, be a liability under regulatory institutional differences at the macro level. Regulatory institutions of different economies often make disparate demands, and a partner from an emerging economy may be called upon to respond quite differently from the compliance expected of its developed country partner. In a trusting relationship partners tend to identify with each other and treat each other's goals and problems as their own (Lewicki & Bunker, 1996). However, accommodating each other's institutional needs might actually interfere with adequate response to their own institutions. In the case of the developed country partner, it involves insufficient adherence to home country standards risking their legitimacy as a result (Goodrick & Salancik, 1996). For the developing country partner, it might involve non-conformity to rule bending activities. Bending the rules in order to get around impediments to business is a typical response to institutional uncertainty in emerging economies (termed *jeitinho* in Brazil, m*ordida* in Mexico, and *pituto* in Chile) (Duarte, 2006; Jarrad, 1995). However, by refraining from such acts an organization risks lagging behind local competition.

Below, we develop our arguments in greater detail and test the hypotheses on a survey sample of 167 international strategic alliances of Latin American firms. Our findings, which confirm our theory, contribute to the interorganizational trust research. There is a substantial body of research that theorizes trust as a key factor for the effective functioning of interorganizational relationships (Dyer, 1997; McEvily et al., 2003; Zaheer et al., 1998). Trust mitigates contractual hazards, fosters mutual identification, and generally helps in conserving the limited cognitive resources of exchange partners, thereby enabling interpartner cooperation and coordination (e.g., Dyer & Chu, 2003; Gulati, Wohlgezogen, & Zhelyazkov, 2012; Mohr & Spekman, 1994; Zaheer et al., 1998). The empirical evidence on the performance benefits of trust in interorganizational relationships has, however, been described as "mixed" and "equivocal" (Katsikeas, Skarmeas, & Bello, 2009, p. 132). Despite multiple calls to unpack how and under what conditions different functions of trust enable or constrain alliance performance, this area of inquiry remains relatively under-examined (Gargiulo & Ertug, 2006; McEvily & Zaheer, 2006; McEvily et al., 2003).

Our study contributes to this research by identifying the conditions under which the identity bridging role of trust benefits or constrains cross-border alliances. The findings suggest that trust allows partners to more easily identify with each other, and this mutual identification is effective under organizational institutional differences. However, under regulatory institutional differences, this quality of trust can interfere with the partners' individual responses to their respective regulatory institutional environments and distract them from contributing to the alliance as they should.

THEORY AND HYPOTHESES

Building on prior trust research, we define interorganizational trust as the expectation held by the exchange partners that each will not exploit its vulnerabilities when faced with the opportunity to do so (Barney & Hansen 1994; Mayer, David & Schoorman,1995; Sako, 1991). This expectation is confirmed when firms (1) demonstrate reliability by carrying out their promises, (2) act fairly when dealing with each other, and (3) exhibit good-will by taking each other's best interests into account even when contractual obligations do not demand it. Our definition thus bases trust on three related components: reliability, fairness, and goodwill (Carson, Madhok, Varman, & John, 2003; Dyer & Chu 2003).

Scholars have highlighted the importance of trust in promoting mutual identification where partners identify with each other's values and needs as though they were their own (Lewicki & Bunker, 1996; McEvily et al., 2003). They have demonstrated that this increases interpartner cooperation and reduces interorganizational conflict (Zaheer et al., 1998). Identifying with each other provides partners the confidence that one will not exploit the vulnerability of the other (Barney & Hansen, 1994; Mayer et al., 1995; Sako, 1991). Studies have shown that such confidence allows partners to give each other the benefit of the doubt, and as a consequence reduces the perceived need for monitoring (Langfred, 2004; McEvily et al., 2003). It also encourages partners to openly communicate with each other and even share valuable and confidential information (Dyer & Chu, 2003). So, scholars generally agree that trust is likely to be highly beneficial in business partnerships.

The identity bridging role of trust is important when alliance partners lack a common institutional framework (Kraatz & Block, 2008; Roy & Oliver, 2009). Hence, in our context, which involves alliances between partners embedded in different institutional frameworks and possessing distinct identities, mutual identification promoted by trust tends to be highly relevant. Pressures imposed on alliance partners by disparate regulatory institutions at the macro level and disparate organizational institutions at the micro level threaten to divide any alliance. As alliance partners are mutually dependent, loose coupling of the partners' objectives as though they were independent entities may not work, requiring cooperation from each other (Kraatz & Block, 2008). When institutional constraints threaten to divide an alliance, trust encourages the partners to adopt cooperative efforts rather than grudgingly tolerate each other.

In the following sections, we argue that the identity bridging benefit of trust is not always a boon; whereas it might be an asset when organizational institutional differences between partnering firms are high, this very same quality becomes a liability when regulatory institutional differences in the partner's respective home countries are high.

Trust, Organizational Institutional Differences, and Alliance Performance

Organizational institution reflects an organization's distinct history and is shaped by the manner in which it responds to internal and external pressures (Selznick, 1957). Its unique set of experiences "infuses [the organization] with value" which involves acquiring distinct values and beliefs and developing "fixed ways of perceiving itself and the world" (Selznick, 1957, pp. 10, 17). Such value infusion bestows a distinctive identity on an organization. Selznick (1957) argues that "as an organization acquires a self, a distinctive identity, it becomes an institution" (p. 21).

The unique histories of organizations shape the values and beliefs they come to adopt (Selznick, 1957). For instance, many Latin American firms have been involved in strategic alliances with developed country firms. They may also have a great deal of exporting experience and have embraced values that emphasize innovation and quality (Reguart, 2005). Such firms tend to be better at innovating than their counterparts who have not had the benefit of learning from such international exposure. Hence, they were able to adjust to the transition from protectionist import orientation policies to liberal export orientation policies (Reguart, 2005). Firms whose organizational histories did not have such exposure were weighed down by the import substitution period that was characterized by limited incentives for innovation, which combined with low investment in R&D resulted in these organizations embracing values that favored imitation (Bortagaray & Tiffin, 2005; Fraga, 2004). Such firms will have difficulty in interacting with their alliance partners whose values are shaped by different set of experiences.

In international alliances, where organizational institutions of partners are shaped by unique organizational histories, values and beliefs are not common, amounting to different work expectations, operating procedures, and interpretation of strategic issues (Park & Ungson, 1997, 2001; Simonin, 1999). Differing beliefs and values might require the partners to deal with more than one identity. Partners with different purposes and disparate perceptions of appropriate behavior must interact regularly to process information and make vital decisions if the alliance is to be successful (Glynn, 2000; Kraatz & Block, 2008).

Disparate belief systems that are deeply embedded in each organization tend to engender conflict and fragmentation, as objectives that are merely different might be viewed as antagonistic (Kraatz & Block, 2008). Such misunderstandings can lead to concerns about the appropriation of know-how. They can also impede devising efficient interorganizational routines (Park & Ungson, 1997, 2001). Overall, alliances where partners possess distinct identities are deprived of a vital pre-requisite for joint action: "congruent expectations" on how work rules are structured, on the importance given to innovativeness, rule orientation and attention to details (Hodgson, 2004; Ring & Van de Ven, 1994, pp. 99–100).

Trust encourages partners to identify with each other which is vital when distinct identities threaten to divide the alliance (Lewicki & Bunker, 1996; McEvily et al., 2003), and the benefits of trust tend to be magnified under organizational institutional differences. As partners exhibit trusting behaviors, they strongly identify with each other's values and beliefs (Lewicki & Bunker, 1996). As a result, partners tend to embrace each other's values and goals as their own, which might compensate for the absence of shared identity in alliances with disparate organizational institutions (McAllister, 1995). Strong identification is shown to increase commitment towards the relationship and to each other (Kramer, 1993; Selznick, 1957), which is especially important in alliances where conflict and fragmentation tend to be high owing to misunderstandings stemming from exposure to multiple values and beliefs. Mutual identification resolves such conflicts as it encourages partners to engage in constructive interpretation of each other's motives. Furthermore, Gulati and Singh (1998) argue that trust encourages partners to be aware of each other's procedures and processes. Such awareness encourages partners to make conscious effort to develop congruent expectations about work rules and orientation (Sirmon & Lane, 2004), thereby allowing them to develop interorganizational routines that facilitate effective communication and coordination.

So overall, trust helps prevent alliance partners' distinctive identities from interfering with the functioning of the alliance, thus improving alliance performance (McAllister, 1995). When organizational institutions are similar, however, trust might be redundant as shared identities are already in place.

Hypothesis 1: *Interorganizational trust is more likely to enhance alliance performance when partnering firms' organizational institutional differences are high than when they are low.*

Trust, Regulatory Institutional Differences, and Alliance Performance

Regulatory institutions specify the "rules of the game" that guide business interactions (Meyer, Estrin, Bhaumik, & Peng, 2009; North, 1990, p. 3). They constrain and formally regulate behaviors by providing a legal system that protects property rights and enforces contracts (Ingram & Clay, 2000; North, 1991; Scott, 2008). In international alliances, partners are often subject to competing institutional prescriptions (Kraatz & Block, 2008, p. 243), which impose disparate demands on partners. Regulatory institutional prescriptions tend to be particularly divergent in alliances involving developed and emerging economy firms. Compared to emerging economies, developed countries have well developed legal frameworks, well defined property rights, and efficient contract enforcement. The regulatory institutions in emerging economies, on the other hand, tend to be weak, the rules guiding economic exchange are inadequate and contract enforcement is often poor (Chan, Isobe, & Makino, 2008; North, 1990).

North (1991) argues that the institutions of Western countries evolved through a series of institutional innovations in Europe from the 11th through the 16th century that laid the foundations of the modern Western world. These innovations involved development of better capital markets and reduced information costs made possible by gradual development in enforcement of contracts by an efficient state. The institutional framework of the Western colonial powers left lasting imprints on the colonies such that institutional practices that were left behind continue to exist in former colonies to this date. The colonization of North America and the eventual declaration of independence coincided with the gaining prominence of the parliament over the crown, giving way to well-protected property rights and better contract enforcement. This trend continued to be reflected in North America post-independence.

In contrast, the Spanish and Portuguese colonization of Latin America coincided with the power of the monarchy and the declining importance of the parliament, resulting in prominence of bureaucratic rules in the colonies. Following independence, Latin American countries reverted to "centralized bureaucratic control" which was characteristic of 19th century Latin America (North, 1991, p. 111). North (1991) argues that although Southern European colonizers managed to revive their regulatory institutions, Latin America, in spite of attempts to reform its economies, still remains in the firm grip of crippling bureaucracy, and "personalized" relationships still hold the key to carrying out business transactions in weak regulatory institutions.

Consequently, the response of Latin American firms and their developed country counterparts to their respective regulatory institutions tend to reflect this discrepancy in their history. Because standards for appropriate behavior are already set, monitoring by stakeholders such as governments, regulators, shareholders, and consumers tend to be more stringent for developed country firms (Gardberg & Fombrun, 2006; van Tulder & van der Zwart, 2006). News reports also suggest that multinational companies face close scrutiny by their home countries when they operate in emerging economies where regulatory institutions are weak. For example, question-able labor practices employed by Apple's partner in China affected Apple's reputation in its home country as was the case for Nike a few years ago (Duhigg & Barboza, 2012). Therefore, when regulatory institutions are well developed and certain, rules and standards are already clearly laid out; and organizations and their stakeholders agree on appropriate actions, leaving little room for organizational discretion—they risk losing legitimacy if they fail to adhere to strict home country standards in their international alliances (Goodrick & Salancik, 1996).

Unlike well-developed institutions exhibiting certainty, when institutions are weak organizations have more discretion to pursue their interests as standards are insufficient to completely constrain organizational actions (Goodrick & Salancik, 1996). A typical response to weak regulatory institutions in emerging economies is to resort to informal personalized relationships with regulatory officials and/or suppliers. Use of such personalized relationships often times take the form of rule bending to get around regulatory hurdles. For instance, Brazilian organizations respond to uncertainty in the regulatory institutions through the use of "*jeitinho*" which involves bending or breaking the law either by outright evasion or by eliciting favors from government officials by adequately motivating them (Duarte, 2006; Stone, Levy, & Paredes, 1996). Specifically, to dodge complex regulatory rules associated with starting a business, organizations tend to approach specialized fixers who work out details in 6 weeks for an affordable fee (Stone et al., 1996). Organizations deal with complex tax laws and labor regulations by selling goods without the required paperwork and by under-reporting the wages paid. When such violations are discovered by government officials, firms can avoid the full force of the law by paying between 5 and 25% of the normal fine directly to the official. Such measures to deal with weak regulatory institutions also exist in other Latin American countries—*mordida*, for example, in Mexico and *pituto* in Chile (Duarte, 2006; Jarrad, 1995). Such measures are of course less acceptable in developed countries.

Alliance partners' disparate needs in dealing with their respective regulatory institutions are bound to trigger interpartner conflict as each partner pushes the other to help it conform to the expectations of its home market. An Indonesian mining firm recently ended its relationship with a British partner because the British firm tried to enforce international corporate governance standards incompatible with the Indonesian situation (Economist, 2012). Because trust allows partners to identify with each other, it is likely to reduce interpartner conflict and increase commitment to the relationship and towards each other (McEvily et al., 2003). However, trust might still prove to be a liability when regulatory institutional differences are high, as such commitment might result in partners compromising on the manner in which they ideally respond to their institutional demands. As trusting partners come to identify with each other, they not only understand and agree with the other's values but also adopt their values as though these were their own (Lewicki & Bunker, 1996). Also, a partner tends to know and appreciate what is really valuable for the other and places the same importance on those needs as the other partner does (McEvily et al., 2003). In a sense, partners come to behave similarly and act to one another's benefit, knowing that there is little need for monitoring the other's behavior closely (Lewicki & Bunker, 1996). A developed country partner might come to appreciate and adopt the way things are done in an emerging economy even if it means violating home country standards. For its part, the emerging economy partner, knowing that the foreign partner needs to adhere to strict home country standards might restrict tendencies to bend local rules to obtain regulatory approvals.

However, the consequences of both adjustments can hurt the alliance. On the one hand, by failing to adhere to home country standards the foreign partner risks losing its legitimacy at home, which is often an important market. Because it belongs to a trusting relationship, the foreign partner might accept certain amount of responsibility for the rule bending acts of the local partner and will hesitate to attribute the questionable act completely to the local partner. In practice, reputed firms such as Apple have attributed questionable labor practices in their emerging economy supply chains to their suppliers (Duhigg & Barboza, 2012). The struggle to safeguard its reputation among home country stake holders will obviously distract the foreign partner from concentrating on activities that improve alliance performance. On the other hand, for the local partner, refraining from rule bending activities means lagging behind competition, which can hurt alliance performance. Specifically, it might be difficult to succeed in emerging economies like Latin American countries if firms do not engage in the local way of getting things done; approvals are delayed and the costs of doing business are higher than they would be with better cooperation from powerful decision makers.

When regulatory institutions are similar, however, rules of exchange tend to be comparable and foreign partners can understand and work with the host country institutions with relative ease making coordination with the local partner less demanding. Hence, the limiting effects of trust tend to be less relevant here as their mutual identification and commitment for each other will not interfere with their response to their own institutional demands that are fairly similar and might even compensate for any uncertainty in the host country institutions (Gambetta, 1988; Ingram & Clay, 2000; Ingram & Silverman, 2002). Hence,

Hypothesis 2: *Interorganizational trust is less likely to enhance alliance performance when regulatory institutional differences between partnering firms' home countries are high than when they are low.*

METHODS

Sample

These propositions were tested using data collected in a survey conducted in Chile, Brazil, and Mexico between 2004 and 2005. This was considered appropriate as published data covering emerging markets either were not available or did not capture the specific variables of interest. Brazil, Mexico, and Chile had then started to encourage international alliances for capability improvement, which makes them a good data source (Falcke, 1996; Vonortas, 2002; Weiss, 1999). The survey instrument was first designed in English and translated into Spanish and Portuguese. The translation-back translation technique was used to verify item equivalence in the different languages. The Spanish and Portuguese versions were content analyzed by academics in Brazil, Chile, and Mexico to ensure the suitability of the items in the respective business settings.

There is no single master directory of internationally oriented firms for any of the three countries, so various sources including Chambers of Commerce, published directories, and business school contacts were used to prepare lists of target firms. In Brazil, 357 firms were initially selected as the target sample. They were first contacted by phone (a total of 1200 calls), and the caller explained the nature of the study and asked the name of a person in charge of the company's international alliances. In this way, 294 of the 357 firms were eventually contacted. In the second stage, 294 questionnaires were mailed out to those firms. A total of 93 Brazilian surveys were returned, of which 60 were complete enough to be useable, for an effective response rate of 20%. In Chile, the target sample consisted of 180 manufacturing firms that traded on the Bolsa de Comercio de Santiago. Given local concerns about the feasibility of mail surveys, only 40 questionnaires were initially sent through the mail and after two reminders and extensive telephone follow-ups, only 3 questionnaires were returned through the mail. Eventually the resources of a prominent local university were deployed to hand-deliver and collect questionnaires. This led to 92 responses, of which 56 were usable, for a response rate of 31%. In Mexico, the data were collected through hand-delivery to 82 firms involved in international alliances identified through contacts at a major business school. All the surveys were returned, and 51 were usable, for a response rate of

62%. Table 4.1 provides details of the sample's characteristics. The English version of the survey is presented in the Appendix.

Table 4.1

Sample Characteristics

Variable	Brazil	Mexico	Chile
Total sales (US$)	$250 million	$163 million	$373 million
Foreign sales (%)	13.2%	43.3%	28.3%
Respondent's experience with the firm (yrs.)	13.56	7.55	8.66
Respondent's experience managing international alliances (yrs.)	8.63	4.55	4.83
Total employment (persons)	3,347	5,735	2,567

While survey research has been useful in understanding organizational behavior, and in certain contexts, may be the only feasible way to get the desired information (Dess & Robinson 1984; Huber & Power, 1985), there are several concerns related to the validity of this data collection methodology. In particular, the following issues have been raised: (i) non-response bias which leads to a systematic exclusion of firms from the population; and (ii) problems related to single informant bias and common method variance (Huber & Power 1985; Podsakoff, MacKenzie, Lee, & Podsakoff, 2003).

All the respondents held upper-management positions, had on average 10 years of experience with their firms and 6.3 years in managing international alliances. Although non-response bias could not be statistically examined (Armstrong & Overton, 1977) due to the fact that comprehensive secondary information was not available and early and late respondents could not be compared as most of the questionnaires were collected in person, the sample characteristics point to the appropriateness of the represented firms to test the model (i.e., firms on average have $150 million in total sales; foreign sales constitute 28.3% of total sales; sample firms belong to different industries).

We undertook several *procedural* and *statistical remedies* to address the possible concern of single informant bias and common method bias. Procedural remedies included *protecting respondent anonymity, reducing item ambiguity,* and *minimizing effects of consistency artifacts.* By assuring the respondents complete anonymity we reduced the respondent's tendency to be socially desirable or acquiescent when responding to the survey (Podsakoff et al., 2003, p. 888). We also took steps to reduce item ambiguity by avoiding vague concepts and double-barreled questions (Tourangeau et al., 2000). In order to further minimize effects of consistency artifacts, open-ended questions were interspersed throughout the instrument and the anchors for scales varied for certain constructs (i.e., use of both Likert and semantic differential scales). Finally, regarding issues related to single informants, we targeted managers of the respective firms who were explicitly responsible for the management of strategic alliances and partnerships with foreign firms.

We adopted the following statistical remedies. First, we used *Harman's one-factor test*. The logic behind this test is that if common method variance is a serious issue in the data, a single factor will emerge accounting for most of the covariance in the independent and dependent variables (Aulakh & Kotabe 1997; Podsakoff & Organ, 1986). An unrotated principal components factor analysis on all the variables measured using the survey instrument revealed four factors with Eigenvalues greater than 1.0 and the first factor did not account for majority of the variance. Related to this, using LISREL's *confirmatory factor analysis*, we compared Model 1 where the items loaded onto their theoretically assigned latent variables—interorganizational trust, alliance performance, and organizational institutional difference—to Model 2 where all the items loaded onto a common method factor (Podsakoff et al., 2003; Stam & Elfring, 2008). The decrease in fit of Model 2 (one common method factor) over the Model 1 (theoretical model) was highly significant ($\Delta\chi2 = 1317.45$ (Δdf = 7), ΔNFI = 0.14, ΔCFI = 0.14, ΔGFI = 0.35, ΔECVI = 17.28).

Second, we conducted *partial correlation adjustment procedure* (Lindell & Whitney, 2001), after which all our significant zero-order correlations remained significant. Third, we *triangulated survey data using archival sources* (Parkhe, 1993). Specifically, we performed a correlation between total sales reported by the respondents and those available from secondary sources. The correlation coefficient for 45 firms for which secondary data were available is 0.896 ($p < .0001$). Finally, all our *interaction effects are significant* suggesting that our results are less likely to be affected by single informant bias as the respondents are unlikely to have deliberately theorized the moderated relationships when responding to the survey (Brockner, Phyllis, Daly, Tyler, & Martin, 1997). Thus, the results of our procedural and statistical remedies indicate that common method bias and single respondent bias were not serious issues in our study.

Dependent Variable

Alliance Performance

The hybrid structure and transitory nature of strategic alliances presents distinct challenges in measuring alliance performance using traditional measures such as survival and financial performance. An alliance's survival may not indicate that it is performing well, as partners might choose to continue with an unprofitable alliance hoping to improve their relationship. At the same time, alliances that did not survive cannot necessarily be counted as failures because they may have ended after attaining their intended objectives (Yan & Zeng, 1999). Financial measures of performance can be biased, but most importantly a majority of alliances do not report their financial results. Owing to such challenges, much alliance research has relied on managers' evaluations of alliance performance, which is appropriate if the respondent belongs to the top management team.

Alliance performance was measured by 6 items with responses on a 5-point Likert scale (see Appendix). The local partner was asked to evaluate the performance of its alliance with the foreign partner. Except for two items that assessed the overall satisfaction of the local partner with the alliance, the rest questioned the respondent on objective performance criterion such as growth potential, profitability and market penetration. Geringer and Hebert's (1991) study on the comparability and reliability of alliance performance measures obtained from both partners shows a significant positive correlation between the local partner's assessment of performance and the foreign partner's assessment of the same. With a Cronbach's Alpha of 0.83, the performance scale demonstrated high reliability (DeVellis, 1991; Nunally, 1978).

Independent Variables

Organizational Institutional Difference

O'Reilly's (OCP) scale (O'Reilly et al., 1991) was adapted to measure organizational institutional difference—the extent to which the local firm and its foreign partner differed on certain values. This measure involving 15 items captures the extent to which partners differed with respect to innovativeness, stability, attention to detail, team orientation, respect for people, outcome orientation and aggressiveness (Alpha = 0.93). The first three dimensions describe how work rules are structured. The innovativeness dimension emphasizes risk taking, while stability emphasizes rule orientation and attention to details stresses precision and accuracy. The team orientation and respect for people dimensions show whether an organization values teamwork and collaboration, and is tolerant and fair towards its employees. The final two dimensions capture what is rewarded in the organization. Outcome orientation places emphasis on achievement and aggressiveness encourages competition.

Regulatory Institutional Difference

We calculated regulatory institutional difference using dimensions from Kaufmann et al.'s (2009) world governance indicators (e.g., Martin, Solomon, & Wu, 2010; Oh & Oetzel, 2011). Specifically, for different countries we used scores for regulation quality—"ability of the government to formulate and implement sound policies and regulations that permit and promote private sector development," and rule of law—"extent to which agents have confidence in and abide by the rules of society, and in particular the quality of contract enforcement, property rights, the police, and the courts" (Kaufmann et al., 2010, p. 3). A regulatory institutional difference score was calculated as the average of squared deviations of the "regulation quality" and "rule of law" scores of each home country from those of the host country. These scores were corrected for the difference in variance of the index across all countries in the sample. We introduced these variables in two models separately owing to the high correlation between them.

Interorganizational Trust

Interorganizational trust was measured in the survey with responses to 7 items using a 5-point Likert scale (see Appendix). Although prior research has not reached a consensus on measuring trust, scholars generally agree on 3 important dimensions – reliability, fairness and goodwill. The items that capture these three dimensions were adapted from Aulakh, Kotabe & Sahay (1996), Carson et al. (2003), and Sako and Helper (1998). We obtained interorganizational trust data from the local partner. Of the nearly 30 studies published in peer reviewed journals that measure interorganizational trust, 97% obtain data from one partner, and the remaining 3% find strong correlation (0.75 to 0.83) between the level of interorganizational trust reported by the local partner and the level of interorganizational trust reported by the foreign partner. Furthermore, the correlation between trust and performance in our study is 0.49, which is well within the range of .34 and .65 reported in prior studies (e.g., Aulakh et al., 1996; Carson et al., 2003; Geyskens, Steenkamp, & Kumar, 1999; Zaheer et al., 1998). Overall, these statistics provide evidence that our measure of trust is reasonable and consistent (Alpha = 0.80).

Control Variables

National Cultural Distance

National cultural distance might be related to alliance performance (Luo 2002a; Pothukuchi, Damanour, Choi, Chen, & Park, 2002). National culture might also influence cognitive cultural framework, hence we controlled for it in our models. Following extant literature, we measured national cultural distance by using Kogut and Singh's (1988) index, based on Hofstede's (1980) four cultural dimensions.

Relationship Duration

Relationships with a longer history might have had enough time to develop mutual understanding and trust (Parkhe, 1998). More experience might also improve the respondent's evaluation of a relationship's performance (Child & Yan, 2003). Relationship duration was measured as the number of years the respondent's firm had been in a relationship with the foreign partner at the time of the survey (e.g., Simonin, 1999).

Level of Equity

The alliance governance mode is likely to affect the manner in which the relationship unfolds and have an impact on alliance performance (Osborn & Baughn, 1990; Saxton, 1997). Equity alliance is a continuous variable with 0 for non-equity alliances and higher values indicative of higher percentage of equity held by the foreign partner (e.g., Luo, 2002b).

Partner Dependence

We measured partner dependence by two items. *Local partner's dependence on foreign partner* is measured using the percentage of the local partner's business that comes from its relationship with the foreign partner. *Foreign partner's dependence on local partner* is measured using percentage of foreign partner's business that comes from its relationship with the local partner. Research shows that dependence affects relationship performance (Gulati & Sytch, 2007). Moreover, research also argues that in order to mitigate the anxiety arising from dependence on a partner, firms tend to attribute trusting behavior to their partner (Weber, Malhotra, & Murnighan, 2005). Because we collected data on interorganizational trust from the local partner, the local partner's dependence on the foreign partner might have resulted in it trusting the foreign partner. By the same token, the knowledge of the foreign partner's dependence on the local partner might have resulted in the local partner believing that the foreign partner trusts it and that there is overall more trust in the relationship. To make sure that such possibilities do not affect the robustness of our findings, we controlled for partners' dependence.

Local Partner Size

We measured local partner size by an item that captures the total number of people employed in the local partner firm worldwide (e.g., Deeds & Rothaermel, 2003). We used a log transformation of this variable. A large local partner might have more resources (Bonaccorsi, 1992) and, hence is in a better position to absorb knowledge from the foreign partner as well as contribute towards improving alliance performance (Parkhe, 1993).

Local Partner's International Experience

We measure local partner's international experience by an item that captures the number of years the local partner has done business overseas. A local partner that has had prior international experience might have learnt about the institutions of other countries, hence might be in a better position to anticipate the challenges involved in partnering with foreign firms whose institutions vary widely from their own.

Local Partner's Alliance Experience

We measure the local partner's alliance experience by an item that captures the number of alliances the local firm has had with foreign partners. A local partner that has had alliance experience with foreign partners might be less vulnerable to institutional constraints and might be better able to work effectively with its current alliance partner.

Demand Volatility in the Host Country Market

Volatility in the local partner's market might increase challenges introduced by institutional differences by affecting the local partner's knowledge absorption as well as affect alliance performance (Lane, Salk, & Lyles, 2001). We measured demand volatility using a single item that asked the local partner to rate the extent of volatility in sales forecast ranging from very low to very high.

Host Country Dummies

We also included host country dummies in our models to control for host country effects. The two host country dummies included in our models represent Brazil and Mexico respectively with Chile being the reference category.

Industry Dummies

We included three dummy variables to control for industry effects. Given that standard industry classifications were not available through secondary sources and the possibility that individual classification systems vary across countries, we asked the respondents to list the primary industry of their product. These were then classified independently by two people and coded into different industry groups. The set of products fell under four broad industry groups (Industry 1: manufactured durables; Industry 2: manufactured non-durables; Industry 3: services; Industry 4: primary and agriculturally-based products).

Analysis

We conducted the measurement analysis using LISREL's 8.8 maximum likelihood program (Joreskog & Sorbom, 1996). Specifically, we performed confirmatory factor analysis using LISREL to check for convergent and discriminant validity. We used ordinary least squares regression to test our hypotheses. Before calculating the interaction terms used to test our hypotheses, the variables involved were mean centered (Aiken & West, 1991).

RESULTS

Reliability and Validity

All of the constructs displayed satisfactory levels of reliability, as indicated by the composite reliabilities ranging from 0.80 to 0.93 (Nunnaly, 1978; see the Appendix for reliabilities of constructs). Convergent validity, the extent to which different attempts to measure a construct agree (Campbell & Fiske, 1959), can be judged by looking at the factor loadings. Each loading (λ) was significantly related to its underlying factor and all standardized item loadings were above the recommended cut-off of 0.50 (Hildebrandt, 1987), supporting the convergent validity of these measures. We also performed factor analyses separately for each of the three samples. The factor structures were similar across the three country samples, thus demonstrating equivalence of the measures.

A series of chi-square difference tests on the factor correlations showed that discriminant validity, the extent to which a construct differs from others, is achieved among all constructs (Bagozzi, 1993; Joreskog, 1971). Discriminant validity was achieved between all our latent constructs. Below we explain how we tested for discriminant validity between *interorganizational trust* and *alliance performance* as these two latent constructs share the highest bivariate correlation ($r = 0.49$) compared to all the other latent constructs. We constrained the estimated correlation parameter between *interorganizational trust* and *alliance performance* to 1.0, and then performed a chi-square difference test on the values obtained for the constrained ($\chi 2 = 541.75$, df = 119, p < 0.000) and unconstrained models ($\chi 2 = 478.62$, df = 118, p < 0.000). The difference in chi-square ($\Delta\chi 2 = 72.84$, Δdf = 1, p < 0.000) is highly significant indicating that the two constructs are not perfectly correlated and that discriminant validity is achieved (see Anderson & Gerbing, 1988). We carried out the same procedures for other constructs too, with similar results.

Tests of Hypotheses

Table 4.2 reports means, standard deviations, and correlations for all variables. Table 4.3 report results of OLS regression models. The regressions were performed on a sample of 167 international alliances.

We tested nine regression equations for alliance performance, as reported in Table 4.3. We included control variables in Model 1. Because Kaufmann's "rule of law" score and "regulation quality" scores are highly correlated, we introduced them in separate models. Models 2 through 5 includes analysis with "rule of law" score and Models 6 through 9 includes analysis with "regulation quality" score. We included main variables in Models 2 and 6. We introduced the two-way interaction effects separately in Models 3, 4, 7, and 8. Specifically, we introduced two-way interaction of trust and organizational institutional difference in Models 3 and 4. Whereas Model 3 included "rule of law" as one of the main variables, Model 7 included "regulation quality" as one of the main variables. We introduced the interaction of trust with regulatory institutional difference using the "rule of law" score in Model 4 and its interaction with regulatory institutional difference using "regulation quality" score in Model 8. Finally, we included both the two-way interactions together in Models 5 and 9. Specifically, along with the interaction of trust with organizational institutional difference Model 5 included the interaction of trust with regulatory institutional difference using "rule of law" score, Model 9 included regulatory institutional difference using "regulation quality" score. Model 1 is significant (p < 0.10), and the control variables explain 10% of the variance in *alliance performance*. *Demand volatility in the host country market*

Table 4.2

Descriptive Statistics and Correlations[a]

Variable	Mean	SD	1	2	3	4	5	6	7	8	9	10	11	12	13
1. Alliance performance	3.74	0.76													
2. National cultural distance	2.32	1.03	.01												
3. Relationship duration	7.41	8.37	.10	-.06											
4. Level of equity	21.25	25.3	.03	.05	-.06										
5. Foreign partner's dependence on local partner	25.9	29.6	.21	.26	-.00	.17									
6. Local partner's dependence on foreign partner	15.55	27.9	.16	.13	-.08	.09	.41								
7. Local partner size[b]	6.42	2.00	-.02	-.22	.17	.03	-.29	-.11							
8. Local partner's international experience	12.28	16.3	-.01	-.11	.19	.09	-.15	-.05	.34						
9. Local partner's alliance experience	7.18	17.6	-.05	.07	.03	-.08	-.10	.21	.04	.04					
10. Demand volatility in the host country market	1.93	1.09	-.11	-.19	.04	-.07	-.06	.05	.16	.11	.05				
11. Organizational institutional difference	2.25	0.74	-.26	-.08	-.01	-.04	-.13	.01	.15	.08	.11	.14			
12. Regulatory institutional difference (RL)	2.18	1.17	.07	.19	-.02	-.01	.30	.22	.02	-.11	-.00	.14	-.15		
13. Regulatory institutional difference (RQ)	1.66	1.03	.10	.26	-.06	-.01	.22	.22	-.02	-.11	-.01	.07	-.16	.83	
14. Interorganizational trust	3.73	0.68	.49	.01	-.01	.11	.11	.05	-.15	-.06	.01	-.19	-.29	-.03	.01

[a]N = 167. [b]Local partner size is the log of the number of employees.

Means and standard deviations reported here are raw scores.

($p < 0.10$) is negatively related to alliance performance in Model 1. Models 2 and 6 are significant ($p < 0.001$), and the variables explain 34% of variance in alliance performance. The incremental variance accounted for by the main effects in Model 2 ($\Delta R^2 = 0.236$, $p < 0.001$) and Model 6 ($\Delta R^2 = 0.227$, $p < 0.001$) are significant. *Interorganizational trust* ($p < 0.001$) is positively related to *alliance performance* in Models 2 and 6 suggesting that trust improves alliance performance in the absence of the moderating effects. *Organizational institutional difference* ($p < 0.10$) is negatively related to alliance performance in Models 2 and 6. The relationship between *regulatory institutional difference* and alliance performance is insignificant using both the "rule of law" and "regulation quality" scores in Models 2 and 6 respectively.

Table 4.3

OLS Regression Coefficients (Alliance Performance as the Dependent Variable)

Variable	Model 1	Model 2	Model 3	Model 4	Model 5
Main effects					
Organizational institutional difference		−.13†	−.14†	−.16*	−.17*
		(.07)	(.08)	(.08)	(.08)
Regulatory institutional difference (RL)		−.10	−.08	−.08	−.06
		(.07)	(.08)	(.07)	(.07)
Regulatory institutional difference (RQ)					
Interorganizational trust		.52***	.49***	.47***	.45***
		(.09)	(.09)	(.09)	(.08)
Two–way interactions					
Organizational institutional difference x Trust			.29*		.23*
			(.11)		(.10)
Regulatory institutional difference (RL) x Trust				−.23**	−.21**
				(.07)	(.06)
Regulatory institutional difference (RQ) x Trust					

(Table continued on next page)

Table 4.3 (Continued)

OLS Regression Coefficients (Alliance Performance as the Dependent Variable)

Variable	Model 1	Model 2	Model 3	Model 4	Model 5
Controls					
National cultural distance	−.04	.02	.01	.02	.01
	(.06)	(.06)	(.06)	(.06)	(.06)
Relationship duration	.01	.01	.01	.01	.01
	(.01)	(.01)	(.004)	(.004)	(.004)
Level of equity	−.07	−.17	−.19	−.11	−.13
	(.26)	(.23)	(.22)	(.22)	(.21)
Foreign partner's dependence on local partner	.29	.25	.28	.27	.29
	(.23)	(.21)	(.21)	(.20)	(.20)
Local partner's dependence on foreign partner	.27	.27	.26	.31	.30
	(.22)	(.19)	(.18)	(.19)	(.18)
Local partner size	.01	.04	.02	.03	.02
	(.04)	(.03)	(.03)	(.03)	(.03)
Local partner's international experience	.0007	.0007	.0002	.0003	.00
	(.004)	(.003)	(.003)	(.003)	(.002)
Local partner's alliance experience	−.002	−.003	−.003	−.002	−.002
	(.002)	(.002)	(.002)	(.002)	(.002)
Demand volatility in the host country market	−.11†	−.02	−.03	−.002	−.003
	(.06)	(.05)	(.04)	(.04)	(.04)
Host country dummy 1	.14	.27	.25	.19	.17
	(.17)	(.21)	(.21)	(.19)	(.20)
Host country dummy 2	.24	.38†	.36	.30	.29
	(.19)	(.21)	(.23)	(.20)	(.21)
Industry dummy 1	.24	.14	.09	.17	.12
	(.21)	(.19)	(.19)	(.18)	(.19)
Industry dummy 2	.04	.19	.16	.21	.18
	(.21)	(.18)	(.19)	(.17)	(.18)
Industry dummy 3	.02	.05	.03	.08	.07

(Table continued on next page)

Table 4.3 (Continued)

OLS Regression Coefficients (Alliance Performance as the Dependent Variable)

Variable	Model 1	Model 2	Model 3	Model 4	Model 5
Controls					
	(.22)	(.19)	(.19)	(.19)	(.19)
Intercept	3.54***	3.08***	3.31***	3.05***	3.25***
	(.36)	(.42)	(.46)	(.41)	(.44)
R^2	0.108	0.344	0.376	0.400	0.421
ΔR^2		.236***	0.032*	0.056**	0.077***

$N = 167$. ΔR^2 in models 3, 4 and 5 is in comparison with the R2 in model 2. ΔR^2 in models 7, 8 and 9 is in comparison with the R^2 in model 6. The coefficients reported are unstandardized estimates, with standard errors in parentheses. *indicates significance at the $p \leq 0.05$ (** $p \leq 0.01$, *** $p \leq 0.001$) level of confidence (two-tailed). The host country dummies represent Brazil and Mexico respectively with the reference category being Chile.

Table 4.3 (Continued)

OLS Regression Coefficients (Alliance Performance as the Dependent Variable)

Variable	Model 6	Model 7	Model 8	Model 9
Main effects				
Organizational institutional difference	–.13†	–.13†	–.16*	–.16*
	(.08)	(.08)	(.08)	(.08)
Regulatory institutional difference (RL)				
Regulatory institutional difference (RQ)	–.01	–.01	–.02	–.003
	(.06)	(.06)	(.06)	(.06)
Interorganizational trust	.52***	.49***	.47***	.45***
	(.07)	(.09)	(.09)	(.08)
Two–way interactions				
Organizational institutional difference x Trust		.30**		.26*
		(.11)		(.10)
Regulatory institutional difference (RL) x Trust				
Regulatory institutional difference (RQ) x Trust			–.27**	–.24**
			(.08)	(.07)

(*Table continued on next page*)

Table 4.3 (Continued)

OLS Regression Coefficients (Alliance Performance as the Dependent Variable)

Variable	Model 6	Model 7	Model 8	Model 9
Controls				
National cultural distance	−.002	−.03	.01	−.02
	(.07)	(.07)	(.06)	(.07)
Relationship duration	.01	.01	.01	.01
	(.01)	(.004)	(.004)	(.004)
Level of equity	−.17	−.19	−.12	−.14
	(.23)	(.22)	(.21)	(.22)
Foreign partner's dependence on local partner	.24	.27	.19	.23
	(.21)	(.21)	(.20)	(.20)
Local partner's dependence on foreign partner	.28	.26	.34	.33
	(.18)	(.18)	(.20)	(.19)
Local partner size	.03	.02	.03	.02
	(.03)	(.03)	(.03)	(.03)
Local partner's international experience	.00	.00	.001	.00
	(.00)	(.00)	(.003)	(.003)
Local partner's alliance experience	−.003	−.003	−.002	−.002
Demand volatility in the host country market	−.03	−.03	−.02	−.02
	(.05)	(.05)	(.04)	(.04)
Host country dummy 1	.12	.09	.09	.07
	(.17)	(.16)	(.16)	(.17)
Host country dummy 2	.21	.19	.20	.19
	(.18)	(.18)	(.18)	(.17)
Industry dummy 1	.15	.10	.21	.16
	(.19)	(.20)	(.19)	(.20)
Industry dummy 2	.20	.16	.21	.18
	(.19)	(.19)	(.18)	(.18)
Industry dummy 3	.03	.02	.05	.04
	(.20)	(.20)	(.19)	(.19)
Intercept	3.28***	3.52***	3.19***	3.41***
	(.39)	(.43)	(.38)	(.42)
R^2	0.335	0.370	0.388	0.413
ΔR^2	0.227***	0.035**	0.053**	0.078***

$N = 167$. $\Delta R2$ in models 3, 4 and 5 is in comparison with the R^2 in model 2. Local partner size is the log of the number of employees. The coefficients reported are unstandardized estimates, with standard errors in parentheses. * indicates significance at the $p \leq 0.05$ (** $p \leq 0.01$, *** $p \leq 0.001$) level of confidence (two–tailed). The host country dummies represent Brazil and Mexico respectively with the reference category being Chile.

Hypothesis 1 predicts that the beneficial effect of *interorganizational trust* on alliance performance will be stronger when *organizational institutional difference* is high. The coefficient of the interaction of *interorganizational trust* with *organizational institutional difference* is significant and positive ($b = 0.29$, $p < 0.05$ in Model 3; $b = 0.23$, $p < 0.05$ in Model 5; $b = 0.30$, $p < 0.01$ in Model 7; $b = 0.26$, $p < 0.05$ in Model 9), supporting Hypothesis 1. These results suggest that the *interorganizational trust* is more beneficial when *organizational institutional difference* between partnering firm is high.

Hypothesis 2 predicts that the beneficial effect of *interorganizational trust* on alliance performance will be weaker when *regulatory institutional difference* is high. We used Kaufmann et al.'s (2010) "rule of law" and "regulation quality" score to construct the *regulatory institutional difference*. The coefficient of the interaction of *interorganizational trust* with *regulatory institutional difference* using "rule of law" score is significant and negative ($b = -0.23$, $p < 0.01$ in Model 4; $b = -0.21$, $p < 0.01$ in Model 5). Likewise, the coefficient of the interaction of *interorganizational trust* with *regulatory institutional difference* using "regulation quality" score is significant and negative ($b = -0.27$, $p < 0.01$ in Model 8; $b = -0.24$, $p < 0.01$ in Model 9), supporting Hypothesis 2. These results suggest that the benefits of *interorganizational trust* diminish under *regulatory institutional difference*.

To further assess the implications of the regression results, we conducted simple slope tests for the two-way interactions. For the two-way interaction between *organizational institutional difference* and *trust*, the simple slope test (Aiken & West, 1991) reveals that the slope of alliance performance regressed on *interorganizational trust* for high *organizational institutional difference* (simple slope: $b = 0.62$, $t = 6.04$, $p < .001$) is highly significant and positive. This highly significant positive effect of alliance performance regressed on *interorganizational trust* disappears for low *organizational institutional difference* (simple slope: $b = -0.76$, $t = -1.3$, $p > .10$). This shows that interorganizational trust is highly beneficial at high levels of *organizational institutional difference* but might be redundant in partnerships having low level of *organizational institutional difference*.

For the two-way interaction between *regulatory institutional difference* and *interorganizational trust*, the simple slope test (Aiken & West, 1991) reveals that the magnitude of the slope of alliance performance regressed on *interorganizational trust* is nearly seven times smaller for high regulatory institutional difference using "rule of law" score (simple slope: $b = 0.23$, $t = 1.89$, $p < .10$) than for low *regulatory institutional difference* (simple slope: $b = 1.60$, $t = 5.29$, $p < .001$). The slope for high regulatory difference using "regulation quality" score (simple slope: $b = 0.22$, $t = 1.71$, $p < .10$) is nearly seven times smaller than for low regulatory difference (simple slope: $b = 1.53$, $t = 5.15$, $p < .001$). This indicates that trust-performance relationship weakens for high level of *regulatory institutional difference*.

All in all, the results support our argument that whereas interorganizational trust might be an asset under organizational institutional difference at the micro level, it is a liability under regulatory institutional difference at the macro level.

DISCUSSION

A majority of the nearly 90 published studies which have examined the relationship between trust and alliance performance have studied international alliances, and nearly 50% of them examined partners from emerging economies. However, such research has usually taken for granted that trust benefits partners even when they come from dissimilar institutional contexts. Our study shows that in alliances where partners belong to different institutional contexts, the benefits of trust might be contingent on the level at which institutional differences occur. Our findings, based on a survey sample of 167 international alliances in Latin America, reveal that whereas the benefits of trust magnify under organizational institutional differences at the micro level, its benefits diminish under regulatory institutional differences at the macro level.

First, our study contributes to the body of research on interorganizational trust which has identified its many benefits as a governance mechanism, but calls for more studies to identify the conditions under which these purported benefits materialize. In this regard, a few studies use the transaction cost reasoning to examine the conditions under which the contractual hazard mitigation function of trust is beneficial (e.g., Aulakh et al., 1996; Carson et al., 2003; Krishnan, Martin, & Noorderhaven, 2006). This perspective maintains a calculative conceptualization of trust where risk calculations are a reflection of the available leverages to constrain possibility of opportunistic behavior (Williamson, 1993). Another perspective suggests that trust involves a cognitive leap of faith which leads to an over-generalization of the available information about the exchange partner, and this generalization rather than verification leads the relationship to blindness which can be detrimental even in the absence of opportunism (Gargiulo & Ertug, 2006). A few studies examine how conservation of resources in high trust relationships could adversely impact the derived benefits. For example, Szulanski, Cappetta, & Jensen (2004) show that trust hampers knowledge transfer when knowledge is causally ambiguous by limiting cognitive efforts. Similarly, Krishnan et al. (2006) and Krishnan, Geyskens, and Steenkamp (2015) show that trust hinders alliance performance under environmental uncertainty by limiting cognitive efforts. Langfred (2004) reveals that by reducing the need to monitor each other trust ends up being harmful when teams are highly autonomous. Thus, there are some emerging studies that identify the boundary conditions which influence the effectiveness of trust related to contractual hazards and cognitive resource conservation.

To date, however, no published research has identified the conditions under which the mutual identification function of trust might be beneficial or harmful, although it has been acknowledged that "over embedded-ness" (Gargiulo & Ertug, 2006; Uzzi, 1997) or over-identification with the partners and internalizing each other's and belief systems (McEvily et al., 2003) could be detrimental to the exchange partnerships. The mutual identification that trust brings about is highly relevant in alliances between partners embedded in disparate institutional frameworks as their distinct institutions bestow distinct identities on partners. Our study shows that the benefits of trust magnify under organizational institutional differences, as trust encourages partners to identify with each other thereby minimiz-ing misunderstandings and allowing partners to focus on activities that improve alliance performance. When regulatory institutional differences are high, however this quality of trust interferes with partners' optimal response to their respective regulatory institutional environments and dis-tracts them from adequately contributing to the alliance.

Second, recent research on neo-institutionalism argues that when regu-latory institutions are weak, trust acts as a private decentralized institution that fills the voids left by regulatory institutions (Ingram & Clay, 2000; Ingram & Silverman, 2002). Our research adds to this stream of research by suggesting that while this might be true in strategic alliances where both partners belong to similar weak regulatory institutions, this is not the case when one partner belongs to a weak regulatory institution whereas the other belongs to a strong regulatory institution. When both partners are from weak regulatory institutions, standards are not well developed, and organizations have sufficient discretion to pursue their interests. Hence, rule bending activities that are pursued in host countries are accepted by foreign partners as they not only understand the way things are done in the host country but also face less scrutiny on such activities by their home country stakeholders. Trusting under such conditions by encouraging partners to identify with each other reduces any appropriation concerns stemming from weak regulatory institutions. However, our findings reveal that this might not be the case when the foreign partner belongs to a well-developed regulatory institution and the host country partner belongs to a weak regulatory environment. Under such conditions, the same quality of trust that encourages partners to identify with each other might prove to be a liability.

In treating each other's values and needs as their own, the foreign part-ner might step outside the limited discretionary boundaries permitted by its home country institution thereby risking its legitimacy, whereas the local partner underutilizes its discretionary prowess by refraining from rule bending activities. Both of which harm alliance performance; while the former distracts the foreign partner from contributing effectively to alliance performance as it deals with home country stakeholders for its actions elsewhere, the latter delays getting things done in the emerging market where most local firms rely on rule bending activities thereby putting the alliance at a disadvantage. As neo-institutional theory suggests, relying on private centralized institutions such as contracts may not yield the expected benefits under such situations because for contracts to be effective, it should be enforceable which is unlikely when regulatory institutions are weak. Our research has implications for neo-institutional research. This finding suggests that organizations are constrained by their regulatory institutions either directly when they are strong or indirectly by the normative response to institutional demands when they are weak. The cooperation facilitated by trust might work at cross-purposes when partners are subject to divergent institutional constraints. As trust is not an effective decentralized institution under such conditions, future research might examine whether informal networks formed by partners with each other's regulatory authorities might be more effective.

Third, Selznickian institutionalism suggests that the manner in which an organization responds to its institutional environment over time infuses it with value. In a sense, organizational institution reflects such history and over the course of such history an organization develops distinct identity. Our chapter examines Selznickian institutionalism in the interorganizational context. For instance, Latin American firms that have not had international exposure either through exporting or strategic alliances might struggle to adjust to the new export orientation era. This manifests itself in the form of insufficient absorptive capacity and absence of an innovation culture. Our research shows that trust, by encouraging partners whose organizational institutions are different to identify with each other's values and needs, allows them to make up for each other's weaknesses, thereby bringing about synergistic benefits. This finding has implications for other contexts, for example, organizations where team members trust each other might be better able to cope with institutional change at the organizational level. Also, trust might be able to bring about successful integration in acquisitions where organizations with distinct identities come together.

Our findings also have some practical implications. Emerging economy firms increasingly rely on strategic alliances with foreign firms to obtain superior capabilities to compete in a globalized environment (Lyles & Salk, 1996). In fact, public policy initiatives in some emerging economies are geared towards initiating alliances and joint ventures with the expressed purpose of building indigenous capability (Vonortas & Safioleas, 1997).

Our findings show that institutional differences between the emerging economy firms and their developed economy partners cannot be underestimated, to the extent that even cooperative solutions, such as trust, might not be able to bridge regulatory institutional differences at the macro level. Hence, emerging economy firms ought to realize that developing cooperative solutions to bridge organizational differences alone may not be enough and would have to go beyond that. In order to obtain high quality assistance from their developed economy partners, emerging economy firms ought to work with their governments to strengthen their formal institutions by improving contract enforcement, reducing corruption and clearly define property rights.

On the other side, our findings also have implications for multinational companies planning to form strategic alliances with firms operating in weak regulatory institutions. There is an emerging view in international strategic management research that multinational companies and local institutions interact in a co-evolutionary process (Cantwell, Dunning, & Lundan, 2010; Meyer, 2004) whereby MNC institutional frameworks (i.e., beliefs, norms, values, etc.) are adopted by the local partners. While influencing partners to adopt the MNCs core values and ways of doing business may be useful to satisfy the home market stakeholders, our findings show the limits of such attempts when the macro-regulatory institutions necessitate distinct approaches to navigate the local landscape. The response of emerging economy firms to their weak regulatory institutions might not be compatible with the response of developed country firms whose strong home country regulatory institutions may not give them enough discretion to pursue their interests. Under such conditions, organizing principles such as trust might be a liability. Hence, managers of multinational corporations and emerging economy firms might be better off maintaining their distinct identities.

Our findings offer opportunities for future research. First, our chapter examined international alliances in Latin American economies. Future research could examine whether our results hold in other emerging economies that have had colonial influences, such as India for example. For example, bureaucratic challenges from the Southern European colonial era still persist in Latin American economies; similarly bureaucratic system left behind by the British colonization of India remains largely unaltered and presents huge challenges to business. Second, national cultural distance is insignificant in our study. Perhaps organizational institutional differences at the micro level matter more to alliance performance than cultural differences at the national level. Sirmon and Lane (2004) show that national cultural difference manifests itself in differences at the organizational level. Future research might examine this link in more detail.

Third, our findings show that trust is likely to be highly beneficial under organizational institutional differences at the micro level. Partners with distinct identities might have work towards cultivating trust in the relationship. Future research might examine whether being aware of the differences might be a good starting point towards cultivating trust in such relationships. Finally, our research shows that the very quality of trust that is beneficial under certain conditions becomes a liability under other conditions giving rise to the paradox of trust. This opens up research possibilities for identifying solutions to managing the paradox of trust. Perhaps partners that have had prior experience working together might have learnt how to work with each other, which in addition to compensating for the limits of trust might allow them to leverage the psychological safety resulting from trust.

REFERENCES

Abdi, M., & Aulakh, P. S. (2012). Do country-level institutional frameworks and interfirm governance arrangements substitute or complement in international business relationships. *Journal of International Business Studies*, *43*(5), 477–497.

Aiken, L. S., & West, S. G. (1991). *Multiple regression: Testing and interpreting interactions*. Thousand Oaks, CA: SAGE.

Anderson, J. C., & Gerbing, D. W. (1988). Structural equation modeling in practice: A review and recommended two-step approach. *Psychological Bulletin*, *103*(3), 411–423.

Armstrong, S. J., & Overton, T. S. (1977). Estimating non-response bias in mail surveys. *Journal of Marketing Research*, *14*(3), 396–402.

Aulakh, P. S., Kotabe, M., & Sahay, A. (1996). Trust and performance in cross-border marketing partnerships: A behavioral approach. *Journal of International Business Studies*, *27*(5), 1005–1032.

Aulakh, P. S., & Kotabe, M. (1997). Antecedents and performance implications of channel integration in foreign markets. *Journal of International Business Studies*, *28*(1), 145–175.

Bagozzi, R. P. (1993). Assessing construct validity in personality research: Applications to measures of self-esteem. *Journal of Research and Personality*, *27*(1), 49–87.

Barney, J. B., & Hansen, M. H. (1994). Trustworthiness as a source of competitive advantage. *Strategic Management Journal*, *15*(S1), 175–190.

Brockner, J., Phyllis, A. S., Daly, J. P., Tyler, T., & Martin, C. (1997). When trust matters: The moderating effect of outcome favourability. *Administrative Science Quarterly*, *42*(3), 558–583.

Bonaccorsi, A. (1992). On the relationship between firm size and export intensity. *Journal of International Business Studies*, *23*(4), 605–635.

Bortagaray, I., & Tiffin, S. (2005). Innovation clusters in Latin America. In D. V. Gibson, M. V. Heitor, & A. Ibarra-Yunez (Eds.), *Learning and knowledge for the network society* (pp. 261–206). West Lafayette, IN: Purdue University Press.

Campbell, D. T., & Fiske, D. W. (1959). Convergent and discriminant validation by the multitrait-multimethod matrix. *Psychological Bulletin*, *56*(2), 81-105.

Cantwell, D. T., Dunning, J. H., & Lundan, S. M. (2010). An evolutionary approach to understanding international business activity: The co-evolution of MNEs and the institutional environment. *Journal of International Business Studies*, *43*(5), 567–586.

Carson, S. J., Madhok, A., Varman, R., & John, G. (2003). Information processing moderators of the effectiveness of trust-based governance in interfirm R&D collaboration. *Organization Science*, *14*(1), 45–56.

Chan, C. M., Isobe, T., & Makino, S. (2008). Which country matters? Institutional development and foreign affiliate performance. *Strategic Management Journal*, *29*(11), 1179–1205.

Child, J., & Yan, Y. (2003). Predicting the performance of international joint ventures: An investigation in China. *Journal of Management Studies*, *40*(2), 283–320.

Deeds, D. L., & Rothaermel, F. T. (2003). Honeymoons and liabilities: The relationship between age and performance in research and development alliances. *Journal of Product Innovation Management*, *20*(6), 468–484.

Dess, G. G., & Robinson, R. B. (1984). Measuring organizational performance in the absence of objective measures: The case of the privately-held firm and conglomerate business unit. *Strategic Management Journal*, *5*(3), 265–273.

DeVellis, R. F. (1991). *Scale development*. Newbury Park, CA: SAGE.

Duarte, F. (2006). Exploring the interpersonal transaction of the Brazilian Jeitinho in bureaucratic contexts. *Organization*, *13*(4), 509–527.

Dyer, J. H. (1997). Effective interfirm collaboration: How firms minimize transaction costs and maximize transaction value. *Strategic Management Journal*, *18*(7), 535–556.

Dyer, J. H., & Chu, W. (2003). The role of trustworthiness in reducing transaction costs and improving performance: Empirical evidence from the United States, Japan, and Korea. *Organization Science*, *14*(1), 57–68.

Duhigg C., & Barboza D. (2012). In China, human costs are built into an IPad. *New York Times*: January-25-2012.

Economist. (2012). Not king coal. The Rothschild-Bakrie marriage hits the rocks, February 11, p. 87.

Falcke, C. O. (1996). Recent experiences with alternative forms of privatization: Case studies and a synthesis with a focus on the role of government. United Nations Industrial Development. Organization Report 1996-03-25; Vienna, UNIDO.

Fraga, A. (2004). Latin America since the 1990s: Rising from the sickbed? *Journal of Economic Perspectives*, *18*(2), 89–106.

Gambetta, D. G. (1988). Can we trust trust? In D. G. Gambetta (Ed.), *Trust: Making and breaking cooperative relations* (pp. 213–237). New York, NY: Basil Blackwell.

Gargiulo, M., & Ertug, G. (2006). The dark side of trust. In R. Bachmann & A. Zaheer (Eds.), *Handbook of trust research* (pp. 165–186). New York, NY: Elgar.

Gardberg, N. A., & Fombrun, C. J. (2006). Corporate citizenship: Creating intangible assets across institutional environments. *Academy of Management Review*, *31*(2), 329–346.

Geringer, J. M., & Hebert, L. (1991). Measuring performance of international joint ventures. *Journal of International Business Studies*, *22*(2), 249–264.

Geyskens, I., Steenkamp, J. B. E. M., & Kumar, N. (1999). A meta-analysis of satisfaction in marketing channel relationships. *Journal of Marketing Research*, *36*(2), 223–239.

Glynn, M. (2000). When cymbals become symbols: Conflicts over organizational identity within a symphony orchestra. *Organization Science*, *11*(3), 285–298.

Goodrick, E., & Salancik, G. R. (1996). Organizational discretion in responding to institutional practices: Hospitals and Cesarean births. *Administrative Science Quarterly*, *41*(1), 1–28.

Gulati, R., & Singh, H. (1998). The architecture of cooperation: Managing coordination costs and appropriation concerns in strategic alliances. *Administrative Science Quarterly*, 43, 781–814.

Gulati, R., & Sytch, M. (2007). Dependence asymmetry and joint dependence in interorganizational relationships: Effects of embeddedness on a manufacturer's performance in procurement relationships. *Administrative Science Quarterly*, *52*(1), 32–69.

Gulati, R., Wohlgezogen, F., & Zhelyazkov, P. (2012). The two facets of collaboration: Cooperation and coordination in strategic alliances. *Academy of Management Annals*, *6*(1), 531–583.

Hildebrandt, L. (1987). Consumer retail satisfaction in rural areas: A reanalysis of survey data. *Journal of Economic Psychology*, *8*(1), 19–42.

Hitt, M. A., Dacin, M. T., Levitas, E., Arregle, J. L., & Borza, A. (2000). Partner selection in emerging and developed market contexts: Resource-based and organizational learning perspectives. *Academy of Management Journal*, *43*(3), 449–467.

Hodgson, G. M. (2004). Opportunism is not the only reason why firms exist. *Industrial and Corporate Change*, *13*(2), 401–417.

Hofstede, G. (1980). *Culture's consequences: International differences in work-related values*. London, UK, SAGE.

Huber, G. P., & Power, D. J. (1985). Retrospective reports of strategic-level managers: Guidelines for increasing their accuracy. *Strategic Management Journal*, *6*(2), 171–180.

Ingram, P., & Clay, K. (2000). The choice-within-constraints new institutionalism and implications for sociology. In K. S. Cook & J. Hagan (Eds.), *Annual review of sociology* (Vol. 26, pp. 525–546). Palo Alto, CA: Annual Reviews.

Ingram, P., & Silverman, B. S. (2002). The new institutionalism in strategic management. In P. Ingram & B. S. Silverman (Eds.), *Advances in strategic management* (Vol. 19, pp. 1–32). Greenwich, CT: JAI Press.

Jarrad, J. (1995). The Brazilianization of alcoholic anonymous. In R. DaMatta & D. J. Hess (Eds), *The Brazilian puzzle: Culture on the borderlands of the Western world* (pp. 209–236). New York, NY: Columbia University Press.

Joreskog, K. G. (1971). Statistical analysis of congeneric tests. *Psychometrika*, *36*(2), 109–133.

Joreskog, K. G., & Sorbom, D. (1996). *LISREL 8: User's reference guide*. Chicago, IL: Scientific Software International.

Katsikeas, C. S., Skarmeas, D., & Bello, D. C. (2009). Developing successful trust-based international exchange relationships. *Journal of International Business Studies, 40*(1), 132–155.

Kaufmann, D., Kraay, A., & Mastruzzi, M. (2009). Governance matters VIII: Aggregate and individual governance indicators for 1996–2008. World Bank Policy Research Working Paper No. 4978. Washington, D.C.

Kaufmann, D., Kraay, A., & Mastruzzi, M. (2010). *The worldwide governance indicators: Methodology and analytical issues*. World Bank Policy Research Working Paper No. 5430. Washington, DC.

Kogut, B., & Singh, H. (1988). The effect of national culture on the choice of entry mode. *Journal of International Business Studies, 19*(3), 411–432.

Kostova, T., & Roth, K. (2002). Adoption of an organizational practice by subsidiaries of multinational corporations: Institutional and relational effects. *Academy of Management Journal, 45*(1), 215–233.

Kraatz, M. S., & Block, E. S. (2008). Organizational implications of institutional pluralism. In R. Greenwood, C. Oliver, K. Sahlin-Andersson, & R. Suddaby (Eds.), SAGE *handbook of organizational institutionalism* (pp. 243–275). Thousand Oaks, CA: SAGE.

Kramer, R. M. (1993). Cooperation and organizational identification. In J. K. Murnighan (Ed.), *Social psychology in organizations: Advances in theory and research* (pp. 244–268). Englewood, NJ: Prentice Hall.

Kriauciunas, A., & Kale, P. (2006). The impact of socialist imprinting and search on resource change: A study of firms in Lithuania. *Strategic Management Journal, 27*(7), 659–679.

Krishnan, R., Geyskens, I., & Steenkamp, J. B. E. M. (2016). The effectiveness of contractual and trust-based governance in strategic alliances under behavioral and environmental uncertainty. *Strategic Management Journal, 37*(12), 2521–2542.

Krishnan, R., Martin, X., & Noorderhaven, N. G. (2006). When does trust matter to alliance performance? *Academy of Management Journal, 49*(5), 894–917.

Lane, P. J., Salk, J. E., & Lyles, M. A. (2001). Absorptive capacity, learning, and performance in international joint ventures. *Strategic Management Journal, 22*(12), 1139–1161.

Langfred, C. W. (2004). Too much of a good thing? Negative effects of high trust and individual autonomy in self-managing teams. *Academy of Management Journal, 47*(3), 385–399.

Lewicki, R., & Bunker, B. B. (1996). Developing and maintaining trust in work relationships. In R. M. Kramer & T. R. Tyler (Eds.), *Trust in organizations: Frontiers of theory and research* (pp. 114–139). Thousand Oaks, CA: SAGE.

Lindell, M. K., & Whitney, D. J. (2001). Accounting for common method variance in cross-sectional designs. *Journal of Applied Psychology, 86*(1), 114–121.

Luo, Y. (2002a). Product diversification in international joint ventures: Performance implications in an emerging market. *Strategic Management Journal, 23*(1), 1–20.

Luo, Y. (2002b). Stimulating exchange in international joint ventures: An attachment-based view. *Journal of International Business Studies*, *33*(1), 169–181.

Lyles, M. A., & Salk, J. E. (1996). Knowledge acquisition from foreign parents in international joint ventures. *Journal of International Business Studies*, *27*(5), 877–904.

Martin, X., Salomon, R. M., & Wu, Z. (2010). The institutional determinants of agglomeration: A study in the global semiconductor industry. *Industrial and Corporate Change*, *19*(6), 1769–1800.

Mayer, R. C., Davis, J. H., & Schoorman, F. D. (1995). An integrative model of organizational trust. *Academy of Management Review*, *20*(3), 709–734.

McEvily, B., Perrone, V., & Zaheer, A. (2003). Trust as an organizing principle. *Organization Science*, *14*(1), 91–103.

McEvily, B., & Zaheer, A. (2006). Does trust still matter? Research on the role of trust in inter-organisational exchange. In R. Bachmann & A. Zaheer (Eds.), *Handbook of trust research* (pp. 280–300). Cheltenham, UK: Edward Elgar.

McAllister, D. J. (1995). Affect and cognition-based trust as foundations for interpersonal cooperation in organizations. *Academy of Management Journal*, *38*(1), 24–59.

Meyer, K. E. (2004). Perspectives on multinational enterprises in emerging economies. *Journal of International Business Studies*, *35*(4), 259–276.

Meyer, K. E., Estrin, S., Bhaumik, S., & Peng, M. W. (2009). Institutions, resources, and entry strategies in emerging economies. *Strategic Management Journal*, *30*(1), 61–80.

Mohr, J., & Spekman, R. (1994). Characteristics of partnership success: Partnership attributes, communication behavior and conflict resolution techniques. *Strategic Management Journal*, *15*(2), 135–152.

North, D. C. (1990). *Institutions, institutional change and economic performance*. Cambridge, MA: Harvard University Press.

North, D. C. (1991). Institutions. *Journal of Economic Perspectives*, *5*(1), 97–112.

Nunnaly, J. (1978). *Psychometric theory*. New York, NY: McGraw-Hill.

Oh, C. H., & Oetzel, J. (2011). Multinationals' response to major disasters: How does subsidiary investment vary in response to the type of disaster and the quality of country governance? *Strategic Management Journal*, *32*(6), 658–681.

O'Reilly III, C., Chatman, J., & Caldwell, D. F. (1991). People and organizational culture: A profile comparison approach to assessing person-organization fit. *Academy of Management Journal*, *34*(3), 487–516.

Osborn, R. N., & Baughn, C. C. (1990). Forms of interorganizational governance for multinational alliances. *Academy of Management Journal*, *33*(3), 503–519.

Park, S. H., & Ungson, G. R. (1997). The effect of national culture, organizational complementarity, and economic motivation on joint venture dissolution. *Academy of Management Journal*, *40*(2), 279–307.

Park, S. H., & Ungson, G. R. (2001). Interfirm rivalry and managerial complexity: A conceptual framework of alliance failure. *Organization Science*, *12*(1), 37–53.

Parkhe, A. (1993). Strategic alliance structuring: A game theoretic and transaction cost examination of interfirm cooperation. *Academy of Management Journal*, *36*(4), 794–829.

Parkhe, A. (1998). Building trust in international alliances. *Journal of World Business*, *33*(4), 417–437.

Podsakoff, P. M., & Organ, D. W. (1986). Self-reports in organizational research: Problems and prospects. *Journal of Management*, *12*(4), 531–544.

Podsakoff, P. M., MacKenzie, S. B., Lee, J. Y., & Podsakoff, N. P. (2003). Common method biases in behavioral research: A critical review of the literature and recommended remedies. *Journal of Applied Psychology*, *88*(5), 879–903.

Pothukuchi, V., Damanpour, F., Choi, J., Chen, C. C., & Park, S. H. (2002). National and organizational culture differences and international joint venture performance. *Journal of International Business Studies*, *33*(2), 243–265.

Reguart, C. C. (2005). Globalization and industrial restructuring in Mexico: The electronics and automobile industries. In Gibson, D. V, Heitor, M. V., Ibarra-Yunez, A. (Eds.), *Learning and knowledge for the network society* (pp. 261–306). West Lafayette, IN: Purdue University Press.

Ring, P. S., & Van de Ven, A. H. (1994). Developmental processes of cooperative interorganizational relationships. *Academy of Management Review*, *19*(1), 90–118.

Roy, J. P., & Oliver, C. (2009). International joint venture partner selection: The role of the host-country legal environment. *Journal of International Business Studies*, *40*(5), 779–801.

Sako, M. (1991). The role of "trust" in Japanese buyer-supplier relationships. *Ricerche Economiche*, 45, 449–474.

Sako, M., & Helper, S. (1998). Determinants of trust in supplier relations: Evidence from the automotive industry in Japan and the United States. *Journal of Economic Behavior & Organization*, *34*(3), 387–417.

Saxton, T. (1997). The effects of partner and relationship characteristics on alliance outcomes. *Academy of Management Journal*, *40*(2), 443–460.

Scott, W. R. (2008). *Institutions and organizations: Ideas and interests* (3rd ed.). Los Angeles, CA: SAGE.

Selznick, P. (1957). *Leadership in administration*. New York, NY: Harper & Row.

Sirmon, D. G., & Lane, P. J. (2004). A model of cultural differences and international alliance performance. *Journal of International Business Studies*, *35*(4), 306–319.

Simonin, B. L. (1999). Ambiguity and the process of knowledge transfer in strategic alliances. *Strategic Management Journal*, *20*(7), 595–624.

Stam, W., & Elfring, T. (2008). Entrepreneurial orientation and new venture performance: The moderating role of intra- and extra-industry social capital. *Academy of Management Journal*, *51*(1), 97–111.

Stone, A., Levy, B., & Paredes, R. (1996). Public institutions and private transactions: A comparative analysis of the legal and regulatory environment for business transactions in Brazil and Chile. In L. J. Alston, T. Eggertsson, & D. C. North. *Empirical studies in institutional change*, (pp. 95–128). New York, NY: Cambridge University Press

Szulanski, G., Cappetta, R., & Jensen, R. J. (2004). When and how trustworthiness matters: Knowledge transfer and the moderating effect of causal ambiguity. *Organization Science*, *15*(5), 600–613.

Tourangeau, R., Rips, L. J., & Rasinski, K. (2000). *The psychology of survey response*. Cambridge, UK: Cambridge University Press.

Uzzi, B. (1997). Social structure and competition in interfirm networks. *Administrative Science Quarterly, 42*(1), 37–69.

Van Tulder, R., & Van der Zwart, A. (2006). *International business-society management*. New York, NY: Routledge.

Vonortas, N. S. (2002). Building competitive firms: Technology policy initiatives in Latin America. *Technology in Society, 24*, 433–459.

Vonortas, N. S., & Safioleas, S. P. (1997). Strategic alliances in information technology and developing country firms: Recent evidence. *World Development, 25*(5), 657–680.

Weber, J. M., Malhotra, D., & Murnighan, J. K. (2005). Normal acts of irrational trust: Motivated attributions and the trust development process. In R. M. Kramer (Ed.), *Research in organizational behavior* (Vol; 27, pp. 75–101). New York, NY: Elsevier/JAI.

Weiss, J. (1999). Trade reforms and manufacturing performance in Mexico: From import substitution to dramatic economic growth. *Journal of Latin American Studies, 31,* 151–166.

Williamson, O. E. (1993). Calculativeness, trust and economic organization. *Journal of Law and Economics, 36*(1), 453-486.

Yan, A., & Zeng, Z. (1999). International joint venture instability: A critique of previous research, a reconceptualization, and directions for future research. *Journal of International Business Studies, 30*(2), 397–414.

Zaheer, A., McEvily, B., & Perrone, V. (1998). Does trust matter? Exploring the effects of interorganizational and interpersonal trust on performance. *Organization Science, 9*(2), 141–159.

APPENDIX

Measures

Alliance performance (for the local partner) ($\alpha = 0.87$)

(Five-point scale point ranging from 1 – strongly disagree to 5 – strongly agree)

1. The alliance with this foreign partner is more profitable that we expected
2. Overall, we consider the alliance to be successful
3. The alliance has shown less growth potential than we expected (R)
4. The alliance has achieved profit goals that were set
5. The partnership with the foreign firm has achieved good market penetration
6. In general, our relationship with this partner is very satisfactory

Organizational institutional difference ($\alpha = 0.93$)

(Five-point scale from 1 – identical to 5 – Opposite)

Please indicate the degree of similarity between your firm and your foreign partner firm for the following organizational values.

(1) Focus on details, (2) Clear philosophy of the firm, (3) Action orientation, (4) Orientation towards results, (5) Emphasis on organizational culture, (6) Employment security, (7) Team orientation, (8) Opportunities for growth in the same firm, (9) Be socially responsible, (10) Innovativeness, (11) Tolerance, (12) Emphasis on quality, (13) Autonomy, (14) Aggressiveness, (15) Orientation towards achievement

Interorganizational Trust ($\alpha = 0.80$)

(Five-point scale point ranging from 1 – strongly disagree to 5 – strongly agree)

1. Promises made by this partner has been reliable
2. This business relationship is characterized by high levels of trust
3. Sometimes our foreign partner alters the facts in order to get concessions from us. (R)
4. Our foreign partner has sometimes promised to do things without actually doing them later. (R)
5. Our foreign partner hesitates to give us information that is not part of the contract (R)
6. In times of crisis in this relationship, we and our foreign partner can depend on each other
7. Whenever an unexpected situation arises, we and our foreign partner cooperate to resolve the issue

Local partner's international experience

For how many years have your firm done business in overseas markets? In Years

Local partner's alliance experience

Besides this foreign partner, with how many firms from foreign countries has your firm had business relationships? Number of Firms

Local partner size

How many people are employed in your firm worldwide?

Relationship duration

Number of years your organization has had a relationship with this firm?

Partner dependence

Local partner's dependence of foreign partner. Approximately what percentage of your firm's total business comes from your firm's relationship with this foreign partner?

Foreign partner's dependence on local partner. Approximately what percentage of this foreign partner's business comes from its relationship with your firm?

Demand volatility

(5 – point item ranging from 1– very low to 5 – very high)
Stability in sales forecast (R)
Note: (R) refers to reverse coded variables.

CHAPTER 5

A CONTINGENT VIEW OF INTERFIRM COOPERATION

The Role of Firm Similarity in the Linkages Between Trust and Contract

Steven S. Lui, James Robins, and Hang-yue Ngo

ABSTRACT

Empirical findings on whether trust and contracting substitute or complement each other in interfirm cooperation have been equivocal. In this study, we suggest that organizational factors associated with observation and interpretation of partner behavior may help to explain the equivocal findings. We examine this idea with data collected from 156 trading companies in buyer-seller relationships. We find that trust and contracting act as substitutes in promoting cooperation between trading companies and their suppliers, but the effectiveness of contracting is contingent on firm similarity between trading partners. We also find that trust plays a dominant role in fostering cooperation. These findings have important implications for research on trust in interfirm exchange and for organizational-economic analysis of exchange.

Managing Interpartner Cooperation in Strategic Alliances, pp. 129–154
Copyright © 2022 by Information Age Publishing
www.infoagepub.com

INTRODUCTION

The study of trust and contracting has taken on a very important role in the dialogue between economic and behavioral approaches to organizations. The organizational economic tradition associated with Williamson (1985) has been one of the most influential approaches to analysis of exchange between firms (Adler, 2001). It has also been a very uncomfortable approach for behavioral scientists, who find the underlying economic assumptions excessively reductive (cf. Donaldson, 1990; Ghoshal & Moran, 1996). The research on conditions for contractual and trust-based exchange has become a key empirical setting where these different views are put to the test.

The central question in the work on contracting and trust has been whether contractual organization of exchange and trust-based organization of exchange are interrelated—as substitutes or complements—or if they are unrelated means of facilitating cooperation between firms (Das & Teng, 1998; de Man & Roijakkers, 2009; Faems, Janssens, Madhok, & van Looy, 2008; Inkpen & Currall, 2004; Klein Woolthuis, Hillebrand, & Nooteboom, 2005; Lui, 2009; Lui & Ngo, 2004; Patzelt & Shepherd, 2008; Poppo & Zenger, 2002; Vlaar, van den Bosch, & Volberda, 2007; Zhou & Poppo, 2010). Alliance creates value beyond either market exchange or hierarchy by fostering cooperation (Dyer & Singh, 1998; Thorgren & Wincent, 2011). Cooperative behavior is therefore an important outcome to study. Empirical findings on this question remain equivocal. Some studies have found complementarity, while others suggest that contracting is a substitute for trust (Puranam &Vanneste, 2009).

In this study, we argue that this ambiguity is partially due to incomplete treatment of an issue that has been very important in organizational economic work. The contract versus trust literature neglects a fundamental aspect of the context in which contracting takes place—the difficulty of partners observing and monitoring each other. In situations where the contracting relationship is relatively transparent—that is, contracts are relatively easy to write and post-contractual performance can be more readily observed—then contracting will be less costly and more efficacious as a means of promoting cooperation between partners (Williamson, 1975, 1979). This can alter the balance between contract and trust as means of promoting interfirm coordination.

The research on monitoring has emphasized the technical side of this problem. Certain types of exchanges are difficult to monitor due to the nature of the good or service exchanged (Carson, Madhok, & Wu, 2006). Contracting will be costly or ineffective in promoting cooperation when exchanges of that type are involved. However, difficulty of monitoring has social as well as technical dimensions, and the organizational context in which monitoring takes place has received less attention in the research. Difficulty of writing contracts and monitoring performance relies, in part, on the transparency of the relationship between firms, that is, the difficulty of observing and interpreting the actions of managers in the partner firm. The ability to observe and interpret behavior in a partner firm can be strongly affected by the similarity between firms. In this way, similarity between firms may alter the balance between contracting and trust.

This study contributes to both behavioral research on cooperation and research on organizational economics. Reintegrating organizational-economic concerns about monitoring into the study of trust and contracting extends the behavioral approach and offers a more comprehensive logic for analysis of interfirm relationships. It helps to address a central debate of research on interfirm cooperation: whether trust and contract act as substitutes in promoting cooperation between firms. We find that they are substitutes, but their substitution effects are conditioned on the potential difficulty of monitoring. This study also makes a contribution to empirical research on organizational economics. Although the role of trust has received increasing recognition in the work on organizational economics (Williamson, 1993), little empirical research has charted the links between trust and more traditional concerns with monitoring and contracting. The three-way interaction of these factors identified in this chapter adds a dimension to the empirical work on these issues.

The chapter is organized in three parts. The first part reviews key ideas from transaction-cost theory and earlier studies of trust and cooperation. Based on these ideas, we develop a set of hypotheses about the roles played by trust, similarity between firms, and contracting in promoting cooperation between firms. The second part reports the empirical analysis of these hypotheses using data collected from garment traders in Hong Kong. The final part of the chapter discusses some of the implications of the work for research on interfirm cooperation and for the management of inter-organizational relationships.

HYPOTHESIS DEVELOPMENT

Trust, Contracting, and Cooperation

The debate on trust and contracting in interfirm cooperation highlights the basic problem of governance in economic exchange (Ring, 2008). In this context, cooperative behavior refers to cooperation between two firms in terms of flexibility, information exchange and joint problem solving (Jap, 1999; Lusch & Brown, 1996). Trust and contracting both deal with threats of opportunism, and both can create an environment in which cooperation may be effective (Das & Teng, 1998; de Man & Roijakkers, 2009; Luo, 2006).

Following Mayer, Davis, and Schoorman (1995), trust is used here to refer to the belief or expectation that an exchange partner will not exploit vulnerabilities in one's own firm when given the opportunity. This belief is built upon the experience of a partner's benevolence and credibility in fulfilling promises, acting fairly, and exhibiting goodwill (Doney & Cannon, 1997; Krishnan, Martin, & Noorderhaven, 2006). It is fundamental to the development of cooperative behavior (Anderson & Narus, 1990; Morgan & Hunt, 1994; Zhang, Cavusgil, & Roath, 2003). To cooperate with another firm involves vulnerability and mutual dependence. Trust reduces the perceived risk of opportunism from vulnerability (Das & Teng, 1998; Lui & Ngo, 2004; Nooteboom, 1996). The reduced vulnerability has been studied as lower transaction costs in Dyer and Chu (2003) and Katsikeas, Skarmeas, and Bello (2009). Moreover, trusted partners are also more likely to follow norms of reciprocity; they communicate more effectively; and they make efforts to build goodwill (Ganesan, 1994; Morgan & Hunt, 1994; Thorgren & Wincent, 2011). This open communication process cultivates mutual dependence among cooperating parties. Thus, trust generally can be expected to foster cooperative behavior between firms. In its simplest form, this suggests the hypothesis:

Hypothesis 1: *Trust is positively associated with cooperative behavior between firms, ceteris paribus.*

The research on trust also has suggested that trust may substitute for formal contracting as means of promoting cooperation. Formal contracting refers to the extent to which an explicit and legally binding agreement is used to specify the scope of an exchange and the obligations of each exchange party (Cavusgil, Deligonul, & Zhang, 2004; Dyer, 1997; Zhou & Poppo, 2010). A formal contract provides explicit terms of exchange and enforceable legal sanctions. This reduces hazards of opportunistic behavior and can facilitate cooperative economic exchange (Cannon & Perreault, 1999).

On the other hand, trust can offer the equivalent of a normative, self-reinforcing contract (Lusch & Brown, 1996, Srinivasan & Brush, 2006). This can serve as a functional substitute for a formal contract. The underlying assumption is that trust and contract serve as different safeguards that accomplish same end – promoting cooperative exchange in a partnership (Das & Teng, 1998; Faems et al., 2008; Gulati, 1995; Parkhe, 1993). In situations where trust is strong, contracts assume less importance as devices for promoting cooperation.

Hypothesis 2: *Trust and contract act as substitutes in their relationship to cooperative behavior between firms, ceteris paribus.*

Contracting, Similarity, and Cooperation

Organizational economists argue that the potential for opportunism is omnipresent. Opportunistic behavior can be controlled by competition in pure market theory, but those controls break down in most exchanges carried out in the real world (Ouchi, 1980). The capabilities, intentions, and actions of trading partners are not fully known, and interfirm relationships commonly involve specific investments that make it costly to switch partners.

The difficulty of monitoring a partner's performance is one of the key issues of the organizational economic approach (e.g., Eisenhardt, 1985; Klein, Crawford, & Alchian, 1978; Williamson, 1985). Monitoring cost is a fundamental form of transaction cost. The power of a contract to prevent appropriation relies on the fact that a partner's behavior is potentially observable and verifiable (Argyres & Mayer, 2007; Klein et al., 1978). Two issues affect the use of monitoring: ease of specifying partner obligations *ex ante*, and how readily managers can observe and interpret the post-contractual behavior of their counterparts in a partner firm (Dyer, 1997; Oxley, 1997). If the outputs of a task are difficult to specify *ex ante* or observe and measure *ex post*, monitoring is problematic and costly, and the use of contracts becomes difficult (Eisenhardt, 1985; Mayer & Nickerson, 2005; Mayer & Salomon, 2006).

The difficulty of observing and measuring contractual performance may be influenced by both technical and social features of the exchange. The characteristics of certain types of goods and services are intrinsically difficult to specify *ex ante* or measure *ex post*. These technical problems of monitoring have been the traditional focus of transaction-cost analysis (cf. Williamson, 1985).

However, the difficulty of monitoring also may be influenced by the organizational context of the exchange. It is easier for managers to understand and interpret the behavior of their counterparts in another firm when the firms are similar in their operations and culture. Similarity in operations, goals and values facilitates recognition of patterned behavior by partners (Parkhe, 1993; Saxton, 1997). This allows more accurate inferences about motives of managers and better prediction of the future actions of partner firms (Sarkar, Aulakh, & Cavusgil, 1998). Partners that are more similar deal with parallel environmental and business issues, and managers in the firms have more homogenous mental maps (Ouchi, 1980).

Similarity also facilitates exchange by improving communication between partners (Saxton, 1997).

These organizational elements facilitate the use of contracting. They affect exchange in ways that are similar to the technical characteristics of goods and services. It is relatively easy to contract for simple, stable goods and services because confidence in the ability of a partner to deliver is higher *ex ante* and monitoring of performance is easier *ex post*. It also is easier to organize exchange by contract when firms are similar. Managers can judge whether a partner is misrepresenting capabilities before the fact and whether the partner is taking actions necessary to fulfill the contract after the fact. Conversely, if similarity is low, judgment of contract fulfillment is difficult to make. Under such conditions, rigid reference to formal contract may easily degenerate into inflexibility formalism (Vlaar et al., 2007) and block joint sensemaking (Faems et al., 2008). This argues for an interaction between contracting and similarity. We expect contracting to be more important as a means of promoting cooperation between firms when the firms are more similar, and reduce cooperation between firms when they are dissimilar.

Hypothesis 3: *The association between contract and cooperative behavior will be stronger when firms have greater similarity.*

Trust, Contracting, Similarity, and Cooperative Behavior

These different influences on cooperation define a complex set of relationships. Both trust and interfirm similarity may affect the importance of contracting in facilitating cooperation between exchange partners. Trust is important to cooperation; cooperation may be strong in a high trust relationship even though formal contracts have little significance. This may be true regardless of whether the partners are very similar; if contracting does not matter, similarity is irrelevant as well. On the other hand, contracting may assume greater importance in promoting cooperation in situations where trust is weak. However, contracting is likely to take on this role only if partners are relatively similar. If partners are not similar, contracting can be expected to be an ineffective alternative to trust, and we would expect to see little effect of contracting.

These relationships define a three-way interaction among trust, contracting and similarity as they affect cooperation. The effect of any one of these factors on cooperation will be contingent on the level of the other two. The decision to use contracting for a specific exchange is the only one of the three factors that managers can control in the short run. Similarity and trust both take a significant amount of time to change and may not truly be "decision variables" in the same sense as contracting. We therefore treat contracting as an independent variable and trust and similarity as covariates. The fundamental problem faced by managers is to determine whether contracting will be effective or necessary under specified conditions of trust and similarity.

The debate in the literature has focused on trade-offs between trust and contract (Das & Teng, 1998; Poppo & Zenger, 2002; Vlaar et al., 2007). As indicated above, this relationship is our primary interest. The focus of the analysis therefore is the way interaction between contract and trust is affected by levels of interfirm similarity. We expect contracts to serve as a substitute for trust only when similarity is relatively high. The role of contracting in promoting cooperation therefore will be most important in high similarity/low trust situations. If similarity is low, we do not expect contracting to be effective in promoting cooperation. This would be true even if trust also is weak. Under those circumstances, we anticipate less cooperation altogether.

Finally, the potential effectiveness of contracting may not matter if trust is high. If contracting acts as a substitute for trust, then there will be no need to rely on contracts with strong trust relations. Under those circumstances, the level of similarity between firms also is immaterial. However, if trust is low, the level of similarity between firms may attenuate the effectiveness of contracting. Highly similar firms may have the potential to rely on contracting to promote cooperation, but they have no need for contracting as trust has done the job already. On the other hand, cooperation suffers in high trust/high contract condition, because ineffectual contracts obstruct the smooth operation of partnership based on trust. In many ways, this is the obverse side of the saying that "good contracts make good partners." Bad contracts may erode the ability of good partners to act on their trust relationships (Klein Woolthius et al., 2005). Terms of contracting are likely to be less appropriate when a partner is very different, and a poorly drawn contract may reduce flexibility and adaptation that could have been facilitated by trust (Vlaar et al., 2007). We can summarize this in a single hypothesis about the independent variable, contracting:

Hypothesis 4: *Contracting will have the strongest positive association with cooperative behavior when trust is low and similarity is high.*

METHODS

Sample

We tested the relationships between contract and cooperative behavior under different conditions of trust and similarity using a sample of garment trading companies in Hong Kong and their suppliers. We selected this setting for several reasons. As indicated above, much of the work on monitoring has emphasized technical dimensions of exchange such as difficulties inherent in exchanging scarce or intangible goods. We are interested in the organizational factors that affect observation and interpretation of partner actions. A single industry study allowed us to hold many of the technical characteristics of exchanges constant and focus on variability due to organizational similarity. The garment trader-supplier relationship is not highly complex and it involves tangible products. This also is a setting where contractual form varies relatively little. We can examine managerial assessments of the role contracting plays in relationships without confounding questions about contractual form.

The study of the garment industry also has practical significance. International garment brands increasingly source their products through Hong Kong garment trading firms, making these firms and their suppliers a crucial link in the global garment supply chain. Our sample was composed of garment trading firms included in the Menswear and Knitwear Directories of the Trade Development Council of Hong Kong. The directories provided business information about the firms and the names of contact persons who were usually the owners or the top executives of the firms. A total of 1,171 firms and their corresponding contact persons were included in the original sampling frame.

Procedures

The questionnaire was first written in English and then translated into Chinese using the conventional back-translation process. After pilot testing, surveys were mailed to the contact persons of the sample firms in March 2005. The mailing was followed by a second survey and then a telephone reminder. Of the 1,171 mailed surveys, 61 were undeliverable or were sent to firms that had left the garment trading industry. We finally received a total of 156 responses from the 1,110 effective sample, representing a 14% response rate. This response rate is typical for mailed surveys to top executives (Hambrick, Geletkanycz, & Fredrickson, 1993). We compared the respondent and non-respondent firms on number of employees and year of establishment, and found no significant differences between the two groups (F-values were 0.004 for number of employees and 0.08 for year of establishment; both non-significant), suggesting that responding firms were representative of the full sample. The reported cooperative relationships have an average history of seven years. Fifty seven percent of the suppliers were the biggest supplier of the trading firms in terms of procurement, and 85% of them were located in China.

We collected information from one informant per firm, since these trading firms usually were small and only one staff member has contact with a supplier. Although single respondent data account for the great majority of all survey research, they do always involve the possibility of common method variance. We addressed this problem using both *ex ante* procedural and *ex post* statistical techniques as suggested by Chang, van Witteloostuijn, and Eden (2010) and Podsakoff, MacKenzie, Lee, and Podsakoff (2003). First, for a test-retest reliability check, we sent a follow-up mini-survey to those who had responded, asking them to once again provide information on trust and partnership satisfaction (cf. Luo, 2005; Yli-Renko, Autio, & Sapienza, 2001). This procedure yielded a sample of 49 for which both first and second responses were received. The correlation coefficient between the two responses on trust was 0.57 (p <0.001) and that on partnership satisfaction was correlated at 0.51 (p <0.001). A paired samples t-test was also conducted, and no significant differences were detected in the profiles of the two groups with respect to trust (t = 0.15, df =41, ns) and partnership satisfaction (t = 0.79, df =41, ns). Second, we conducted a Harman single factor test on the dependent and the independent variables, and six factors with eigenvalues larger than 1 were identified. These six factors explained a total of approximately 66% of the variance, with the first one explaining 33%. Thus, we did not find evidence that a single factor explained the variance of the study variables.

The survey focused the respondents on a particular relationship by asking them to answer the questions with respect to "a supplier that you have recently dealt with." We collected data from the trader side of the dyad, and we looked at variables that are either specific to the trader or that the trader can legitimately interpret and explain. The fact that buyer's and supplier's perceptions of exchange have been quite consistent in prior research makes informant bias less likely (Heide & John, 1992; Zaheer, McEvily, & Perrone, 1998). We focus on the trader's trust in the supplier because procurement partnerships in the garment industry usually are led by the trader, making the trader's trust in the supplier a core element of the relationship.

Measures

All variables in the study were measured using 5-point Likert-type scales, with 1 indicating "strongly disagree" and 5 indicating "strongly agree." Table 5.1 lists the questionnaire items measuring each variable and reports the internal reliability (Cronbach's alpha) of the scales formed by the items.

Table 5.1

Measures and Items of Dependent and Independent Variables

Measures and items *5-point scale ranged from strongly disagree (1) to strongly agree (5)*	Reliability	Source
Trust 1. We feel that this supplier cares about what happens to us. 2. This supplier has always been frank and truthful in its dealing with us. 3. This supplier would go out of its way to make sure our firm is not damaged or harmed in this relationship. 4. This supplier sometimes promises to do things without actually doing them later.[r]	.75	Adapted from Johnson et al. (1996)
Firm similarity 1. We and this supplier have the same long term plans and goals for our relationship. 2. Managers from both of our firms have similar philosophies and approaches to business dealing. 3. The procedures and practices of our two firms are very different.[r]	.68	Adapted from Sarkar et al. (1998)
Formal contract 1. We do not have specific, well detailed agreements with this supplier.[r] 2. We have formal agreements that detail the obligations of both parties. 3. Our relationship with this supplier is governed primarily by written contract.	.66	Adapted from Cannon and Perreault (1999) and Jap and Ganesan (2000)
Cooperative behavior *Flexibility* 1. Flexibility in response to requests for changes is a characteristic of this relationship. 2. It is expected that the parties will be open to modifying their agreements if unexpected events occur. 3. Changes in fixed terms are willingly made by the parties, if it is considered necessary.	.82	Items taken from Pearce (2001) based on Heide and Miner (1992)

(Table continued on next page)

Table 5.1 (Continued)

Measures and Items of Dependent and Independent Variables

Measures and items

5-point scale ranged from strongly disagree (1) to strongly agree (5)	Reliability	Source
Information exchange		
4. In this relationship, it is expected that any information that may help the other party will be provided to them.		
5. Exchange of information in this relationship takes place frequently, informally, and openly.		
6. It is expected that we keep each other informed about events or changes that may affect the other party.		
Joint problem solving		
7. In most aspects of this relationship the parties are jointly responsible for getting things done.		
8. Problems that arise in the course of this relationship are treated by the parties as joint rather than individual responsibilities.		
9. The parties in this relationship do not mind owing each other favors.		

r = reverse coded item

Trust

We measured the trader's trust in the supplier using four items from the scale developed by Johnson, Cullen, Sakano, and Takenouchi (1996). These items reflected the extent of reliability, fairness, and benevolence that a supplier exhibited. The Cronbach alpha of the scale was 0.75 in this study.

Firm Similarity

This was measured by the respondent's perception of similarity between the respondent and supplier firms, using a three-item scale in Sarkar et al. (1998). When partners are similar and compatible, communication and mutual understanding are better. This in turn increases relationship transparency and mutual understanding, which reduces problems in specifying and monitoring contractual relationships. The scale had a Cronbach alpha of 0.68 in this study.

Formal Contract

This was measured by the scale of legal bonds developed by Cannon and Perreault (1999) and the scale by Jap and Ganesan (2000). These items reflected the extent and details of the contract provided for the partnership. The scale had a Cronbach alpha of 0.66.

We conducted a confirmatory factor analysis to examine the convergent validity and the multidimensionality of the three independent variables. The fit indexes indicated that the model fitted the data well ($\chi^2 = 44.32$ (32), $p > 0.05$, ns; CFI = 0.95, GFI = 0.93, RMSEA = 0.05). All items loaded on their respective constructs, and all loadings were substantial and significant at the 0.001 level. This supports the dimensionality of the constructs. To assess the discriminant validity of each scale, we estimated a series of chi-square difference tests between a model in which the correlation between a pair of constructs was constrained to unity, and a model without this constraint (Gerbing & Anderson, 1988). We found that all chi-square differences were significant at the 0.05 level, indicating that the fit of the unconstrained model was significantly better than that of the constrained model. This provided evidence of discriminant validity.

Cooperative Behavior

Cooperative behavior was operationalized as having three dimensions: flexibility, information exchange, and shared problem solving (Griffith & Myers, 2005; Pearce, 2001). We followed Pearce (2001) in measuring each dimension using three items. A factor analysis on the nine items produced one single factor which explained 41% of the variance. The result was consistent with the idea that cooperative behavior is a second order factor that arises from three first order factors. This nine-item scale had a Cronbach alpha of 0.84 in this study.

We chose this approach to measuring interfirm cooperation because it has good content validity as a property of the relationship between firms. The measure chosen also is focused on generalized capabilities for exchange, not affective relationships between individuals in the firms. Performance outcomes have been the major alternative approach to a dependent measure for studies of exchange (e.g., Patzelt & Shepherd, 2008; Poppo & Zenger, 2002). However, performance outcomes may be difficult to interpret in our analysis. Performance may be influenced by a number of exogenous factors, and it may not be directly linked to the organization and governance of the relationship between firms. Cooperation in this case is cooperation within the context of the relationship. An outcome such as cost performance could be the result of something unrelated such as a vendor having favorable access to materials. The measures used here are antecedent conditions of performance and they have a tighter logic linking them to the independent variables of the study.

Control Variables

We included six control variables that may affect cooperative behavior in the model. Dependence may make less powerful firms more vulnerable to the exercise of power by the more powerful partners (Subramani & Venkatraman, 2003). To measure the *supplier dependence*, we asked each respondent whether the relationship was more important to the supplier than to themselves. A high value represented higher supplier dependence. *Cost focus* reflects the level of task complexity in a partnership. Cost typically is a major consideration in a partnership when the tasks involved in the partnership are less complex and more standardized (White & Lui, 2005). Although the industry and sample were chosen in part because products and exchanges are relatively simple, we added the additional control to pick up effects of variability within those limits. We asked respondents to rate the extent price affected their choice of the supplier in order to capture cost focus in a relationship.

Partners also tend to cooperate more with each other if they have longer working history (Saxton, 1997). We measured *history* by asking how long the respondent has been working with the supplier. Specific asset investment may lock partners into cooperating with each other (Dyer & Singh, 1998; Saxton, 1997). *Asset specificity* was measured by a 3-item scale developed by Jap (1999). Some of the suppliers are not located in China and cultural differences with trading firms may exist. We used *location* to identify the location of the suppliers. It was labeled 1 if the supplier was located in China and 0 if not. Finally, the performance of a partnership may affect cooperation (Parkhe, 1993). We used the log of the percentage of *on-time delivery* to measure the performance of a partnership. Higher on-time delivery represented higher performance.

RESULTS

Means, standard deviations, and correlations among all study variables are presented in Table 5.2. We tested the hypotheses using moderated hierarchical regression analysis. We mean-centered trust, similarity, and contract in the regression. The control variables, formal contract, and firm similarity were first entered into the regression equation in Step 1, followed by trust in Step 2, the two-way interaction terms in Step 3, and the three-way interaction term in Step 4.

Table 5.3 displays the results of the analyses of cooperative behavior. Step 2 of Table 5.3 shows that the coefficient of trust was significant (β = 0.41, p < 0.001) and the addition of trust significantly improved the R^2 of the regression model (ΔR^2 = 0.10, p < 0.001). Hypothesis 1 therefore was supported.

Step 3 of Table 5.3 shows that the two-way interaction terms collectively created a significant increase in the explained variance in cooperative behavior (ΔR^2 = 0.04, p < 0.05). As predicted in Hypotheses 2 and 3, the interaction of trust and contract (β = –0.23, p < 0.05) and of similarity and contract (β = 0.25, p < 0.01) had significant associations with cooperative behavior, above and beyond their direct effects.

We followed procedures suggested by Aiken and West (1991) to interpret the nature of the interaction. We used the unstandardized regression coefficients and constant from the final regression equation to conduct simple slope tests and to plot the relationship between contract and cooperative behavior at high and low levels of trust. The procedure was repeated for high and low levels of similarity. The interaction pattern shown in the plot was consistent with what we hypothesized in Hypothesis 2. Figure 5.1 Panel A shows that the association between contract and cooperative behavior was more positive when trust was low, showing that trust and contract act as substitutes for each other (b = –0.15, p <0.05 in high trust group; b = 0.10, $n.s.$ in low trust group). Hypothesis 2 was thus supported. Figure 5.1 Panel B shows that the association between contract and cooperative behavior was more positive when similarity was high (b = 0.12, p <0.10 in high similarity group; b = – 0.16, p<0.05 in low similarity group). Hypothesis 3 also was supported.

The significance of the three-way interaction effect was indicated in the increase in R^2 of Step 4 over Step 3 in Table 5.3 (ΔR^2 = 0.03; p <0.01). Consistent with Hypothesis 4, the three-way interaction of trust, similarity and contract made a significant (β = 0.22, p < 0.01) contribution to explained variance in cooperative behavior. Support for hypothesis 4 also requires a pattern of results consistent with the prediction we made. We used Aiken and West's (1991) approach to take a closer look at the three-way interaction. We plotted the relationship of contracting with cooperation for different combinations of trust and similarity. As revealed in Figure 5.2, Panel B, the positive association between contract and cooperation is greatest when trust is low, and similarity is high. This is consistent with the prediction in Hypothesis 4. This panel also provides some indication of the dominant role of trust in cooperative behavior. In situations where trust and similarity both are high, the graph for contracting is essentially parallel to the X-axis. This suggests that contracting will not improve cooperation if trust is already high, even with a similar partner. In all, these findings provide support for Hypothesis 4.

Table 5.2

Means, Standard Deviations, and Correlations Among Studied Variables

Variable	Mean	SD	1	2	3	4	5	6	7	8	9
1 Cooperative behavior	3.76	.42									
2 Trust	3.42	.60	.52***								
3 Firm similarity	3.23	.63	.44***	.60***							
4 Formal contract	2.96	.68	-.03	-.03	.01						
5 Supplier dependence	3.34	.66	.33***	.11	.27**	-.02					
6 Cost focus	3.79	.88	.09	-.10	.02	.25**	.05				
7 Cooperation history (ln year)	1.84	.74	.04	.21**	.18*	.12	-.03	-.09			
8 Asset specificity	3.68	.62	.18*	.16	.20*	.02	-.04	.07	.06		
9 Location (China=1)	0.86	.34	.05	.00	-.06	-.07	.04	.01	.01	-.02	
10 On-time delivery (ln %)	4.35	.21	.28***	.42***	.38***	-.14	.09	-.17*	.08	.10	-.12

Notes: N = 127;

* $p < .05$

** $p < .01$

*** $p < .001$

143

Table 5.3

Regression Results: Cooperative Behavior

Variables	Cooperative behavior			
	Step 1: Controls and main effects	Step 2: Trust	Step 3: Two-way interaction	Step 4: Three-way interaction
Control Variables				
Supplier dependence	.23**	.24**	.26***	.28***
	(2.84)	(3.23)	(3.48)	(3.84)
Cost focus	.10	.12	.15*	.15*
	(1.20)	(1.66)	(1.97)	(2.03)
History	-.00	-.04	-.05	-.08
	(-0.07)	(-.62)	(-.76)	(-1.09)
Asset specificity	.11	.10	.09	.11
	(1.45)	(1.35)	(1.32)	(1.53)
Location	.07	.05	.05	.06
	(1.00)	(.74)	(.79)	(.84)
On-time delivery	.15	.06	.04	.07
	(1.72)	(.74)	(.47)	(.92)
Direct Effect				
Formal contract	-.03	-.03	-.04	-.13
	(-.43)	(-.42)	(-.57)	(-1.65)
Firm similarity	.30***	.09	.08	.09
	(3.41)	(.99)	(.91)	(.98)
Trust		.41***	.43***	.38***
		(4.37)	(4.56)	(4.00)
2-way Interaction				
Trust X Formal contract			-.23*	-.18
			(-2.25)	(-1.75)
Firm similarity X Formal contract			.25**	.14
			(2.52)	(1.32)
Trust X Firm similarity			-.03	-.05
			(-.47)	(-.67)

(Table continued on next page)

Table 5.3 (Continued)

Regression Results: Cooperative Behavior

Variables	Cooperative behavior			
	Step 1: Controls and main effects	Step 2: Trust	Step 3: Two-way interaction	Step 4: Three-way interaction
3-way Interaction				
Trust X Firm similarity X Formal contract				.22** (2.5)
ΔR^2		.10	.04	.03
ΔF		19.15***	2.57*	6.27**
Adjusted R^2	.25	.35	.37	.40
F value	6.13***	8.41***	7.20***	7.44***

Notes: Standardized coefficients are reported with t values in parenthesis.

$\dagger p < .10$, $* p < .05$, $** p < .01$, $*** p < .001$

Figure 5.1

Relationship Between Contract and Cooperative Behavior (2-Way Interaction)

Panel A. Interaction between contract and trust

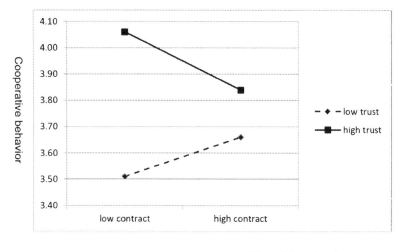

(Figure 5.1 continued on next page)

Figure 5.1 (Continued)

Relationship Between Contract and Cooperative Behavior (2-Way Interaction)

Panel B. Interaction between contract and similarity

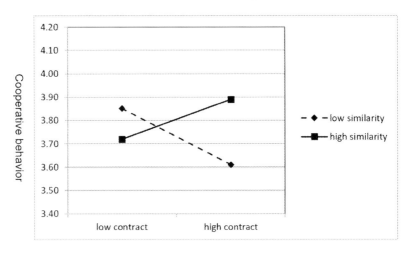

Figure 5.2

Relationship Between Contract and Cooperative Behavior for Different Levels of Similarity and Trust (3-Way Interaction)

Panel A. When similarity is low

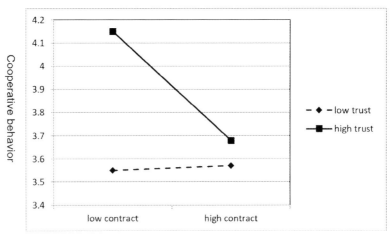

(Figure 5.2 continued on next page)

Figure 5.2 (Continued)

Relationship Between Contract and Cooperative Behavior for Different Levels of Similarity and Trust (3-Way Interaction)

Panel B. When similarity is high

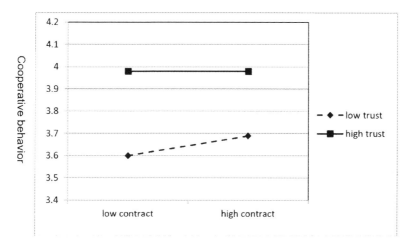

DISCUSSION

In this chapter, we move beyond the basic relationship between trust and contract to examine a more complex set of inter-relationships among trust, potential monitoring difficulty, and contracting. Our working hypothesis is that the interplay of all three factors determines interfirm cooperation. The results of this study highlight two important points: first, trust plays a key role in promoting cooperation between exchange partners. Although contracts can help to make up for a deficit of trust, they do not improve cooperation if trust is strong. In situations where trust is high, contracts make no additional contribution to cooperation, even if relationship transparency is high as well (as shown in Figure 5.2, panel B).

Second, the role of contracting as an alternative to trust is contingent on the similarity between firms. The latter is supported by the significant three-way interaction of trust, contracting, and similarity on cooperative behavior. If similarity is high, contracts promote cooperation in low-trust conditions. If similarity is low under the same low-trust conditions, contracts have no effect on cooperation (as shown in Figure 5.2).

As noted above, there has been debate whether trust and contracting function as substitutes or complements. We find evidence of substitution, but our analysis does not provide any support for complementarity. Our results also indicate one reason why a substitution effect between trust and contract might not have been appeared in some prior studies. Prior research has not taken account of the implications of organizational similarity. Contracts may have been ineffective substitutes for trust simply because there was too little transparency in the relationship between firms to make contracts specifiable and enforceable.

The findings also highlight some important areas for future research. Longitudinal study of these relationships may help to answer questions that cannot be addressed by our cross-sectional data. The dynamic evolution of trust and contract may change the roles they play in a partnership (Faems et al., 2008; Klein Woolthuis et al., 2005; Mayer & Argyres, 2004). For example, Puranam and Vanneste (2009) have provided a longitudinal framework that accommodates the complementary and substitution effects between trust and contract when they are studied over time.

We recognize that trust and cooperation tend to reinforce each other in a virtuous circle, which points to another limitation of the study. Relationships between trust and cooperation are likely to involve feedback effects that cannot be analyzed with our data. The factors that contribute to cooperative behavior also may have reciprocal relationships with other variables in the analysis; the formalization of contract at the beginning of a partnership may depend on trust and transparency in previous partnerships. Analysis of these issues would require non-recursive models based on either an instrumental-variable approach such as two-stage least squares or a longitudinal analysis. The cross-sectional data we collected does not offer suitable instrumental variables for non-recursive modeling, nor does it permit longitudinal analysis. With a few notable exceptions (e.g., Poppo & Zenger, 2002), this has been typical of the majority of studies on this topic. However, it is an important avenue for future research. Although panel data are very difficult to collect, longitudinal data could make it possible to carry out a more comprehensive analysis of the origins and effects of cooperation. Finally, studies of both trust and contract have suggested that each of these constructs involves a number of underlying dimensions (e.g., Das & Teng, 1998; Luo, 2005; McAllister, 1995). In the interest of making the study manageable, we have not attempted to collect detailed data on these separate dimensions. The additional interactions would make the study extremely complex. In many ways, this study is a first cut at a larger and complex program of research designed to expand our understanding of issues that have seen largely in terms of a dichotomy between extremes —contracting and trust.

The use of single industry data, and the collection of data from one side of trading dyads, creates limits as well as benefits for the study. Single industry data provide control for a number of key issues and increase internal validity, but they also diminish external validity. We cannot assume that findings generalize to other industries.

CONCLUSION

The study sheds new light on the long-standing debate over trust and contracting. The findings suggest that the equivocal nature of previous research on trust and contracting may reflect an excessively simple approach to contracting. Reintroduction of one of the basic concepts of organizational economics—the idea that specifiability of contracts and ease of monitoring are important variables in the analysis of exchange—reveals a relationship between trust and contracting that has eluded prior studies. This also has important implications for organizational-economic research. Trust may play as significant role in facilitating exchange as some of the technical factors that have been the focus of organizational-economic research. Although there has been prior discussion of this issue (cf. Williamson, 1993), little empirical work has been done in this area.

This study also has some important practical implications for managers. There has been growing pressure to substitute market-like arrangements for more personal relationships in global supply chains. The "disintermediation" of supply chains through the substitution of electronic marketplaces has been promoted as a means of improving efficiency. This study suggests that managers should approach this move toward contracting with caution. Cooperation often may be best facilitated by trust. Reliance on contracts under the wrong circumstances may be ineffective or even detrimental to the smooth functioning of interfirm exchange. Of course, the level of trust also changes along different stages of a partnership (MacDuffie, 2011). A more careful partnership management involving both trust and contracting seems to be a more sensible approach for managers (Faems et al., 2008; Puranam & Vanneste, 2009; Verbeke & Greidanus, 2009).

The larger message in this research probably is the importance of more comprehensive approaches to the study of inter-organizational exchange. Behavioral and economic views of exchange have had an uneasy history together (Hirsch, Michaels, & Friedman, 1987; Robins, 1987). They have come together in certain key problems, such as the study of utility, but researchers in each area often have adopted a narrow view of the other perspective. Behavioral scientists sometimes have neglected the complexity of organizational-economic theories, while organizational-economic approaches have reduced subtle issues of motivation and perception to stylized assumptions about human behavior. More inclusive approaches to empirical work offer a route to a richer and deeper understanding of exchange between firms.

ACKNOWLEDGMENTS

This chapter, save some minor changes, was earlier published as Lui, Steven S., Robins, James, and Ngo, Hang-yue (2011). A contingent view of inter-firm cooperation: The role of firm similarity in the linkages between trust and contract. In T. K. Das (Ed.), *Behavioral perspectives on strategic alliances* (pp. 83–107). Charlotte, NC: Information Age Publishing. This chapter was partly supported by the UNSW Goldstar Research Grant (#PS19146) awarded to the first author.

REFERENCES

Adler, P. S. (2001). Market, hierarchy, and trust: The knowledge economy and the future of capitalism. *Organization Science, 12*, 215–234.

Aiken, L. S., & West, S. G. (1991). *Multiple regression: Testing and interpreting interactions.* Newbury Park: SAGE.

Anderson, J. C., & Narus, J. A. (1990). A model of distributor firm and manufacturer firm working partnerships. *Journal of Marketing, 54* (Jan), 42–58.

Argyres, N., & Mayer, K. J. (2007). Contract design as a firm capability: An integration of learning and transaction cost perspectives. *Academy of Management Review, 32*, 1060–1077.

Cannon, J. P., & Perreault, W. D. Jr. (1999). Buyer-seller relationships in business markets. *Journal of Marketing Research, 36*, 439–460.

Carson, S. J., Madhok, A., & Wu. T. (2006). Uncertainty, opportunism and governance: The effects of volatility and ambiguity on formal and relational contracting. *Academy of Management Journal, 49*, 1058–1077.

Cavusgil, S. T., Deligonul, S., & Zhang, C. (2004). Curbing foreign distributor opportunism: An examination of trust, contracts, and the legal environment in international channel relationships. *Journal of International Marketing, 12*(2), 7–27.

Chang, S., van Witteloostuijn, A., & Eden, L. (2010). Common method variance in international business research. *Journal of International Business Studies, 41*, 178–184.

Das, T. K., & Teng. B. (1998). Between trust and control: Developing confidence in partner cooperation in alliances. *Academy of Management Review, 23*, 491–512.

de Man, A-P, & Roijakkers, N. (2009). Alliance governance: Balancing control and trust in dealing with risk. *Long Range Planning, 42*, 75–95.

Donaldson, L. (1990). The ethereal hand: Organizational economics and management theory. *Academy of Management Review, 15*, 369–381.

Doney, P. M., & Cannon, J. P. (1997). An examination of the nature of trust in buyer-seller relationships. *Journal of Marketing, 61*(April), 35–51.

Dyer, J. H. (1997). Effective interfirm collaboration: How firms minimize transaction costs and maximize transaction value. *Strategic Management Journal, 18*, 535–556.

Dyer, J. H., & Chu, W. (2003). The role of trustworthiness in reducing transaction costs and improving performance: Empirical evidence from the United States, Japan and Korea. *Organization Science, 14*, 57–68.

Dyer, J. H., & Singh. H. (1998). The relational view: Cooperative strategy and sources of interorganizational competitive advantage. *Academy of Management Review, 23*, 660–679.

Eisenhardt, K. M. (1985). Control: Organizational and economic perspectives. *Management Science, 31*, 134–149.

Faems, D., Janssens, M., Madhok, A., & van Looy, B. (2008). Toward an integrative perspective on alliance governance: Connecting contract design, trust dynamics, and contract application. *Academy of Management Journal, 51*, 1053–1078.

Ganesan, S. (1994). Determinants of long-term orientation in buyer-seller relationships. *Journal of Marketing, 58*(April), 1–19.

Gerbing, D. W., & Anderson. J. C. (1988). An updated paradigm for scale development incorporating unidimensionality and its assessment. *Journal of Marketing Research, 25*, 186–192.

Ghoshal, S., & Moran. P. (1996). Bad for practice: A critique of the transaction cost theory. *Academy of Management Journal, 21*, 13–47.

Griffith, D. A., & Myers. M. B. (2005). The performance implications of strategic fit of relational norm governance strategies in global supply chain relationships. *Journal of International Business Studies, 36*, 254–269.

Gulati, R. (1995). Does familiarity breed trust? The implications of repeated ties for contractual choice in alliances. *Academy of Management Journal, 38*, 85–112.

Hambrick, D. C., Geletkanycz, M. A., & Federickson. J. W. (1993). Top executive commitment to the status quo: Some tests of its determinants. *Strategic Management Journal, 18*, 401–418.

Heide, J., & John. G. (1992). Do norms matter in marketing relationships? *Journal of Marketing, 56*(April), 32–44.

Heide, J., & Miner. A. (1992). The shadow of the future: Effects of anticipated interaction and frequency of contact on buyer-supplier cooperation. *Academy of Management Journal, 35*, 265–291.

Hirsch, P., Michaels, S., & Friedman, R. (1987). 'Dirty hands' versus 'clean models': Is sociology in danger of being seduced by economics? *Theory & Society, 16*, 317–336.

Inkpen, A. C., & Currall. S. C. (2004). The coevolution of trust, control, and learning in joint ventures. *Organization Science, 15*, 586–599.

Jap, S. D. (1999). Pie-expansion efforts: Collaboration processes in buyer-supplier relationships. *Journal of Marketing Research, 36*, 461–475.

Jap, S. D., & Ganesan, S. (2000). Control mechanisms and the relationship life cycle: Implications for safeguarding specific investments and developing commitment. *Journal of Marketing Research, 37*, 227–245.

Johnson, J. L., Cullen, J. B., Sakano, T., & Takenouchi. H. (1996). Setting the stage for trust and strategic integration in Japanese-U.S. cooperative alliances. *Journal of International Business Studies, 27*, 981–1004.

Katsikeas, C. S., Skarmeas, D., & Bello, D. C. (2009). Developing successful trust-based international exchange relationships. *Journal of International Business Studies, 40*, 132–155.

Klein, B., Crawford, R., & Alchian, A. (1978). Vertical integration, appropriable rents and the competitive contracting process. *Journal of Law and Economics, 21*, 297–326.

Klein Woolthuis, R., Hillebrand, B., & Nooteboom, B. (2005). Trust, contract, and relationship development. *Organization Studies, 26*, 813–840.

Krishnan, R., Martin, X., & Noorderhaven, N. G. (2006). When does trust matter to alliance performance? *Academy of Management Journal, 49*, 894–917.

Lui, S. (2009). The roles of competence trust, formal contract, and time horizon in interorganizational learning. *Organization Studies, 30*, 333–353.

Lui, S., & Ngo, H. Y. (2004). The role of trust and contractual safeguards on cooperation in non-equity alliances. *Journal of Management, 30*, 471–485.

Luo, Y. (2005). Transactional characteristics, institutional environment and joint venture contracts. *Journal of International Business Studies, 36*, 209–230.

Luo, Y. (2006). Opportunism in cooperative alliances: Conditions and solutions. In O. Shenkar & J. J. Reuer (Eds.), *Handbook of strategic alliances* (pp. 55–79). Thousand Oaks, CA: Sage.

Lusch, R. F., & Brown, J. R. (1996). Interdependency, contracting, and relational behavior in marketing channels. *Journal of Marketing, 60*(Oct), 19–38.

MacDuffie, J. P. (2011). Interorganizational trust and dynamics of distrust. *Journal of International Business Studies, 42*, 35–47.

Mayer, K. J., & Argyres, N. S. (2004). Learning to contract: Evidence from the personal computer industry. *Organization Science, 15*, 394–410.

Mayer, K. J., & Nickerson, J. A. (2005). Antecedents and performance implications of contracting for knowledge workers: Evidence from information technology services. *Organization Science, 16*, 225–242.

Mayer, K. J., & Salomon, R. M. (2006). Capabilities, contractual hazards, and governance: Integrating resource-based and transaction cost perspectives. *Academy of Management Journal, 49*, 942–959.

Mayer, R. C., Davis, J. H., & Schoorman, F. D. (1995). An integrative model of organizational trust. *Academy of Management Review, 20*, 709–734.

McAllister, D. J. (1995). Affect and cognition based trust as foundations for interpersonal cooperation in organizations. *Academy of Management Journal, 38*, 24–59.

Morgan, R. M., & Hunt, S. D. (1994). The commitment-trust theory of relationship marketing. *Journal of Marketing, 58*(Jul), 20–38.

Nooteboom, B. (1996). Trust, opportunism and governance: A process and control model. *Organization Studies, 17*, 985–1010.

Ouchi, W. G. (1980). Market, bureaucracies, and clans. *Administrative Science Quarterly, 25*, 129–141.

Oxley, J. (1997). Appropriability hazards and governance in strategic alliances: A transaction cost approach. *Journal of Law, Economics, & Organization, 13*, 387–409.

Parkhe, A. (1993). Strategic alliance structuring: a game theoretic and transaction cost examination of interfirm cooperation. *Academy of Management Journal*, *36*, 794–829.

Patzelt, H., & Shepherd, D. A. (2008). The decision to persist with underperforming alliances: The role of trust and control. *Journal of Management Studies*, *45*, 1217–1243.

Pearce, R. J. (2001). Looking inside the joint venture to help understand the link between inter-parent cooperation and performance. *Journal of Management Studies*, *38*, 557–582.

Podsakoff, P. M., MacKenzie, S. B., Lee, J. Y., & Podsakoff, N. P. (2003). Common method biases in behavioral research: A critical review of the literature and recommended remedies. *Journal of Applied Psychology*, *88*, 879–903.

Poppo, L., & Zenger, T. (2002). Do formal contracts and relational governance function as substitutes or complements? *Strategic Management Journal*, *23*, 707–725.

Puranam P., & Vanneste, B. S. (2009). Trust and governance: Untangling a tangled web. *Academy of Management Review*, *34*, 11–31.

Ring, P. S. (2008). Theories of contract and their use in studying inter-organizational relations. In S. Cropper, M. Ebers, C. Huxham, & P. S. Ring (Eds.), *Inter-organizational relations* (pp. 502–524). New York, NY: Oxford University Press

Robins, J. (1987). Organization economics: Notes on the use of transaction-cost theory in the study of organizations. *Administrative Science Quarterly*, *32*, 68–86.

Sarkar, M. B., Aulakh, P. S., & Cavusgil, S. T. (1998). The strategic role of relational bonding in interorganizational collaborations: An empirical study of the global construction industry. *Journal of International Management*, *4*, 85–107.

Saxton, T. (1997). The effect of partner and relationship characteristics on alliance outcomes. *Academy of Management Journal*, *40*, 443–461.

Srinivasan, R., & Brush, T. H. (2006). Supplier performance in vertical alliances: The effects of self-enforcing agreements and enforceable contracts. *Organization Science*, *17*, 436–452.

Subramani, M. R., & Venkatraman, N. (2003). Safeguarding investments in asymmetric interorganizational relationships: Theory and evidence. *Academy of Management Journal*, *46*, 46–62.

Thorgren, S., & Wincent, J. (2011). Interorganizational trust: Origins, dysfunctions and regulation of rigidities. *British Journal of Management*, *22*, 21–41.

Verbeke, A., & Greidanus, N. S. (2009). The end of the opportunism vs. trust debate: Bounded reliability as a new envelop concept in research on MNE governance. *Journal of International Business Studies*, *40*, 1471–1495.

Vlaar, P. W. L., Van den Bosch, F. A. J., & Volberda, H. W. (2007). On the evolution of trust, distrust, and formal coordination and control in interorganizational relationships: Towards an integrative framework. *Group & Organization Management*, *32*, 407–428.

White, S., & Lui, S. (2005). Distinguishing costs of cooperation and control in alliances. *Strategic Management Journal*, *26*, 913–932.

Williamson, O. (1975). *Market and hierarchies*. New York: Free Press.

Williamson, O. (1979). Transaction cost economics: The governance of contractual relations. *Journal of Law & Economics, 22*, 233–262.

Williamson, O. (1985). *The economic institutions of capitalism: Firms, markets, relational contracting*. New York: Free Press.

Williamson, O. (1993). Calculativeness, trust, and economic organization. *Journal of Law & Economics, 36*, 453–486.

Yli-Renko, H., Autio, E., & Sapienza, H. J. (2001). Social capital, knowledge acquisition, and knowledge exploitation in young technology-based firms. *Strategic Management Journal, 22*, 587–613.

Zaheer, A., McEvily, B., & Perrone, V. (1998). Does trust matter? Exploring the effects of interorganizational and interpersonal trust on performance. *Organization Science, 9*, 141–159.

Zhang, C., Cavusgil, S. T., & Roath, A. S. (2003). Manufacturer governance of foreign distributor relationships: Do relational norms enhance competitiveness in the export market? *Journal of International Business Studies, 34*, 550–566.

Zhou, K. Z., & Poppo, L. (2010). Exchange hazards, trust, and contract in China: The contingent role of legal enforceability. *Journal of International Business Studies, 41*, 861–881.

CHAPTER 6

AFFILIATED OR ALIGNED?

Orchestration Modes of Multipartner Innovation Among Incumbent Firms and New Ventures

Pia Kerstin Neudert and Markus Kreutzer

ABSTRACT

As technologies become increasingly specialized and customers require more modular, flexible, and interconnected solutions, single firms face increasing difficulties in serving these demands on their own. Hence, joint innovation of multiple firms gains in importance. While earlier research stressed the co-membership in networks and associations as catalyst for creating innovations together with diverse partners, more recent research focuses on ecosystems thriving on complementarity and modularity—independent of membership contracts—as drivers of multipartner innovation. However, the increasing divergence between these two perspectives, that is, ecosystem-as-affiliation and ecosystem-as-structure, impedes a structured decision-making process among the different options for multipartner innovation. We therefore delineate an integrative framework of four member-based modes of orchestrating multipartner innovation (i.e., following the ecosystem-as-affiliation paradigm) and of four value-proposition-based modes of orchestrating multipartner innovation (i.e., following the ecosystem-as-structure paradigm), depending on the type of orchestrator: (1) no orchestrator (i.e., based on standards), (2) incumbent firms as orchestrators, (3) third-party organizations as orchestrators, and (4) new ventures as orchestrators. By distinguishing

Managing Interpartner Cooperation in Strategic Alliances, pp. 155–199
Copyright © 2022 by Information Age Publishing
www.infoagepub.com
155

these orchestration modes from the perspectives of incumbent firms and new ventures, we provide clarity on the objectives of each type of firm to derive key challenges (e.g., determining memberships, selecting complementors) and opportunities (e.g., pooling common interests to commercialize novel technologies, creating novel value propositions). We conclude with two mode choice frameworks—one for incumbent firms and one for new ventures—that explain key decision criteria for each orchestration mode.

INTRODUCTION

In the age of increasing specialization, resources for innovation often lie outside of the firm boundaries (Estrada, Martín-Cruz, & Pérez-Santana, 2012; Malone, Laubacher, & Johns, 2011). Firms therefore regularly engage in *multipartner innovation*, which refers to a "group of partners with varying skills and knowledge" that pursue "exploratory projects on emerging technologies" (Gillier & Piat, 2011, p. 242) and often have different industry backgrounds (Gillier, Piat, Roussel, & Truchot, 2010). Sometimes also referred to as distributed innovation (Boudreau, 2010; Howells, James, & Malik, 2003; Jeppesen & Lakhani, 2010; von Hippel, 2005) or multipartner initiatives (Hettich & Kreutzer, 2021; Leten, Vanhaverbeke, Roijakkers, Clerix, & Van Helleputte, 2013), multipartner innovation refers to situations in which decision making and the innovation process are shared by multiple firms, allowing them to create and commercialize innovations across firm boundaries.[1]

However, governance modes for orchestrating multipartner innovation vary widely. Multipartner alliances focusing on research and development (R&D) (Furr, O'Keeffe, & Dyer, 2016; Kherrazi, 2021; Singh, Lavie, & Lechner, 2007) and innovation networks (Aarikka-Stenroos & Ritala, 2017; Hofman, Halman, & Looy, 2016; Hofman, Halman, & Song, 2017; Tidd & Bessant, 2018) are just two concepts that researchers have developed to capture the diversity of multipartner innovation orchestration. An innovation network, for instance, is described as "loosely coupled systems of autonomous firms," usually led by a hub firm that assumes a "central position in the network structure" (Dhanaraj & Parkhe, 2006, p. 659) and coordinates the distributed resources and capabilities of the innovation network's members. This definition can then be operationalized in the form of R&D consortia, government-sponsored industrial programs (i.e., closed forms of innovation networks), incubators, national and regional agencies, and SME associations (Giudici, Reinmoeller, & Ravasi, 2018). As a result, scholars and practitioners alike encounter problems in deriving insights from the diversity of concepts alluding to multipartner innovation.

At the same time, the motivations of firms engaging in multipartner innovation can differ. Particularly, when investigating incumbent firms and new ventures different objectives become visible (Katila, Piezunka, Reineke, & Eisenhardt, 2022). Incumbent firms characteristically seek new ventures' complementary resources (e.g., knowledge), goods, and services to solve their innovation-related problems (Reischauer, Güttel, & Schüssler, 2021; Shipilov, Furr, & Studer Andersson, 2020). For instance, as of April 8, 2021, Siemens AG partnered with 163 new ventures, Daimler AG with 132 new ventures, and Bosch with 97 new ventures to co-create innovations (GlassDollar UG, 2021). New ventures are thus traditionally considered as providers of novel technologies, which incumbent firms can leverage at scale (Dedehayir, Mäkinen, & Roland Ortt, 2016). To gain market access and commercialize their technologies at scale, new ventures therefore tend to engage in "big ponds" (Katila et al., 2022, p. 51), which allow them to leverage technologies, processes, and other innovation assets with multiple other firms at the same time (Nambisan & Baron, 2013).

To bring clarity to this diversity of concepts and motivations for multipartner innovation, we apply an ecosystem perspective, which can be applied to different types of interorganizational relationships. More specifically, we use Adner's (2017) distinction between *ecosystem-as-affiliation* and *ecosystem-as-structure* as overarching framework. By focusing on either membership affiliation (i.e., ecosystem-as-affiliation) or on co-creating a joint value proposition (i.e., ecosystem-as-structure), we present a two-by-four matrix of how incumbent firms and new ventures can participate in and orchestrate (Kreutzer & Neudert, 2021; Leten, Vanhaverbeke, Roijakkers, Clerix, & Van Helleputte, 2013; Oskam, Bossink, & de Man, 2021) multipartner innovation.

Based on this core part of our analysis, we derive two choice frameworks—one for incumbent firms and one for new ventures—that provide structured decision processes for choosing an orchestration mode of multipartner innovation. With these orchestration mode choice frameworks, we extend established "make, buy, or ally" corporate development mode choice frameworks like those of Capron and Mitchell (2010) and Kreutzer (2012) in an innovation context. Since we zoom in on different "ally" options, our frameworks provide guidance as to which multipartner innovation orchestration mode is most suitable for incumbent firms or new ventures, depending on what motivates these types of firms to engage in multipartner innovation.

With this chapter, we therefore enable scholars and practitioners to structure their mental models about how incumbent firms and new ventures can engage in multipartner innovation. In this manner, we provide clarity about the increasingly diverse opportunities to co-create innovative goods and services across firm boundaries. We thereby add to lacking research on "how firms of different sizes and ecosystem positions act strategically upon innovation ecosystems," providing evidence on "how to align internal innovation activities with technological progress in the ecosystem" (Visscher, Hahn, & Konrad, 2021, p. 620).

ECOSYSTEM-AS-AFFILIATION AND ECOSYSTEM-AS-STRUCTURE PARADIGM

Initially, Adner (2017) delineated the ecosystem-as-affiliation and ecosystem-as-structure concepts to differentiate between two paradigms of orchestrating interorganizational relationships, without a specific focus on innovation. On the one hand, the ecosystem-as-affiliation paradigm alludes to the collaboration of multiple firms that are part of a specific community—or, in simpler terms, by memberships. This paradigm relies on aggregating member firms' contributions such that consensus, community-related enhancements, and a shared vision guide governance decision (Moore, 1993). These forms of interorganizational relationships arise either because different organizations can be uniquely associated with a certain geography (i.e., the organizations are members of a particular region) or because several organizations establish formal rules of admission and behavior that other firms must follow to become members. Classic examples are "the Silicon Valley ecosystem" (Adner, 2017, p. 41), which subsumes all new ventures in a certain regional location, or meta-organizations like the Star Alliance in which airlines of a certain quality standard can become members (Berkowitz & Dumez, 2016; Findeisen & Sydow, 2016; Gomes-Casseres & Judd, 2021).

On the other hand, the ecosystem-as-structure paradigm refers to interorganizational relationships that are bound together by an alignment toward a focal value proposition (Adner, 2017). According to Jacobides, Cennamo, and Gawer (2018), such an ecosystem-as-structure represents "a set of actors with varying degrees of multilateral, nongeneric complementarities that are not fully hierarchically controlled" (p. 2264). Consequently, multiple firms jointly deliver a customer-facing solution without corporate hierarchies in place that could enforce control with regard to single complementary goods and services (Adner, 2006). Classic examples are e-commerce ecosystems (Burford, Shipilov, & Furr, 2022), such as those curated by the no-code website design platforms Wix or Squarespace. Depending on what Wix's or Squarespace's customers need for their e-commerce activities, customers can choose from a wide range of third-party providers that offer scheduling, content creation, and other services that complement Wix's and Squarespace's no-code website design solutions. Via the Wix app market (Wix, 2022) or Squarespace extensions (Squarespace, n.d.), the two orchestrating firms curate complementary, modular services from independent, external firms that are compatible with their no-code website design offers. Complementors' solutions are, however, also available as standalone offerings for customers that seek to independently program their websites.

Multipartner innovations following the ecosystem-as-structure paradigm often develop in a non-linear manner, partly because of the fuzzy boundaries and implicit connections between ecosystem actors (Visscher, Hahn, & Konrad, 2021). The underlying interdependence between ecosystem actors can have a negative impact on the ecosystem's overall chances of success (Adner & Feiler, 2019; Brusoni & Prencipe, 2013) as the actors' embeddedness influences the creation and distribution of value within the ecosystem-as-structure, both in positive and negative manners (Dattée, Alexy, & Autio, 2018; Oskam, Bossink, & de Man, 2021).

In recent years, research on these two paradigms has developed in different directions. The ecosystem-as-affiliation perspective culminated in a rich body of research on accelerator networks (Cohen, Fehder, Hochberg, & Murray, 2019; Wright, Siegel, & Mustar, 2017), on entrepreneurial ecosystems (Autio, Nambisan, Thomas, & Wright, 2018; Carayannis, Provance, & Grigoroudis, 2016; Spigel & Harrison, 2018; Thompson, Purdy, & Ventresca, 2018), and on clusters and science parks (Ben Letaifa & Rabeau, 2013; Ng, Appel-Meulenbroek, Cloodt, & Arentze, 2019; Pitelis, 2012). Conversely, the ecosystem-as-structure perspective largely focused on complementarity and modularity (Jacobides et al., 2018; Shipilov & Gawer, 2020), investigating questions of ecosystem orchestration (Lingens, Huber, & Gassmann, in press; Neudert & Kreutzer, 2021; Oskam et al., 2021), value creation and capture (Adner & Lieberman, 2021; de Vasconcelos Gomes, Facin, Salerno, & Ikenami, 2018; Ritala, Agouridas, Assimakopoulos, & Gies, 2013), and coopetition (Ansari, Garud, & Kumaraswamy, 2016; Bacon, Williams, & Davies, 2020; Hannah & Eisenhardt, 2018), independent of an affiliation with a certain closed group or regional co-location.

When co-creating innovation is the guiding motivation to form an ecosystem, researchers usually delineate them as innovation ecosystems (de Vasconcelos Gomes et al., 2018; Granstrand & Holgersson, 2020). The question thus arises "how innovation ecosystems … contribute to new, open forms of governance" (Bogers et al., 2017, p. 28) when co-creating innovations. This is what our conceptual framework illuminates. By bringing together more established research streams, such as research on standardization alliance networks (Axelrod, Mitchell, Thomas, Bennett, & Bruderer, 1995) and accelerators (Cohen, Fehder, et al., 2019; Pauwels, Clarysse, Wright, & Van Hove, 2016), with novel research on innovation ecosystems (Adner, 2006; Adner & Kapoor, 2010; Granstrand & Holgersson, 2020) we provide an answer to the following research question: *Using an ecosystem lens, what are the opportunities and challenges for incumbent firms and new ventures when engaging in different orchestration modes of multipartner innovation?*

Our analyses focus on product innovation, that is, a "market introduction of a new or significantly improved good or service with respect to its capabilities, user friendliness, components [*sic*] or subsystems" (Tavassoli & Karlsson, 2015, p. 1899). Particularly, we investigate how technology-driven innovations (Ansari et al., 2016; Bianchi, Frattini, Lejarraga, & Di Minin, 2014) can be orchestrated across firm boundaries. Other types of innovation, such as process or organizational innovation (De Propris, 2002; Kim & Lui, 2015), are not investigated. Business model innovation (Zott, Amit, & Massa, 2011) is covered to a certain degree, namely in relation to the value proposition and innovation-related aspects (Foss & Saebi, 2017). Our choice stems from our focus on how firms co-create value for customers (Adner, 2006, 2017). A cross-level analysis of how the different modes of multipartner innovation orchestration impact processes internal to a firm is beyond the scope of our chapter.

For both paradigms (i.e., ecosystem-as-affiliation and ecosystem-as-structure), we thus show four manners how firms can collaborate for innovation purposes, depending on the type of firm that takes on the role of orchestrator: (1) There can be no dedicated orchestrator, which means that multiple partners develop innovations exclusively on the basis of common standards (Axelrod et al., 1995; Miller & Toh, 2022; Toh & Miller, 2017; Wen, Qualls, & Zeng, 2020). Alternatively, (2) incumbent firms, (3) new ventures, or (4) dedicated third-party organizations that specialize in ecosystem building and orchestration can assume this focal role (Hou & Shi, 2021; Lingens, Böger, & Gassmann, 2021; Lingens, Miehé, & Gassmann, 2021). For each of the eight orchestration modes, we present exemplary cases that illustrate our theoretical explanations. Table 6.1 synthesizes this two-by-four matrix of multipartner orchestration modes and serves as guiding framework for the ensuing sections.

ECOSYSTEM-AS-AFFILIATION ORCHESTRATION MODES OF MULTIPARTNER INNOVATION

In the following sections, we will delineate how interorganizational relationships underlying the ecosystem-as-affiliation paradigm lead to innovation. Consequently, we present four different manners how economic actors can be affiliated to a joint community and, based on this affiliation, co-create innovations.

Table 6.1

Orchestration Modes for Multipartner Innovation

Type of orchestrator ➔	No orchestrator	Incumbent firm	Third-party organization	New ventures
Ecosystem-as-affiliation	Standardization alliance network	Meta-organization	Accelerator network	Entrepreneurial ecosystem
Exemplary studies	Axelrod et al. (1995); Delcamp & Leiponen (2014); Wen et al. (2020)	Ahrne & Brunsson (2005); Berkowitz & Dumez (2016); Cropper & Bor (2018)	Cohen, Bingham, et al. (2019); Cohen, Fehder, et al. (2019); Hallen et al. (2020)	Autio et al. (2018); Isenberg (2010); Spigel & Harrison (2018); Thompson et al. (2018)
Exemplary case(s)	Connectivity Standard Alliance	Star Alliance	Y Combinator; Techstars	OptoNet Photonics Network Thuringia
Collaborative mechanisms	Jointly lobby technological standards to standard-setting organizations to commercialize novel technologies; membership contracts	Align on common interests and lobby them toward external stakeholders; membership contracts	Predominantly dyadic, equity-based relationships between incumbent firms and new ventures catalyzed through accelerator; informal support among new ventures	Emergent, self-organized collaboration; serendipitous discoveries through regional co-location; distinct partnerships with similar actors in other geographies
Innovation mechanism	Exploitation of emerging standards by establishing them as de jure standard	Exploitation of technological developments by jointly adopting single member's innovations	Provision of capital and mentoring for new ventures with promising innovations; organizational learning within alumni network and between new ventures and incumbent firms	Similar organizations exchange ideas and interests in a certain region to foster innovation through entrepreneurship; entrepreneurial intentions guide innovation success

(Table continued on next page)

Table 6.1 (Continued)

Orchestration Modes for Multipartner Innovation

Type of orchestrator ➜	No orchestrator	Incumbent firm	Third-party organization	New ventures
Ecosystem-as-affiliation	Standardization alliance network	Meta-organization	Accelerator network	Entrepreneurial ecosystem
Underlying technologies	Emerging technologies that need more interoperability and specification to unfold their commercial potential (e.g., DNA computing)	Technologies with proven commercial potential but small customer base (e.g., face recognition technology in the airline and travel industry)	Disruptive technologies (e.g., adaptive machine learning) with substantial growth potential that need fine-tuning of the business model for commercialization	Novel technologies for both gradual (e.g., improving precision) and radical (e.g., replacing existing methods) innovations, needing assistance in firm founding and funding
Incumbent firms' objectives	Create industry-wide standards for broad commercialization of technologies; avoid malinvestments into other technologies	Share and lobby joint interests of member organizations with similar business models	Gain information about novel trends in the industry and attract new ventures to fuel corporate innovation pipeline	Receive information about emerging new ventures and general trends in the entrepreneurial scene; scout ventures to acquire
New ventures' objectives	Challenge existing standards; capitalize on incumbent firms' standard development efforts without active involvement	Inspire meta-organizations' members to innovate; contribute novel ideas as external input	Learn from consultation with third parties (e.g., accelerator, venture capitalist) and mentors from incumbent firms; engage in alumni network of new ventures and as mentors themselves	Derive common challenges across entrepreneurs focusing on similar technologies; lobby interests toward public regulatory bodies and incumbents

(Table continued on next page)

Table 6.1 (Continued)

Orchestration Modes for Multipartner Innovation

Type of orchestrator ➜	No orchestrator	Incumbent firm	Third-party organization	New ventures
Ecosystem-as-affiliation	Standardization alliance network	Meta-organization	Accelerator network	Entrepreneurial ecosystem
Exemplary studies	Henfridsson et al. (2018); Miller & Toh (2022)	Adner (2006); Dedehayir & Sepänen (2015); Hannah & Eisenhardt (2018)	Gulati et al. (2012); Prexl et al. (2019); Shipilov et al. (2020)	Lingens, Böger, et al. (2021); Lingens, Miché, et al. (2021)
Exemplary case(s)	Catena-X open automotive ecosystem	Bain Alliance Ecosystem; Novartis Biome digital health ecosystem	InnoCentive; Sopra Steria Scale up; Startup Autobahn	Solarisbank's banking-as-a-service ecosystem
Collaborative mechanisms	Exploration of joint standards via use cases; co-specialized investments into standards required; usually no formal standard-setting organizations involved	A central incumbent firm attracts, selects, and aligns complementors to its innovation ecosystem	Third-party organizations build and manage a community that serves as starting point to form multilateral partnerships that eventually grow into an ecosystem	A new venture attracts, selects, and aligns complementors to its innovation ecosystem
Innovation mechanism	Users co-create the innovation ecosystem based on complementary, modular components; firms develop the nuclei of their own innovation ecosystems within a standard-based innovation ecosystem	Complementors provide specialized expertise for innovative solutions that extend an incumbent firm's own value proposition	Third-party organizations lend ecosystem-building capabilities to other firms; nuclei for firms' own innovation ecosystems arise from guided exchange	Incumbent firms serve as complementors that provide customer access and thereby scale a new venture's novel technology; new ventures determine the overarching value proposition and value capture mechanisms

(Table continued on next page)

Table 6.1 (Continued)

Orchestration Modes for Multipartner Innovation

Type of orchestrator ➜	No orchestrator	Incumbent firm	Third-party organization	New ventures
Ecosystem-as-affiliation	Standardization alliance network	Meta-organization	Accelerator network	Entrepreneurial ecosystem
Underlying technologies	Emerging technologies that need more interoperability and specification to unfold their commercial potential (e.g., DNA computing)	Technologies with proven commercial potential but unspecified value proposition from a customer perspective (e.g., embedded AI)	Technologies with proven commercial potential but unspecified value proposition from a customer perspective (e.g., embedded AI)	Technologies with proven commercial potential but unspecified value proposition from a customer perspective (e.g., embedded AI)
Incumbent firms' objectives	Attract complementors based on open-standards ecosystem; build nuclei for incumbent-led innovation ecosystems based on increasingly accepted standards	Secure long-term performance by binding innovative new ventures into ecosystems' value propositions; improve offerings to existing clients based on new ventures' innovative solutions	Obtain ecosystem-building capabilities from third-party orchestrator(s); build nuclei for incumbent firms' innovation ecosystems by means of an exploratory exchange with a diverse range of new ventures	Use new ventures' fast processes and technology platforms as accelerators for innovation efforts
New ventures' objectives	Contribute to multiple incumbent firms' emerging technologies as complementors; "big pond" strategy to scale commercial success of novel technologies	Scale commercially as complementor in incumbent firms' ecosystems; disrupt incumbent firms' innovation ecosystems	Develop use cases with several incumbents in parallel; prolonged exploratory interaction with incumbents without committing as complementor or handing out equity stakes	Secure autonomy about the ecosystem's purpose and vision; fast and flexible development of the ecosystem

Standardization Alliance Networks

During the 2000s, two technological standards competed for high-definition optical disc formats: the Blu-ray Disc (Sony) and the HD DVD (NEC/Toshiba) in which the Blu-ray Disc technology eventually became the dominating standard (Daidj, Grazia, & Hammoudi, 2010). This example shows how the success of firms' innovations depends on the ability to commercialize novel technologies based on the alignment with other complementary goods and services (Bianchi et al., 2014; Nevens, Summe, & Uttal, 1990). In a race for commercialization, different technological standards may compete with each other, leading to standard wars (Shapiro & Varian, 1999). Such standard wars are more likely once commercial advantages increase when a core technology becomes more widely adopted, especially when external network effects are present (Stango, 2004).

Standard wars usually entail the formation of coalitions between firms that aim at commercializing a certain standard (Calcei & M'Chirgui, 2012; Vanhaverbeke & Noorderhaven, 2001). When no central organization exists that sets a de jure standard (e.g., via standard-setting organizations such as the American National Standards Institute) or a de facto standard (e.g., via a firm with a high market power) (Stango, 2004), multiple firms often decide to "join together into one or more standard-setting alliances" so as "to develop standard technology and to sponsor adoption of a standard" (Axelrod et al., 1995, p. 1493). A *standardization alliance network* therefore thrives on the incentive to avoid costly malinvestments in a technology that might lose a standard war.

Membership contracts usually define the boundaries of standardization alliance networks (Axelrod et al., 1995; Nambisan, 2013). The objective of such memberships is to "discuss, test, or promote certain technologies, or ... develop new technical specifications that will subsequently be submitted to formal standard setting organizations for official approval" (Delcamp & Leiponen, 2014, p. 37). Standardization alliance networks therefore serve as standard-developing organizations (SDOs) that lobby their recommendations to formal standard-setting organizations (SSOs) (Blind & Mangelsdorf, 2016; Teece, 2018).

For instance, the Connectivity Standard Alliance works on increasing the accessibility, security, and usability of Internet of Things technologies, for example, in the field of smart home goods and services, energy, lighting, and commercial real estate. Exemplary member firms are incumbent firms (e.g., Texas Instruments, IKEA), leading technology firms (e.g., Amazon, Google), and new ventures (e.g., signify, Tuya). Together, these firms develop a joint library of protocols around Internet of Things applications, improving interoperability and connectedness. The standardization alliance network thus fosters the adoption rate of Internet of Things technologies not only by bringing together developers' reference designs, specifications, and model libraries but also by providing certifications on goods and services.

While incumbent firms create standardization alliance networks to grow the market for their newly developed technologies, new ventures usually have difficulties in setting standards due to their lack of credibility (Vanhaverbeke & Noorderhaven, 2001). An option for new ventures is therefore to join such standardization alliances as adopters, thereby capitalizing on incumbent firms' standard development without incurring expenditures (Keil, 2002). By gaining information from incumbent firms, new ventures' risks of malinvestments into alternative standards decline and market access—especially in supranational standardization alliance networks—increases (Blind & Mangelsdorf, 2016; Wen et al., 2020).

Alternatively, new ventures can position themselves as challengers to the emerging standard, which pays off in markets where customers appreciate variety. Accordingly, when the heterogeneity of customer demand is high, new ventures may position themselves as incompatible with existing standards in novel niche markets, thereby consciously forgoing potential network externalities by adopting a certain standard (Sheremata, 2004). The semiconductor and printer industry are two examples of such markets with demand heterogeneity, as the breadth between high-end technology segments (i.e., at the leading edge of technology) and low-end technology segments (e.g., for home appliances) leaves room for market niches outside of existing standards. For instance, PoooliPrint has developed an inkless pocket printing solution based on thermal printing technologies. While thermal printing has traditionally been used in fax machines and for prints from medical devices, PoooliPrint repurposed the technology for smartphone users, thereby creating a novel market outside of existing business-to-consumer (B2C) printing systems (PoooliPrint, 2022).

Meta-Organizations

In the 2000s, researchers observed that—independent of standards—multiple firms began to form *meta-organizations* in which "membership is voluntary, and members can withdraw at will. The purpose of a meta-organization is to work in the interests of all its members, with all members being equally valuable and membership being based on some form of similarity" (Ahrne & Brunsson, 2005, p. 11). Meta-organizations operate legally autonomously without any member firm enforcing residual control rights over other member firms (Heine & Kerk, 2017). Consequently, meta-organizations usually do not create distinct goods or services but rather provide information in the form of best-practice reports, industry data, and common guidelines (Berkowitz & Bor, 2018). Still, meta-organizations create a shared identity, establish a social order, and lobby the interests of members toward other external institutions, such as policymakers (König, Schulte, & Enders, 2012). While the original definition allows for a variety of associations to be considered as meta-organizations, for example, the European Union, the World Trade Organization, and global union federations (Berkowitz & Dumez, 2016; Garaudel, 2020), we focus on commercially oriented meta-organizations, such as the Star Alliance (Berkowitz & Dumez, 2016; Findeisen & Sydow, 2016; Gomes-Casseres & Judd, 2021), and depict how these meta-organizations develop innovations from the interaction of multiple partners.

Traditionally, meta-organizations consisted predominantly of incumbent firms. Inertial forces within incumbents' meta-organizations can therefore impede innovation in this form of ecosystems-as-affiliation (König et al., 2012). Particularly, the closed membership model may foster elitist perceptions that make members less willing to include external, novel views and instead adapt established manners of doing business. As a remedy for this potential drawback, König et al. (2012) suggested that meta-organizations should create a culture that welcomes innovation champions and establish efficient governance processes among members to allow for adapting to changes in the external environment.

Following the call of König et al. (2012) for more openness toward external innovators, meta-organizations increasingly consider the role that new ventures can play in this form of multipartner innovation. Battisti, Agarwal, and Brem (2022), for instance, depict how a meta-organization that focuses on the commercial application of artificial intelligence (AI) technologies supports incumbent firms in finding sponsors and potential partners in AI-based new ventures. This perspective corroborates the suggestion that selected "active non-members could be recognized as playing a potentially important role, if not in the governance, then in the energy and action radius of the meta-organization" (Cropper & Bor, 2018, p. 17). Consequently, although new ventures may not fulfill all membership criteria for meta-organizations, their selected input may help meta-organizations in overcoming inertial forces.

The Star Alliance, for example, operates the Connecting Partners program that allows non-member airlines to offer integrated services with the member airlines of Star Alliance (e.g., Lufthansa German Airlines, United, and Thai Airways). Newer carriers with a low-frills business model like Juneyao Airlines (established in 2006) and Thai Smile (established in 2011) can therefore offer a number of the services to their customers that a full membership at Star Alliance would entail, such as seamlessly forwarding bags to the final destination (Star Alliance, 2022). The full-service carriers that are members of the Star Alliance thereby guarantee a certain level of openness toward innovative business models and stay in exchange with new ventures about changing needs of more distant customer segments without abandoning their membership hurdles.

Accelerator Networks

When third parties orchestrate multipartner innovation efforts with an affiliation-based approach, these activities usually happen within a type of *accelerator network*. Accelerators are defined as "limited-duration programs, lasting roughly three to six months, that help cohorts of startup ventures with their entrepreneurial processes and aspirations" (Cohen, Fehder, et al., 2019, p. 1781). Accelerators as orchestrating firms therefore help provide access to capital, to working space, to networks, and also to education and mentoring. Accordingly, while new ventures are the main members of accelerators, incumbent firms play an important role as mentors and educators (Cohen, Bingham, & Hallen, 2019). Instead of relying on trial-and-error strategies, new ventures therefore benefit from "broad, intensive, and paced consultation with external parties" (Hallen, Cohen, & Bingham, 2020, p. 379), enhancing search and limiting the exploration of potentially unattractive opportunities.

After taking part as an active member in an accelerator's cohort, new ventures usually join accelerators' alumni network (Hallen et al., 2020). Y Combinator, often referred to as the first accelerator (Kohler, 2016), highlights the benefits of its alumni network as follows:

> Y Combinator has a huge alumni network, and there's a strong ethos of helping out fellow YC founders. So, whatever your problem, whether you need beta testers, a place to stay in another city, advice about a browser bug, or a connection to a particular company, there's a good chance someone in the network can help you. (Y Combinator, 2020, para. 19)

Consequently, when new ventures join an accelerators' cohort, alumni from preceding cohorts may provide valuable insights, thereby fostering entrepreneurial learning across cohorts (Pauwels et al., 2016).

Incumbent firms—in their role as mentors—gain information about novel trends in their industries, as new ventures' pitches are often available publicly (Cohen, Bingham, et al., 2019). Furthermore, incumbent firms can use accelerators to position their firms as potential partners for aspiring new ventures. This tie-formation process usually results in dyadic relationships first, as "highly desirable partners are most likely to exclusively partner with one another, leaving less desirable partners to partner with others who are also less desirable" (Hallen et al., 2020, pp. 381–382).

Alternatively, incumbent firms partner with accelerators to scout new ventures that can quickly sell their goods and services to incumbent firms, even though such activities are not the focus of accelerators (Cohen, Fehder, et al., 2019). Plug and Play, for instance, "match[es] large corporations with the brightest startups" so as to "increase operational efficiencies, lower costs, find new product lines, and become more innovative from the core" (Plug and Play, n.d.-c, para. 2). As a result, the accelerator has created an ecosystem-as-affiliation with "30,000+ startups, 500+ world-leading corporations, and hundreds of venture capital firms, universities, and government agencies across multiple industries" (Plug and Play, n.d.-a, para. 4). Exemplarily, in a cooperative 12-week program with BNP Paribas, Plug and Play therefore sought new ventures that "can negotiate pilots and sell … product[s] rapidly and efficiently" (Plug and Play, n.d.-b, para. 6).

Entrepreneurial Ecosystems

Entrepreneurial ecosystems have their conceptual roots in the idea of innovation clusters, which Porter (1998) described as "geographic concentrations of interconnected companies and institutions in a particular field" (p. 78) that produce above-average innovative goods and service. Examples are the Italian leather fashion cluster and the Californian wine cluster. Porter (1998) observed that new ventures grew particularly well in such clusters due to better awareness of market opportunities, pre-existing relationships with incumbent firms, and investor expertise in the cluster's field.[2] Isenberg (2010) then labeled these regionally co-located forms of new ventures as "entrepreneurship ecosystems" (p. 42). As the idea of entrepreneurial ecosystems matured, definitions increasingly focused on their generative potential, depicting entrepreneurial ecosystems as "complex contexts for activity, characterized by resource interdependencies and diverse connections, second-order consequences, and the potential to generate variety" (Thompson et al., 2018, p. 98).

Often, policymakers' activities are related to the formation of entrepreneurial ecosystems. However, public funding that instigates entrepreneurial action does not always lead to the intended outcome of long-term, innovation-driven economic growth (Brown & Mawson, 2019). Instead, the intentionality of entrepreneurs—that is, "the tendency towards [*sic*] a goal that first appears in the individual's mind as a purpose"—and the coherence of entrepreneurs' activities sustain entrepreneurial ecosystems' long-term success (Roundy, Bradshaw, & Brockman, 2018, p. 5).

At the end of the 2010s, scholars therefore increasingly recognized the central role that new ventures assumed in this orchestration mode of multipartner innovation (Autio et al., 2018; Goswami, Mitchell, & Bhagavatula, 2018; Thompson et al., 2018). Positive feedback loops among successful entrepreneurs foster the long-term viability of entrepreneurial ecosystems, as even more founders join entrepreneurial ecosystems once they position themselves in the global race to innovate (Autio, Kenney, Mustar, Siegel, & Wright, 2014). Central themes in entrepreneurial ecosystem research therefore are "academic entrepreneurship, innovation and regional development, social entrepreneurship, sustainability, networks, and clusters" (Theodoraki, Dana, & Caputo, 2022, p. 11).

Successful entrepreneurial ecosystems thus usually rely on mechanisms of self-organization among the entrepreneurial ventures. Auerswald and Dani (2017), for instance, observed how a biotechnology-related entrepreneurial ecosystem in the U.S. moved through an "adaptive life cycle [*sic*]" (p. 97), as new ventures, complementary incumbent firms, and research organizations iteratively exploited, conserved, released, and reorganized their activities among each other. As a result, a well-functioning entrepreneurial ecosystem "emerges out of the logic of the socially embedded nature of the entrepreneurship process, which involves a wide array of actors, resources, and capabilities" (Spigel & Harrison, 2018, p. 157).

While new ventures are the driving forces of entrepreneurial ecosystems, incumbent firms participate in entrepreneurial ecosystems "to pursue their 'corporate entrepreneurship' strategy" because they "depend on absorbing and exploiting new technologies and innovations" (Cantner, Cunningham, Lehmann, & Menter, 2021, p. 408). While the role of incumbent firms in entrepreneurial ecosystems is still somewhat underexplored, emerging evidence points to a winner-picking function in entrepreneurial ecosystems: Incumbent firms tend to make technological acquisitions of promising new ventures, providing an additional source of capital compared to public funding (Shin, Han, Kang, & Marhold, 2019).

While Porter (1998) and Isenberg (2010) formed their ideas on the basis of regional co-location, activities in entrepreneurial ecosystems nowadays can span the entire globe. Exemplarily, the OptoNet Photonics Network Thuringia encompasses 105 industry and research members active in optics and mechanics, laser and radiation sources, optoelectronics, and other photonics technologies to facilitate networking, technology transfer, projects, workshops, and training (OptoNet, n.d.). Despite its regional focus on eastern Germany, the entrepreneurial ecosystem also includes organizations like the Shenzhen-based technology consultancy Sinolumina Technology Ltd. and Photonics Austria, an Austrian-based meta-organization funded by the Austrian Federal Ministry of Traffic, Innovation, and Technology.

ECOSYSTEM-AS-STRUCTURE ORCHESTRATION MODES OF MULTIPARTNER INNOVATION

After elaborating on ecosystem-as-affiliation orchestration modes for multipartner innovation (i.e., when the actors are connected by belonging to a specific membership-based network or a specific regional location), we now present ecosystem-as-structure orchestration modes for multipartner innovation. Firms in these forms of multipartner innovation are bound together by a joint value proposition to a customer (Adner, 2017), building on complementary and modular goods and services (Jacobides, Cennamo, & Gawer, 2018; Shipilov & Gawer, 2020).

Standard-Based Innovation Ecosystems

When standards are the only coordination mechanism in innovation ecosystems (i.e., no central firm guides the development and implementation of a joint value proposition), we refer to a *standard-based innovation ecosystem*. A standard, in this case, refers to "a set of interaction rules between system components that is shared to facilitate future technological developments" and to "ensure compatibility across components, rather than performance standards specifying certain output parameters" (Toh & Miller, 2017, p. 2216). For example, Miller and Toh (2022) show how individual firms contributing to a standard-based ecosystem disclose intellectual property to an SSO, which serves as an intermediary between the different firms. In contrast to standardization alliance networks, which focus on developing the standards and lobbying them to formal SSOs, standard-based innovation ecosystems immediately entail a relationship to a user (i.e., either a consumer or a business client) that derives value from the individual combination of the complementary components. Consequently, users determine what makes up their ecosystems, combining complementary goods and services according to their preferences (Henfridsson, Nandhakumar, Scarbrough, & Panourgias, 2018)

For instance, the Catena-X open automotive ecosystem considers itself as "an extensible ecosystem in which automotive manufacturers and suppliers, dealer associations and equipment suppliers, including the providers of applications, platforms and infrastructure, can all participate equally" (Mercedes-Benz Group AG, 2022, para. 4). Consequently, not only large automotive manufacturers are part of this standard-based innovation ecosystem but also complementary firms like Bosch, the German Aerospace Center, Deutsche Telekom AG, small and medium-sized firms as well as new ventures like Circunomics, Fetch.ai, and Apheris (Catena-X, 2021, p. 4). Operating under the guiding values of openness and neutrality, the standard-based innovation ecosystem postulates the mission "to create a uniform standard for information and data-sharing throughout the entire automotive value chain" (Mercedes-Benz Group AG, 2022, para. 4). The participating firms therefore contribute or develop complementary goods and services with increasingly standardized interfaces. These standardization efforts (e.g., via application programming interfaces) then allow for nongeneric complementarities to arise, building the nuclei of emerging ecosystems (e.g., customized urban mobility ecosystems). These standards are not as generic as, for instance, a USB or WiFi standard but require co-specialization on all firms' sides.

Standard-based innovation ecosystems can even help incumbent firms work together to attract new ventures as complementors. Since complementors have to justify their investments in specific ecosystems (Boudreau, 2010; Jacobides et al., 2018), a standard-based innovation ecosystem consisting of several incumbent firms increases the attractiveness of investing in it. New ventures' activities in such "big ponds" (Katila et al., 2022) therefore reduce risks of malinvestments. For instance, BigchainDB and Fetch.ai "contribute to Catena-X complementary areas of expertise in token-based ecosystems. They will all support the development of decentralized technologies and business models, as well as incentive systems within Catena-X" (Ocean Protocol Foundation, 2021, para. 4). Consequently, new ventures consider themselves as complementary sparring partners and technology providers for incumbent firms, contributing with their specialized expertise to develop the standard-based innovation ecosystem.

Both incumbent firms and new ventures face the tradeoff between disclosing standards—such that other firms can co-create novel goods and services based on these standards—and keeping non-disclosed complementary components proprietary such that the single firm can capture value from them (Miller & Toh, 2022). Engagement in standard-based innovation ecosystems often precedes the creation of firm-led ecosystems in which incumbent firms or new ventures orchestrate the de novo ecosystems based not only on standards but also on their corporate objectives. We can therefore understand standard-based innovation ecosystems as incubators for the nuclei of incumbent-led or startup-led innovation ecosystems (as depicted in the subsequent sections).

Consequently, a high degree of exploration characterizes the engagement in standard-based innovation ecosystems. The members of the Catena-X open automotive ecosystem, for instance, experiment with use cases concerning logistics, supply chain management, quality management, maintenance, and sustainability. For the latter use case of sustainability, Atos—a global information technology company active in the fields of cybersecurity as well as cloud and high-performance computing—contributes expertise in decarbonization efforts. Subsequently, Atos extracts the results from these experimentation efforts and includes these nuclei in its Software République ecosystem for intelligent and sustainable mobility (Atos, 2021).

Incumbent-Led Innovation Ecosystems

Incumbent-led innovation ecosystems are the best-known form of ecosystem-as-structure orchestration modes for multipartner innovation. In his seminal article on innovation ecosystems, Adner (2006) shaped the concept as "the collaborative arrangements through which firms combine their individual offerings into a coherent, customer-facing solution" (p. 98). An example is the innovation ecosystem around the Airbus A380, which prompted complementors, such as airports and aircraft machinery manufacturers (e.g., de-icing vehicles), to invent goods and services that are compatible with the focal innovation (Adner & Kapoor, 2010). Incumbent firms use ecosystems with new ventures predominantly to shepherd "external communities for key value creating and capturing activities" outside of firm boundaries (Altman, Nagle, & Tushman, 2022, p. 14). Often, this orchestration mode of multipartner innovation serves incumbent firms' explorative needs, for instance, by partnering with new ventures that operate on innovative data-driven business models (Radziwon, Bogers, Chesbrough, & Minssen, 2022).

Innovation ecosystems' growth depends on how well complementors develop and expand the value proposition and how well customers accept the modular, complementary solutions (Dedehayir & Seppänen, 2015; Wang & Miller, 2020). In 2017, for instance, the strategy consulting firm Bain & Company launched their Bain Alliance Ecosystem with "best-of-breed tool, technology, and service providers that complement [their] consulting expertise" (Bain & Company, 2017, para. 1) to generate "breakthrough innovation, growth, and efficiency initiatives at unprecedented speed" (Bain & Company, 2017, para. 3). With this innovation ecosystem, Bain & Company aims at "redefining the strategy consulting business—while incorporating cutting-edge innovations from other industries in [their] offerings" (Bain & Company, 2017, para. 4).

Depending on the client's needs, Bain & Company can therefore select several complementors that provide the necessary specialized expertise (e.g., on certain technologies) to co-create innovative, customer-tailored consulting offerings. Complementors predominantly provide their solutions based on specialized technologies, which is different from Bain's Advisor Network, which extends their classic business model with freelance expertise: "Our partnership ecosystem is complemented by the Bain Advisor Network, a proprietary group of hundreds of external experts spanning all sectors, functions and geographies, who are matched to client needs by a dedicated Bain team" (Bain & Company, 2022).

While incumbent firms orchestrate innovation ecosystems, new ventures also participate in them (Garnsey & Leong, 2008), such as depicted by Rohrbeck, Hölzle, and Gemünden (2009) for Deutsche Telekom's open innovation ecosystems. Another example of such an incumbent-led innovation ecosystem that includes new ventures is the Novartis Biome digital health ecosystem. "By co-creating scalable digital solutions," the Novartis Biome ecosystem consists of "strong partnerships that are combining expertise of all areas involved" so as "to exploit the numerous new technological possibilities available and to make use of the opportunities the new legal framework is offering" (Novartis AG, 2022, para. 5). For instance, Novartis partners with the Moorfields Eye Hospital NHS Foundation Trust "to source tech collaborators to build in patient education to an existing system, with the long-term goal to widen the development to many other eye clinics in hospitals" (Novartis AG, 2021, para. 14). Consequently, two incumbent firms (i.e., Novartis und Moorfields) collaborate in a multilateral manner with technology-based ventures "to drive a much wider cross-industry collaboration to advance health outcomes" (Novartis AG, 2021, para. 20). Partnerships with leading technology firms, such as Novartis' collaboration with Microsoft (Novartis AG, 2019), characteristically complement these innovation ecosystems.

New ventures benefit in several manners from their contributions to innovation ecosystems, such as "access to established markets, enhanced reputation, and increased opportunities for IPOs," as incumbent firms' innovation ecosystems form the "value creation and value appropriation infrastructure for entrepreneurs and their ventures, thereby mitigating their liability of newness" (Nambisan & Baron, 2021, p. 520). These benefits depend on a new venture's abilities to sense and seize opportunities within the innovation ecosystem (Nambisan & Baron, 2013). When new ventures collectively discover and exploit opportunities, innovation ecosystems tend to expand; however, new ventures usually face competitive risks when interacting with other ecosystem actors (Overholm, 2015). Consequently, new ventures strategically engage in innovation ecosystems to scale their businesses, by exploiting an incumbent firm's platform, rebuilding interfaces for allowing complementors to multi-home, or injecting resources to capture a share of an innovation ecosystem's value (Karhu & Ritala, 2021).

Third-Party-Led Innovation Ecosystems

As the prominence of innovation ecosystems grew, incumbent firms noticed that they often do not have all capabilities in-house to navigate this "ecosystem transition" (Altman et al., 2022, p. 23). Increasingly, incumbent firms choose to engage in *third-party-led innovation ecosystems* to create the nuclei for their own innovation ecosystems. Siota, Prats, Fernandéz, and Pérez (2020) call these orchestrating firms "enablers," that is, "an institution or individual, within an innovation ecosystem, that facilitates a resource or activity in the collaboration between an established corporation and a start-up, in order for the corporation to attract and adopt innovation" (p. 5). Gulati, Puranam, and Tushman (2012) similarly portrayed how the innovation intermediary InnoCentive connected clients with new ventures to explore and develop the nuclei for incumbent firms' own innovation ecosystems.

Accelerators, for instance, can develop into orchestrators of third-party-led innovation ecosystems. For instance, Cohen, Fehder, et al. (2019) allude to Techstars's novel business activities in forming partnerships with corporate firms as a noteworthy exception to accelerators' classic business activities. Prexl, Hubert, Beck, Heiden, and Prügl (2019) corroborate this development, since they describe "white-label accelerators" (p. 630) as a third party that adopts the role to catalyze innovation among multiple firms. In a similar vein, Pauwels et al. (2016) refer to "ecosystem builder" accelerators that "match … customers with start-ups and build corporate ecosystem[s]" (p. 20). These accelerators thus "enable incumbent corporations to profit from the collaboration with start-ups while sparing them the complex set-up procedure" (Prexl et al., 2019, p. 630).

Other types of organizations can also serve as third parties that orchestrate innovation ecosystems that are open to incumbent firms searching for complementors. Bettenmann, Giones, Brem, and Gneiting (2022) illustrate this phenomenon using the example of Startup Autobahn, an "open corporate accelerator" consisting of 30 incumbent firms—"including automotive OEMs and suppliers, as well as firms from other industries, such as IT, logistics, and chemicals"—that "screen thousands of startups, execute more than 150 pilot projects, and implement 17 innovative solutions" (pp. 39–40). Compared to the (ecosystem-as-affiliation) accelerator network, the (ecosystem-as-structure) third-party-led innovation ecosystem therefore "emphasizes and accelerates the strategic fit" and "harnesses the network effects of open innovation and platforms by inviting the participation of multiple sponsors, startups, and other stakeholders rather than establishing exclusive sponsor-startup relationships" (Bettenmann et al., 2022, p. 40). The focus of the orchestrating third party therefore rests on catalyzing nongeneric complementarities and modularizing existing goods and services to enable ecosystem formation.

Shipilov, Furr, and Studer Andersson (2020) relate to Sopra Steria Scale up, a cross-country initiative of the consulting firm Sopra Steria, as "an ecosystem-based innovation initiative" (para. 2) in which Sopra Steria Scale up assumes the role of a third-party orchestrator for their clients' emerging innovation ecosystems. As a client of Sopra Steria Scale up states, "they [i.e., Sopra Steria Scale up] create innovation and possibilities by connecting the large players and the young startups. We have participated since the beginning, and have established relations that has led to cooperation and interesting projects" (Sopra Steria, 2022, last para.). This phenomenon reflects how innovation intermediaries (Howells, 2006) increasingly serve to build ecosystems (De Silva, Howells, & Meyer, 2018; Reischauer, Güttel, & Schüssler, 2021).

Third-party-led innovation ecosystems enable incumbent firms to gain capabilities in ecosystem building and orchestration, such as curating and cultivating a set of relevant complementors. Indeed, innovation ecosystems require a delicate balance between sufficient variety of complementors and sufficient specificity of complementors (Wareham, Fox, & Cano Giner, 2014). Consequently, third parties like accelerators and innovation intermediaries assume the responsibility to create a "mix of common and uncommon partners," solving the problem that "you need to have the uncommon partners find you" (Shipilov et al., 2020, para. 9). Likewise, third parties fuel ecosystem formation when they possess relevant knowledge and experience in the domain of the particular ecosystem; solely providing financial resources, however, is not sufficient for successful ecosystem formation (Breznitz, Forman, & Wen, 2018).

Incumbent firms thus gain access to third-party organizations' orchestration capabilities (Altman et al., 2022; Sieg, Wallin, & von Krogh, 2010), essentially paying a neutral orchestrator for its market knowledge and network (Lingens, Miehé, et al., 2021). New ventures, conversely, benefit from partnering with such third-party orchestrators, as they have access to several incumbent firms in parallel without giving away equity (Bettenmann et al., 2022; Weiblen & Chesbrough, 2015). When the relationships between an orchestrating firm and new ventures or between incumbent firms and new ventures are not based on equity, the innovation ecosystem can develop more autonomously instead of signaling that corporations are "picking winners and losers" (Weiblen & Chesbrough, 2015, p. 84) by investing in certain new ventures but abstaining from investments in other new ventures. Engaging in a third-party-led innovation ecosystem therefore represents another "big pond" type of corporate-startup relationship (Katila et al., 2022), which enables new ventures to co-create innovations with incumbent firms without the necessity to immediately form dyadic ties.

Startup-Led Innovation Ecosystems

Recent research has shown that new ventures can position themselves as orchestrators of their own *startup-led innovation ecosystems* and capture value from their orchestrating activities (Lingens, Böger, et al., 2021; Lingens, Miehé, et al., 2021). These new insights are at odds with established narratives that have viewed incumbent firms as the only players capable of orchestrating ecosystems (Iansiti & Levien, 2004; Moore, 1993). The original reasoning was that "ecosystem leaders" (Dedehayir, Mäkinen, & Roland Ortt, 2016, p. 22) need to undertake multiple resource-intensive tasks during ecosystem initiation, such as designing ecosystem governance, forging partnerships, building, and managing a platform, and determining value creation and capture mechanisms. According to these narratives of the mid-2000s, orchestrators "improve the overall health of their ecosystems by providing a stable and predictable set of common assets" (Iansiti & Levien, 2004, p. 73), such as in the form of platforms, services, tools, and technologies. New ventures, however, were deemed as resource constrained and therefore not able to orchestrate a multipartner innovation effort (Dedehayir et al., 2016; Fuller, Jacobides, & Reeves, 2019).

Recently, however, new ventures have successfully demonstrated that they are capable of building and orchestrating ecosystems themselves. New ventures' increasing power to orchestrate ecosystems stems from their capabilities to develop highly innovative goods and services based on new technologies and scale their digital offerings globally (Rohrbeck et al., 2009). As a result, new ventures' strengths as orchestrators of innovation ecosystems particularly lie in the flexibility and fast development as well as in the technological innovations that serve as nuclei of innovation ecosystems. Garnsey and Leong (2008), for instance, described how resource-constrained new ventures grew their niche markets into innovation ecosystems, as they "influence[d] their own selection experience" and sought "actively to create an innovative ecosystem favourable [*sic*] to their innovation" (pp. 684–685).

Solarisbank's banking-as-a-service ecosystem serves as a vivid example of how a new venture has successfully positioned itself as an orchestrator of its innovation ecosystem. Founded in 2016, Solarisbank considers itself a "technology company with a German banking license" (Solarisbank, n.d., para. 1). Application programming interfaces connect multiple players via its banking-as-a-service platform, enabling both B2C (e.g., the sustainable bank Tomorrow) and business-to-business services (e.g., Penta as bank for small and medium-sized firms). Solarisbank thereby provides its banking license and technology not only to other new ventures (such as Tomorrow and Penta) but also to incumbent firms. For instance, Samsung Electronics, Visa, and Solarisbank jointly created the mobile payment solution Samsung

Pay in which Samsung Electronics contributes the smartphones' hardware and software, Visa provides virtual credit cards, and Solarisbank adds the compliant processes to identify customers and connect their virtual Visa card to an existing bank account (Bessenbach, 2020).

This example shows how incumbent firms benefit from acting as complementors to new ventures' innovation ecosystems, as they appreciate the access to new ventures' innovative technologies without having to acquire stakes in them (Neudert & Kreutzer, 2021). Increasing modularization due to digitalization spurs this development (Baldwin, 2021), as incumbent firms can deploy their established goods and services into new ventures' customer-centric innovation ecosystems, such as insurance firms in mobility ecosystems (Tanguy, Lorenz, Nandan, Sharma, & Waschto, 2018). However, research thus far has only sparsely examined how incumbent firms contribute as complementors to new ventures' innovation ecosystems (Jacobides et al., 2018; Lingens, Böger, et al., 2021).

MULTIPARTNER INNOVATION MODE CHOICE FRAMEWORK FOR INCUMBENT FIRMS

To provide guidance on which orchestration mode of multipartner innovation fits which incumbent firms' objectives, we have outlined a corresponding choice framework in Figure 6.1.

Figure 6.1

Multipartner Innovation Mode Choice Framework for Incumbent Firms

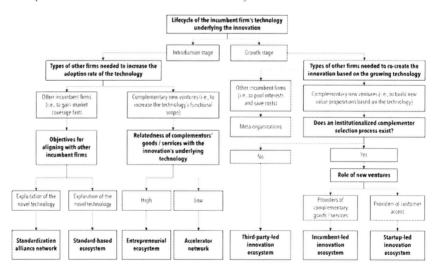

At the outset, incumbent firms should assess the lifecycle stage of the technologies underlying the innovation project. In the introduction stage—what Taylor and Taylor (2012) refer to as "embryonic" (p. 545)—the market for the technology and its adoption rate is still low; likewise, the uncertainty of investing in the technologies is high (Rogers, 1983; Taylor & Taylor, 2012). The viability of the technology forming the basis for the innovative good, service, or value proposition therefore still needs to be proven.

At this point in the technology life cycle, entrepreneurial ecosystems, accelerator networks, standardization alliance networks, and standard-based innovation ecosystems are the preferred modes for scaling the underlying technologies. Due to the uncertainties described above, either a very tight coupling of actors as in standardization alliance networks and standard-based innovation ecosystems or a very loose coupling of actors as in entrepreneurial ecosystems or accelerator networks[3] appears best: On both sides of the coordination spectrum, losses from malinvestments (Jacobides et al., 2018) in emerging technologies shall be reduced, either via tightly knit technical agreements and alignments (to guarantee reciprocal payoffs) or via self-organization (to guarantee the voluntary nature of investments).

In the next step, incumbent firms need to assess whether other incumbent firms (i.e., to gain market coverage fast) or complementary new ventures (i.e., to increase the technology's functional scope) are necessary to increase the adoption rate of the technology. When an incumbent firm has the clear objective how to commercially exploit a novel technology, a standardization alliance network is most useful to increase the commercial viability of the technology. A standard-based innovation ecosystem, on the other hand, provides a space to experiment with standard-based use cases and, thereby, to develop the nuclei of incumbent firms' ecosystems, which then evolve into incumbent-led innovation ecosystems.

When complementary new ventures should serve to increase the technology's functional scope, incumbent firms should assess the relatedness of the technology at stake with complementors' goods and services. In case of a high relatedness, incumbent firms should have enough knowledge to actively contribute to an entrepreneurial ecosystem and decide for themselves which ventures they want to engage in a dialogue with. In case of a low relatedness, an accelerator network provides mediated access to a broad community of new ventures in which specialized innovation scouts can curate potential complementors for the incumbent firm.

The four other orchestration modes are better suited when technologies are in the growth stage. This means that the adoption rate of the technology increases rapidly, leaving behind the introduction stage that is characterized by a rather slow adoption rate (Haupt, Kloyer, & Lange, 2007; Rogers, 1983; Taylor & Taylor, 2012). During this stage, technology investments are most attractive (Andersen, 1999). This strengthens the common interests of similar firms that join a meta-organization (Cropper & Bor, 2018) and accelerates the necessary co-specializations that orchestrators seek to grow their innovation ecosystems (Jacobides et al., 2018; Teece, 1986). Consequently, when technology adoption rates appear to grow rapidly, either a meta-organization or the different types of innovation ecosystems (i.e., incumbent-led, startup-led, and third-party-led innovation ecosystems) are most appealing as orchestration modes.

To decide among the four orchestration modes, firms must evaluate the types of other firms that are necessary to co-create the innovation based on the growing technology. If other incumbent firms should serve to pool interests and save costs during the commercialization of the innovation (i.e., like bundling their market power with regard to suppliers or customers), a meta-organization with delineated boundaries in the form of membership contracts appears as the most viable option (Cropper & Bor, 2018; Gulati et al., 2012; Radnejad, Vredenburg, & Woiceshyn, 2017). However, if complementary new ventures are necessary to co-create innovative value propositions based on the growing technology, the question arises whether incumbent firms have the capabilities to identify and align with such complementors (Altman et al., 2022; Sieg et al., 2010). The ensuing question is therefore whether incumbent firms are able to strategically select complementors and position themselves as complementors of innovation ecosystems, or whether they lack such an institutionalized complementor selection process (Visscher et al., 2021).

Typical considerations in this complementor selection process are the assessment of the type of complementarities (Jacobides, 2019; Jacobides et al., 2018) and the position in the ecosystem (Burford et al., 2022; Shipilov & Gawer, 2020). Such a process also entails considerations that challenge established industry thinking and forces incumbent firms to perceive business opportunities rather in "temporary clusters of semifluid relationships, spanning traditional industry boundaries" (Fuller et al., 2019, p. 7). Relevant capabilities in this regard are organizational processes to "transition from hierarchical closed governance to more open ecosystem structures" and "embracing more than one governance structure at the same time" (Altman et al., 2022, pp. 23–24)

When incumbent firms have an institutionalized complementor selection process in place (Visscher et al., 2021), they can systematically assess whether to take on the role of orchestrator themselves or whether to let new ventures assume the role of orchestrator (Lingens, Böger, et al., 2021; Lingens, Miehé, et al., 2021). When new ventures are to serve as providers of complementary goods or services to incumbent firms' existing technologies, incumbent firms are most likely to play the role of orchestrator. However, when new ventures create customer access through a focal good or service (e.g., a customer-friendly app), incumbent firms should position themselves as complementors in startup-led innovation ecosystems.

When incumbent firms do not have an institutionalized complementor selection process in place, collaborating with third-party organizations specializing in ecosystem building, such as accelerators, innovation intermediaries, and consulting firms, appears most reasonable (Bettenmann et al., 2022; Shipilov et al., 2020). In these third-party-led innovation ecosystems, incumbent firms and new ventures experiment together with use cases under the guidance of a neutral orchestrator to create the nuclei of incumbent firms' or new ventures' innovation ecosystems.

MULTIPARTNER INNOVATION MODE CHOICE FRAMEWORK FOR NEW VENTURES

After depicting a multipartner innovation mode choice framework for incumbent firms, Figure 6.2 portrays the corresponding mode choice framework for new ventures. The type of decisions that new ventures must take are in many instances the same as those that incumbent firms must take; however, certain decision points differ and, even in case of the same decision points, the resulting options for new ventures may differ, depending on their situation as young, growth-oriented technology-driven firms

Figure 6.2

Multipartner Innovation Mode Choice Framework for New Ventures

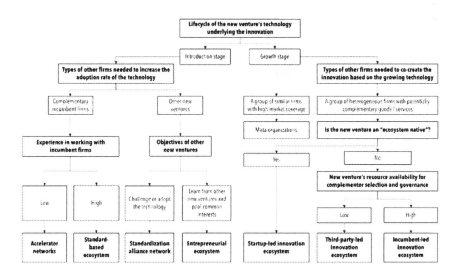

Like incumbent firms, new ventures must first assess the lifecycle stage of the technology underlying the innovation. When the underlying technology is still in the introduction stage, adoption rate is low and investments in these emerging technologies are still uncertain (Rogers, 1983; Taylor & Taylor, 2012). Such situations rather point to membership-based standardization alliance networks, accelerator networks, and entrepreneurial ecosystems or structurally aligned standard-based innovation ecosystems.

Again, the type of other firms that are necessary to co-create the innovation based on the growing technology decides upon the next steps in selecting the right orchestration mode. When complementary incumbent firms are required to scale the technology in the introduction stage, new ventures can use two paths to access these diverse complementary actors despite their resource and attention constraints (Cozzolino & Rothaermel, 2018; Katila, Rosenberger, & Eisenhardt, 2008). The first path is to become part of an accelerator network that promises curated access to mentors from incumbent firms who can bring their perspectives (but not necessarily complementary goods or services) to the multipartner commercialization strategy of the new venture's underlying technology. Alternatively, standard-based innovation ecosystems provide immediate access to incumbent firms interested in experimenting with emerging technologies. These multilateral interactions with potential complementors in standard-based innovation ecosystems promise to identify commercially viable value propositions; however, new ventures may lack experience in aligning with incumbent firms, leading to a potentially high invest of human and time resources into finding and approaching complementors. Accelerator networks' mediators who catalyze matches between new ventures and incumbent firms can thus help overcome this lack of experience in aligning with incumbent firms.

When interaction with other new ventures is deemed necessary to increase the technology's adoption rate, joining either a standardization alliance network or actively engaging in an entrepreneurial ecosystem is recommended. When new ventures want to simply adopt a certain standard (e.g., to create a superior customer experience based on this standard) or—consciously—challenge it, becoming a member of a standardization alliance network appears as the best option. The alternative option, actively engaging in an entrepreneurial ecosystem, usually does not require an application to a formal organization. This option appears most viable for new ventures when learning from other new ventures (also regarding general entrepreneurial concerns like funding, hiring, and scaling) and pooling common interests (e.g., toward policymakers) are the prime objectives of their interaction with other new ventures.

The four other orchestration modes apply when the innovation's underlying technology is already in the growth stage, that is, when the technology's rate of adoption increases most rapidly and investments into the technology appears most attractive. In this stage of the technology lifecycle, meta-organizations, third-party-led innovation ecosystems, incumbent-led, or startup-led innovation ecosystems appear as most viable orchestration modes for new ventures' multipartner innovation engagements.

On the one hand, when a homogeneous group of similar firms (e.g., an industry association of incumbent firms) is necessary to swiftly cover a large market, applying to be a dedicated partner firm of a meta-organization may be the most viable path. Similar incumbent firms that learn of the new venture's innovation may be more easily convinced to collectively adopt the technology for their own goods or services, which leverages the new venture's potential to scale while keeping the investment into orchestrating multiple dyadic relationships low. On the other hand, when a group of heterogeneous complementors is necessary (e.g., to leverage complementary resources), innovation ecosystems appear most promising.

When deciding among the different orchestration modes of innovation ecosystems, also new ventures must assess whether they have an institutionalized complementor selection process in place (Visscher et al., 2021). Interestingly, for several new ventures this complementor selection process represents an integral part of their business model, which is the reason why we delineate these new ventures as *ecosystem natives*. This means that the selection of complementors and/or the conscious decision to act as a complementor to multiple other ecosystems are deeply ingrained in a new venture's business model. An exemplary ecosystem native is Doconomy. This ecosystem native claims that "from the very start, [it has] been developing an ecosystem of financial tools to educate and drive positive change" (Doconomy AB, 2021a, para. 1), which started by allying with "Ålandsbanken, the UNFCCC [*sic*] and MasterCard" (Doconomy AB, 2021a, para. 2). Subsequently, Doconomy enlarged their innovation ecosystem by collaborating with S&P Global, Patch, Parley for the Oceans, paybox Bank AG, Giesecke+Devrient, BNP Paribas Bank Polska, and other diverse firms (Doconomy AB, 2021b).

New ventures that do not start as ecosystem natives may have to institutionalize such complementor selection processes, which can be resource consuming. In this case, new ventures can start by strategically assessing a complementary incumbent firm's existing customer base as a vehicle to offer their complementary solutions by joining an incumbent firm's existing innovation ecosystem (Visscher et al., 2021). Alternatively, when new ventures do not have the resources to scout attractive incumbent firms and govern their ecosystem engagement with these incumbent firms, a third-party-led innovation ecosystem may provide alleviation. In this manner, third parties that specialize in ecosystem building (e.g., accelerators, innovation intermediaries, and consulting firms) identify potentially complementary incumbent firms and guide the potential ecosystem actors along the first steps toward developing their own innovation ecosystems' nuclei.

CONCLUSION

Summary

In this chapter, we presented different orchestration modes of multi-partner innovation, taking an ecosystem lens. We therefore distinguished between the ecosystem-as-affiliation and the ecosystem-as-structure paradigm (Adner, 2017) and the type of orchestrating firm (Jacobides et al., 2018; Leten, Vanhaverbeke, Roijakkers, Clerix, & Van Helleputte, 2013; Lingens, Böger, et al., 2021; Lingens, Miehé, et al., 2021), leading to a two-by-four matrix of multipartner innovation orchestration modes whose definitions are summarized in Table 6.2.

Table 6.2

Definitions of Orchestration Modes of Multipartner Innovation

	Orchestration mode	Definition	Source
Ecosystem-as-affiliation	Standardization alliance network	"Firms to join together into one or more standard-setting alliances in order to develop standard technology and to sponsor adoption of a standard."	Axelrod et al. (1995, p. 1493)
	Meta-organization	"The purpose of a meta-organization is to work in the interests of all its members, with all members being equally valuable and membership being based on some form of similarity;" membership is voluntary and can be withdrawn at the member's will	Ahrne & Brunsson (2005, p. 11)
	Accelerator network	The network of alumni of new ventures that have participated in "a fixed-term, cohort-based program for startups, including mentorship and/or educational components, that culminates in a graduation event" and incumbent firms' mentors	Authors' definition based on Cohen et al. (2019, p. 1782)

(Table continued on next page)

Table 6.2 (Continued)

Definitions of Orchestration Modes of Multipartner Innovation

	Orchestration mode	Definition	Source
Ecosystem-as-affiliation	Entrepreneurial ecosystem	"Complex contexts for activity, characterized by resource interdependencies and diverse connections, second-order consequences, and the potential to generate variety"	Thompson et al. (2018, p. 98)
	Standard-based innovation ecosystem	An innovation ecosystem that is predominantly coordinated via standards; hence, no central firm guides the development and implementation of an innovative value proposition toward a customer	Authors' definition
	Incumbent-led innovation ecosystem	"The collaborative arrangements through which firms combine their individual offerings into a coherent, customer-facing solution," orchestrated by one or more incumbent firm(s) to expand the incumbent firm's / firms' value proposition(s) by means of new ventures' complementary technologies	Authors' definition based on Adner (2006, p. 98)
Ecosystem-as-structure	Third-party-led innovation ecosystem	A third-party orchestrator "emphasizes and accelerates the strategic fit" and "harnesses the network effects of open innovation and platforms by inviting the participation of multiple sponsors, startups, and other stakeholders rather than establishing exclusive sponsor-startup relationships."	Authors' definition based on Bettenmann et al. (2022, p. 40)
	Startup-led innovation ecosystem	"The collaborative arrangements through which firms combine their individual offerings into a coherent, customer-facing solution," orchestrated by one or more new venture(s) and focusing on fast development, flexibility, and technological innovation	Authors' definition based on Adner (2006, p. 98)

Per orchestration mode, we outlined the distinct opportunities and challenges for both incumbent firms and new ventures. From the perspective of incumbent firms, we depicted how membership-based ecosystem-as-affiliation orchestration modes can serve to pool common innovation initiatives via meta-organizations (Berkowitz & Dumez, 2016; König et al., 2012; Rad-nejad et al., 2017) or to jointly commercialize technological standards via standardization alliance networks (Axelrod et al., 1995; Wen et al., 2020). Furthermore, engagement in accelerator networks (Cohen, Fehder, et al., 2019; Hallen et al., 2020) and entrepreneurial ecosystems (Auerswald & Dani, 2017; Autio et al., 2018; Spigel & Harrison, 2018) can provide new knowledge and inspiration about emerging technologies.

From the perspective of new ventures, several ecosystem-as-affiliation orchestration modes of orchestrating multipartner innovation appear dominated by incumbent firms, such as meta-organizations and stan-dardization alliance networks. However, formerly closed-membership meta-organizations and standardization alliance networks selectively open themselves for partnerships with new ventures as drivers of innovation (Battisti et al., 2022; Cropper & Bor, 2018). Accelerator networks provide new ventures with guided mentoring at the price of equity handed out to accelerators and incumbent firms seeking partnerships (Cohen, Bingham, et al., 2019; Cohen, Fehder, et al., 2019). Entrepreneurial ecosystems, on the other hand, rely on mechanisms of self-organization among entrepre-neurs (Auerswald & Dani, 2017), lacking a dedicated orchestrating firm but capitalizing on entrepreneurial intention.

When orchestrating innovation with multiple firms through an eco-system-as-structure orchestration mode, the focus shifts to a shared value proposition that different players need to co-create. Incumbent firms can either take on the role of an orchestrator (i.e., attract complementors and bring about alignment between them) or position themselves as comple-mentors for new ventures' innovation ecosystems (Lingens, Böger, et al., 2021; Lingens, Miehé, et al., 2021). New ventures—particularly, ecosystem natives—accordingly gain importance both as complementors for incum-bent firms' innovation ecosystems and as creators of novel innovation ecosystems in which incumbent firms can offer their goods and services as complementors.

In addition to these two more common orchestration modes, we out-lined two novel views on orchestrating multipartner innovation, namely third-party-led innovation ecosystems (Bettenmann et al., 2022; Shipilov et al., 2020) and standard-based innovation ecosystems (Miller & Toh, 2022). Both orchestration modes enable incumbent firms and new ventures to incubate the nuclei of emerging innovation ecosystems, either under the guidance of a specialized accelerator, innovation intermediary, or consult-ing firm (i.e., third-party-led innovation ecosystem) or by experimenting with emerging standards (i.e., standard-based innovation ecosystem).

Limitations and Outlook for Future Research

We focused on product innovations, touching only marginally on other types of innovation, such as process, organizational, and business model innovation (De Propris, 2002; Kim & Lui, 2015; Zott et al., 2011). Existing research, for instance, has shown that modular and architectural types of innovation influence the relationship between the degree of partner coupling and commercial or innovation performance (Hofman, Halman, & Looy, 2016; Hofman, Halman, & Song, 2017). Future research could therefore investigate how different innovation types affect each orchestration mode. For instance, can business model innovations from the interaction of incumbent firms and new ventures better arise in ecosystem-as-affiliation modes or in ecosystem-as-structure modes? Do more loosely coupled orchestration modes lead to better innovation performance? Do organizations learn differently in each orchestration mode, and if so, how?

Moreover, the eight orchestration modes that we conceptually outlined in this chapter represent ideal types of multipartner innovation. However, mixed forms of these orchestration modes exist and will, most likely, even gain in popularity. For instance, corporate venturing ecosystems represent crossovers between accelerator networks and incumbent-led innovation ecosystems; however, researchers still formulate their understanding about what a corporate venturing ecosystem actually defines (Burford et al., 2021; Dushnitsky & Kang, 2018). Particularly, combinations of equity-based and non-equity-based corporate-startup relationships (Veit, Kramer, Kanbach, & Stubner, 2021) may potentially combine the upside potentials of membership-based, rather closed forms of multipartner innovation and value-proposition-based, rather open forms of multipartner innovation. However, balancing the different types of relationships might increase complexity of orchestration, potentially leading to distinct tensions (e.g., stability versus change, exploration versus exploitation)—another exciting avenue for future research. Moreover, orchestration modes of multipartner innovation may change and transform over time, for instance, when standard-based innovation ecosystems develop into incumbent-led or startup-led innovation ecosystems as the nuclei of single firms' ecosystems grow and certain firms, in parallel, enact orchestration opportunities.

Lastly, our chapter focused on commercial firms as orchestrators, omitting public initiatives and universities as orchestrators of pre-commercial multipartner innovation, for example, research-driven innovation networks like the Academic Health Science Networks in the United Kingdom. These types of pre-commercial multipartner innovations are usually orchestrated by universities, research institutions, and knowledge creators, which bring incumbent firms and new ventures together to work on foundational ideas to be commercialized (Levén, Holmström, & Mathiassen, 2014). Investigating orchestration modes of public-private multipartner innovation (Asplund, Björk, Magnusson, & Patrick, 2021; Li & Garnsey, 2014) may therefore be an intriguing avenue for future research to combine the upside potential of market-based innovation success with policy-driven market intervention mechanisms.

NOTES

1. In contrast to multipartner innovation, *collaborative innovation* refers to situations in which "contributors ... share the work of generating a design and also reveal the outputs from their individual and collective design efforts openly for anyone to use;" hence, "(1) the participants are not rivals with respect to the innovative design ... and (2) they do not individually or collectively plan to sell products or services incorporating the innovation or intellectual property rights related to it" (Baldwin & von Hippel, 2011, p. 1403). Collaborative innovation, for instance, alludes to open-source software projects in which the participating actors do not aim at directly commercializing the invented designs. In this chapter, however, we focus on commercially oriented product innovations that are co-created by incumbent firms and new ventures.
2. For a comprehensive review of the differences between the cluster view and the entrepreneurial ecosystem view, see Spigel and Harrison (2018, p. 157).
3. We consider the majority of multilateral interactions in an accelerator's alumni network as loosely coupled; however, the dyadic, usually equity-based corporate-startup relationships established from formal accelerator programs should be considered as tightly coupled.

ACKNOWLEDGMENTS

We would like to thank Katrin Burmeister-Lamp for her questions about the different types of ecosystems, which inspired us to develop these frameworks. Furthermore, we are grateful for Thomas Draschbacher's helpful feedback on a previous version of this manuscript.

REFERENCES

Aarikka-Stenroos, L., & Ritala, P. (2017). Network management in the era of ecosystems: Systematic review and management framework. *Industrial Marketing Management, 67*, 23–36.

Adner, R. (2006). Match your innovation strategy to your innovation ecosystem. *Harvard Business Review, 84*(4), 98–107.

Adner, R. (2017). Ecosystem as structure: An actionable construct for strategy. *Journal of Management, 43*(1), 39–58.

Adner, R., & Feiler, D. (2019). Interdependence, perception, and investment choices: An experimental approach to decision making in innovation ecosystems. *Organization Science, 30*(1), 109–125.

Adner, R., & Kapoor, R. (2010). Value creation in innovation ecosystems: How the structure of technological interdependence affects firm performance in new technology generations. *Strategic Management Journal, 31*(3), 306–333.

Adner, R., & Lieberman, M. (2021). Disruption through complements. *Strategy Science, 6*(1), 91–109.

Ahrne, G., & Brunsson, N. (2005). Organizations and meta-organizations. *Scandinavian Journal of Management, 21*(4), 429–449.

Altman, E. J., Nagle, F., & Tushman, M. L. (2022). The translucent hand of managed ecosystems: Engaging communities for value creation and capture. *Academy of Management Annals, 16*(1), 70–101.

Andersen, B. (1999). The hunt for S-shaped growth paths in technological innovation: A patent study. *Journal of Evolutionary Economics, 9*(4), 487–526.

Ansari, S., Garud, R., & Kumaraswamy, A. (2016). The disruptor's dilemma: TiVo and the U.S. television ecosystem. *Strategic Management Journal, 37*(9), 1829–1853.

Asplund, F., Björk, J., Magnusson, M., & Patrick, A. J. (2021). The genesis of public-private innovation ecosystems: Bias and challenges. *Technological Forecasting and Social Change, 162*, Article No. 120378. https://doi.org/10.1016/j.techfore.2020.120378

Atos. (2021, October 15). *Atos joins Catena-X: The automotive industry network to strengthen and secure data exchange & innovation across* [Press release]. https://atos.net/en/2021/press-release_2021_10_15/atos-joins-catena-x-the-automotive-industry-network-to-strengthen-and-secure-data-exchange-innovation-across-europe

Auerswald, P. E., & Dani, L. (2017). The adaptive life cycle of entrepreneurial ecosystems: The biotechnology cluster. *Small Business Economics, 49*(1), 97–117.

Autio, E., Kenney, M., Mustar, P., Siegel, D., & Wright, M. (2014). Entrepreneurial innovation: The importance of context. *Research Policy, 43*(7), 1097–1108.

Autio, E., Nambisan, S., Thomas, L. D. W., & Wright, M. (2018). Digital affordances, spatial affordances, and the genesis of entrepreneurial ecosystems. *Strategic Entrepreneurship Journal, 12*(1), 72–95.

Axelrod, R., Mitchell, W., Thomas, R. E., Bennett, D. S., & Bruderer, E. (1995). Coalition formation in standard-setting alliances. *Management Science, 41*(9), 1493–1508.

Bacon, E., Williams, M. D., & Davies, G. (2020). Coopetition in innovation ecosystems: A comparative analysis of knowledge transfer configurations. *Journal of Business Research, 115*, 307–316.

Bain & Company. (2017, November, 17). *Bain & Company forms Bain Alliance Ecosystem to help clients achieve breakthrough results* [Press release]. https://www.bain.com/about/media-center/press-releases/2017/bain-forms-bain-alliance-ecosystem/

Bain & Company. (2022). *Bain Alliance Ecosystem*. https://www.bain.com/vector-digital/partnerships-alliance-ecosystem/ (accessed March 11, 2022).

Baldwin, C., & von Hippel, E. (2011). Modeling a paradigm shift: From producer innovation to user and open collaborative innovation. *Organization Science, 22*(6), 1399–1417.

Baldwin, C. Y. (2021). *Design rules, volume 2: How technology shapes organizations*. https://www.researchgate.net/project/Design-Rules-Volume-2-How-Technology-Shapes-Organizations (accessed January 14, 2022).

Battisti, S., Agarwal, N., & Brem, A. (2022). Creating new tech entrepreneurs with digital platforms: Meta-organizations for shared value in data-driven retail ecosystems. *Technological Forecasting and Social Change, 175*, Article No. 121392. https://doi.org/10.1016/j.techfore.2021.121392

Ben Letaifa, S., & Rabeau, Y. (2013). Too close to collaborate? How geographic proximity could impede entrepreneurship and innovation. *Journal of Business Research, 66*(10), 2071–2078.

Berkowitz, H., & Bor, S. (2018). Why meta-organizations matter: A response to Lawton et al. and Spillman. *Journal of Management Inquiry, 27*(2), 204–211.

Berkowitz, H., & Dumez, H. (2016). The concept of meta-organization: Issues for management studies. *European Management Review, 13*(2), 149–156.

Bessenbach, J. (2020, September 24). How Solarisbank and Visa enable Samsung Pay in Germany. *Solarisbank*. https://www.solarisbank.com/blog/solarisbank-enables-samsung-pay-in-germany/

Bettenmann, D., Giones, F., Brem, A., & Gneiting, P. (2022). Break out to open innovation. *MIT Sloan Management Review, 63*(2), 39–43.

Bianchi, M., Frattini, F., Lejarraga, J., & Di Minin, A. (2014). Technology exploitation paths: Combining technological and complementary resources in new product development and licensing. *Journal of Product Innovation Management, 31*(S1), 146–169.

Blind, K., & Mangelsdorf, A. (2016). Motives to standardize: Empirical evidence from Germany. *Technovation, 48–49*, 13–24.

Bogers, M., Zobel, A.-K., Afuah, A., Almirall, E., Brunswicker, S., Dahlander, L., … Ter Wal, A. L. J. (2017). The open innovation research landscape: Established perspectives and emerging themes across different levels of analysis. *Industry and Innovation, 24*(1), 8–40.

Boudreau, K. (2010). Open platform strategies and innovation: Granting access vs. devolving control. *Management Science, 56*(10), 1849–1872.

Breznitz, D., Forman, C., & Wen, W. (2018). The role of venture capital in the formation of a new technological ecosystem: Evidence from the cloud. *MIS Quarterly, 42*(4), 1143–1169.

Brown, R., & Mawson, S. (2019). Entrepreneurial ecosystems and public policy in action: A critique of the latest industrial policy blockbuster. *Cambridge Journal of Regions, Economy and Society, 12*(3), 347–368.

Brusoni, S., & Prencipe, A. (2013). The organization of innovation in ecosystems: Problem framing, problem solving, and patterns of coupling. In R. Adner, J. E. Oxley, & B. S. Silverman (Eds.), *Collaboration and competition in business ecosystems* (pp. 167–194). Bingley, U.K.: Emerald Group Publishing Limited.

Burford, N. J., Kang, S., Dushnitsky, G., Shipilov, A. V., Altman, E. J., Cennamo, C., … Zhu, F. (2021). Where do ecosystems come from? The origins of ecosystem structure and performance. *Proceedings of the Annual Meeting of the Academy of Management*, 13345. Virtual, July 29 – August 4, 2021. https://doi.org/10.5465/AMBPP.2021.13345symposium

Burford, N. J., Shipilov, A. V., & Furr, N. R. (2022). How ecosystem structure affects firm performance in response to a negative shock to interdependencies. *Strategic Management Journal, 43*(1), 30–57.

Calcei, D., & M'Chirgui, Z. (2012). Coalition building dynamics in video format wars. *Innovation: Management, Policy and Practice, 14*(3), 324–336.

Cantner, U., Cunningham, J. A., Lehmann, E. E., & Menter, M. (2021). Entrepreneurial ecosystems: A dynamic lifecycle model. *Small Business Economics, 57*(1), 407–423.

Capron, L., & Mitchell, W. (2010). Finding the right path. *Harvard Business Review, 88*(7–8), 102–107.

Carayannis, E. G., Provance, M., & Grigoroudis, E. (2016). Entrepreneurship ecosystems: An agent-based simulation approach. *The Journal of Technology Transfer, 41*(3), 631–653.

Catena-X. (2021). *Catena-X Automotive Network: Building the first operating system for a data driven value chain.* https://catena-x.net/fileadmin/user_upload/intro_praesenationen/catena-x_im_ueberblick_de_v2.3.pdf

Cohen, S. L., Bingham, C. B., & Hallen, B. L. (2019). The role of accelerator designs in mitigating bounded rationality in new ventures. *Administrative Science Quarterly, 64*(4), 810–854.

Cohen, S. L., Fehder, D. C., Hochberg, Y. V, & Murray, F. (2019). The design of startup accelerators. *Research Policy, 48*(7), 1781–1797.

Cozzolino, A., & Rothaermel, F. T. (2018). Discontinuities, competition, and cooperation: Coopetitive dynamics between incumbents and entrants. *Strategic Management Journal, 39*(12), 3053–3085.

Cropper, S., & Bor, S. (2018). (Un)bounding the meta-organization: Co-evolution and compositional dynamics of a health partnership. *Administrative Sciences, 8*(3), 42. https://doi.org/10.3390/admsci8030042

Daidj, N., Grazia, C., & Hammoudi, A. (2010). Introduction to the non-cooperative approach to coalition formation: The case of the blu-ray/HD-DVD standards' war. *Journal of Media Economics, 23*(4), 192–215.

Dattée, B., Alexy, O., & Autio, E. (2018). Maneuvering in poor visibility: How firms play the ecosystem game when uncertainty is high. *Academy of Management Journal, 61*(2), 466–498.

De Propris, L. (2002). Types of innovation and inter-firm co-operation. *Entrepreneurship and Regional Development, 14*(4), 337–353.

De Silva, M., Howells, J., & Meyer, M. (2018). Innovation intermediaries and collaboration: Knowledge–based practices and internal value creation. *Research Policy, 47*(1), 70–87.

de Vasconcelos Gomes, L. A., Facin, A. L. F., Salerno, M. S., & Ikenami, R. K. (2018). Unpacking the innovation ecosystem construct: Evolution, gaps and trends. *Technological Forecasting and Social Change, 136*, 30–48.

Dedehayir, O., Mäkinen, S. J., & Roland Ortt, J. (2016). Roles during innovation ecosystem genesis: A literature review. *Technological Forecasting and Social Change, 136*, 18–29.

Dedehayir, O., & Seppänen, M. (2015). Birth and expansion of innovation ecosystems: A case study of copper production. *Journal of Technology Management & Innovation, 10*(2), 145–154.

Delcamp, H., & Leiponen, A. (2014). Innovating standards through informal consortia: The case of wireless telecommunications. *International Journal of Industrial Organization, 36*, 36–47.

Dhanaraj, C., & Parkhe, A. (2006). Orchestrating innovation networks. *Academy of Management Review, 31*(3), 659–669.

Doconomy AB. (2021a). *About Doconomy.* https://doconomy.com/about/ (accessed December 14, 2021).

Doconomy AB. (2021b). *News.* https://doconomy.com/news/ (accessed December 14, 2021).

Dushnitsky, G., & Kang, S. (2018). Seeding a star or constructing a constellation? Corporate venturing as an ecosystem strategy. *Proceedings of the Annual Meeting of the Academy of Management Proceedings, 11361*. Chicago, IL, August 10–14, 2018. https://doi.org/10.5465/AMBPP.2018.11361abstract

Estrada, I., Martín-Cruz, N., & Pérez-Santana, P. (2012). Multi-partner alliance teams for product innovation: The role of human resource management fit. *Innovation: Management, Policy & Practice, 15*(2), 2224–2247.

Findeisen, H., & Sydow, J. (2016). Star Alliance: Adapting the management institutions of an interorganizational network. In J. Sydow, E. Schüßler, & G. Müller-Seitz (Eds.), *Managing interorganizational relations: Debates and cases* (pp. 124–130). London, U.K.: Palgrave-Macmillan.

Foss, N. J., & Saebi, T. (2017). Fifteen years of research on business model innovation. *Journal of Management, 43*(1), 200–227.

Fuller, J., Jacobides, M. G., & Reeves, M. (2019, February 25). The myths and realities of business ecosystems. *MIT Sloan Management Review.* https://sloanreview.mit.edu/article/the-myths-and-realities-of-business-ecosystems/

Furr, N., O'Keeffe, K., & Dyer, J. H. (2016). Managing multiparty innovation. *Harvard Business Review, 94*(11), 76–83.

Garaudel, P. (2020). Exploring meta-organizations' diversity and agency: A meta-organizational perspective on global union federations. *Scandinavian Journal of Management, 36*(1), Article No. 101094. https://doi.org/10.1016/j.scaman.2020.101094

Garnsey, E., & Leong, Y. Y. (2008). Combining resource-based and evolutionary theory to explain the genesis of bio-networks. *Industry and Innovation, 15*(6), 669–686.

Gillier, T., & Piat, G. (2011). Exploring over: The presumed identity of emerging technology. *Creativity and Innovation Management, 20*(4), 238–252.

Gillier, T., Piat, G., Roussel, B., & Truchot, P. (2010). Managing innovation fields in a cross-Industry exploratory partnership with C-K design theory. *Journal of Product Innovation Management, 27*(6), 883–896.

Giudici, A., Reinmoeller, P., & Ravasi, D. (2018). Open-system orchestration as a relational source of sensing capabilities: Evidence from a venture association. *Academy of Management Journal, 61*(4), 1369–1402.

GlassDollar UG. (2021). *Most innovative companies in Europe 2021.* https://ranking.glassdollar.com/ (accessed January 12, 2022).

Gomes-Casseres, B., & Judd, J. (2021). *Star Alliance in 2020.* Ivey ID: 9B21M010. https://www.iveypublishing.ca/s/product/star-alliance-in-2020/01t5c00000CwqLu

Goswami, K., Mitchell, J. R., & Bhagavatula, S. (2018). Accelerator expertise: Understanding the intermediary role of accelerators in the development of the Bangalore entrepreneurial ecosystem. *Strategic Entrepreneurship Journal, 12*(1), 117–150.

Granstrand, O., & Holgersson, M. (2020). Innovation ecosystems: A conceptual review and a new definition. *Technovation, 90–91*(February–March), Article No. 102098. https://doi.org/10.1016/j.technovation.2019.102098

Gulati, R., Puranam, P., & Tushman, M. (2012). Meta-organization design: Rethinking design in interorganizational and community contexts. *Strategic Management Journal, 33*(6), 571–586.

Hallen, B. L., Cohen, S. L., & Bingham, C. B. (2020). Do accelerators work? If so, how? *Organization Science, 31*(2), 378–414.

Hannah, D. P., & Eisenhardt, K. M. (2018). How firms navigate cooperation and competition in nascent ecosystems. *Strategic Management Journal, 39*(12), 3163–3192.

Haupt, R., Kloyer, M., & Lange, M. (2007). Patent indicators for the technology life cycle development. *Research Policy, 36*(3), 387–398.

Heine, K., & Kerk, M. (2017). Conflict resolution in meta-organizations: The peculiar role of arbitration. *Journal of Organization Design, 6*(1), 3. https://doi.org/10.1186/s41469-017-0013-2

Henfridsson, O., Nandhakumar, J., Scarbrough, H., & Panourgias, N. (2018). Recombination in the open-ended value landscape of digital innovation. *Information and Organization, 28*(2), 89–100.

Hettich, E., & Kreutzer, M. (2021). Strategy formation across organizational boundaries: An interorganizational process model. *British Journal of Management, 32*(1), 147–199.

Hofman, E., Halman, J. I. M., & Looy, B. van. (2016). Do design rules facilitate or complicate architectural innovation in innovation alliance networks? *Research Policy, 45*(7), 1436–1448.

Hofman, E., Halman, J. I. M., & Song, M. (2017). When to use loose or tight alliance networks for innovation? Empirical evidence. *Journal of Product Innovation Management, 34*(1), 81–100.

Hou, H., & Shi, Y. (2021). Ecosystem-as-structure and ecosystem-as-coevolution: A constructive examination. *Technovation, 100*, Article No. 102193. https://doi.org/10.1016/j.technovation.2020.102193

Howells, J. (2006). Intermediation and the role of intermediaries in innovation. *Research Policy, 35*(5), 715–728.

Howells, J., James, A., & Malik, K. (2003). The sourcing of technological knowledge: Distributed innovation processes and dynamic change. *R&D Management, 33*(4), 395–409.

Iansiti, M., & Levien, R. (2004). Strategy as ecology. *Harvard Business Review, 82*(3), 68–78.

Isenberg, D. J. (2010). The big idea: How to start an entrepreneurial revolution. *Harvard Business Review, 88*(6), 40–50.

Jacobides, M. G. (2019). In the ecosystem economy, what's your strategy? *Harvard Business Review, 97*(5), 129–137.

Jacobides, M. G., Cennamo, C., & Gawer, A. (2018). Towards a theory of ecosystems. *Strategic Management Journal, 39*(8), 2255–2276.

Jeppesen, L. B., & Lakhani, K. R. (2010). Marginality and problem-solving effectiveness in broadcast search. *Organization Science, 21*(5), 1016–1033.

Karhu, K., & Ritala, P. (2021). Slicing the cake without baking it: Opportunistic platform entry strategies in digital markets. *Long Range Planning, 54*(5), Article No. 101988. https://doi.org/10.1016/j.lrp.2020.101988

Katila, R., Piezunka, H., Reineke, P., & Eisenhardt, K. M. (2022). Big fish vs. big pond? Entrepreneurs, established firms, and antecedents of tie formation. *Academy of Management Journal, 65*(2), 427–452.

Katila, R., Rosenberger, J. D., & Eisenhardt, K. M. (2008). Swimming with sharks: Technology ventures, defense mechanisms and corporate relationships. *Administrative Science Quarterly, 53*(2), 295–332.

Keil, T. (2002). De-facto standardization through alliances—Lessons from Bluetooth. *Telecommunications Policy, 26*(3–4), 205–213.

Kherrazi, S. (2021). Management control of collaborative innovation: Design and structuring mode. *European Journal of Innovation Management, 24*(3), 848–869.

Kim, Y., & Lui, S. S. (2015). The impacts of external network and business group on innovation: Do the types of innovation matter? *Journal of Business Research, 68*(9), 1964–1973.

Kohler, T. (2016). Corporate accelerators: Building bridges between corporations and startups. *Business Horizons, 59*(3), 347–357.

König, A., Schulte, M., & Enders, A. (2012). Inertia in response to non-paradigmatic change: The case of meta-organizations. *Research Policy, 41*(8), 1325–1343.

Kreutzer M. (2012). Selecting the right growth mechanism: The choice between internal development, strategic alliances, and mergers & acquisitions. In G. Mennillo, T. Schlenzig, & E. Friedrich (Eds.), *Balanced growth: Management for professionals* (pp. 77–94). Berlin / Heidelberg, Germany: Springer.

Kreutzer, M., & Neudert, P. (2021). Ecosystem orchestration—Much more than strategic alliance management. *EFMD Global Focus, 15*(2), 11–15.

Leten, B., Vanhaverbeke, W., Roijakkers, N., Clerix, A., & Van Helleputte, J. (2013). IP models to orchestrate innovation ecosystems: IMEC, a public research institute in nano-electronics. *California Management Review, 55*(4), 51–64.

Levén, P., Holmström, J., & Mathiassen, L. (2014). Managing research and innovation networks: Evidence from a government sponsored cross-industry program. *Research Policy, 43*(1), 156–168.

Li, J. F., & Garnsey, E. (2014). Policy-driven ecosystems for new vaccine development. *Technovation, 34*(12), 762–772.

Lingens, B., Böger, M., & Gassmann, O. (2021). Even a small conductor can lead a large orchestra: How startups orchestrate ecosystems. *California Management Review, 63*(3), 118–143.

Lingens, B., Huber, F., & Gassmann, O. (in press). Loner or team player: How firms allocate orchestrator tasks amongst ecosystem actors. *European Management Journal.* https://doi.org/10.1016/j.emj.2021.09.001

Lingens, B., Miehé, L., & Gassmann, O. (2021). The ecosystem blueprint: How firms shape the design of an ecosystem according to the surrounding conditions. *Long Range Planning, 54*(2), Article No. 102043. https://doi.org/10.1016/j.lrp.2020.102043

Malone, T., Laubacher, R. J., & Johns, T. (2011). The age of hyperspecialization. *Harvard Business Review, 89*(7–8), 56–65.

Mercedes-Benz Group AG. (2022). *The European vehicle industry is linking up.* https://www.daimler.com/innovation/digitalisation/industry-4-0/article.html (accessed March 11, 2022).

Miller, C. D., & Toh, P. K. (2022). Complementary components and returns from coordination within ecosystems via standard setting. *Strategic Management Journal, 43*(3), 627-662.

Moore, J. F. (1993). Predators and prey: A new ecology of competition. *Harvard Business Review, 71*(3), 75–86.

Nambisan, S. (2013). Industry technical committees, technological distance, and innovation performance. *Research Policy, 42*(4), 928–940.

Nambisan, S., & Baron, R. A. (2013). Entrepreneurship in innovation ecosystems: Entrepreneurs' self-regulatory processes and their implications for new venture success. *Entrepreneurship: Theory and Practice, 37*(5), 1071–1097.

Nambisan, S., & Baron, R. A. (2021). On the costs of digital entrepreneurship: Role conflict, stress, and venture performance in digital platform-based ecosystems. *Journal of Business Research, 125*, 520–532.

Neudert, P. K., & Kreutzer, M. (2021). Ecosystem orchestration: Matching new ventures and established organizations to catalyze innovation. *Proceedings of the Annual Meeting of the Academy of Management*, 12926. Virtual, July 29–August 4, 2021. https://doi.org/10.5465/AMBPP.2021.183

Nevens, M. T., Summe, G. L., & Uttal, B. (1990). Commercializing technology: What the best companies do. *Harvard Business Review, 68*(3), 154–163.

Ng, W. K. B., Appel-Meulenbroek, R., Cloodt, M., & Arentze, T. (2019). Towards a segmentation of science parks: A typology study on science parks in Europe. *Research Policy, 48*(3), 719–732.

Novartis AG. (2019, October 10). *Novartis and Microsoft announce collaboration to transform medicine with artificial intelligence* [Press release]. https://www.novartis. com/news/novartis-and-microsoft-announce-collaboration-transform-medicine-artificial-intelligence

Novartis AG. (2021, September 7). *Responding to health service goals to improve patient access to healthcare* [Press release]. https://www.biome.novartis.com/stories/responding-health-service-goals-improve-patient-access-healthcare

Novartis AG. (2022). Novartis Biome Germany. https://www.biome.novartis.com/innovation-hubs/novartis-biome-germany (accessed March 11, 2022).

Ocean Protocol Foundation. (2021, May 20). *Ocean Protocol, represented by BigchainDB, Bosch, and Fetch.ai have joined Catena-X, bringing their collective expertise in market, mechanism, and token design* [Press release]. https://oceanprotocol.com/press/2021-05-20-bigchaindb-bosch-fetchai-join-catenax

OptoNet. (n.d.). *Members.* https://optonet-jena.de/members/?lang=en (accessed March 11, 2022).

Oskam, I., Bossink, B., & de Man, A.-P. (2021). Valuing value in innovation ecosystems: How cross-sector actors overcome tensions in collaborative sustainable business model development. *Business & Society, 60*(5), 1059–1091.

Overholm, H. (2015). Collectively created opportunities in emerging ecosystems: The case of solar service ventures. *Technovation, 39–40*(May–June), 14–25.

Pauwels, C., Clarysse, B., Wright, M., & Van Hove, J. (2016). Understanding a new generation incubation model: The accelerator. *Technovation, 50–51*(April–May), 13–24.

Pitelis, C. (2012). Clusters, entrepreneurial ecosystem co-creation, and appropriability: A conceptual framework. *Industrial and Corporate Change, 21*(6), 1359–1388.

Plug and Play. (n.d.-a). *About PlugAndPlay.* https://www.plugandplaytechcenter.com/about/ (accessed March 11, 2022).

Plug and Play. (n.d.-b). *BNP Paribas-Plug and Play.* https://www.plugandplaytechcenter. com/bnp-paribas-plugandplay/ (accessed March 11, 2022).

Plug and Play. (n.d.-c). *Corporate innovation.* https://www.plugandplaytechcenter. com/corporations/ (accessed March 11, 2022).

PooliPrint. (2022). *About PooliPrint.* https://www.poooliprint.com/pages/our-story (accessed March 11, 2022).

Porter, M. E. (1998). Clusters and the new economics of competition. *Harvard Business Review, 76*(6), 77–90.

Prexl, K.-M., Hubert, M., Beck, S., Heiden, C., & Prügl, R. (2019). Identifying and analysing the drivers of heterogeneity among ecosystem builder accelerators. *R&D Management, 49*(4), 624–638.

Radnejad, A. B., Vredenburg, H., & Woiceshyn, J. (2017). Meta-organizing for open innovation under environmental and social pressures in the oil industry. *Technovation, 66–67*, 14–27.

Radziwon, A., Bogers, M. L., Chesbrough, H., & Minssen, T. (2022). Ecosystem effectuation: Creating new value through open innovation during a pandemic. *R&D Management, 52*(2), 376–390.

Reischauer, G., Güttel, W. H., & Schüssler, E. (2021). Aligning the design of intermediary organisations with the ecosystem. *Industry and Innovation, 28*(5), 594–619.

Ritala, P., Agouridas, V., Assimakopoulos, D., & Gies, O. (2013). Value creation and capture mechanisms in innovation ecosystems: A comparative case study. *International Journal of Technology Management, 63*(3/4), 244–267.

Rogers, E. M. (1983). *Diffusion of innovations* (3rd ed.). New York, NY: Free Press.

Rohrbeck, R., Hölzle, K., & Gemünden, H. G. (2009). Opening up for competitive advantage—How Deutsche Telekom creates an open innovation ecosystem. *R&D Management, 39*(4), 420–430.

Roundy, P. T., Bradshaw, M., & Brockman, B. K. (2018). The emergence of entrepreneurial ecosystems: A complex adaptive systems approach. *Journal of Business Research, 86*(May), 1–10.

Shapiro, C., & Varian, H. R. (1999). Art of standard wars. *California Management Review, 41*(2), 8–32.

Sheremata, W. A. (2004). Competing through innovation in network markets: Strategies for challengers. *Academy of Management Review, 29*(3), 359–377.

Shin, S. R., Han, J. S., Kang, J., & Marhold, K. (2019). Do incumbent firms' technological M&As affect startup growth in the entrepreneurial ecosystem? *Proceedings of the Annual Meeting of the Academy of Management Proceedings,* 13617. Boston, MA, August 9–13, 2019. https://doi.org/10.5465/AMBPP.2019.13617abstract

Shipilov, A., Furr, N., & Studer Andersson, T. (2020, May 27). *Looking to boost innovation? Partner with a startup.* Harvard Business Review. https://hbr.org/2020/05/looking-to-boost-innovation-partner-with-a-startup

Shipilov, A., & Gawer, A. (2020). Integrating research on interorganizational networks and ecosystems. *Academy of Management Annals, 14*(1), 92–121.

Sieg, J. H., Wallin, M. W., & von Krogh, G. (2010). Managerial challenges in open innovation: A study of innovation intermediation in the chemical industry. *R&D Management, 40*(3), 281–291.

Singh, H., Lavie, D., & Lechner, C. (2007). The performance implications of timing of entry and involvement in multipartner alliances. *Academy of Management Journal, 50*(3), 578–604.

Siota, J., Prats, M. J., Fernandéz, D., & Pérez, T. (2020). *Open innovation: Improving your capability, deal flow, cost and speed with a corporate venturing ecosystem.* IESE Insight. https://media.iese.edu/research/pdfs/74686.pdf

Solarisbank. (n.d.). *Solarisbank.* https://www.solarisbank.com/en/ (accessed March 11, 2022).

Sopra Steria. (2022). *Scale up: For startups.* Steria: https://soprasteriascaleup.com/startups (accessed March 11, 2022).

Spigel, B., & Harrison, R. (2018). Toward a process theory of entrepreneurial ecosystems. *Strategic Entrepreneurship Journal, 12*(1), 151–168.

Squarespace. (n.d.). *Squarespace extensions.* https://www.squarespace.com/extensions/home (accessed March 11, 2022).

Stango, V. (2004). The economics of standards wars. *Review of Network Economics, 3*(1). https://doi.org/10.2202/1446-9022.1040

Star Alliance. (2022). *Connecting Partners.* https://www.staralliance.com/en/cp-overview (accessed March 11, 2022).

Tanguy, C., Lorenz, J.-T., Nandan, J., Sharma, S., & Waschto, A. (2018, January 10). *Insurance beyond digital: The rise of ecosystems and platforms.* McKinsey & Company. https://www.mckinsey.com/industries/financial-services/our-insights/insurance-beyond-digital-the-rise-of-ecosystems-and-platforms

Tavassoli, S., & Karlsson, C. (2015). Persistence of various types of innovation analyzed and explained. *Research Policy, 44*(10), 1887–1901.

Taylor, M., & Taylor, A. (2012). The technology life cycle: Conceptualization and managerial implications. *International Journal of Production Economics, 140*(1), 541–553.

Teece, D. J. (1986). Profiting from technological innovation: Implications for integration, collaboration, licensing and public policy. *Research Policy, 15*(6), 285–305.

Teece, D. J. (2018). Profiting from innovation in the digital economy: Enabling technologies, standards, and licensing models in the wireless world. *Research Policy, 47*(8), 1367–1387.

Theodoraki, C., Dana, L.-P., & Caputo, A. (2022). Building sustainable entrepreneurial ecosystems: A holistic approach. *Journal of Business Research, 140*(February), 346-360.

Thompson, T. A., Purdy, J. M., & Ventresca, M. J. (2018). How entrepreneurial ecosystems take form: Evidence from social impact initiatives in Seattle. *Strategic Entrepreneurship Journal, 12*(1), 96–116.

Tidd, J., & Bessant, J. R. (2018). *Managing innovation: Integrating technological, market and organizational change* (6th ed.). Hoboken, NJ: John Wiley & Sons.

Toh, P. K., & Miller, C. D. (2017). Pawn to save a chariot, or drawbridge into the fort? Firms' disclosure during standard setting and complementary technologies within ecosystems. *Strategic Management Journal, 38*(11), 2213–2236.

Vanhaverbeke, W., & Noorderhaven, N. G. (2001). Competition between alliance blocks: The case of the RISC microprocessor technology. *Organization Studies, 22*(1), 1–30.

Veit, P., Kramer, A., Kanbach, D., & Stubner, S. (2021). Revising the taxonomy of corporate accelerators: Moving towards an evolutionary perspective. *International Journal of Entrepreneurial Venturing, 13*(6), 568–599.

Visscher, K., Hahn, K., & Konrad, K. (2021). Innovation ecosystem strategies of industrial firms: A multilayered approach to alignment and strategic positioning. *Creativity and Innovation Management, 30*(3), 619–631.

von Hippel, E. (2005). Democratizing innovation: The evolving phenomenon of user innovation. *Journal für Betriebswirtschaft, 55*(1), 63–78.

Wang, R. D., & Miller, C. D. (2020). Complementors' engagement in an ecosystem: A study of publishers' e-book offerings on Amazon Kindle. *Strategic Management Journal, 41*(1), 3–26.

Wareham, J., Fox, P. B., & Cano Giner, J. L. (2014). Technology ecosystem governance. *Organization Science, 25*(4), 1195–1215.

Weiblen, T., & Chesbrough, H. W. (2015). Engaging with startups to enhance corporate innovation. *California Management Review, 57*(2), 66–90.

Wen, J., Qualls, W. J., & Zeng, D. (2020). Standardization alliance networks, standard-setting Influence, and new product outcomes. *Journal of Product Innovation Management, 37*(2), 138–157.

Wix. (2022). *Wix app market*. https://www.wix.com/app-market (accessed March 11, 2022).

Wright, M., Siegel, D. S., & Mustar, P. (2017). An emerging ecosystem for student start-ups. *The Journal of Technology Transfer, 42*(4), 909–922.

Y Combinator. (2020). *About Y Combinator*. https://www.ycombinator.com/about/ (accessed March 11, 2022).

Zott, C., Amit, R., & Massa, L. (2011). The business model: Recent developments and future research. *Journal of Management, 37*(4), 1019–1042.

CHAPTER 7

R&D COLLABORATION AND MULTIMARKET CONTACT

How Overlap and Asymmetry Influence Partner Selection

Ha Hoang

ABSTRACT

This study examines how interpartner cooperation can occur between firms who are also rivals in markets outside the alliance domain. Building on recent extensions of multimarket contact theory, I examine how R&D alliances are facilitated by competitive overlap and asymmetry at the partner selection stage. The study is set in the biopharmaceutical industry and competitive overlap and asymmetry are captured, respectively, by the extent to which potential partners' R&D projects are conducted in the same therapeutic markets and the difference in investment levels therein. By comparing realized alliances between 62 market entrants and 52 incumbents operating in 58 markets with counterfactual dyads involving the same entrants paired with non-allied incumbents, I find that: (1) overlap facilitates the partner selection process due to greater familiarity that reduces partner search costs; and (2) asymmetry decreases the perceived threat of competitive loss due to knowledge appropriation. Taken together, the effects of overlap and asymmetry suggest a pathway based on multimarket contact whereby firms identify and partner with new collaborators despite competitive tension.

Managing Interpartner Cooperation in Strategic Alliances, pp. 201–224
Copyright © 2022 by Information Age Publishing
www.infoagepub.com
201

INTRODUCTION

Research and development (R&D) alliances are inter-firm agreements focused on discovery and commercialization that can increase the likelihood of project success and speed up development times (Gulati, 1995; Hagedoorn, 1993, 2002). Such forms of interpartner cooperation can make participating firms stronger competitors (Chen, 2008; Chen & Miller, 2015; Gimeno, 2004; Klein, Semrau, Albers, & Zajac, 2020; Silverman & Baum, 2002; Singh & Mitchell, 2005) by increasing competitive pressure on non-allied firms (Chen, Su, & Tsai, 2007). While acknowledging their advantages, scholars have also made substantial inroads delineating the numerous challenges and tensions that may result in R&D collaborations falling short of their intended goals (Park & Ungson, 2001; Parmigiani & Rivera-Santos, 2011). In particular, firms face erosion of their competitive position due to unanticipated knowledge leakage or opportunistic transfer of valuable knowledge by a partner (Khanna, Gulati, & Nohria, 1998) which leaves the focal firm in a weak competitive position and undermines the value of subsequent collaborations (Larsson, Bengtsson, Henriksson, & Sparks, 1998). Preventing private benefits or gains that are not related to the stated objectives of the alliance is difficult because appropriated knowledge is leveraged beyond the scope of the alliance and involves tacit knowledge transfer (Samant & Kim, 2021; Yang, Zheng, & Zaheer, 2015).

Due to uncertainty and the potential for opportunism, there is a well-documented tendency to turn to prior partners across a broad array of inter-firm collaborations including R&D alliances (Gulati, 1998). However, scholars have noted that a continued reliance on past partners can affect subsequent gains caused by eventual limits to the novelty of the knowledge that is pooled and recombined (Hagedoorn & Frankort, 2008). This study examines an important pathway for identifying a new partner that occurs when firms "meet" due to R&D projects that competitively overlap in multiple markets.[1] For example, competitive overlap arises when two firms conduct separate R&D projects to find treatments for diabetes and angina and this may affect their decision to ally in a third domain. Multimarket contact is a common occurrence in R&D intensive industries (Snyder & Vonortas, 2005) but has not been investigated for its role in partner selection, a key stage of the alliance formation process.

This study builds on recent extensions of multimarket contact (MMC) theory that relate competitive overlap to greater accessibility of information and lower appropriation risk. I posit that competitive overlap raises awareness of a smaller subset of firms and increases familiarity regarding a partner's capabilities and future behavior that can lower search and evaluation costs. Greater overlap will thus increase the likelihood of two firms selecting each other as partners thus facilitating alliance formation.

Moreover, I consider the extent of asymmetry in their overlapping markets arising from differences in firms' investment levels and argue that greater asymmetry reduces the perceived risk of knowledge appropriation. By reducing appropriation concerns, asymmetry can enhance the motivation of both firms to form an R&D alliance. Taken together, the effect of R&D MMC overlap and asymmetry suggests a pathway whereby firms identify new collaborators despite competitive tension.

The empirical analysis to test these arguments focuses on R&D collaboration by firms in the U.S. biopharmaceutical industry over the 2000–2009 time period. I compare the allying firms (62 entrants and 52 incumbents) to counterfactual dyads that consist of the entrants and all remaining active non-allied incumbents in the market. I leverage detailed R&D project data of 3,102 incumbents operating in 58 markets which allows for controls at the firm, dyad, and market levels. After accounting for a variety of factors, I find support for the impact of overlap and asymmetry. The chapter concludes with a discussion of how this work extends research on the interplay of competitive and cooperative dynamics, alliance formation and implications of multimarket competition in contexts of high uncertainty.

THEORY AND HYPOTHESIS DEVELOPMENT

Research focused on the interplay of competitive and cooperative dynamics has yielded insights on the strategic benefits of alliances. Cooperation can enhance a firm's competitive potency by accessing resources of its partner while placing non-allied rivals at a disadvantage (Park & Zhou, 2005) and at risk of higher failure rates (Silverman & Baum, 2002). In the case of R&D alliances, the destabilizing effects on rivals arise when collaboration leads to increases in innovative activity and pace of new product introductions thereby broadening a firm's repertoire and frequency of competitive actions (Andrevski, Brass, & Ferrier, 2016; Eisenhardt & Martin, 2000; Mitchell & Singh, 1993).

This dynamic can also be observed in collaborations that are formed between market entrant and incumbent (Singh & Mitchell, 2005) because they increase competitive pressure on rivals in the market. Empirical work in this research stream has highlighted a further set of strategic conditions that stimulate collaborative entry which is the empirical context for this study (Jensen, 2008; Mitchell & Singh, 1996; Singh & Mitchell, 2005). Based on the duration of its market presence and extent of its investments, an incumbent can provide valuable experience and supporting assets which increase its attractiveness as a potential partner. The entrant lacks operating experience in the focal market by definition but holds new technology or knowledge that the market incumbent lacks (Haveman, 1993; Srinivasan,

Haunschild, & Grewal, 2007). Recent work has highlighted that entrants must overcome additional challenges to collaborating which arise from their greater need to preempt similar rivals (Morreale, Robba, Nigra, & Roma, 2017). This can lead an entrant to offer favorable alliance terms so that the incumbent is inclined to start a cooperation.

Despite these insights, we have yet to fully understand how firms overcome uncertainty which is particularly acute for entrants due to their lack of operating history compared to the market incumbents who are already present in the market. This raises the concern that an entrant may bring poor quality projects for collaboration which can divert resources from an incumbent's own projects (Danzon, Nicholson, & Pereira, 2005). R&D collaboration, owing to their knowledge-intensive nature, also give rise to a threat of knowledge leakage or opportunistic appropriation (Gulati & Singh, 1998; Oxley, 1997) which contributes to differential value capture by the partners (Lavie, 2006). The concern that knowledge appropriation will weaken a firm's competitive position is particularly acute when R&D alliances are formed between competitors (Dussauge, Garrette, & Mitchell, 2000; Oxley & Sampson, 2004). As a result, R&D collaboration requires reducing uncertainty surrounding partner behavior and capability assessments by engaging in extensive information gathering and systematic evaluation.

Prior work suggests that geographic proximity can decrease the costs of evaluating a new partner's resources and capabilities (Reuer & Lahiri, 2014; Ryu, McCann, & Reuer, 2018). In addition, scholars have noted that cues arising from knowledge spillovers can raise a firm's awareness of potential partners which narrow and focus the search process (Rosenkopf & Padula, 2008). Phene and Tallman (2014) for example find that firms can identify new partners by observing who builds on their knowledge and are motivated to form collaborations in order to learn and to control the direction of technology development. However, the extent of firms' patents in the area of the knowledge spillover was found to negatively impact the decision to collaborate, suggesting concerns of knowledge appropriation. Because research to date does not account directly for contact that arises from R&D project overlap, additional insight can be gained by exploring how the partner selection process accommodates appropriation concerns particularly between new partners. Recent extensions of multimarket contact theory suggest that overlapping R&D positions may facilitate cooperation.

Extending MMC Theory to R&D Collaboration

Researchers in the multimarket contact stream of literature analyze competitive dynamics that ensue among firms that encounter each other across multiple product markets (Bernheim & Whinston, 1990; Jayachandran, Gimeno, & Varadarajan, 1999). A basic tenet underlying this work is that a high level of multimarket competition leads firms to recognize their interdependencies and hence lowers the probability of their engagement in intense competition as captured by market share (Chuang, Dahlin, Thomson, Lai, & Yang, 2018), profits (Hughes & Oughton, 1993; Scott, 1991) and prices (Evans & Kessides, 1994; Kang, Bayus, & Balasubramanian, 2010). For two multimarket firms, a competitive action by one firm in one product market may meet with a retaliatory action in the other remaining markets where the firms meet. The related literature stream of competitive dynamics (Chen, 1996; Upson, Ketchen, Connelly, & Ranft, 2012), similarly asserts that greater market contact resulting from market entry increases information flows that lead to a greater understanding of competitors' likely reactions (Chen et al., 2007; Stephan, Murmann, Boeker, & Goodstein, 2003). Either due to the recognition of interdependence or due to familiarity, MMC serves as a basis for mutual forbearance or reduction of competitive tensions which has been found to influence firm's market entry behavior (Jayachandran et al., 1999).

A small number of studies have subsequently examined the link between alliance activity and MMC. Chuang et al. (2018) examined how the extent of a firm's alliance activity can enhance the benefits of MMC by: (1) increasing its access to resources which can increase the potency of retaliation, and (2) dampen the impact of others' aggressive actions. Related studies have linked multimarket overlap to alliance formation (Amir, Lavie, & Hashai, 2019) and technology partner selection (Ryu, Reuer, & Brush, 2020). They confirm how firms operating in multiple markets can decrease the risk that competitive behaviors within an alliance would overwhelm the gains from cooperation.

Of the few studies that examine R&D overlap, early research explored how interdependencies that arise through participation in multiple R&D consortia could lead to mutual forbearance between collaborating firms (Vonortas, 2000). However, recent work by Anand, Mesquita, and Vassolo (2009) examining R&D overlap in the biopharmaceutical industry emphasized the uncertainty of the R&D process and the inability to accurately predict the outcomes of retaliatory actions. They argued instead for the role of overlap in increasing familiarity with the actions of a subset of firms and facilitating the imitation of strategic actions. Consistent with this view, they found that firms enter the markets of competitors with whom they overlap and are less likely to exit those markets.

Because conditions of uncertainty and lack of information also surround the decision to engage in collaborative R&D, I argue that competitive overlap in R&D projects can act as a cue that narrows an entrant firm's attention to a subset of incumbents who may be potential partners. As has been noted in the MMC literature (Boeker, Goodstein, Stephan, & Murmann, 1997), market overlap yields a "database of competitive intelligence" (Stephan, Murmann, Boeker, & Goodstein, 2003) on overlapping firms' competitive behaviors which can influence decision-making. Supported by information available in commercial databases, industry and academic conferences and publications, overlapping firms are well-placed to appraise each other's project portfolios. This familiarity can reduce the costs associated with partner evaluation and assessment of joint gains when deciding to collaborate in a R&D market (Reuer, Zollo, & Singh, 2002).

> **Hypothesis 1:** *The likelihood of an R&D alliance between an entrant and an incumbent increase as R&D MMC overlap increases between them.*

Role of Asymmetry

My arguments thus far have assumed that firms have similar positions in the markets where they overlap and that they view each market to be of similar strategic importance. However, multimarket rivals that meet across product markets can hold dominant positions in a few markets (Gimeno, 1999; Jayachandran et al., 1999; Upson et al., 2012) which give rise to spheres of influence. Indeed, an incumbent that invests to a greater extent and thus holds valuable experience and complementary resources will be a more attractive partner to an entrant considering collaboration.

The distinction between footholds and spheres of influence in the product MMC literature implies that firms may also hold different positions across their overlapping R&D markets. These positions emerge from firm-specific choices including project initiation and continuance and are due to underlying heterogeneity in firm resources and capabilities as noted in the resource-based view (Barney, 1991; Helfat, 1994; Lavie, 2006; Mahoney & Pandian, 1992) and due to characteristics of the decision-makers involved in R&D investments (Daellenbach, McCarthy, & Schoenecker, 1999; Ener, 2019).

In the biopharmaceutical industry such differences can be observed in the high share of R&D projects relative to its overall portfolio that are conducted in certain therapeutic areas. It entails knowledge and resource sharing across multiple projects and supporting coordination and multi-project portfolio management capabilities (Biedenbach, 2011). A high proportion of projects focused on a therapeutic area represents a firm's significant commitment to develop and commercialize new products in that domain. Significant investments are likely to receive more attention and will weigh more heavily in perceived competitive gains or losses that arise from alliance knowledge appropriation.

Defined as the difference in investment levels that firms make in their overlapping markets, R&D MMC asymmetry is the situation that can influence partner selection by bolstering potential partners' assessments that they hold strategically compatible positions. Figure 7.1 provides illustrative depictions of high (low) levels of asymmetry that are driven by large (small) differences between partners' investments in the markets where they overlap. When there is high asymmetry, the consequences of knowledge appropriation are assessed differently between the firm and its partner (Chen, 1996). In the overlapping markets, the possible transfer of alliance knowledge to projects in the areas that constitutes an entrant's sphere of influence will be viewed by the incumbent partner who holds a foothold in those areas as less strategically damaging because it is less invested in those domains. This implies that the partner's investments are weighted toward non-overlapping areas which further emphasizes differences in resource endowments and capabilities between them. Competitive tension is further reduced because of lower prospects that they will compete vigorously in the same downstream product markets (Markman, Gianiodis, & Phan, 2009).

Asymmetry in investment levels in overlapping markets can thus increase the motivation of rivals to seek a cooperative tie by reducing concerns of competitive loss due to knowledge appropriation. In contrast, when investment levels are comparable for firm and partner, they are

Figure 7.1

Illustrative High and Low R&D Asymmetry

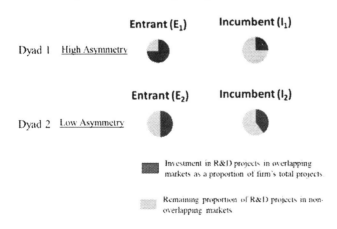

strategically similar which can heighten concern that competition for key factor resources will spill over to the collaboration (Shipilov, 2009; Yang, Zheng, & Zaheer, 2015).

In support of the view that appropriation can have significant performance consequences, scholars conducting event studies of alliance announcements have linked differential abnormal stock market returns to stronger learning and knowledge transfer abilities (Kumar, 2010; Yang et al., 2015). These studies, however, are not able to differentiate the extent to which gains are due to greater capture of common benefits generated from the alliance, private benefits that arise from knowledge appropriation or both. The construct of R&D MMC asymmetry accounts for firms' positions in the overlapping markets which are directly implicated in generating private benefits. This focus on asymmetry suggests the following:

Hypothesis 2: *Greater R&D MMC asymmetry between an entrant and an incumbent increases the likelihood of R&D alliance formation.*

METHOD

Data and Sample

The empirical setting is the global biopharmaceutical industry. Biopharmaceutical firms make concurrent R&D investments in multiple markets and face stringent reporting requirements which renders this setting appropriate for empirical investigation of R&D MMC. In this study, I use data on R&D projects carried out by biopharmaceutical firms that develop and commercialize new human therapeutic products. A typical R&D project cycle in this industry starts with early-stage preclinical research, followed by successive phases of clinical trials which are reported due to regulatory requirements. If successful in these previous stages, approval is sought from the US Food and Drug Administration (FDA) to market and sell the drug.

The main data source is IMS Lifecycle©, a commercially available database that maintains comprehensive information on R&D projects and their development progress carried out by organizations in the biopharmaceutical industry. Details of each project enable the identification of market entrants and incumbents. I also accessed Compustat (NA and Global) and CapitalIQ databases to obtain data on R&D intensity and the disambiguated Harvard patent database for patent information (Li, Lai, D'Amour, Doolin, Sun, Torvik, Yu, & Fleming, 2014).

I identified R&D alliance formation between a market entrant and active firms already present in the market from 2000 to 2009. Using Compustat, I retained those market entrants that were publicly listed in order to gather important firm-level control variables. Whenever a firm initiated its first R&D project in a market, I recorded that event as the firm's entry into that specific market for the first time for the first-stage model. I next identified and collected information on the market incumbents that had collaborated with an entrant. There are 62 market entrants and 52 market incumbents who formed 135 R&D alliances across 58 markets over the 2000–2009 time period.

In addition to realized alliances between market entrants and incumbent, the dataset includes counterfactual partner dyads that did not ally (Sorenson & Stuart, 2008; Zhelyazkov & Gulati, 2016). Using the IMS database, I paired each market entrant with the pool of potential incumbent partners consisting of all non-allied, for-profit firms active in the focal market within a five-year window including the focal year. This raised the number of market incumbents to a total of 3,102 which included both private and publicly traded firms. Including the counterfactual dyads resulted in a total of 110,775 dyads.

Dependent Variable

The dependent variable is a binary variable coded as "1" when an R&D alliance is observed between entrant and incumbent within a focal therapeutic market and "0" otherwise.

Independent Variables

The first independent variable is "R&D MMC Overlap" and builds on the count of markets where the firm dyads have overlapping ongoing R&D projects at t-1. Half of the dyads have at least one market in which they overlap. Following prior work (Baum & Korn, 1996; Fuentelsaz & Gomez, 2006), I then divided the number of common markets by the total number of markets in which both firms in the dyad are active. I further mean centered this variable to facilitate a robustness check.

The second predictor of market incumbent-entrant R&D alliance formation is "R&D MMC Asymmetry." I compute the variable as follows:

$$\text{R\&D MMC Asymmetry}_{ij} = \sum_{N=1}^{n} (P_{Ni}/P_i) - \sum_{N=1}^{n} (P_{Nj}/P_j)$$

N represents the set of overlapping markets where both the market entrant and the incumbent have ongoing R&D projects in t-1. P_{Ni} and P_{Nj}

are the counts of ongoing R&D projects in an overlapping market for an entrant and an incumbent, respectively, in t-1. P_i and P_j represent the total number of ongoing R&D projects in the entrant and the incumbent's R&D portfolio, respectively, in t-1. This measure captures the differential levels of R&D investments for each entrant-incumbent dyad in their overlapping markets (Baum & Korn, 1999). I posited that growing asymmetry in R&D investment will increase the likelihood of R&D alliance formation (H2).

Control Variables

Among the entrant-incumbent pairs, some firms have engaged in prior ties hence 'Prior Collaborations' is operationalized as a count of prior ties (in any market) between an entrant and market incumbent. Among the collaborative entry events, 16 percent were preceded by a prior collaboration. To assess the extent to which the alliance will generate more common benefits which can influence alliance formation, I captured relevant dimensions of entrant and incumbent quality that can contribute to collaboration success (Cummings & Holmberg, 2012). All measures are captured for incumbents in the realized and counterfactual cases and are lagged by one year. Potential contributions by the incumbent are based on its focal market investment; "Incumbent Focal Market Investment" is measured as the proportion of ongoing R&D projects that the incumbent has in the therapeutic domain of the alliance divided by the total number of active R&D projects in its portfolio. By definition, entrants in the sample have no other projects in the focal market. Poor commercialization capabilities may also limit alliance benefits (Higgins & Rodriguez, 2006). I thus measured the cumulative count of the incumbent's failed R&D projects in the focal market ("Incumbent Cumulative R&D Failures in Focal Market").

Entrants that invest more in R&D are more likely to contribute to knowledge development in the alliance. Using Compustat, I included a measure of the R&D expense of the entrant as a percentage of its revenue ("Entrant R&D Intensity"). I also captured the stock of patents assigned to a focal entrant ("Entrant Patents"). I accounted for entrant age calculated as the difference between the founding year of the entrant firm and the current year ("Entrant Age").

A firm's relative bargaining power is likely to inform the partnership decision (Adegbesan & Higgins, 2011). Firms with greater R&D scale and those who hold large alliance portfolios would be better positioned to appropriate value from the alliance and the common benefits that are generated compared to smaller firms (Lavie, 2007). Because these measures are highly correlated, I summed the total number of ongoing R&D projects and the total number of ongoing R&D alliances in time t-1 to form a portfolio size measure. In the sample, the average portfolio size of an entrant was 9 and 6 respectively while that of an incumbent was 6 and 4 respectively. "Entrant Portfolio Size" and "Incumbent Portfolio Size" are entered separately and as a multiplicative interaction term ("Entrant Portfolio Size X Incumbent Portfolio Size").

Because incumbents with greater development experience may be more likely to be selected as R&D alliance partners (Diestre & Rajagopalan, 2012), I counted the number of marketed drugs that the incumbent has in the focal market ("Incumbent Marketed Drugs in Focal Market") and in its remaining markets ("Incumbent Marketed Drugs in Remaining Markets"). As none of the entrants in the sample had marketed drugs during the time period of this study, I could not create a similar variable for the entrants.

The degree of technological overlap between a market entrant and incumbent could affect alliance gains (Mowery, Oxley, & Silverman, 1998) so I took information sourced by IMS from patents, research publications, and interviews regarding the technological processes that both firms are capable of using to produce a drug in the early, discovery phase (e.g., chemical synthesis and fermentation). "Technological Overlap" is a count of the processes that the market entrant and the incumbent had in common. The final firm dyad control, "Count Shared Partners" is a count of the shared R&D collaborators between entrant and incumbent and assesses the extent of indirect ties between them (Gulati & Gargiulo, 1999).

There may also be systematic differences across markets that can affect the extent to which firms will enter a focal market via alliance (Ang, 2008; Haveman & Nonnemaker, 2000). In particular, due to prior failures in R&D efforts that may motivate risk sharing via inter-firm collaborations, I controlled for the number of prior collaborative first entries as a proportion of total number of first entries in the focal market ("Proportion Collaborative First Entries"). Finally, unobserved market characteristics may facilitate market entrant-incumbent R&D alliance formation. I account for this by creating five R&D Market Dummies for markets that witnessed a greater number of entrant-incumbent alliances.

Analytical Approach

I ran a first-stage Heckman maximum-likelihood probit selection model to account for market entry (Heckman, 1979). The dataset for analyses consisted of 62 new entrants and 189 markets for the 2000–2009 period. The model incorporated R&D MMC at the market level (Anand et al., 2009) as the main predictor of new market entry. To account for the likelihood that firms might enter the markets of their prior collaborators, I created a variable for prior collaboration with market incumbents, measured as the count of prior ties (in any market) with each of the market incumbents divided by the total number of active incumbents in the market. I also controlled for a firm's prior entry experience, age, R&D portfolio size, patent count, and R&D expenses. At the market level, I controlled for the intensity of competition by assessing market density and attractiveness (cumulative project failures, cumulative new entries: solo and collaborative). I also accounted for unobserved time effects by using year dummies. I used the estimated Inverse Mills Ratio from this first-stage regression as a control in the second-stage regressions to account for endogeneity of market entry and partner selection.

In light of the low incidence rate of realized alliances, I used a rare event logit model (King & Zeng, 2001) to derive the estimates. This estimation procedure has been used extensively in prior studies of alliance formation (Sorenson & Stuart, 2001; Zhelyazkov & Gulati, 2016). As the dataset is dyadic, I also face the issue of non-independence of the dyads. Any firm within a dyad could potentially appear in multiple other dyads giving rise to incorrect standard errors. To account for this problem, I estimated the standard errors clustered on both firms of a dyad using *clus_nway* (Cameron, Gelbach, & Miller, 2011; Kleinbaum, Stuart, & Tushman, 2013).

RESULTS

Table 7.1 and Table 7.2 provide the bivariate correlations and descriptive statistics respectively for the sample. To assess multicollinearity, I calculated the mean VIF for the full model and obtained 2.64, which is well below the recommended threshold of 10 (Neter, Wasserman, & Kutner, 1989).

Table 7.3 reports the results of the regression analysis that predict collaborative R&D entry between a market entrant and incumbent in a focal therapeutic area. Model 1 represents the baseline model with control variables. Models 2 and 3 test the effect of R&D MMC overlap (Hypothesis 1) and asymmetry (Hypothesis 2) on collaborative R&D. Model 4 is the full model and includes effects of both R&D MMC overlap and asymmetry.

The baseline results show that incumbent investment in the focal market has a positive impact on being selected as a partner by increasing the alliance common benefits (Model 1: $\beta = 1.246$, $p < 0.001$). I additionally find a positive and significant effect of prior R&D collaborations (Model 1: $\beta = 0.510$, $p < 0.01$) which is consistent with prior work (Gulati, 1995). Incumbent portfolio size has a positive and statistically significant effect on market entrant-incumbent R&D alliance formation (Model 1: $\beta = 0.018$, $p < 0.001$). Dyad technological overlap is also significant ($p < 0.001$ across all models) and suggests that technological overlap increases the common benefits in R&D alliances (Lane & Lubatkin, 1998). Having a greater

Table 7.1

Bivariate Correlations

Variables	(1)	(2)	(3)	(4)	(5)	(6)	(7)	(8)	(9)	(10)	(11)	(12)	(13)	(14)
(1) RD MMC Overlap	1.000													
(2) RD MMC Asymmetry	−0.142	1.000												
(3) Prior Collaborations	0.078	0.043	1.000											
(4) Incumbent Focal Market Investment	−0.137	0.057	−0.014	1.000										
(5) Incumbent Cumulative RD Failures in Focal Market	0.022	0.122	0.043	0.087	1.000									
(6) Entrant RD Intensity	0.034	−0.262	0.056	−0.063	−0.019	1.000								
(7) Entrant Age	0.042	−0.088	0.035	−0.040	−0.026	0.297	1.000							
(8) Entrant Patents	0.025	−0.130	0.038	−0.045	−0.014	0.362	0.491	1.000						
(9) Entrant Portfolio Size	0.104	−0.421	0.073	−0.124	−0.033	0.702	0.442	0.426	1.000					
(10) Incumbent Portfolio Size	0.131	0.296	0.237	−0.065	0.248	−0.004	0.010	0.010	0.001	1.000				
(11) Incumbent Marketed Drugs in Focal Market	0.068	0.194	0.167	−0.017	0.190	0.003	0.014	0.002	0.004	0.733	1.000			
(12) Incumbent Marketed Drugs in Remaining Markets	0.049	0.174	0.188	−0.027	0.162	−0.001	0.010	0.002	−0.001	0.806	0.857	1.000		
(13) Technological Overlap	0.271	0.021	0.178	−0.073	0.123	0.250	0.198	0.136	0.411	0.375	0.246	0.196	1.000	
(14) Count Shared Partners	0.207	0.091	0.286	−0.055	0.104	0.226	0.100	0.089	0.264	0.454	0.332	0.313	0.485	1.000
(15) Proportion Collaborative First Entries	0.025	−0.014	0.003	−0.057	−0.019	0.094	0.090	0.190	0.088	−0.012	−0.028	−0.016	0.021	0.012

Note: All $|r| > 0.005$ is significant at $p < 0.01$.

Table 7.2

Descriptive Statistics

Variable	Mean	Std. Dev.	Min	Max
(1) RD MMC Overlap	0	0.108	–.073	2.927
(2) RD MMC Asymmetry	–0.123	0.484	–6.706	2.622
(3) Prior Collaborations	0.008	0.153	0	12
(4) Incumbent Focal Market Investment	0.108	0.266	0	1
(5) Incumbent Cumulative RD Failures in Focal Market	0.057	0.343	0	13
(6) Entrant RD Intensity	166.033	294.102	.313	2314
(7) Entrant Age	6.322	6.646	0	26
(8) Entrant Patents	6.314	12.755	0	94
(9) Entrant Portfolio Size	16.385	19.579	0	96
(10) Incumbent Portfolio Size	10.257	27.457	0	453
(11) Incumbent Marketed Drugs in Focal Market	0.311	1.568	0	48
(12) Incumbent Marketed Drugs in Remaining Markets	1.016	7.766	0	224
(13) Technological Overlap	0.693	1.009	0	9
(14) Count Shared Partners	0.215	0.835	0	26
(15) Proportion Collaborative First Entries	0.503	0.158	0	1

number of marketed drugs in the focal market increases an incumbent's likelihood of collaborating with a market entrant (Model 1: $\beta = 0.159$, $p < 0.001$) but having more products in its remaining markets decreases this probability (Model 1: $\beta = -0.037$, $p < 0.05$).

Model 2 in Table 7.3 tests Hypothesis 1 by examining the effect of R&D MMC overlap between an entrant and incumbent on their likelihood of forming an R&D alliance. The co-efficient of R&D MMC is positive and significant (Model 2: $\beta = 2.196$, $p < 0.001$).

Model 3 shows that R&D MMC asymmetry (Hypothesis 2) is positive and significant (Model 3: $\beta = 0.701$, $p < 0.01$). The result indicates that collaboration is more likely when the entrant has a greater investment compared to that of the incumbent in their overlapping markets.

The results of Model 4 confirm that both factors remain statistically significant after accounting for firm, firm-dyad, and market-level control variables. However, high levels of statistical significance do not necessarily imply a high effect magnitude. To assess effect size, I find that a one

Table 7.3

Rare Event Logit Model Predicting the Likelihood of R&D Alliance Formation

	Model 1	Model 2	Model 3	Model 4
R&D MMC Overlap		2.196 ***		2.333 **
		(0.517)		(0.512)
R&D MMC Asymmetry			0.701 **	0.715 ***
			(0.241)	(0.237)
Prior Collaborations	0.510 **	0.498 **	0.518 **	0.507 ***
	(0.172)	(0.169)	(0.183)	(0.180)
Incumbent Focal Market Investment	1.246 ***	1.391 ***	1.322 ***	1.488 **
	(0.334)	(0.342)	(0.336)	(0.349)
Incumbent Cumulative R&D Failures in Focal Market	0.127	0.127	0.138	0.136
	(0.120)	(0.120)	(0.110)	(0.110)
Entrant R&D Intensity	0.000	0.000	0.000	0.000
	(0.001)	(0.001)	(0.001)	(0.001)
Entrant Age	0.015	0.019	0.014	0.018
	(0.024)	(0.023)	(0.025)	(0.024)
Entrant Patents	-0.008	-0.007	-0.006	-0.005
	(0.014)	(0.014)	(0.013)	(0.013)
Entrant Portfolio Size	-0.027 *	-0.029 *	-0.017	-0.019
	(0.012)	(0.013)	(0.013)	(0.014)
Incumbent Portfolio Size	0.018 ***	0.018 ***	0.016 ***	0.016 **
	(0.005)	(0.004)	(0.004)	(0.004)
Entrant Portfolio Size X Incumbent Portfolio Size	0.000	0.000	0.000	0.000
	(0.00)	(0.00)	(0.00)	(0.00)
Incumbent Marketed Drugs in Focal Market	0.159 ***	0.160 ***	0.149 ***	0.151 **
	(0.038)	(0.037)	(0.037)	(0.036)
Incumbent Marketed Drugs in Remaining Markets	-0.037 *	-0.037 *	-0.032 *	-0.033 *
	(0.015)	(0.015)	(0.014)	(0.014)
Technological Overlap	0.474 ***	0.436 ***	0.409 ***	0.365 **
	(0.078)	(0.080)	(0.074)	(0.075)
Count Shared Partners	0.075 *	0.065 *	0.073	0.065
	(0.033)	(0.033)	(0.038)	(0.075)
Proportion Collaborative First Entries	0.442	0.457	0.198	0.222
	(0.300)	(0.312)	(0.248)	(0.253)
R&D Market Dummies	YES	YES	YES	YES
Inverse Mills Ratio	YES	YES	YES	YES
Constant	-7.717	-7.840	-7.628	-7.966
	(0.243)	(0.251)	(0.234)	(0.240)

Note. N=10775. Standard errors are in parentheses.
*p<.05, **p<.01, ***p<.001; Significance levels based on two-tailed tests.

standard deviation increase in R&D MMC overlap increases the likelihood of R&D alliance formation by 24% when all control variables are evaluated at their means and there are no prior ties. Results also indicate that the likelihood of R&D alliance formation increases by 41% with a one standard deviation increase in R&D MMC asymmetry and no prior ties. The results further confirm the importance of prior ties on the likelihood of alliance formation: an entrant-incumbent with one prior tie is 68% more likely to engage in collaborative R&D than a dyad with no ties. While the effect sizes of overlap and asymmetry are smaller in comparison, it is an important pathway for identifying new partners despite competitive tension. Moreover, for firms poorly embedded in the alliance network such as new ventures, overlap and asymmetry can play an important role in facilitating collaboration.

Robustness Checks

A possible curvilinear impact of MMC overlap which has been examined in prior studies (Amir et al., 2019) may alter the interpretation of the main effects. I find the results are robust to including a market overlap squared term which itself was not statistically significant. Due to the definition of market incumbent when creating the counterfactual dyads, I have dyads with no overlapping markets which may be confounded with dyads holding the same level of investment as they both lead to an attribution of symmetry. To examine whether this affects the results, I generated a sample consisting of entrant-incumbent dyads with at least one shared market and found that the effect of asymmetry remained positive and significant.

Some scholars have noted that a large number of counterfactual dyads may contribute little information to the analysis and suggest selecting a random subsample of counterfactual dyads at a fixed ratio to the number of realized dyads to confirm the main results (King & Zeng, 2001; Wang & Zajac, 2007). I followed this procedure using a ratio of 1 realized dyad to 10 unrealized dyads. I find that the results are similar to those reported with both overlap and asymmetry remaining statistically significant.

DISCUSSION

This study examines how collaboration is facilitated at the partner selection stage by overlap and asymmetry. Comparing characteristics of observed and counterfactual alliances between entrants and incumbents in the biopharmaceutical industry, I find that overlap facilitates partner selection by increasing familiarity with a smaller subset of firms. I also find that firm dyads characterized by high asymmetry are more likely to enter into an alliance, suggesting compatible strategic positions within overlapping markets may help to reduce knowledge appropriation concerns. The findings are also notable because I draw on an extensive literature on R&D alliance formation to include important control variables that capture alliance benefits and bargaining power in the models as well as the occurrence of prior ties.

Echoing calls for greater theoretical integration of competitive-cooperative relations in order to understand their interplay (Chen, 2008; Hoffman, Lavie, Reuer, & Shipilov, 2018), this study drew on concepts from both the MMC and alliance literature to better understand how partner selection may allow firms to reduce uncertainty without incurring high search and evaluation costs. As the R&D context does not allow for a clear retaliation threat that will predictably affect a firm's performance or profits, I built on recent extensions of multimarket contact theory that emphasize familiarity and uncertainty reduction (Anand, Mesquita, & Vassolo, 2009; Hsieh & Vermeulen, 2013; Kalnins, 2004; Markman et al., 2009). While confirming the importance of prior ties on alliance formation, I nevertheless find an important role of overlap and asymmetry in explaining how new R&D partnerships are formed. Furthermore, this study's focus on R&D collaboration extends the MMC literature's narrow view of market entry solely as a precursor to product-market overlap and rivalrous behavior (Yu & Cannella, 2013).

The findings of this study contribute to the literature on alliances which has traditionally been concerned with the drivers of alliance benefits or joint value creation but has become increasingly focused on understanding the determinants of opportunism and value appropriation (Das & Rahman, 2010). The concept of asymmetry is particularly germane to the discussion but it has typically been captured by firm size and age differences, in part because such data are readily observable. By attending to firms' differential investment in overlapping markets, I further specify a source of asymmetry that is implicated in value appropriation due to opportunistic knowledge transfer. Using detailed R&D data, I demonstrated how asymmetric R&D market positions are an important factor in partner selection and facilitate collaboration.

The findings are significant for their managerial implications because they address the important issue of how firms anticipate and mitigate key challenges to R&D collaboration as early as the partner selection process. The results suggest that managers can limit R&D partner search and evaluation costs by recognizing that market overlap may engender greater familiarity which can increase alliance opportunities, particularly for firms such as new ventures that are poorly embedded in the alliance network. Finally, a partner selection process could usefully include asymmetric market contact which can reduce competitive concerns and lead to identification of a feasible set of partners.

Limitations and Future Research

A limitation of this work is that it is a single industry study which limits variation in technological and product development conditions that may yield boundary conditions for the effect of R&D overlap and asymmetry. Notably, the biopharmaceutical industry has high R&D project failure rates which is due in part to incomplete understanding of the complex biological mechanisms that underlie many human diseases (Bains, 2004). This suggests that examining collaboration in other industry contexts could be useful to capture a broader range of conditions and thus address the generalizability of the results.

This work also does not account for product market overlap as none of the market entrants in the sample had downstream products. It is therefore useful to extend this research to account for the role of product MMC (Anand et al., 2009; Vonortas, 2000). This will allow us to understand how shared product market presence influences partner selection and to examine its impact on R&D alliance formation. Such an endeavor would improve our understanding of how competitive interactions in product markets influence R&D collaboration and thus how competitive and cooperative actions are linked across the value chain.

Because this work is focused on the partner selection stage and leverages secondary data, future process-oriented work is needed to examine how partners balance competition and cooperation over the lifecycle of R&D collaboration. Such work could yield important insights on how MMC dynamics influence other firm behaviors and outcomes. Because of similarities across corporate-level activities, for example, alliances may yield fungible experience that facilitates the execution of more integrative resource combination via merger and acquisition. Hence, it would be interesting to examine how collaboration facilitates subsequent M&A activity which has the effect of foreclosing rivals' partnership opportunities (Wang & Zajac, 2007).

NOTE

1. Strict regulatory disclosure rules allow for mapping of biopharmaceutical firm projects to specific R&D markets and allows for the identification of market entrants and incumbents. R&D markets in this context are defined by stakeholders including regulatory agencies and industry associations to encompass distinct classes of therapeutics that are intended to target specific disease conditions (e.g., diabetes). They reflect closely the downstream markets that yield revenues from product sales. This study defines markets at the ATC 3rd level which includes categories such as Human Insulin and Analogues (A10C) and Anti-ulcerants (A2B). In contrast to higher levels of therapeutic classification (such as ATC 1st level "Alimentary tract and Metabolism" which aggregate many diverse treatments, the level of granularity chosen is meaningful to participants and regulators.

ACKNOWLEDGEMENTS

I received helpful comments and suggestions on this work from Hakan Ener, Joanne Oxley, Javier Gimeno, Freek Vermeulen, Densia Mindruta, Kai-Yu Hsieh, Adam M. Kleinbaum, Pavel Zhelyazkov, Elisa Operti, Matthias Tröbinger, Himanshu Bhatt, and Marco Galo as well as seminar participants at Imperial College London and MTEC-ETH Zurich. Invaluable research support was provided by Archita Sarmah.

REFERENCES

Adegbesan, J. A., & Higgins, M. J. (2011). The intra-alliance division of value created through collaboration. *Strategic Management Journal, 32*, 187–211.

Amir, Y., Lavie, D., & Hashai, N. (2019). Multimarket competition and alliance formation. In F. J. Contractor & J. J. Reuer (Eds.), *Advancing the frontiers of alliance research* (pp. 305–321). Cambridge, UK: Cambridge University Press.

Anand, J., Mesquita, L. F., & Vassolo, R. S. (2009). The dynamics of multimarket competition in exploration and exploitation activities. *Academy of Management Journal, 52*, 802–821.

Andrevski, G., Brass, D. J., & Ferrier, W. J. (2016). Alliance portfolio configurations and competitive action frequency. *Journal of Management, 42*(4), 811–837.

Ang, S. H. (2008). Competitive intensity and collaboration: Impact on firm growth across technological environments. *Strategic Management Journal, 29*, 1057–1075.

Bains, W. (2004). Failure rates in drug discovery and development—Will I ever get any better? *Drug Discovery World, 5*, 9–19.

Barney, J. (1991). Firm resources and sustained competitive advantage. *Journal of Management, 17*, 99–120.

Baum, J. A. C., & Korn, H. J. (1996). Competitive dynamics of interfirm rivalry. *Academy of Management Journal, 39*, 255–291.

Baum, J. A. C., & Korn, H. J. (1999). Dynamics of dyadic competitive interaction. *Strategic Management Journal, 20*, 251–278.

Biedenbach, T. (2011). The power of combinative capabilities: Facilitating the outcome of frequent innovation in pharmaceutical R&D projects. *Project Management Journal, 42*, 63–80.

Bernheim, B. D., & Whinston, M. D. (1990). Multimarket contact and collusive behavior. *RAND Journal of Economics, 21*, 1–26.

Boeker, W., Goodstein, J., Stephan, J., & Murmann, J. P. (1997). Competition in a multimarket environment: The case of market exit. *Organization Science, 8*, 126–142.

Cameron, C. A., Gelbach, J. B., & Miller, D. L. (2011). Robust Inference with Multiway Clustering. *Journal of Business and Economic Statistics, 29*, 238–249.

Chen, M. J. (1996). Competitor analysis and interfirm rivalry: Toward a theoretical integration. *Academy of Management Review, 21*, 100–134.

Chen, M. J. (2008). Reconceptualizing the competition-cooperation relationship: A transparadox perspective. *Journal of Management Inquiry, 17*, 288–304.

Chen, M. J., & Miller, D. (2015). Reconceptualizing competitive dynamics: A multidimensional framework. *Strategic Management Journal, 36*, 758–775.

Chen, M. J., Su, K. H., & Tsai, W. (2007). Competitive tension: The awareness-motivation-capability perspective. *Academy of Management Journal, 50*, 101–118.

Chuang, Y. T., Dahlin, K. B., Thomson, K., Lai, Y. C., & Yang, C. C. (2018). Multimarket contact, strategic alliances, and firm performance. *Journal of Management, 44*, 1551–1572.

Cummings, J. L., & Holmberg, S. R. (2012). Best-fit alliance partners: The use of critical success factors in a comprehensive partner selection process. *Long Range Planning, 45*, 136–159.

Daellenbach, U. S., McCarthy, A. M., & Schoenecker, T. S. (1999). Commitment to innovation: The impact of top management team characteristics. *R&D Management, 29*(3), 199–208.

Danzon, P. M., Nicholson, S., & Pereira, N. S. (2005). Productivity in pharmaceutical–biotechnology R&D: The role of experience and alliances. *Journal of Health Economics, 24*(2), 317–339.

Das, T. K., & Rahman, N. (2010). Determinants of partner opportunism in strategic alliances: A conceptual framework. *Journal of Business & Psychology, 25*, 55–74.

Diestre, L., & Rajagopalan, N. (2012). Are all 'sharks' dangerous? New biotechnology ventures and partner selection in R&D alliances. *Strategic Management Journal, 33*, 1115–1134.

Dussauge, P., Garrette, B., & Mitchell, W. (2000). Learning from competing partners: Outcomes and durations of scale and link alliances in Europe, North America and Asia. *Strategic Management Journal, 21*, 99–126.

Eisenhardt, K. M., & Martin, J. A. (2000). Dynamic capabilities: What are they? *Strategic Management Journal, 21*, 1105–1121.

Ener, H. (2019). Do prior experiences of top executives enable or hinder product market entry? *Journal of Management Studies, 56*, 1345–1376.

Evans, W. N., & Kessides, I. N. (1994). Living by the "golden rule": Multimarket contact in the US airline industry. *Quarterly Journal of Economics, 109*, 341–366.

Fuentelsaz, L., & Gomez, J. (2006). Multipoint competition, strategic similarity and entry into geographic markets. *Strategic Management Journal, 27*, 477–499.

Gimeno, J. (1999). Reciprocal threats in multimarket rivalry: Staking out spheres of influence in the US airline industry. *Strategic Management Journal, 20*, 101–128.

Gimeno, J. (2004). Competition within and between networks: The contingent effect of competitive embeddedness on alliance formation. *Academy of Management Journal, 47*(6), 820–842.

Gulati. R. (1995). Social structure and alliance formation patterns: A longitudinal analysis. *Administrative Science Quarterly, 40*, 619–652.

Gulati. R. (1998). Alliances and networks. *Strategic management Journal, 19*(4), 293–317.

Gulati. R., & Gargiulo, M. (1999) Where do interorganizational networks come from? *American Journal of Sociology, 104*, 1439–1493.

Gulati, R., & Singh, H. (1998). The architecture of cooperation: Managing coordination costs and appropriation concerns in strategic alliances. *Administrative Science Quarterly, 43*, 781–814.

Hagedoorn, J. (1993). Understanding the rationale of strategic technology partnering: Interorganizational modes of cooperation and sectoral differences. *Strategic Management Journal, 14*, 371–385.

Hagedoorn, J. (2002). Inter-firm R&D partnerships: An overview of major trends and patterns since 1960. *Research Policy, 31*, 477–492.

Hagedoorn, J., & Frankort, H. T. (2008). The gloomy side of embeddedness: The effects of overembeddedness on inter-firm partnership formation. *Advances in Strategic Management, 25*, 503–530.

Haveman, H. A. (1993). Follow the leader: Mimetic isomorphism and entry into new markets. *Administrative Science Quarterly, 38*(4), 593–627.

Haveman, H. A., & Nonnemaker, L. (2000). Competition in multiple geographic markets: The impact on growth and market entry. *Administrative Science Quarterly, 45*, 232–267.

Heckman. J. J. (1979). Sample selection bias as a specification error. *Econometrica, 47*, 153–161.

Helfat, C. E. (1994). Firm-specificity in corporate applied R&D. *Organization Science, 5*, 173–184.

Higgins, M. J., & Rodriguez, D. (2006). The outsourcing of R&D through acquisitions in the pharmaceutical industry. *Journal of Financial Economics, 80*, 351–383.

Hoffmann, W., Lavie, D., Reuer, J. J., & Shipilov, A. (2018). The interplay of competition and cooperation. *Strategic Management Journal, 39*(12), 3033–3052.

Hsieh, K. Y., & Vermeulen, F. (2013). The structure of competition: How competition between one's rivals influences imitative market entry. *Organization Science, 25*, 299–319.

Hughes, K., & Oughton, C. (1993). Diversification, multimarket contact and profitability. *Economica, 60*, 203–224.

Jayachandran, S., Gimeno, J., & Varadarajan, R. P. (1999). The theory of multimarket competition: A synthesis and implications for marketing strategy. *Journal of Marketing, 63*(3), 49–66.

Jensen, M. (2008). The use of relational discrimination to manage market entry: When do social status and structural holes work against you? *Academy of Management Journal, 51*(4), 723–743.

Kalnins, A. (2004). Divisional multimarket contact within and between multiunit organizations. *Academy of Management Journal, 47*, 117–128.

Kang, W., Bayus, B. L., & Balasubramanian, S. (2010). The strategic effects of multimarket contact: Mutual forbearance and competitive response in the personal computer industry. *Journal of Marketing Research, 47*, 415–427.

Khanna, T., Gulati, R., & Nohria, N. (1998). The dynamics of learning alliances: Competition, cooperation, and relative scope. *Strategic Management Journal, 19*(3), 193–210.

King, G., & Zeng, L. (2001). Logistic regression in rare events data. *Political Analysis, 9*, 137–163.

Klein, K., Semrau, T., Albers, S., & Zajac, E. J. (2020). Multimarket coopetition: How the interplay of competition and cooperation affects entry into shared markets. *Long Range Planning*, *53*(1), Article 101868.

Kleinbaum, A. M., Stuart, T. E., & Tushman, M. L. (2013). Discretion within constraint: Homophily and structure in a formal organization. *Organization Science*, *24*, 1316–1336.

Kumar, M. S. (2010). Differential gains between partners in joint ventures: Role of resource appropriation and private benefits. *Organization Science*, *21*, 232–248.

Lane, P. J., & Lubatkin, M. (1998). Relative absorptive capacity and interorganizational learning. *Strategic Management Journal*, *19*, 461–477.

Larsson, R., Bengtsson, L., Henriksson, K., & Sparks, J. (1998). The interorganizational learning dilemma: Collective knowledge development in strategic alliances. *Organization Science*, *9*(3), 285–305.

Lavie, D. (2006). The competitive advantage of interconnected firms: An extension of the resource-based view. *Academy of Management Review*, *31*, 638–658.

Lavie, D. (2007). Alliance portfolios and firm performance: A study of value creation and appropriation in the US software industry. *Strategic Management Journal*, *28*, 1187–1212.

Li, G.-C., Lai, R., D'Amour, A., Doolin, D. M., Sun, Y., Torvik, V. I., Yu, A. Z., & Fleming, L. (2014). Disambiguation and co-authorship networks of the US patent inventor database (1975–2010). *Research Policy*, *43*(6), 941–955.

Mahoney, J. T., & Pandian, R. J. (1992). The resource-based view within the conversation of strategic management. *Strategic Management Journal*, *13*, 363-380.

Markman, G. D., Gianiodis, P. T., & Phan, P. H. (2009). Factor-market rivalry. *Academy of Management Review*, *34*, 423–441.

Mitchell, W., & Singh, K. (1993). Death of the lethargic: Effects of expansion into new technical subfields on performance in a firm's base business. *Organization Science*, *4*(2), 152–180.

Mitchell, W., & Singh, K. (1996). Survival of businesses using collaborative relationships to commercialize complex goods. *Strategic Management Journal*, *17*(3), 169–195.

Morreale, A., Robba, S., Nigro, G. L., & Roma, P. (2017). A real options game of alliance timing decisions in biopharmaceutical research and development. *European Journal of Operational Research*, *261*(3), 1189–1202.

Mowery, D. C., Oxley, J. E., & Silverman, B. S. (1998). Technological overlap and interfirm cooperation: Implications for the resource-based view of the firm. *Research Policy*, *27*, 507–523.

Neter, J., Wasserman, W., & Kutner, M. (1989). *Applied linear regression models*. Boston, MA: Irwin.

Oxley, J. E. (1997). Appropriability hazards and governance in strategic alliances: A transaction cost approach. *The Journal of Law, Economics, and Organization*, *13*(2), 387–409.

Oxley, J. E., & Sampson, R. C. (2004). The scope and governance of international R&D alliances. *Strategic Management Journal*, *25*, 723–749.

Park, S. H., & Ungson, G. R. (2001). Interfirm rivalry and managerial complexity: A conceptual framework of alliance failure. *Organization Science*, *12*, 37–53.

Park, S. H., & Zhou, D. (2005). Firm heterogeneity and competitive dynamics in alliance formation. *Academy of Management Review, 30*(3), 531–554.

Parmigiani, A., & Rivera-Santos, M. (2011). Clearing a path through the forest: A meta-review of interorganizational relationships. *Journal of Management, 37*, 1108–1136.

Phene, A., & Tallman, S. (2014). Knowledge spillovers and alliance formation. *Journal of Management Studies, 51*, 1058–1090.

Reuer, J. J., & Lahiri, N. (2014). Searching for alliance partners: Effects of geographic distance on the formation of R&D collaborations. *Organization Science, 25*, 283–298.

Reuer, J. J., Zollo, M., & Singh, H. (2002). Post-formation dynamics in strategic alliances. *Strategic Management Journal, 23*, 135–151.

Rosenkopf, L., & Padula, G. (2008). Investigating the microstructure of network evolution: Alliance formation in the mobile communications industry. *Organization Science, 19*, 669–687.

Ryu, W., McCann, B. T., & Reuer, J. (2018). Geographic co-location of partners and rivals: Implications for the design of R&D alliances. *Academy of Management Journal, 61*, 945–965.

Ryu, W., Reuer, J. J., & Brush, T. H. (2020). The effects of multimarket contact on partner selection for technology cooperation. *Strategic Management Journal, 41*, 267–289.

Samant, S., & Kim, J. (2021). Determinants of common benefits and private benefits in innovation alliances. *Managerial Decision Economics, 42*, 294–307.

Scott, J. T. (1991). Multimarket contact among diversified oligopolists. *International Journal of Industrial Organization, 9*, 225–238.

Shipilov, A. V. (2009). Firm scope experience, historic multimarket contact with partners, centrality, and the relationship between structural holes and performance. *Organization Science, 20*, 85–106.

Silverman, B. S., & Baum, J. A. (2002). Alliance-based competitive dynamics. *Academy of Management Journal, 45*, 791–806.

Singh, K., & Mitchell, W. (2005). Growth dynamics: The bidirectional relationship between interfirm collaboration and business sales in entrant and incumbent alliances. *Strategic Management Journal, 26*, 497–521.

Snyder, C. M., & Vonortas, N. S. (2005). Multiproject contact in research joint ventures: evidence and theory. *Journal of Economic Behavior and Organization, 58*, 459–486.

Sorenson, O., & Stuart, T. E. (2001). Syndication networks and the spatial distribution of venture capital investments. *American Journal of Sociology, 106*, 1546–1588.

Sorenson, O., & Stuart, T. E. (2008). Bringing the context back in: Settings and the search for syndicate partners in venture capital investment networks. *Administrative Science Quarterly, 53*, 266–294.

Srinivasan, R., Haunschild, P. R., & Grewal, R. (2007). Vicarious learning in new product introductions in the early years of a converging market. *Management Science, 53*(1), 16–28.

Stephan, J., Murmann, J. P., Boeker, W., & Goodstein, J. (2003). Bringing managers into theories of multimarket competition: CEOs and the determinants of market entry. *Organization Science, 14*, 403–421.

Upson, J. W., Ketchen, D. J., Connelly, B. L., & Ranft, A. L. (2012). Competitor analysis and foothold moves. *Academy of Management Journal, 55*, 93–110.

Vonortas, N. S. (2000). Multimarket contact and inter-firm cooperation in R&D. *Journal of Evolutionary Economics, 10*, 243–271.

Wang, L., & Zajac, E. J. (2007). Alliance or acquisition? A dyadic perspective on interfirm resource combinations. *Strategic Management Journal, 28*(13), 1291–1317.

Yang, H., Zheng, Y., & Zaheer, A. (2015). Asymmetric learning capabilities and stock market returns. *Academy of Management Journal, 58*, 356–374.

Yu, T., & Cannella, A. A., Jr. (2013). A comprehensive review of multimarket competition research. *Journal of Management, 39*, 76–109.

Zhelyazkov, P. I., & Gulati, R. (2016). After the break-up: The relational and reputational consequences of withdrawals from venture capital syndicates. *Academy of Management Journal, 59*, 277–301.

CHAPTER 8

THE EFFECT OF KNOWLEDGE FLOWS ON THE DECISION TO COOPERATE

Differences for Sector and Firm Size

Eva-María Mora-Valentín, Marta Ortiz-de-Urbina-Criado, and Ángeles Montoro-Sánchez

ABSTRACT

The goal of this chapter is to determine the effects of internal and external knowledge flows on the propensity of firms to enter into R&D alliances. Specifically, this chapter examines these effects by distinguishing between industrial and service firms and between large, small and medium-sized firms. To achieve this aim, a large sample of small, medium, and large firms in the industrial and service sectors is analyzed. The data come from the Technological Innovation Survey, which is part of the General Plan for Statistics on Science and Technology approved by EReeurostat. The results highlight the importance of knowledge flows for R&D alliances, confirming that internal and external knowledge flows have a positive effect on the decision to cooperate on R&D.

Managing Interpartner Cooperation in Strategic Alliances, pp. 225–245
Copyright © 2022 by Information Age Publishing
www.infoagepub.com
225

INTRODUCTION

As part of the recent interest in stimulating innovation, much attention has been paid to the subject of R&D alliances (López, 2008). From an academic perspective, the resource-based view states that one of the crucial motivations for the creation of alliances is the desire of partners to acquire resources and capabilities that firms do not have and cannot obtain from an external source (Mowery, Oxley, & Silverman, 1998). However, R&D cooperation has also become a major topic of interest for policy makers. Most international and national private and public R&D funding is directed at stimulating cooperation both between firms, and between firms and other private or public institutions such as universities and research organisms, among others (Acosta & Modrego, 2001).

Due to the desire to either obtain innovative resources and capabilities from other parties or to fund R&D activities, innovative firms are conscious of the need to enter into R&D alliances (or R&D cooperation) to obtain expertise which cannot be generated in-house. Collaboration with other firms facilitates access to the external resources necessary for the development of R&D activities and also offers the possibility of efficient knowledge transfer, resource exchange and organizational learning (Becker & Dietz, 2004). Therefore, innovation boundaries are shifting from a situation where firms mainly perform R&D activities internally (Mowery, 1983) to a reality where corporate partnering, collaboration and external sourcing of R&D are widespread, corresponding to an open innovation model (Chesbrough, 2003a, 2003b).

Firms involved in R&D cooperation activities have denser knowledge flows than non-allied firms, and external knowledge is more effective for the innovation process when the firm engages in own R&D (Cohen & Levinthal, 1989). Work on interorganizational relationships, knowledge and innovation has increasingly recognized the importance of links for obtaining knowledge spillovers from external sources, such as collaboration, and their significant impact on innovation processes and economic development. In addition, the link between cooperation and knowledge spillovers has been analyzed from different perspectives and in both directions, that is, on the one hand, how alliances allow these knowledge flows to be obtained, and, on the other hand, how obtaining information and knowledge is a precursor to collaboration.

Some studies have analyzed the effects of the location of the partners involved in the R&D alliances on the generation of knowledge flows. Most of these studies focus on the importance of different institutional instruments, such as science and technology parks, incubators or districts and clusters (Chen & Choi, 2004; Colombo & Delmastro, 2002; Hansson, 2007; Montoro-Sánchez, Mora-Valentín, & Ortiz-de-Urbina-Criado, 2012; Montoro-Sánchez, Ortiz-de-Urbina-Criado, & Mora-Valentín, 2011). Other studies have focused on the social network perspective, analysing the process of how networking firms share knowledge, what mechanisms firms use to govern knowledge sharing, and what the consequences are for the sharing firms (Balestrin, Vargas, & Fayard, 2008; Mu, Love, & Peng, 2008; Schilling & Phelps, 2007). Similarly, some studies have analyzed the conditions under which firms benefit from the research efforts of other organizations, that is, R&D spillovers (Kafouros & Buckley, 2008).

Many recent studies have analyzed the factors influencing the decision to enter into R&D alliances. Some factors traditionally studied as determinants of R&D cooperation are: cost, risk sharing, complementarities, absorptive capacity of the firm, appropriability, R&D intensity, types of innovation, purchase of external R&D, and firm size and location (Colombo & Gerrone, 1996; López, 2008; Tether, 2002). However, other factors have been attracting the interest of researchers recently, such as internal and external knowledge flows (Belderbos, Carree, Diederen, & Lokshin, & Veugelers, 2004; Cassiman & Veugelers, 2002; Kaiser, 2002; López, 2008). Nevertheless, while there is some evidence on R&D cooperation and knowledge flows, some questions remain unanswered. More studies and empirical evidence are needed to understand the effect of internal and external knowledge flows in order to arrange R&D cooperative agreements, and in addition, we need to establish whether there are differences between partners according to firm sector and size.

The contribution of this chapter to the empirical literature on R&D cooperation is two-fold. Firstly, we analyze the effects of internal and external knowledge flows on the propensity of firms to enter into R&D alliances. Secondly, and considering the importance that the existing literature has placed on partner characteristics when explaining cooperative R&D relationships, we analyze the differences between partners according to firm sector and size. Specifically, this chapter examines these effects by distinguishing between industrial and service firms and between large, medium and small firms. To achieve this aim, a large sample of small, medium and large firms from the industrial and service sectors is analyzed. The data come from the Technological Innovation Survey, which is part of the General Plan for Statistics on Science and Technology approved by Eurostat. We hope to find that knowledge flows have a positive effect on the decision to cooperate in R&D. This result would highlight the importance of knowledge flows for R&D alliances.

BACKGROUND: KNOWLEDGE FLOWS AND R&D ALLIANCES

Knowledge Flows

According to organizational theory, knowledge and knowledge creation occurs at both the individual and interorganizational level. Models focussing on the individual level analyze the knowledge creation process as a series of activities taking place primarily inside an organization and based on the individual as the knowledge creator. At the interorganizational level, knowledge and knowledge creation are explained using a more collective approach, and knowledge is understood not as individual or due to personal qualities, but instead as an activity based on complex processes between groups of individuals, teams, collectives, or organizations (Hansson, 2007). In this chapter we focus on the second approach, based on the relationships between knowledge organizations and the exchange processes within and between organizations.

According to Verspagen and De Loo (1999), there are different kinds of knowledge, depending on the characteristics of the generating organizations. So, the academic community (performing basic research) thrives on openness, and (ultimately) making research results public is the explicit aim of researchers in this part of the innovation system. Researchers in public labs may in many cases work for specific contractors. The knowledge developed in this sector is thus, in principle, open to everyone (who pays), but the contractor may decide not to pursue dissemination actively. In contrast, research undertaken by firms is often kept as secret as possible, in order to prevent competitors from using the knowledge.

Knowledge flows comprise the set of processes, events, and activities through which data, information, and knowledge are transferred from one entity to another. The end results are knowledge capture, creation, retention, and application (Mu et al., 2008). Knowledge flows consist of intangible knowledge that arises inside firms and through market transactions or exchanges between firms or between firms and institutions (Verspagen & De Loo, 1999). They therefore occur when a firm exploits knowledge and ideas developed by other firms (Kafouros & Buckley, 2008). The extent to which knowledge flows from one agent to another, and the manner in which it does so, both differ significantly according to the type of knowledge.

Verspagen and De Loo (1999) introduced the term R&D or technology spillovers. They consider that R&D spillovers arise because (technological) knowledge cannot be completely appropriated by the firm or person developing the knowledge. Therefore, when one firm makes an innovation, other firms may use the knowledge embodied in this innovation for their activities.

Most of the literature identifies two distinct types of knowledge flows that are often confused. The first of these are so-called rent-flows, which are related to the flow of goods between firms. If goods are used as inputs in the production process of another firm, the latter firm will receive some product innovation as a flow from that input (Verspagen, 1997). The second are so-called "pure" knowledge flows. This refers to the effect of research performed in economic unit *i* (a firm, an industry or a country) improving the technology in a second economic unit *j* without *j* having to pay for it (Griliches, 1992). Pure knowledge flows are usually seen as enhancing the productivity of a firm's own R&D (Verspagen, 1997).

Similarly, Belderbos et al. (2004) define incoming spillovers as the measure of the importance of external information flows for the firm's innovation process, and outgoing spillovers as a firm's attempt to appropriate the benefits of their innovations by controlling information flows out of the company. Spillovers can refer to both involuntary leakage and voluntary transfers of knowledge between market participants. When spillovers are considered to be at least partly voluntary, firms that are partners in R&D cooperation can improve the incoming knowledge transfer through information sharing (Kamien, Muller, & Zang, 1992; Katsoulacos & Ulph, 1998).

Other papers concerned with knowledge flows differentiate between horizontal and vertical flows. If the firm that is the knowledge recipient operates in a different field from the sender, knowledge flows are defined as intra-industry or vertical (for example, from suppliers and clients), whereas inter-industry or horizontal flows occur when the recipient and sender firms operate in the same field of business, for example, between competitors (Kaiser, 2002).

In this chapter we distinguish between internal and external knowledge flows. Internal knowledge flows are flows of information and knowledge circulating and coming from inside firms. External knowledge flows, more commonly referred to as knowledge spillovers, come from outside the firm and from vertical and horizontal sources of information, such as suppliers, customers, competitors, and even other sources, such as public and institutional agents.

Effects of Knowledge Flows on R&D Alliances

Nonaka and Takeuchi (1995) analyzed the creation of new knowledge based on the interaction between individuals, groups, and organizations. For the authors, knowledge emerges at an individual level, and is expanded by the dynamic knowledge-socialization interaction at an organizational and, subsequently, an interorganizational level. The exchange of data, information and knowledge in a given interorganizational network project may converge to a single point for the creation of strategic knowledge for the competitiveness of organizations.

There has been great interest over the last few years in the analysis of knowledge flows and their effect on the propensity of firms to enter into R&D cooperation agreements. As stated above, these knowledge flows start inside firms and through transactions or relationships between different firms or between firms and other types of institution (Verspagen & De Loo, 1999). The knowledge generated, in many cases through the innovative activity of the firm (Kaiser, 2002), is available for other organizations so that anything that is useful can be freely exploited (Kafouros & Buckley, 2008). In addition, taking into account that at times knowledge is easily transferable through various means (magazines, reverse engineering, cooperation, etc.), firms can take advantage of this knowledge without having to pay for it (Verspagen, 1997). This free appropriation of knowledge flows generated by other firms takes place as a result of failures in the mechanisms put in place by firms to protect their innovations.

When firms can easily access the knowledge flows generated by other firms, they usually devote fewer resources to their own R&D investment. However, another way of internalizing these knowledge flows is through R&D cooperation, so firms obtain greater benefits than they would in the absence of cooperation. In this context, the exchange of knowledge flows normally takes place at the start of the cooperative relationships between the parties. Once the initial stages of the relationship have been completed, much more complex and formal cooperation agreements are usually developed. From among all the possible interorganizational relationships, cooperation on R&D is the one requiring the greatest face-to-face contact to guarantee success. This is because this type of relationship requires a high degree of commitment and trust between the parties (Montoro-Sánchez et al., 2011; Simonen & McCann, 2008).

Some academics have focused their attention on the effect that knowledge flows have on the decision to collaborate on R&D (Belderbos et al., 2004; Cassiman & Veugelers, 2002; Kaiser, 2002; López, 2008; López-Fernández, Serrano-Bedia, & García-Piqueres, 2008). However, the relationship between different knowledge flows and R&D cooperation is complex.

Cassiman and Veugelers (2002) show the importance of distinguishing between incoming spillovers and appropriability when we use these measures to analyze their impact on the decision of firms to engage in cooperative R&D agreements. They find that firms that rate generally available external information sources more highly as important inputs to their innovation process (the incoming spillovers) are more likely to be actively engaged in cooperative R&D agreements. In addition, firms that are more effective in appropriating the results from their innovation process are also more likely to cooperate in R&D. Nevertheless, it is also conceivable that a firm that is better prepared to appropriate knowledge might be less keen to cooperate (López, 2008).

Belderbos et al. (2004) explore heterogeneities in the determinants of the decisions by innovating firms to engage in R&D cooperation, differentiating between four types of cooperation partners (competitors, suppliers, customers, and universities and research institutes) and they concentrate specifically on the impact of different types of spillovers. They find that the determinants of R&D cooperation differ significantly across cooperation types. The positive impact of incoming source-specific spillovers is weaker for competitor cooperation, reflecting greater appropriability concerns. Institutional spillovers are more generic in nature and positively affect all cooperation types.

Other studies have focused on the relationship between incoming and outgoing spillovers and R&D cooperation. When spillovers are considered to be at least partly voluntary, firms that are partners in R&D cooperation can improve the incoming knowledge transfer through information sharing (Kamien et al., 1992; Katsoulacos & Ulph, 1998). So, spillovers increase incentives to cooperate, particularly if cooperation allows firms to enhance knowledge transfers among the collaborating partners. However, if incoming spillovers are associated with outgoing spillovers they have a more ambiguous effect on competitor collaboration, as collaborating product market rivals benefit more from a firm's R&D effort. These appropriability considerations are much less important for vertical (supplier, customer) and institutional collaboration. Firms that increase their absorptive capacity through larger R&D investments are more likely to benefit from cooperation. In the case of competitor cooperation, higher R&D investment leads to a greater pool of know-how on which the partner firms can potentially free-ride (Belderbos et al., 2004).

Finally, as many previous studies have found, different R&D partnerships may be established for different purposes, with customer cooperation more focused on bringing to market adapted or improved products, and supplier cooperation more focused on cost reduction (Belderbos et al., 2004). Differences can also be expected in the impact of knowledge spillovers on collaboration depending on firm sector and size. We therefore include both variables to explore whether differences exist in the link between knowledge spillovers and R&D cooperation.

Knowledge spillover processes have sometimes been interpreted as processes for equalizing knowledge flows over sectors. For example, in terms of R&D expenditures, it is a well-known fact that these are relatively concentrated in a number of so-called "high-tech" sectors, such as computers, electronics, pharmaceuticals, instruments, and aerospace.

Spillover matrices, such as the ones mentioned above, may be interpreted as describing the mechanism by which these concentrated R&D efforts are distributed over sectors. This process may then result in a more or less even (or equal) distribution of knowledge (or R&D) over sectors. In addition, the size of firms can also act to enhance, or not enhance, knowledge flows as a precursor for R&D collaboration. Although this variable is usually considered to be a control variable, previous studies have focussed on its role in this link or process. As a result, in this study we explore its effects and any differences found.

METHODOLOGY: SAMPLE AND VARIABLES

Sample

For the empirical study, a sample of firms was selected from the Technological Innovation Panel (PITEC) drawn up by the *Instituto Nacional de Estadística* (INE). This panel was taken from the Technological Innovation Survey, which is part of the General Plan for Statistics on Science and Technology, approved by the Statistical Office of the European Union (Eurostat). The panel's information collection tool was a questionnaire that included all relevant aspects of the company profile (turnover, staff, activity type, geographic market, etc.) and of the possible innovative activities (their conditions and effects). PITEC has been used in pioneering studies analyzing innovation in the manufacturing and service sectors (e.g., see Castro, Montoro-Sánchez, & Ortiz-de-Urbina-Criado, 2011; Montoro-Sánchez et al, 2011, 2012; Romero-Martínez, Ortiz-de-Urbina-Criado, & Ribeiro, 2010; Un, Romero-Martínez, & Montoro-Sánchez, 2009; Vega-Jurado, Gutiérrez-Gracia, & Fernández-de-Lucio, 2009).

The sample was chosen using PITEC data for the last available five years (2005-2009). From among the companies appearing in PITEC, we selected those companies belonging to the industrial and service sectors. We filtered the sample by removing companies without data, leaving a final sample of 7,383 companies, of which 36.7% cooperated on R&D and the rest did not.

The sample has the following characteristics. The majority of companies (58.3%) do not belong to a business group. Looking at company size, we observe that 51% (3762) of the firms are small, 39.6% (2926) are medium-sized and 9.4% (695) are large. By activity sector, 36.2% (2671) of the firms belong to the service sector. Most of the companies are privately owned (96%), 2.1% are public enterprises, and only 1.8% are research centres.

Variables

To analyze the factors that determine the propensity to establish R&D alliances, the dependent variable is a category variable (ALLIANCE) that takes two values: a value of 1 if the company has engaged in R&D cooperation, and a value of 0 if it has not.

We analyzed the effect on cooperation of the following variables: internal knowledge flows and external knowledge flows. A major problem when handling knowledge flows in empirical research is that they cannot be measured precisely. Many researchers rely on proxy variables, which can be more or less crude, based on measures of proximity or technological distance between firms, sectors or regions. The non-measurability of research spillovers implies that testing in the strict sense is impossible. However, the growing availability of innovation survey data and, especially, the creation of the Community Innovation Survey (CIS), not only enables researchers to obtain new measures of knowledge flows, but also provides proxy variables for the accuracy of spillover measures (Kaiser, 2002). Thus, the PITEC Panel provides information regarding the significance of different types of knowledge flows. So, internal knowledge flows (FK_INTERNAL) is measured using a continuous variable which represents the importance (from 1 to 4) of internal knowledge flows for firms. In terms of external knowledge flows (or knowledge spillovers), we firstly measure (from 1 to 4) each type of knowledge spillover, classifying them in a similar way to Belderbos et al. (2004): supplier (SUPPLIER_SPILLOVER), customer (CUSTOMER_SPILLOVER), competitor (COMPETITOR_SPILLOVER), institutional (INSTITUTIONAL_SPILLOVER) and public (PUBLIC_SPILLOVER). Secondly, we use a whole measure of the global significance of all the types of knowledge spillovers (KW_SPILLOVER) using a continuous variable on a scale of 5 to 20. This is the sum of the importance of all spillover types.

Finally, we also consider two additional variables, size (SIZE) and the firm's activity sector (SECTOR) to control for and demonstrate differences in the impact of knowledge flows on R&D collaboration. Table 8.1 sets out the variables, along with a description and their descriptive statistics.

RESULTS

We used binomial logistic regression to analyze the effect of internal knowledge flows and knowledge spillovers on the propensity of firms to cooperate. This technique allows us to analyze the impact of knowledge flows on a firm's propensity to cooperate on R&D. Specifically, binomial logistic regression is used when the dependent variable can take two values, and in that model, the odds ratio (or marginal effects) reflects the probability ratio, that is, the probability that a specific event will occur compared with the probability that it will not occur.

Table 8.1

Summary of Measurements of the Independent and Control Variables

VARIABLE	ABBREVIATION	MEASUREMENT	SOURCE	DESCRIPTIVES
R&D cooperation/ alliances	ALLIANCE	Dummy: 1-Firm cooperates on R&D (2007-2009); 0-no	PITEC 2009	1 (yes): 2706 (36.7%) 0 (no):4677 (63.3%)
Flows of internal knowledge	FK_INTERNAL	Importance of the firm's inside information (2005-2007) (scale of 1 to 4: 1 none – 4 high)	PITEC 2007	Mean: 3.37 TD: 0.88
Knowledge spillovers	KW_SPILLOVER	Importance of knowledge spillovers as source of knowledge for firm innovation as the sum of the importance of all types of spillovers. Values: 5 (none) - 20 (high)	PITEC 2007	Mean: 11.82 TD: 3.61
Types of knowledge spillovers	SUPPLIER_ SPILLOVER	Importance of suppliers as source of knowledge for firm innovation (2005-2007) (scale of 1 to 4: 1 none – 4 high)	Adapted from Belderbos et al. (2004)	Mean: 2.56 TD: 1.04
	CUSTOMER_ SPILLOVER	Importance of customers as source of knowledge for firm innovation (2005-2007) (scale of 1 to 4: 1 none – 4 high)		Mean: 2.58 TD: 1.13
	COMPETITOR_ SPILLOVER	Importance of competitors as source of knowledge for firm innovation (2005-2007) (scale of 1 to 4: 1 none – 4 high)		Mean: 2.20 TD: 1.04
	INSTITUTIONAL_ SPILLOVER	Average of importance of universities, innovation centres, and research institutions as sources of knowledge for firm innovation (2005-2007) (scale of 1 to 4: 1 none – 4 high)	PITEC 2007	Mean: 2.16 TD: 0.86
	PUBLIC_ SPILLOVER	Average of importance of patents, databases, trade literature and fairs as source of knowledge for firm innovation (2005-2007) (scale of 1 to 4: 1 none – 4 high)		Mean: 2.32 TD: 1

(Table continued on next page)

Table 8.1 (Continued)

Summary of Measurements of the Independent and Control Variables

VARIABLE	ABBREVIATION	MEASUREMENT	SOURCE	DESCRIPTIVES
Size	SIZE	Categorical variable: value 1 for small firms (less than 50 employees); value 2 for medium firms (between 50 and 500 employees) and value 3 for large firms (more than 500)	Adapted from Belderbos et al. (2004); López (2008) and López-Fernández et al. (2008) PITEC 2009	1 (Small): 3762 (51%) 2 (Medium): 2926 (39.6%) 3 (Large): 695 (9.4%)
Sector	SECTOR	Categorical variable: value 0: industrial sector (CNAE2009: 05-43) and value 1: service sector (CNAE93: 45-96)	PITEC 2009	1 (Service): 2671 (36.2%) 0 (Industrial): 4712 (63.8%)

Before calculating these models, we have analyzed the correlation between the independent and dependent variables. The tests have shown a moderate or high correlation between the different types of knowledge spillovers (supplier, customer, competitor, institutional and public). Based on these correlations, we have estimated various regression models analysing the effect of each type of spillover separately. Table 8.2 shows the results of the logistic regression models. All the regression models display a good fit.

Model 1, Table 8.2 shows the effect of internal knowledge flows and knowledge spillovers on a firm's propensity to cooperate. All independent variables (FK_INTERNAL and KW_SPILLOVER) have a significant positive effect, that is, the greater the importance that a firm attaches to internal knowledge flows and knowledge spillovers, the greater that firm's propensity to cooperate. This result supports the idea that information and knowledge are strategic resources that impact on the decisions made by the firm (Belderbos et al., 2004). In this case, the firms that consider knowledge highly important normally cooperate more on R&D (Cassiman & Veugelers, 2002).

In addition, positive and significant effects have been found for each type of knowledge spillover (Models 2–6, Table 8.2). Institutional spillovers offer the greatest effect (2.30) on the propensity to cooperate. In this sense, the more important a firm believes this type of spillover is, the greater the probability that it will establish R&D alliances. The information available about other institutions and organizations determines the decision to cooperate, since the firm has information allowing it to identify the organization with which it can establish good cooperative relationships, and the means of cooperation with this organization that could be beneficial for the firm. When a firm decides to cooperate on R&D activities, it needs information about the other companies and institutions, and about the environment, in order to choose the best partners and thus establish successful collaborations (Montoro-Sánchez et al., 2011).

Several authors suggest that when spillovers are considered to be at least partly voluntary, firms who are partners in R&D cooperation can improve incoming knowledge transfers through information sharing (Belderbos et al., 2004; Katsoulacos & Ulph, 1998). Recent literature has paid attention to the relationship between R&D cooperation activity and spillovers. Cassiman and Veugelers (2002) find that firms' external information sources (incoming spillovers) have a significant effect on the probability of R&D cooperation. López (2008) found evidence supporting the existence of a significant spillover effect on R&D cooperation and concluded that spillovers have a positive and significant impact on the probability of R&D cooperation. Other papers have studied the relationship between spillovers and R&D cooperation (e.g., Belderbos et al., 2004; Kaiser, 2002; López-Fernández et al., 2008; Veugelers & Cassiman, 2005). However, many of these studies analyze spillovers in general, without distinguishing between specific types: customer, supplier, competitor, institutional and public (Montoro-Sánchez et al., 2011). The results of this study support and add to the existing body of empirical evidence by showing that the effect of all knowledge spillovers is both positive and significant.

To analyze differences in the effects of internal knowledge flows and spillovers on the propensity for R&D cooperation across sectors and for different firm sizes, the sample has been divided into subsamples (service sector and industrial sector; and small, medium, and large firms) and logistic regression has been used. Table 8.3 shows the results for sector subsamples and Table 8.4 shows the results for size subsamples.

The results shown in Table 8.3 demonstrate that, for firms in both the service sector and the industrial sector, the effects of internal knowledge flows and spillovers on the propensity to cooperate are positive and significant. For firms in the service sector, the firms rating knowledge flows more highly are 1.14 times more likely to cooperate than those rating them less highly. For firms in the industrial sector the effect is 1.07. For this variable, there are no significant differences between the firms in the two sectors in terms of the size of the effect, exp (b); this can be seen in the variation

Table 8.2

R&D Alliances and Spillovers

R&D alliances & Spillovers	Model 1 B	Model 1 Exp (B)	Model 2 B	Model 2 Exp (B)	Model 3 B	Model 3 Exp (B)	Model 4 B	Model 4 Exp (B)	Model 5 B	Model 5 Exp (B)	Model 6 B	Model 6 Exp (B)
FK_INTERNAL	0.10***	1.11	0.24***	1.27	0.18***	1.20	0.21***	1.24	0.11***	1.11	0.16***	1.18
KW_SPILLOVER	0.13***	1.14	—	—	—	—	—	—	—	—	—	—
SUPPLIER_SPILLOVER	—	—	0.07***	1.08	—	—	—	—	—	—	—	—
CUSTOMER_SPILLOVER	—	—	—	—	0.22***	1.24	—	—	—	—	—	—
COMPETITOR_SPILLOVER	—	—	—	—	—	—	0.22***	1.25	—	—	—	—
INSTITUTION_SPILLOVER	—	—	—	—	—	—	—	—	0.83**	2.30	—	—
PUBLIC_SPILLOVER	—	—	—	—	—	—	—	—	—	—	0.36***	1.44
SIZE (small vs large)	-0.70***	0.50	-0.69***	0.50	-0.77***	0.46	-0.71***	0.49	-0.68***	0.51	-0.75***	0.47
SIZE (medium vs large)	-0.43***	0.65	-0.40***	0.67	-0.46***	0.63	-0.42***	0.66	-0.45***	0.64	-0.44***	0.64
SECTOR (Service)	0.33***	1.39	0.31***	1.37	0.32***	1.38	0.32***	1.38	0.28***	1.33	0.31***	1.37
Constant	-2.04***	0.13	-1.17***	0.31	-1.28***	0.28	-1.37***	0.25	-2.36***	0.09	-1.53***	0.22
Chi-square	514.02***		222.883***		304.010***		208.312***		943.030***		414.488***	
–2 log likelihood	9188.369		9479.505		9398.379		9404.077		8750.358		9287.901	
R² Cox and Snell	0.067		0.030		0.040		0.040		0.120		0.055	
R² Nagelkerke	0.092		0.041		0.055		0.054		0.164		0.075	
Matrix of Classification (%)	65.19		63.54		64.17		63.66		68.62		65.11	

*** $p < 0.01$; ** $p < 0.05$; * $p < 0.1$

intervals for exp (b) at 95%. Similar results are obtained for the variable KW_SPILLOVER; in this case the effect of this variable on the propensity of firms to cooperate is very similar (1.15 for service sector firms and 1.13 for industrial firms). If we analyze each type of spillover separately, the results show the same trend seen in the previous cases; the effects of each type of spillover are positive and significant and in most cases (supplier, customer, competitor, institutional) there are no differences in the size of the effect between service sector and industrial sector firms. As seen in Model 5, Table 8.2, in the results obtained for each sector (Table 8.3), institutional spillovers are those that have the greatest effect (2.35 for the service sector and 2.37 for the industrial sector). In terms of public spillovers, there are significant differences in the size of the effect between the service sector and industrial sector. Specifically, the effect is significantly greater for firms in the service sector since exp (B) at 95% CI has higher values for service sector firms ([1.51–1.77]) than for industrial sector firms ([1.30–1.48]). The results show that the service sector firms rating public spillovers more highly are 1.64 times more likely to cooperate; while the industrial firms rating this type of spillover more highly are 1.39 times more likely to cooperate than those that give a lower importance rating to this type of spillover.

Table 8.4 shows the results obtained on the basis of the size of the firm. The sample has been divided into three subsamples; one for small firms, a second for medium-sized firms and a third for large firms. The analysis has been repeated for each subsample, and the results obtained for knowledge spillovers are similar to those obtained for the complete sample (Table 8.2) and for the sub-samples by sector (Table 8.3). In other words, for firms of any size, knowledge spillovers are determining factors in the propensity to cooperate in R&D. In each case the effect is positive, and the effect is particularly significant for institutional spillovers (2.42; 2.29; 2.30 respectively). If we analyze the differences in the size of the effects based on the size of firm for each type of spillover, we can state that there are no significant differences apart from supplier spillovers comparing large and small companies. In this case, the effect of supplier spillovers on the propensity to cooperate is significantly greater for large firms (1.34; CI: [1.15–1.56]) than for the small firms (1.06; CI: [0.99–1.13]).

If we analyze the results obtained for the variable FK_INTERNAL (Table 8.4), we see that, for large and small firms, the effect of this variable is not significant. In other words, the importance of internal knowledge flows to this type of firm does not determine the propensity of firms to enter into R&D alliances.

Table 8.3

Sector: R&D Alliances and Spillovers

SECTOR R&D alliances & Spillovers	Service sector B	Exp (B)	IC Exp (B): 95%	Goodness-of-fit: Chi-square; -2 log likelihood; R2 Nagelkerke; Matrix of Classification (%)	Industrial sector B	Exp (B)	IC Exp (B): 95%	Goodness-of-fit: Chi-square; -2 log likelihood; R2 Nagelkerke; Matrix of Classification (%)
FK_INTERNAL	0.13**	1.14	[1.03-1.26]	186.56***; 3435.57; 0.091; 62.22%	0.07**	1.07	[0.99-1.16]	319.49***; 5721.52; 0.091; 67.72%
KW_SPILLOVER	0.14***	1.15	[1.13-1.18]		0.12***	1.13	[1.10-1.15]	
SIZE (small vs large)	n.s.				-1.20***	0.30	[0.24-0.39]	
SIZE (medium vs large)	n.s.				-0.82***	0.44	[0.35-0.56]	
Constant	-2.50***	0.08			-1.40***	0.25		
SUPPLIER_SPILLOVER	0.09**	1.09	[1.02-1.18]	5.56**; 3616.57; 0.003; 58.67%	0.16***	1.17	[1.10-1.24]	27.68***; 6013.34; 0.008; 66.00%
CUSTOMER_SPILLOVER	0.28***	1.32	[1.23-1.41]	62.99***; 3559.14; 0.031; 58.70%	0.23***	1.26	[1.19-1.33]	67.49***; 5973.52; 0.029; 66.00%
COMPETITOR_SPILLOVER	0.30***	1.35	[1.25-1.45]	58.01***; 3564.12; 0.029; 58.44%	0.23***	1.26	[1.19-1.34]	63.58***; 5977.44; 0.019; 66.00%
INSTITUTION_SPILLOVER	0.86***	2.35	[2.13-2.60]	330.90***; 3291.23; 0.157; 67.24%	0.86***	2.37	[2.19-2.58]	404.98***; 5546.03; 0.138; 68.48%
PUBLIC_SPILLOVER	0.49***	1.64	[1.51-1.77]	156.13***; 3466.00; 0.076; 61.21%	0.33***	1.39	[1.30-1.48]	106.40***; 5934.53; 0.031; 66.00%

*** $p < 0.01$; ** $p < 0.05$; * $p < 0$.

n.s.: not significant. Complete models can be requested from marta.ortizdeurbina@urjc.es

239

Table 8.4

Size: R&D Alliances and Spillovers

SIZE R&D alliances & Spillovers	Small Firms				Medium Firms			
	B	Exp (B)	IC Exp (B): 95%	Goodness-of-fit: Chi-square; −2 log likelihood; R2 Cox and Snell; R2 Nagelkerke; Matrix of Classification (%)	B	Exp (B)	IC Exp (B): 95%	Goodness-of-fit: Chi-square; −2 log likelihood; R2 Cox and Snell; R2 Nagelkerke: Matrix of Classification (%)
FK_INTERNAL	n.s.				0.15***	1.16	[1.05–1.28]	
KW_SPILLOVER	0.12***	1.13	[1.10–1.15]	196.30***; 4539.89; 0.071; 68.31%	0.13***	1.14	[1.12–1.17]	190.19***; 3716.86; 0.085; 63.23%
Sector (service)	0.53***	1.71	[1.48–1.97]		0.29***	1.33	[1.12–1.58]	
Constant	−2.38***	0.09			−2.69***	0.07		
SUPPLIER_SPILLOVER	0.06*	1.06	[0.99–1.13]	2.90**; 4733.29; 0.001; 67.65%	0.12***	1.13	[1.05–1.22]	10.78***; 3896.27; 0.005; 61.24%
CUSTOMER_SPILLOVER	0.22***	1.24	[1.17–1.32]	48.15***; 4688.04; 0.018; 67.65%	0.28***	1.33	[1.24–1.42]	69.00***; 3838.06; 0.032; 61.24%
COMPETITOR_SPILLOVER	0.18***	1.20	[1.12–1.28]	29.06***; 4707.14; 0.011; 67.65%	0.30***	1.35	[1.25–1.45]	64.60***; 3842.45; 0.030; 60.39%
INSTITUTION_SPILLOVER	0.88***	2.42	[2.21–2.64]	415.98***; 4320.21; 0.146; 69.19%	0.83***	2.29	[2.08–2.53]	314.35***; 3592.70; 0.138; 66.44%
PUBLIC_SPILLOVER	0.35***	1.41	[1.32–1.52]	96.33***; 4639.86; 0.035; 67.65%	0.43***	1.54	[1.42–1.66]	121.14***; 3785.91; 0.055; 62.06%

(Table continued on next page)

240

Table 8.4 (Continued)

Size: R&D Alliances and Spillovers

SIZE R&D alliances & Spillovers	B	Exp (B)	Large Firms	
			IC: Exp (B): 95%	Goodness-of-fit: Chi-square; −2 log likelihood; R2 Cox and Snell; R2 Nagelkerke; Matrix of Classification (%)
FK_INTERNAL	n.s.			
KW_SPILLOVER	0.17***	1.18	[1.13–1.24]	67.18***; 895.97; 0.123; 63.74%
Sector (service)	−0.42***	0.65	[0.48–0.90]	
Constant	−1.77***	0.17		
SUPPLIER_SPILLOVER	0.29***	1.34	[1.15–1.56]	14.49***; 948.66; 0.028; 55.54%
CUSTOMER_SPILLOVER	0.30***	1.35	[1.17–1.55]	18.08***; 945.07; 0.034; 56.40%
COMPETITOR_SPILLOVER	0.40***	1.49	[1.27–1.74]	26.30***; 936.85; 0.050; 58.56%
INSTITUTION_SPILLOVER	0.83***	2.30	[1.89–2.81]	77.87***; 885.28; 0.141; 62.88%
PUBLIC_SPILLOVER	0.50***	1.64	[1.40–1.93]	39.82***; 923.33; 0.074; 59.28%

*** $p < 0.01$; ** $p < 0.05$; * $p < 0.1$.

Complete models can be requested from marta.ortizdeurbina@urjc.es

CONCLUSIONS

There has been growing interest in the literature in analyzing R&D partnerships. Some studies examining this issue have focussed on aspects such as the reasons and factors determining cooperation or have analyzed the cooperation process and the effects of cooperation. Moreover, these studies have often been context-specific, studying domestic or international partnerships (Ortiz-de-Urbina-Criado, Montoro-Sánchez, & Romero-Martínez, 2011) or taking into account company location and the links that arise between different types of companies on account of their proximity (Montoro-Sánchez et al., 2012; Montoro-Sánchez et al., 2011). Given this, it is interesting to consider both sector and size as factors in the study of R&D alliances.

The purpose of this chapter has been to determine the effects of internal and external knowledge flows (knowledge spillovers) on the propensity of firms to enter into R&D alliances. Specifically, this chapter has examined these effects by distinguishing between industrial and service sector firms and between large, medium and small firms. To achieve this aim, a large sample has been analyzed and the results have highlighted the importance of knowledge flows for R&D alliances.

The results suggest that knowledge spillovers have a positive influence on the likelihood that firms will establish R&D cooperation agreements. The same results hold for specific types of spillover, that is the greater the importance that a firm attaches to competitor, supplier, customer, institutional or public spillovers, the greater its propensity to engage in R&D cooperation. These findings bear out the conclusions reached by other authors who state that firms who show a greater ability to capture knowledge from external sources and who are better prepared to protect their own knowledge have a higher probability of cooperating on R&D (Abramovsky, Kremp, López, Schmidt, & Simpson, 2009; Cassiman & Veugelers, 2002). In that sense, some authors (Belderbos et al., 2004; Kaiser, 2002; López, 2008) have shown that firms that attach the greatest importance to external knowledge flows have a greater propensity to initiate R&D cooperation agreements. The tacit nature of knowledge associated with production and innovation often involves physical or geographical proximity, which facilitates the transfer of that knowledge.

This study makes several important contributions to the literature. Flows of knowledge and, specially, spillovers are difficult to measure, which is why we have used two approaches in this chapter: one that reflects the importance to the firm of all knowledge spillovers, and another that analyzes the importance of each specific type of spillover (competitor, customer, supplier, institutional and public). This chapter provides more detailed information on the possible effects of knowledge flows, since it sheds light on the effect of each specific type of knowledge spillover and how it influences R&D cooperation. Finally, this study empirically analyzes the effect of knowledge flows on R&D cooperation taking into account firm size and sector, issues that have not been studied previously.

However, as in all research, the results should be interpreted taking into account the limitations imposed by using secondary information sources. Future studies will try to overcome these constraints by obtaining additional qualitative information about knowledge flows. It would be of great interest to study these relationships and effects based on the nature of the partner with whom the company cooperates. It would also be interesting to perform similar analyses in other geographic areas in order to compare the results and make them more generally applicable.

ACKNOWLEDGMENTS

This chapter, save some minor changes, was earlier published as Mora-Valentín, Eva-María, Ortiz-de-Urbina-Criado, Marta, and Montoro-Sánchez, Ángeles (2013). The effect of knowledge flows on the decision to cooperate: Differences for sector and firm size. In T. K. Das (Ed.), *Managing knowledge in strategic alliances* (pp. 139–158). Charlotte, NC: Information Age Publishing. This study was financed by Project ECO2009-13818 and Project ECO2009-10358 of the Ministry of Science and Innovation, Cátedra Bancaja Jóvenes Emprendedores Complutense University of Madrid and Cátedra Iberdrola de Investigación en Administración y Dirección de Empresas of the Rey Juan Carlos University, and Caja Madrid Foundation (Visiting Scholar of Ángeles Montoro-Sánchez at Management Department, Wharton School, University of Pennsylvania).

REFERENCES

Abramovsky, L., Kremp, E., López, A., Schmidt, T., & Simpson, H. (2009). Understanding co-operative R&D activity: Evidence from four European countries. *Economics of Innovation and New Technology, 18*, 243–265.

Acosta, J., & Modrego, A. (2001). Public financing of cooperative R&D projects under the national R&D plan? *Research Policy, 30*, 625–641.

Balestrin, A., Vargas, L. M., & Fayard P. (2008). Knowledge creation in small-firm network. *Journal of Knowledge Management, 12*(2), 94–106.

Becker, W., & Dietz, J. (2004). R&D cooperation and innovation activities of firms –Evidence for the German manufacturing industry. *Research Policy, 33*, 209–223.

Belderbos, R., Carree, M., Diederen, B., Lokshin, B., & Veugelers, R. (2004). Heterogeneity in R&D cooperation strategies. *International Journal of Industrial Organization*, *22*, 1237–1263.

Cassiman, B., & Veugelers, R. (2002). R&D cooperation and spillovers: Some empirical evidence from Belgium. *American Economic Review*, *92*, 1169–1184.

Castro, L. M., Montoro-Sánchez, A., & Ortiz-de-Urbina-Criado, M. (2011). Innovation in service industries: Current and future trends. *Service Industries Journal*, *31*, 7–20.

Chen, S., & Choi, C. J. (2004). Creating a knowledge-based city: The example of Hsinchu Science Park. *Journal of Knowledge Management*, *8*(5), 73–82.

Chesbrough, H. W. (2003a). A better way to innovate. *Harvard Business Review*, *81*(7), 12–13.

Chesbrough, H. W. (2003b). *Open innovation - The new imperative for creating and profiting from technology*. Cambridge, MA: Harvard Business School Press.

Cohen, W. M., & Levinthal, D. A. (1989). Innovation and learning: The two faces of R&D. *Economic Journal*, *99*(397), 569–596.

Colombo, M., & Delmastro, M. (2002). How effective are technology incubators? Evidence from Italy. *Research Policy*, *31*, 1103–1122.

Colombo, M. G., & Gerrone, P. (1996). Technological cooperative agreements and firms R&D intensity. A note on causality relations. *Research Policy*, *25*, 923–932.

Griliches, Z. (1992). The search for R&D spillovers. *Scandinavian Journal of Economics*, *94*(Suppl.), S29–S47.

Hansson, F. (2007). Science parks as knowledge organizations – the *ba* in action? *European Journal of Innovation Management*, *10*(3), 348–366.

Kafouros, M. I., & Buckley, P. J. (2008). Under what conditions do firms benefit from the research efforts of other organizations? *Research Policy*, *37*, 225–239.

Kaiser, U. (2002). Measuring knowledge spillovers in manufacturing and service: An empirical assessment of alternative approaches. *Research Policy*, *31*, 125–144.

Kamien, M. I., Muller, E., & Zang, I. (1992). Research joint ventures and R&D cartels. *American Economic Review*, *82*, 1293–1992.

Katsoulacos, Y., & Ulph, D. (1998). Endogenous spillovers and the performance of research joint ventures. *Journal of Industrial Economics*, *46*, 333–357.

López, A. (2008). Determinants of R&D cooperation: Evidence from Spanish manufacturing firms. *International Journal of Industrial Organization*, *26*(1), 113–136.

López-Fernández, M. C., Serrano-Bedia, A. M., & García-Piqueres, G. (2008). Exploring determinants of company-university R&D collaboration in Spain. *Journal of Manufacturing & Technology Management*, *19*, 361–373.

Montoro-Sánchez, A., Mora-Valentín, E. M., & Ortiz-de-Urbina-Criado, M. (2012). R&D cooperation in science and technology parks: The advantages of location. In T. K. Das (Ed.), *Strategic alliances for value creation* (pp. 73–99). Charlotte, NC: Information Age Publishing.

Montoro-Sánchez, A., Ortiz-de-Urbina-Criado, M., & Mora-Valentín, E. M. (2011). Effects of knowledge spillovers on innovation and collaboration in science and technology parks. *Journal of Knowledge Management*, *15*, 948–970.

Mowery, D. (1983). The relationship between intrafirm and contractual forms of industrial research in American manufacturing. *Explorations in Economic History*, *20*(4), 351−374.

Mowery, D., Oxley, J., & Silverman, B. (1998). Technological overlap and interfirm cooperation: Implications for the resource-based view of the firm. *Research Policy*, *27*(5), 507−523.

Mu, J., Love, E., & Peng G. (2008). Interfirm networks, social capital, and knowledge flow. *Journal of Knowledge Management*, *12*(4), 86−100.

Nonaka, I., & Takeuchi, H. (1995). *The knowledge-creating company*. New York, NY: Oxford University Press.

Ortiz-de-Urbina-Criado, M., Montoro-Sánchez, A., & Romero-Martínez, A. M. (2011). Domestic and international corporate entrepreneurship through alliances. *Canadian Journal of Administrative Sciences*, *28*, 317−327.

Romero-Martínez, A. M., Ortiz-de-Urbina-Criado, M., & Ribeiro-Soriano, D. (2010). Evaluating European Union support for innovation in Spanish small and medium enterprises. *Service Industries Journal*, *30*, 671−683.

Schilling, M. A., & Phelps, C. C. (2007). Interfirm collaboration networks: The impact of large-scale network structure on firm innovation. *Management Science*, *53*, 1113−1126.

Simonen, J., & McCann, P. (2008). Innovation, R&D cooperation and labor recruitment: Evidence from Finland. *Small Business Economics*, *31*(2), 181−194.

Tether, B. (2002). Who co-operates for innovation, and why an empirical analysis? *Research Policy*, *31*, 947−967.

Un, C. A., Romero-Martínez, A. M., & Montoro-Sánchez, A. (2009). Determinants of R&D collaboration of service firms. *Service Business: An International Journal*, *3*, 373−394.

Vega-Jurado, J., Gutiérrez-Gracia, A., & Fernández-de-Lucio, I. (2009). Does external knowledge sourcing matter for innovation? Evidence from the Spanish manufacturing industry. *Industrial & Corporate Change*, *18*, 637−670.

Verspagen, B. (1997). Measuring intersectoral technology spillovers: Estimates from the European and US patent office databases. *Economic Systems Research*, *9*(1), 47−65.

Verspagen, B., & De Loo, I. (1999). Technology spillovers between sectors and over time. *Technological Forecasting and Social Change*, *60*, 215−235.

Veugelers, R., & Cassiman, B. (2005). R&D cooperation between firms and universities. Some empirical evidence from Belgian manufacturing. *International Journal of Industrial Organization*, *23*, 355−379.

CHAPTER 9

A NETWORK APPROACH TO OPEN INNOVATION AND STRATEGIC ALLIANCES

Amalya L. Oliver and Gordon Müller-Seitz

ABSTRACT

Though research on open innovation (OI) and strategic alliances has flourished tremendously, the literature could benefit from incorporating theoretical or analytical insights from the field of interorganizational network research. We address this opportunity by proposing ways to analyze the network structures of strategic alliances among organizations. Herein, we contribute to the literature by focusing firstly beyond egocentric perspectives, moving to the whole network level. Second, we incorporate a stakeholder systems approach incorporating different forms of actors. Third, we differentiate between different forms of openness (inbound and outbound innovation) and pecuniary as well as non-pecuniary forms of knowledge exchange in strategic alliances. Finally, we call for longitudinal perspectives to better understand open innovation and strategic alliances processes. We offer propositions that provide conjunctures between network governance features or structures and the concept of open innovation and strategic alliances. These include network features of reciprocity, homogeneity and heterogeneity, tie strength, and network structures and forms of exchanging knowledge in strategic alliances.

Managing Interpartner Cooperation in Strategic Alliances, pp. 247–273
Copyright © 2022 by Information Age Publishing
www.infoagepub.com
247

INTRODUCTION

Innovations are of utmost importance for organizations. This also appertains to strategic alliances between two or more organizations, whereby different assets are complemented for joint purposes (Hess & Rothaermel, 2011). Innovation activities within strategic alliances are per se what Chesbrough (2003a) has coined open innovation (OI). The open innovation conception has flourished in the past 18 years, generating interest from scholars in the organizational and strategy research fields (Bogers, Chesbrough, & Moedas, 2018; Chesbrough & Bogers, 2014; Randhawa, Wilden, & Hohberger, 2016; Spieth, Laudien, & Meissner, 2020), as well as from science and technology policy research (West & Bogers, 2014). The concept has also been widely diffused in managerial practice ever since Chesbrough (2003a, 2003b) coined the term. The key feature of what open innovation means is the assumed beneficial opening up of organizational boundaries, blurring these very boundaries towards the environment (Dahlander & Gann, 2010), which can take manifold forms, exempli gratia (e.g.) including dealing with intellectual property rights (Henkel, Schöberl & Alexy, 2014; Laursen & Salter, 2014), users (lead users in particular), suppliers, venture capitalists and even competitors (e.g., Gassmann & Reepmeyer, 2005; Von Hippel, 1986). The new inbound knowledge can be utilized using various forms of knowledge governance; some are more beneficial than others (Lakemond, Bengtsson, Laursen, & Tell, 2016). This approach makes the concept applicable to a variety of organizations and sectors. However, the downside of this broad applicability is the observation that the OI field is becoming fragmented (Gianiodis, Ellis, & Secchi, 2010; Huizingh, 2011). Moreover, while the literature offers various definitions and foci points for OI, it could still benefit from incorporating theoretical or analytical insights from interorganizational network research to facilitate the generation of theoretically embedded questions and hypotheses-driven empirical testing. This would enable OI research, against the backdrop of strategic alliances, to frame and analyze a large number of OI phenomena as networks of OI, beyond the general conceptual specifications and detailed case studies.

Hence, venturing beyond the innovation management literature can offer insights that support a more solid theoretical foundation of open innovation research in light of strategic alliances and beyond (Bouncken, Fredrich, Kraus, & Ritala, 2020; Randhawa et al., 2016). While interactions with crowds (Afuah & Tucci, 2012) or dyadic interactions between two organizations (e.g., in the form of dyadic strategic alliances; Child, Faulkner, & Tallman, 2005) are comparatively well understood, fewer theory-building efforts have targeted strategic alliances' networks, understood as three or more organizations collaborating for a joint purpose (Powell, 1990). In a recent review, West and Bogers (2014, pp. 44–45) state that there is a need to focus more on network collaboration within the framework of open innovation: "Another important extension has been moving beyond the bilateral collaborations of Chesbrough (2003) to various network typologies of collaboration... These network forms include alliances, communities, consortia, ecosystems, and platforms, and require firms to orchestrate (or negotiate) the joint value creation and value capture of the firms across the network.... Little OI research has been done on such networks." Randhawa and colleagues (2016, p. 758) join this chorus, arguing that the "[m]anagement of OI networks is a theme that has attracted limited research." Towards this end, we draw upon the established literature on interorganizational networks and collaborations among organizations (Borgatti & Foster, 2003; Cropper, Ebers, Huxham, & Ring 2008; DeBresson & Amesse, 1991; Dougherty, 2017; Huggins, 2010; Huxham & Vangen, 2005; Jarillo, 1988; Oliver & Kalish, 2011; Parkhe, Wasserman, & Ralston 2006; Provan, Fish, & Sydow, 2007; Sydow, Schüßler, & Müller-Seitz, 2016; Zaheer, Gözübüyük, & Milanov, 2010), as well as between universities and industry, which has been predominantly addressed against the backdrop of science-based and knowledge intensive industries (Oliver, 2009; Powell, White, Koput, & Owen-Smith, 2005) and innovation ecosystems (e.g. Adner, 2017; Davis, 2016).

In this debate, there are also network methodologies that allow for examining network structures among organizations (Borgatti, Everett, & Johnson, 2013; Kastelle & Steen, 2010; Knoke & Yang, 2007; Oliver & Kalish, 2011; Wasserman & Faust, 1994). These very network structures can become a major facilitating force that can enhance large-scale open innovation processes; increase knowledge sharing and reciprocating, and increase firm, industry, regional, and national levels of innovation (Belussi, Sammarra, & Sedita, 2010; Cooke, 2001; Dhanaraj & Parkhe, 2006; Lundvall, 1992). Studies rooted in the area of interorganizational networks and collaborations, as well as network-methodology driven contributions, seldom explicitly use the term open innovation (Sydow et al., 2016; West, Salter, Vanhaverbeke, & Chesbrough, 2014).

In what follows, we seek to expand on open innovation and strategic alliance research by informing both debates theoretically and methodologically. Building thereupon, it is our goal to theorize how open innovation can be conceptualized on the clusters (Cooke, 2002; Vörös & Snijders, 2017) or on the whole network level of analysis (Provan et al., 2007; Xue, 2018). We suggest that this level of analysis needs further theorizing if we want to better understand how open innovation takes place within networks (Nieto & Santamaría, 2007; Randhawa et al., 2016; West & Bogers, 2014; Zeng, Xie, & Tam, 2010). Hence, we focus on the context wherein open innovation in strategic alliances' networks takes place. In particular, we seek to include different actors, network structures and types of interorganizational knowledge exchanges.

Our main effort lies in refining the concept of open innovation in a number of directions. First, venturing from the egocentric hub-organizational level to the cluster or a whole network level answers recent calls for venturing beyond the firm-centric focus of OI research (e.g., Randhawa et al., 2016). Towards this end, we concentrate upon concepts of network research dealing with the structural underpinnings of interorganizational networks (Borgatti et al., 2013; Wasserman & Faust, 1994) related to network governance (e.g., tie strength) and network structure (e.g., density). Secondly, we move the focus from firms only to a wider, stakeholder systems approach, suggesting the inclusion of actors such as universities, research institutes and crowds, which responds to similar calls by Adner (2017) or Davis (2016). Third, we will follow the conceptual distinction made by Dahlander and Gann (2010) between different forms of openness (inbound and outbound innovation), also including non-pecuniary, informal, and not-for-profit knowledge exchange processes into the way we reflect upon interorganizational networks. Fourth, we extend the perspective from an emphasis on a cross-sectional approach to a process-based longitudinal approach, and claim that this will allow us to better understand open innovation processes. These suggested refinements can open the field for empirical, theory-driven studies that contain wider foci and more precise analytical distinctions.

We start by reviewing the literature on open innovation and discussing the various definitions offered. Then we move on to offering a stakeholder analysis of the potential participants in open-innovation-based collaborations and show how a stakeholder systems approach (Roelofsen, Boon, Kloet, & Broerse, 2011) maps the wide spectrum of potential open-innovation collaborative frameworks. Figure 9.1 also depicts the underlying idea of an integration between stakeholders within the ecosystem and the connecting compatibilities within the process of the formation of open-innovation networks (Paredes-Frigolett, & Pyka, 2017). In the following section, we offer an integration of network-based concepts that can enhance open innovation as a key for network management and policy development.

OPEN INNOVATION: DEFINITIONS AND IMPLICATIONS

The concept of open innovation (Chesbrough, 2006) calls for externalizing knowledge to the network of alliances' partners and internalizing knowledge from the network of alliances' partners, yet the network is not well-defined in terms of characteristics and structure (Huizingh, 2011). While we seek to inform the literature on open innovation via insights from

Figure 9.1

The General Process Approach to Networks of Open Innovation

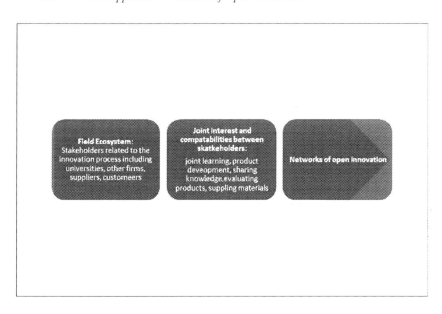

the literature on interorganizational networks, we aim to widen the open innovation paradigm to include new models in which network characteristics and structure become inherent features of various research questions.

From the different definitions presented in Table 9.1, we can see that the use of the concept of open innovation is not uniform. Open innovation is described in different places as a paradigm (Chesbrough, 2003a), a model (Chesbrough, 2003b), a strategy (Laursen & Salter, 2006) or a system (Dittrich & Duysters, 2007), and there is no discussion about the meaning of the concept or the theoretical implications of these descriptive variations. In addition, the concept of open innovation deals with both inflow and outflow of ideas and knowledge (Chesbrough, 2003a, 2003b; Dahlander & Gann, 2010; Laursen & Salter, 2006). Yet, these writers are not specific about the nature of the exchanged knowledge and about the conditions under which we observe inflows and outflows, or whether the knowledge exchange is symmetrical, compatible, or complimentary (e.g., Matutes & Regibeau, 1998; Nielsen, 2002). Following this challenge, we suggest clarifying who the external parties are that provide the ideas or knowledge for the inflow, as well as who those are who benefit from the outflow and their role in any possible reciprocation process. Beyond the opacities mentioned above, the open innovation literature is depicted egocentrically, from the perspective of a single organization and its OI exchanges, while an ecosystem, network-based approach can provide a broader perspective.

Table 9.1

Definitions of Open Innovation

Author(s)	Definition
Chesbrough (2003a)	Open Innovation is a paradigm that assumes that firms can and should use external ideas as well as internal ideas, and internal and external paths to market, as the firms look to advance their technology. Open Innovation combines internal and external ideas into architectures and systems whose requirements are defined by a business model:
	"The use of purposive inflows and outflows of knowledge to accelerate internal innovation, and expand the markets for external use of innovation, respectively." (p. 1)
Chesbrough (2003b)	In this new model of open innovation, firms commercialize external (as well as internal) ideas by deploying outside (as well as in-house) pathways to the market. Specifically, companies can commercialize internal ideas through channels outside of their current businesses in order to generate value for the organization.
Chesbrough & Bogers (2014)	"A distributed innovation process based on purposively managed knowledge flows across organizational boundaries, using pecuniary and non-pecuniary mechanisms in line with the organization's business model" (p. 17)
Chesbrough, Vanhaverbeke, & West (2006)	"the use of purposive inflows and outflows of knowledge to accelerate internal innovation, and to expand the markets for external use of innovation, respectively" (p. vii)
Dittrich & Duysters (2007)	"Thus, an open-innovation system may result in a complex network of relationship with other organizations, serving different purposes in different periods." (p. 513)
Laursen & Salter (2006)	Not explicitly defined but measured as the breadth and depth of engaging with multiple knowledge sources (market, institutional, specialized and others) "different external search strategies for innovative ideas across different knowledge sources" (p. 147)
Poot & Faems (2009)	In a closed innovation model, firms internalize their firm-specific R&D activities, and commercialize them through internal development, manufacturing, and distribution processes. This model considers R&D as an inherent part of a vertically integrated system within firms. [...] In contrast, an open innovation model is characterized by the use of purposive inflows and outflows of knowledge to accelerate internal innovation, and expand the markets for external use of innovation, respectively. This model treats R&D as an open system in which external ideas and external paths to market are placed on the same level of importance as internal ideas and paths to market. (p. 3)

The literature further suggests that the role of coexisting and potentially competing governance models has not been analyzed so far. In particular, we know little about how competing governance models coexist against the backdrop of innovation networks (Browning & Shetler, 2000; Müller-Seitz & Sydow, 2012). For instance, cross-sector actors have been shown to exhibit colliding logics in the course of collaborating in innovation networks (Al-Tabbaa, Leach & Khan, 2019; Browning & Shetler, 2000; Gambardella & Panico, 2014; Koschmann, Kuhn, & Pfarrer, 2012). These very settings cannot be managed in a merely hierarchical fashion, as the underlying organizations are unlikely to be managed in the same way. A case in point might be the usage and redistribution of data or knowledge produced in the context of intellectual property rights. Whereas public organizations might have a rather lax attitude when it comes to distributing the knowledge generated, for-profit companies vying for market shares might be less interested in freely sharing the knowledge generated, and more inclined to engage in the protection of knowledge integration (Alexy, George, & Salter, 2013; Dhanaraj & Parkhe, 2006; Oliver & Kalish, 2011). This complexity is depicted well in the argument by Laursen and Salter (2014) on the "paradox of openness." Their argument claims that a firm's openness may demand more attention to issues of knowledge protection. By following Arrow (1962) they claim that

> Appropriating the benefits deriving from an innovation requires considerable managerial attention and effort, such as applying for patents, establishing a market lead time, keeping key technologies secret from competitors, and gaining access to complementary assets.... Following the open innovation literature, we contend that these efforts have a major influence on the firm's approach to the external environment in relation to who it works with, where it looks for ideas, and how it organizes its own innovative activities. (Laursen & Salter, 2014, p. 868)

Using a similar logic, Henkel (2006) found that firms using Linux are using a co-existing sharing strategy and revealing their knowledge selectively. They reveal about half of the code they have developed, while protecting the other half by various means.

Finally, industry characteristics might also be associated with open innovation. In some industries, such as biotechnology, it is assumed that no products can be developed based on knowledge, capabilities or resources that exist within a single organization. Thus, knowledge-based collaborations have been widely studied in this industry (Bianchi, Cavaliere, Chiaroni, Frattini, & Chiesa, 2011; Oliver, 2004, 2009; Oliver & Liebeskind, 1997; Powell, Koput, & Smith-Doerr, 1996; Powell et al., 2005). Recent studies show how knowledge in biotechnology is exchanged informally through the scientific networks that have emerged in the industry through conferences and joint workshops between firms (Maurer & Ebers, 2006; Powell & Grodal, 2005; Swan et al., 2005; Whittington, Owen-Smith, & Powell, 2009). This is a general issue of the context dependency of open innovation that is not clear (Huizingh, 2011), as well as the internal and external environments that affect performance.

Similar observations in terms of being sensitive to opening up the innovation process can be made in the field of complex product systems (CoPS), such as the aerospace industry (Hobday, 1998). For the semiconductor manufacturing industry, the SEMATECH consortium is portrayed as being an example where open innovation appears to be mandatory due to the complexity of the products as well as the large amounts of investments needed to pursue future technological options (Browning, Beyer, & Shetler, 1995; Browning & Shetler, 2000; Lange, Müller-Seitz, Sydow, & Windeler, 2013).

From a network perspective, the introduction of the open flows idea and knowledge, while retaining an egocentric view, limits our understanding of the potential in this perspective. This is because no organization is acting in isolation within a vacuum (Richardson, 1972) or within a single relationship. Indeed, organization theory in the past 40 years has been based on the assumption of open ecosystems (Kenis & Knoke, 2002; Scott & Davis, 2015) and organizations operating within the pressures and constraints of organizational fields (DiMaggio & Powell, 1983). Following these basic assumptions, any dyadic exchange between two organizations occurs within a larger context of potential collaborative, competitive or neutral firms who can benefit from enhancing or blocking this knowledge flow. We therefore claim that the ideas of open innovation have to be introduced within a larger structure of interorganizational networks, as is theorized and analyzed in the interorganizational learning networks literature (Dyer & Nobeoka, 2000; Oliver, 2009; Powell et al., 2005; to mention a few).

Furthermore, we seek to offer operationalization measures for "open innovation" for both theory development and network-level propositions. If we are to compare two firms on their level of open innovation, what can be measured? There are potentially a few directions. One can focus on the subjective estimation of organizational members regarding the degree to which ideas are shared with external actors. On a more objective level, one can measure the collaborative relations not under formal contractual arrangements, which may depict trust-based relations (Das & Teng, 1996, 2001; Nooteboom, 2004).

In the next section, we introduce a wider contextual frame for studying open innovation. We will introduce the multiplicity of actors that operate within networks in a knowledge intensive industry, organizational fields, or a sector. In addition, we will review related interorganizational network research and make initial propositions.

STRATEGIC ALLIANCES AS INTERORGANIZATIONAL INNOVATION NETWORKS

Mapping an interorganizational ecosystem that surrounds strategic alliances (Bouncken et al., 2020) of related actors is an important step before defining the boundaries of the potential networks of interorganizational learning needs (Adner, 2017). We make a distinction between firms that are similar to or different from the focal firm in terms of the products they develop or services they provide. This resonates with similar inquiries by Belderbos, Faems, Leten, and Looy (2014) who distinguish between intra-industry partners, inter-industry partners and universities. By doing so, we can map compatibilities and potential for competition (primarily among similar firms) or collaborations (primarily among different firms). In this distinction we include start-up firms that are knowledge intensive and large firms that can offer development and market capabilities to start-ups in the same knowledge or product domain (Oliver, 2009). We add universities that act as important actors of knowledge development (Casanueva & Gallego, 2014; Perkman & Walsh, 2007), especially in knowledge intensive industries such as biotechnology or information technology, and that can offer a flow of information or knowledge (Oliver, 2009; Powell et al., 1996) or be partners for collaborative research (Belderbos et al., 2014).

In the spirit of the open innovation literature, we also add another set of stakeholders; that is, the public/users as the end-line actors that may hold important information for learning or needs related to innovation for certain actors within an industry (Afuah & Tucci, 2012; Alexy et al., 2013; Greer & Lei, 2012). We know that the users can contribute to innovation by being asked to offer their reactions to the product, process, or service or by offering information based on their own choices and preferences. Take, for example, the navigation software WAZE, which incorporates information from their users while optimizing their navigations services.

The analysis can range from dyadic analysis of any two collaborating actors, to knowledge flow or information flow, to egocentric networks where one firm is at the center and all other collaborating actors to/from whom knowledge is flowing surround the firm, and to whole networks where all the collaborating actors and their exchanges within a certain domain are mapped (Provan et al., 2007; Xue, 2018).

To illustrate with some examples, we can typify two main facets of open innovation: the various collaborating actors, as well as their main characteristics. In terms of the collaborating actors involved, at the early stages of the concept's use, firms were considered the main collaborating actors (Chesbrough, 2003a). But the open innovation approach can be applied to both firms and universities (Belderbos et al., 2014), as well as firms and the public (Lakhani, Boudreau, Guinan, Baldwin, MacCormack, Lonstein,

Lydon, & Arnaout, 2013) or users of innovative products (von Hippel, 1995) and the general public as future users interested in the product/process or service offered by the focal firm. Thus, the collaborating actors who participate in this process are diverse key actors who hold knowledge valuable to the innovation process.

We can also focus on different levels of analysis, ranging from the dyadic relations between two R&D firms to larger constellations or clusters of networks such as university-industry consortia with universities, R&D firms, and established firms. The largest constellation can include various types of actors. To clarify, we offer two illustrative examples. One could conduct the analysis when the collaboration is between two R&D firms, and this may be in the nature of a horizontal collaboration, where the exchange is based on compatibility of knowledge. Another project could conduct the analysis of a constellation of firms and universities (for example, a university-industry science consortia) where some potential users from the public can also participate. In this case, different types of multiple knowledge exchanges can lead to the development of a technology or a product. To address this wide variety of options, in the following section we offer a framework that is subsequently enriched by insights from structural measures.

RESEARCH ON INTERORGANIZATIONAL NETWORKS AND COLLABORATIONS

The Framework

To fully capture the broad spectrum of possibilities in terms of how open innovation can unfold within and across networks, we propose a holistic conception of potential collaboration constellations (see left side of Figure 9.1). First, we seek to incorporate different kinds of actors that operate in a cluster or network, or an ecosystem venturing beyond egocentric perspectives (see Adner, 2017, who offers a critique and a structuralist approach to conceptualizing the ecosystem construct). Second, we allow for a dynamic perspective of how knowledge is generated, exchanged, and acquired (Ebers, 1999). Third, we allow for various kinds of knowledge to be exchanged; relating to Dahlander and Gann (2010), we are interested not only in pecuniary, formalized knowledge exchange processes, but also in non-pecuniary, informal, and not-for-profit knowledge exchange processes.

Figure 9.2 depicts a hypothetical arena of open innovation, where we illustrate (a) the range of network actors in a field, (b) different types of knowledge exchanged, and (c) the change in the network over time. Thus, we offer the contextualization of open innovation in terms of the actors, the knowledge exchanged and the changes over time. Towards this end, we

Figure 9.2

*A Network-Related, Theoretically Refined Framework of Open Innovation Research
Against the Backdrop of Strategic Alliances Across Sectors*

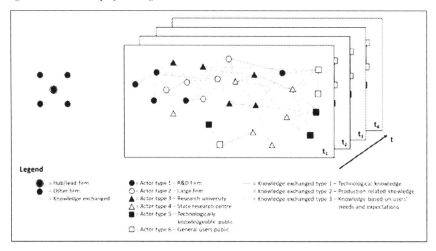

argue that each specific context offers opportunities and constraints that
influence the actors' preferences for and degrees of engaging in closed
and/or open innovation activities (see Figure 9.3). The ability to innovate,
then, is dependent upon two key features of structural network analysis,
namely network governance and network structure. Such an approach
merits attention as it allows for a theoretical or analytical platform that
can facilitate theoretically embedded questions and hypotheses-driven
empirical testing.

Overview: Network Models, Governance Forms and Contexts That Can Enhance Open Innovation

Building upon the variety of interorganizational OI constellations, we
propose an integrative approach that brings the notion of open innovation
elements into the features and structure of the interorganizational network. In doing so, we seek to offer network-related propositions that can
offer conjunctures between network structures and features and expected
patterns of open innovation (see Figure 9.3). With such specification of
network features and structures modelled as independent variables or
dependent variables, propositions related to open innovation can be examined empirically with organizational level datasets.

Figure 9.3

The Context and Network Features of Open Innovation Processes in Light of Strategic Alliances

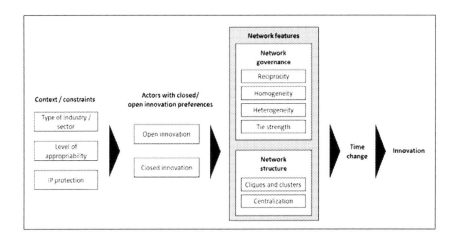

We distinguish between two main network categories: network governance (Jones, Hesterly & Borgatti, 1997; Provan & Kenis, 2008) and network structure (Reagans & McEvily, 2003; Schilling & Phelps, 2007). The category of "Network governance [...] involves a select, persistent, and structured set of autonomous firms (as well as nonprofit agencies) engaged in creating products or services based on implicit and open-ended contracts to adapt to environmental contingencies and to coordinate and safeguard exchanges. These contracts are socially—not legally—binding" (Jones et al., 1997, p. 914). Thus, by network governance, we refer to any coordinated interorganizational systems with strong safeguards and strong norms of reciprocity. The main argument is that under conditions of demand uncertainty and task complexity, the organizations within the network will tend to form socially embedded transactions, and this will lead to governance mechanisms that include restricted access and collective sanctions on opportunistic behavior and reputation as the basis for exchanges within the network.

For the category of network structure, we refer to measures that characterize the network as a structure that depicts various forms of ties between the actors, and the structures of such ties when two or more actors are involved (Capaldo, 2007; Oliver, 2009; Oliver & Ebers, 1998; Reagans & McEvily, 2003; Schilling & Phelps, 2007). Such measures can include, on the dyadic level, ties strength and frequency; and on the network level, social cohesion and network range (Reagans & McEvily, 2003), network density, cliques and clustering (Schilling & Phelps, 2007), as well as various types of centralities (e.g. "reach" Schilling & Phelps, 2007) or network centralization (Ferriani & MacMillan, 2017).

In the next section, we describe the concepts suggested and provide some propositions that provide conjunctures between network governance features or structures and the concept of open innovation.

Network Governance

Network governance depicts the "shielding" coordinative features of networks of interorganizational collaborations under high levels of ambiguity and environmental complexities, and represents strong norms of trustworthy behavior (Jones et al., 1997). Below, we offer an integration of these parameters into the open innovation paradigm. Towards this end, we introduce the ideas of reciprocity, homogeneity, heterogeneity, and tie strength.

The term *reciprocity* is not commonly used in the context of organization studies. In technical language of networks, reciprocity measures the tendency of vertex pairs to form mutual connections. In the social networks approach, reciprocity is usually studied in the context of community building and establishing shared norms. We know from the literature that norms of reciprocity facilitate social integration (Gouldner, 1960) and encourage long-term commitment to giving and sharing. In a group of networking organizations, norms of reciprocity emerge when there are high levels of compatibility and trust between the collaborating organizations, and when the levels of community norms and interorganizational trust (Liebeskind & Oliver, 2000; Liebeskind, Oliver, Zucker, & Brewer, 1996; Oliver, 1997; Perrons, 2009) facilitate generosity in knowledge sharing as normative systems of reciprocity. This means that organizations are attending to the needs of other organizations for knowledge, technology, materials, and capabilities and are willing to give each other these resources, regardless of secrecy keeping and protection motivations. This is in the belief and trust that, if they have such a need, other firms will be likely to return favors (Muthusamy & White, 2005). The trust and reciprocity benefit is expected to increase joint problem-solving efforts and searching within various knowledge combinations that can be reached by different partners and lead to higher rates of innovation (Capaldo, 2007; Dyer & Nobeoka, 2000; Savino, Petruzzelli, & Albino, 2017). Consistent with this argument, we comprehend "rates of innovation" as the tendency to engage in open innovation activities. We thus suggest that:

Proposition 1: *Higher levels of trust between network members will be associated with reciprocity in sharing information and knowledge within a network of firms, leading to more open innovation activities.*

It is important to note that our use of reciprocity is more general than merely a sharing of ideas. It also can include an exchange of materials available to one firm but hard to find for the collaborating partner, as well as pooling together shared interests and motivation to act jointly on technology policy issues, and to collaborate in establishing consortia to access resources needed for a group of firms.

The next two measures—"homogeneity" and "heterogeneity" of the network—are opposites of each other. However, they are both perceived in the literature as associated with a greater level of innovative performance. There is no contradiction in claiming that both are relevant to the issue of open innovation. Firms can benefit from ties with homogeneous partners, based on the redundancy of knowledge and capabilities that may lead to a higher level of trust and spillover of knowledge. At the same time, firms can benefit from heterogeneous partners that can provide access to complementarities and a greater range of knowledge and capabilities.

In terms of *homogeneity*, a group is homogeneous when it is uniform in composition or character with regard to the technology used, product area, research focus, and so forth. We know from the literature that homogeneity is associated with a tendency to gather together, and with higher levels of trust among members (Borgatti & Foster, 2003; Sydow & Windeler, 2003). In the context of knowledge intensive firms, homogeneity is associated with similar knowledge and related capabilities. This generates redundancies of knowledge, and these redundancies increase actors' ability to evaluate the knowledge and capabilities that the collaborative partner has, and to estimate the potential benefits from open knowledge exchanges, along with a higher level of trust (Das & Teng, 2001; Muthusamy & White, 2006). Breschi and Malerba (2005, pp. 189–190) studied regional clusters and networks in industrial districts in Italy and argue that the knowledge and capability redundancy of firms within the same district who perform similar but slightly different functions is associated with facilitating the diffusion of information. We thus propose that:

Proposition 2: *In homogeneous networks of firms with similar types of knowledge, capabilities, and technologies, sharing of knowledge will increase due to the higher level of trust between network members, leading to higher rates of open innovation.*

When it comes to *heterogeneity*, this term relates to diversity in kind or nature. In the context of open innovation, it is expected that when firms in a network are dissimilar, having different knowledge market experience and technological capabilities, open innovation will be enhanced and lead to a higher rate of exposure to heterogeneous knowledge and innovation outcomes. Sammarra and Biggiero (2008) found that innovation is a complex process that requires and benefits from exposure to heterogeneous knowledge at both individual and organizational levels. Similarly, Rodan and Galunic (2004) found that access through networks to the heterogeneous knowledge in other firms is of importance for overall managerial performance and of greater importance for innovation performance.

Proposition 3: *In networks where firms can access heterogeneous knowledge through collaborations with other firms, there will be higher rates of open innovation.*

With regard to *tie strength*, this term relates to two collaborating organizations, whereby tie strength in effect facilitates the transfer of knowledge between organizations. Strong ties reflect a greater degree of commitment and emotional attachment between actors; therefore, if the source of knowledge and the recipient have a strong relationship, the knowledge source is expected to agree to spend more time and effort sharing knowledge with the knowledge recipient (Tortoriello, Reagans, & McEvily, 2012). Reagans and McEvily (2003, p. 261) also found that, beyond the effect of network density on knowledge transfer processes, tie strength significantly eases the transfer of knowledge (p. 259). The relationship between tie strength and the sharing of knowledge was found to exist, yet was mediated by competence and benevolence-based trust (Levin & Cross, 2004). Thus, we posit:

Proposition 4: *The higher the tie strength, the more likely it is that knowledge exchange will be facilitated across firms, leading to higher rates of open innovation.*

Network Structure

In this section we introduce a set of network structure measures that can be associated with open innovation. These include network cliques and clusters, and centralization. We describe each measure and explain its relevance to open innovation.

The definition of *cliques* in network research is "a small close-knit group of people who do not readily allow others to join them" (Oxford, 2021). *Clusters* are somewhat different and refer to places where firms form a cluster that is regionally interconnected. Hence, cliques can be defined as exhibiting a strong interconnectedness, while clusters emerge in a spatial context. In the context of organizations, these structures refer to cases where a group of interconnected organizations have various collaborative exchanges within the group yet restrict the entry of additional actors. This can be the case of a formal R&D consortium with clear boundaries or a set of subsidiary firms (all connected through a shared parent organization) that collaborate only among themselves. On the informal level, it can relate to firms who voluntarily choose to collaborate on shared ideas, compatible knowledge, or technology development—in a certain region, district, or industry—yet act to keep this structure closed to other external actors (Xue, 2018).

In such social structures, it is expected that strong norms of sharing and collaboration will emerge in the form of open innovation, under the assumption that each firm is giving and receiving knowledge based on its needs (Alexy et al., 2013). When the trust level within such cliques increases, it is expected that fears of knowledge appropriation will be reduced, while open sharing of knowledge, based on expected reciprocity, will increase. In this context, Schilling and Phelps (2007) studied over one thousand firms in 11 industry-level alliance networks and found that firms embedded in alliance networks characterized by high clustering and frequent short path length to other firms have a greater innovative output than firms that are not embedded in such networks. Similarly, Baptista and Swann (1998) found that firms located in clusters innovate more. Thus, we suggest that:

Proposition 5: *Closed structures of firms in the form of cliques or clusters will be associated with a higher level of trustworthiness and, thus, a higher level of knowledge sharing, leading to higher rates of open innovation.*

Centralization in a network is associated with a strong central formal position or a strong informal position (Dhanaraj & Parkhe, 1994; Ferriani & MacMillan, 2017). In a formal network, a centralizing organization can include the position of a managing organization in the role of monitoring other organizations in the network over specific tasks, or when acting as a central organization in terms of distributing resources to other organizations in the system (Capaldo, 2007; Lorenzoni & Lipparini, 1999). In an informal network characterized by volunteer exchanges, a strong informal centralizing position can be in the form of network leadership (Dyer & Nobeoka, 2000; Huxham & Vangen, 2000; Müller-Seitz, 2012), such as organizing activities toward policy design or change. Previous research has pointed out that it is highly likely that a central organization within a network can enhance norms of knowledge sharing that will benefit the entire network of organizations that surrounds it (Dhanaraj & Parkhe, 2006; Lorenzoni & Lipparini, 1999). For example, a network with a strong central actor, such as a large pharmaceutical company that has formed collaborations with universities and smaller biotechnology firms, can enhance a higher level of knowledge sharing among members of the networks due to the interests established by the centralized actor (Oliver, 2009). This centralized actor also has the power to monitor trustworthy sharing, reciprocity, and openness, as well as sanction any misbehavior of organizations in the network. Thus, we propose that:

Proposition 6: *Networks with high centralization will benefit from a strong central actor that can diffuse the adoption of high rates of open innovation.*

There are three additional important refinements that can enlarge the scope of OI research. The first is to classify the direction of the knowledge exchanged and its nature. The second is to follow the longitudinal development of OI networks, and the third refers to governance forms that can enhance OI. In the next section, we elaborate on these.

Explicitly dealing with open innovation and reviewing the literature, Dahlander and Gann (2010) propose a differentiation between different forms of exchanging knowledge, *pecuniary versus non-pecuniary knowledge exchanges*. Pecuniary knowledge exchange deals with commercializing inventions and technologies through selling or licensing out resources developed in other organizations. Non-pecuniary knowledge exchange deals with how firms reveal internal resources without immediate financial rewards, seeking indirect benefits for the focal firm (Alexy et al. 2013; Henkel et al., 2014). Thus, they identify two inbound open innovation processes of acquiring knowledge (i.e., in a market-oriented transaction, licensing out) and sourcing knowledge (i.e., searching for external knowledge informally), and two outbound processes, selling (e.g., licensing out knowledge) and revealing knowledge (i.e., purposefully disclosing non-patented knowledge to actors outside of the focal organization without immediate financial rewards). As pointed out, we are interested in and open to both pecuniary and non-pecuniary forms of knowledge exchange mechanisms.

Following Dahlander and Gann's (2010) distinction, we suggest that any network-based study of open innovation needs to distinguish between inbound and outbound knowledge exchange processes, between single-directional or reciprocal processes, and between pecuniary or non-pecuniary knowledge resources. Moreover, in our view, there is a hierarchy in the exchange of knowledge, and the more "pure" cases of OI exist when firms exchange non-pecuniary knowledge resources. However, it is important to be able to depict cases where the exchange of knowledge is not for immediate financial gains. With this view, Dahlander and Gann (2010) suggest that revealing internal knowledge as a form of non-pecuniary outbound innovation may be a double-edged sword. On the one hand, it can make an organization vulnerable (e.g., Helfat & Quinn, 2006) and maybe ineffective, as it does not have "absorptive capacity capabilities" (Spithoven, Clarysse, & Knockaert, 2011); alternatively, this very vulnerability can also be a source of gaining legitimacy (see, e.g., Alexy et al., 2013). In addition, being too "open" towards a broad range and number of ideas might be difficult, if not impossible, to process (Laursen & Salter, 2006).

Although understanding *knowledge exchange longitudinal dynamics in networks* is important, there is a need for more studies of networks focusing on knowledge exchanges over time (Ahuja, 2000; Oliver, 2009; Paruchuri, 2010; Powell et al., 1996). Depicting the longitudinal evolution of collaborative networks is hard, and data are not always available for such projects. Yet, with the aim of better understanding OI processes, future research should explore how OI at stage 1 is associated with OI at stage 2, and so forth. For example, using a longitudinal perspective over time, Phelps (2010) found that the technological diversity of a firm's alliance partners is associated with an increase in its exploratory innovation. In another longitudinal study of an automobile supply network, Dyer and Hatch (2006) found that greater knowledge sharing by Toyota resulted in a faster rate of learning for the suppliers' manufacturing operations that were devoted to Toyota. Another study (Oliver, 2001) found a life-cycle pattern according to which biotechnology firms establish learning alliances. Oliver claimed that alliance-based learning is vital to biotechnology firms at the early stages of their formation, when learning is associated with exploration, while at later phases of the life-cycle, learning is internally exploited through intrafirm networks. By adding a time dimension to OI studies, scholars will be able to better understand the conditions that facilitate and those that hinder OI, as well as how OI can change the product outcomes of firms and the landscape of OI networks.

DISCUSSION AND CONCLUDING REMARKS

Open innovation can operate on the dyadic level (i.e., between two collaborative actors forming a strategic alliance) or within a network of collaborating actors as strategic alliances. In this inquiry we provide an initial effort to combine the concept of open innovation with the literature and ideas of interorganizational collaborations and strategic alliances. We discuss network features, network structures and network governance forms in order to develop propositions that can be tested in specific studies.

We summarize with some disclaimers about open innovation and network boundaries. How open can open innovation be? Innovation strategic alliances by definition demand a certain degree of permeability in terms of the knowledge boundaries of the firm, as well as the knowledge boundaries of the network, to enable collaboration across network partners; blurring these boundaries demands either one-way permeability (e.g., licensing a product to an external partner) or two-way or multilateral permeability (e.g., generating novel products for joint purposes and uses). How this engagement ought to unfold and what the nature of the relations is between the organization and the network and in parallel, the network and its environment, has not been conceptualized so far. We suggest that a theoretically and methodologically sound perspective of open innovation in strategic alliances can be achieved by informing the debate with insights from network research. Features proposed, such as reciprocity, contribute to a dynamic perspective on how open innovation unfolds in networks over time (Gouldner, 1960), which helps to elucidate how and why organizations collaborate in loosely coupled fashions. Such a perspective is in line with recent research on network dynamics in innovative settings, such as innovation ecosystems (Adner, 2017; Davis, 2016), and allows us to shed light on how networks evolve by not necessarily assuming that a network remains a fixed entity over time.

Despite advancing the open innovation management debate by means of introducing structural measures to better comprehend the way open innovation unfolds in networks, we feel that several challenges remain to explore in future research. First, are there patterns of measures relating to strategic alliances' governance and strategic alliances' structure that can be observed across settings, which result in particularly successful or failure-prone open innovation strategic alliance activities? Though we inform the open innovation debate concerning the network features introduced, several patterns await exploration, such as those concerning indicators of financial turnover, the rate of innovations or the degree of innovativeness of the ensuing outputs (e.g., radical versus incremental innovations).

Second, methodologically and relating to the concept of embeddedness (Granovetter, 1985) and the idea of a theory of fields (Fligstein & McAdam, 2012), an ongoing challenge for empirical studies involves where to draw the boundary of the setting to be analyzed (Adner, 2017). This challenge requires that studies of open innovation and strategic alliances aim for an uncontested, shared definition and measurement of fields in term of time frame, actors and types of knowledge exchanged. This would allow for comparative studies of open innovation strategic alliances in different industry contexts and would advance the understanding of open innovation.

Third, several of our suggestions await empirical confirmation across settings so as to derive industry or sector-specific recommendations. While it was not our goal to offer such recommendations, in order to remain theoretically sound and abstract, the generalizability of our assumptions comes at the expense of a detailed, rich account of how open innovation strategic alliances operate in different settings. While the technology and R&D driven settings seem comparatively well explored (e.g., Oliver, 2009; Powell et al., 1996), we lack a better understanding of network dynamics in other settings. For instance, service settings might exhibit different characteristics worth taking into account, as opposed to the predominantly industry driven theoretical and empirical advancements documented. This can be traced back to the key features of most services, which differ from "traditional" industrial production settings, such as the uno-actu principle (i.e., the immediate consumption of the service on delivery) or perishability of services provided (e.g., Zeithaml, Berry, & Parasuraman, 1996). In fact, Van de Vrande, De Jong, Vanhaverbeke, and de Rochemont (2009) found differences between manufacturing and services industries (for example, manufacturing firms have adopted R&D outsourcing more often than service firms) as well as between small and medium sized firms in terms of their open innovation practices.

Our goal is to bring to the fore the importance of shifting the focus of open innovation from the dyadic level to the whole network level (Provan et al., 2007). Since knowledge exchanges and collaborations take place in larger groups of firms, it is of value to incorporate strategic alliances' features and structures. The basic proposition is that certain features and structures facilitate or inhibit firms' openness beyond the dyadic level. As we zoom out of the dyadic level, we are better able to see the roles of strategic alliances and their structures in enhancing open innovation—a timely topic awaiting future fruitful exchanges across disciplinary silos. Towards this end, we posit that measures of network governance and network structure help to improve our understanding of how open innovation is influenced by different features of the focal strategic alliances. We view this effort as the start of an ongoing engagement between the fields of innovation and strategic alliance management.

REFERENCES

Adner, R. (2017). Ecosystem as structure: An actionable construct for strategy. *Journal of Management*, *43*(1), 39–58.

Afuah, A., & Tucci, C. L. (2012). Crowdsourcing as a solution to distant search. *Academy of Management Review*, *37*(3), 355–375.

Ahuja, G. (2000). Collaboration networks, structural holes, and innovation: A longitudinal study. *Administrative Science Quarterly, 45*(3), 425–455.

Alexy, O., George, G., & Salter, A. (2013). Cui bono? The selective revealing of knowledge and its implications for innovative activity. *Academy of Management Review*, *38*(2), 270–291.

Al-Tabbaa, O., Leach, D., & Khan, Z. (2019). Examining alliance management capabilities in cross-sector collaborative partnerships. *Journal of Business Research, 101*, 268–284

Arrow, K. J. (1962). Economic welfare and the allocation of resources for invention. In K. J. Arrow (Ed.), *The rate and direction of inventive activity* (pp. 609–625). Princeton, N.J.: Princeton University Press.

Baptista, R., & Swann, P. (1998). Do firms in clusters innovate more? *Research Policy, 27*(5), 525–540.

Belderbos, R., Faems, D., Leten, B., & Looy, B. V. (2014). Co-ownership of intellectual property: Exploring the value-appropriation and value-creation implications of co-patenting with different partners. *Research Policy, 43*(5), 841–852.

Belussi, F., Sammarra, A., & Sedita, S. R. (2010). Learning at the boundaries in an "Open Regional Innovation System": A focus on firms' innovation strategies in the Emilia Romagna life science industry. *Research Policy, 39*(6), 710–721.

Bianchi, M., Cavaliere, A., Chiaroni, D., Frattini, F., & Chiesa, V. (2011). Organisational modes for open innovation in the bio-pharmaceutical industry: An exploratory analysis. *Technovation, 31*(1), 22–33.

Bogers, M., Chesbrough, H., & Moedas, C. (2018). Open innovation: Research practices, and policies. *California Management Review, 60*(2), 5–16.

Borgatti, S. P., Everett, M. G., & Johnson, J. C. (2013). *Analyzing social networks*. London, UK: SAGE.

Borgatti, S. P., & Foster, P. C. (2003). The network paradigm in organizational research: A review and typology. *Journal of Management, 29*(6), 991–1013.

Bouncken, R. B., Fredrich, V., Kraus, S., & Ritala, P. (2020). Innovation alliances: Balancing value creation dynamics, competitive intensity and market overlap. *Journal of Business Research, 112*, 240–247.

Breschi, S., & Malerba, F. (2005). *Clusters, networks and innovation*. Oxford, UK: Oxford University Press.

Browning, L. D., Beyer, J. M., & Shetler, J. C. (1995). Building cooperation in a competitive industry: Sematech and the semiconductor industry. *Academy of Management Journal, 38* (1), 113–151.

Browning, L. D., & Shetler, J. C. (2000). *Sematech: Saving the U.S. semiconductor industry*. College Station, TX: A&M University Press.

Capaldo, A. (2007). Network structure and innovation: The leveraging of a dual network as a distinctive relational capability. *Strategic Management Journal, 28*(6), 585–608.

Casanueva, C., & Gallego, Á. (2010). Social capital and individual innovativeness in university research networks. *Innovation, 12*(1), 105–117.

Chesbrough, H. (2003a). *Open innovation: The new imperative for creating and profiting from technology*. Boston, MA: Harvard Business School Press.

Chesbrough, H. (2003b). The era of open innovation. *MIT Sloan Management Review, 44*(3), 35–41.

Chesbrough, H. (2006). Open innovation: A new paradigm for understanding industrial innovation. In H. Chesbrough, W. Vanhaverbeke, & J. West (Eds.), *Open innovation: Researching a new paradigm* (pp. 1–12). Oxford, UK: Oxford University Press.

Chesbrough, H., & Bogers, M. (2014). Explicating open innovation: Clarifying an emerging paradigm for understanding innovation. In H. Chesbrough, W. Vanhaverbeke, & J. West (Eds.), *New frontiers in open innovation* (pp. 3–28). Oxford, UK: Oxford University Press.

Chesbrough, H., Vanhaverbeke, W., & West, J. (Eds.) (2006). *Open innovation: Researching a new paradigm*. London, UK: Oxford University Press.

Child, J., Faulkner, D., & Tallman, S. (2005). *Cooperative strategy: Managing alliances, networks and joint ventures* (2nd). Oxford, UK: Oxford University Press.

Cooke, P. (2001). Regional innovation systems, clusters, and the knowledge economy. *Industrial and Corporate Change*, *10*(4), 945–974.

Cooke, P. (2002). *Knowledge economies: Clusters, learning and cooperative advantage*. London, UK: Oxford University Press.

Cropper, S., Ebers, M., Huxham, C., & Ring, P. S. (Eds.) (2008). *The Oxford handbook of inter-organizational relations*. Oxford, UK: Oxford University Press.

Dahlander, L., & Gann, D. M. (2010). How open is innovation? *Research Policy*, *39*(6), 699–709.

Das, T. K., & Teng, B. (1996). Risk types and inter-firm alliance structures. *Journal of Management Studies*, *33*(6), 827–843.

Das, T. K., & Teng, B. (2001). Trust, control, and risk in strategic alliances: An integrated framework. *Organization Studies*, *22*(2), 251–283.

Davis, J. P. (2016). The group dynamics of interorganizational relationships: Collaborating with multiple partners in innovation ecosystems. *Administrative Science Quarterly*, *61*(4), 621–661.

DeBresson, C., & Amesse, F. (1991). Networks of innovators: A review and introduction to the issue. *Research Policy*, *20*(5), 363–379.

Dhanaraj, C., & Parkhe, A. (2006). Orchestrating innovation networks. *Academy of Management Review*, *31*(3), 659–669.

DiMaggio, P., & Powell, W. W. (1983). The iron cage revisited: Institutional isomorphism and collective rationality in organizational fields. *American Sociological Review*, *48*(2), 147–160.

Dittrich, K., & Duysters, G. (2007). Networking as a means to strategy change. The case of open innovation in mobile telephony. *Journal of Product Innovation Management*, *24*(6), 510–521.

Dougherty, D. (2017). Organizing for innovation in complex innovation systems, *Innovation*, *19*(1), 11–15.

Dyer, J. H., & Hatch, N. W. (2006). Relation-specific capabilities and barriers to knowledge transfers: Creating advantage through network relationships. *Strategic Management Journal*, *27*(8), 701–719.

Dyer, J. H., & Nobeoka, K. (2000). Creating and managing a high-performance knowledge-sharing network: The Toyota case. *Strategic Management Journal*, *21*(3), 345–367.

Ebers, M. (1999). The dynamics of inter-organizational relationships. *Research in the Sociology of Organizations*, *16*, 31–56.

Ferriani, S., & MacMillan, I. (2017). Performance gains and losses from network centrality in cluster located firms: A longitudinal study. *Innovation*, *19*(3), 307–334.

Fligstein, N., & McAdam, D. (2012). *A theory of fields*. Oxford, UK: Oxford University Press.

Gambardella, A., & Panico, C. (2014). On the management of open innovation. *Research Policy, 42*(5), 903–913.

Gassmann, O., & Reepmeyer, G. (2005). Organizing pharmaceutical innovation: From science-based knowledge creators to drug-oriented knowledge brokers. *Creativity and Innovation Management, 14*(3), 233–245.

Gianiodis, P. T., Ellis, S.C., & Secchi, E. (2010). Advancing a typology of open innovation. International. *Journal of Innovation Management, 14*(4), 531–572.

Gouldner, A. W. (1960). The norm of reciprocity: A preliminary statement. *American Sociological Review, 25*(2), 161–178.

Granovetter, M. (1985). Economic action and social structure: The problem of embeddedness. *American Journal of Sociology, 91*(3), 481–510.

Greer, C. R., & Lei, D. (2012). Collaborative innovation with customers: A review of the literature and suggestions for future research. *International Journal of Management Reviews, 14*(1), 63–84.

Helfat, C. E., & Quinn, J. B. (2006). Book review of open innovation: The new imperative for creating and profiting from technology. *Academy of Management Perspectives, 20*(2), 86–88.

Henkel, J. (2006). Selective revealing in open innovation processes: The case of embedded Linux. *Research Policy, 35*(7), 953–969.

Henkel, J., Schöberl, S., & Alexy, O. (2014). The emergence of openness: How and why firms adopt selective revealing in open innovation. *Research Policy, 43*(5), 879–890.

Hess, A. M., & Rothaermel, F. T. (2011). When are assets complementary? Star scientists, strategic alliances, and innovation in the pharmaceutical industry. *Strategic Management Journal, 32*(8), 895–909.

Hobday, M. (1998). Product complexity, innovation and industrial organisation. *Research Policy, 26*(6), 689–710.

Huggins, R. (2010). Forms of network resource: Knowledge access and the role of inter-firm networks. *International Journal of Management Reviews, 12*(3), 335–352.

Huizingh, E. K. (2011). Open innovation: State of the art and future perspectives. *Technovation, 31*(1), 2–9.

Huxham, C., & Vangen, S. (2000). Leadership in the shaping and implementation of collaboration agendas: How things happen in a (not quite) joined-up world. *Academy of Management Journal, 43*(6), 1159–1175.

Huxham, C., & Vangen, S. (2005). *Managing to collaborate*. London, UK: Routledge.

Jarillo, J.C. (1988). On strategic networks. *Strategic Management Journal, 9*(1), 31–41.

Jones, C., Hesterly, W. S., & Borgatti, S. P. (1997). A general theory of network governance: Exchange conditions and social mechanisms. *Academy of Management Review, 22*(4), 911–945.

Kastelle, T., & Steen, J. (2010). Introduction. *Innovation, 12*(1), 2–4.

Kenis, P., & Knoke, D. (2002). How organizational field networks shape interorganizational tie-formation rates. *Academy of Management Review, 27*(2), 275–293.

Knoke, D., & Yang, S. (2007). *Social network analysis* (2nd edition). London, UK: SAGE.

Koschmann, M. A., Kuhn, T.R., & Pfarrer, M. D. (2012). A communicative framework of value in cross-sector partnerships. *Academy of Management Review*, 37(3), 332–354.

Lakemond, N., Bengtsson, L., Laursen, K., & Tell, F. (2016). Match and manage: The use of knowledge matching and project management to integrate knowledge in collaborative inbound open innovation. *Industrial and Corporate Change*, 25(2), 333–352.

Lakhani, K. R., Boudreau, K. J., Guinan, E. C., Baldwin, C. Y., MacCormack, A., Lonstein, E., Lydon, M., & Arnaout, R. A. (2013). Prize-based contests can provide solutions to computational biology problems. *Nature Biotechnology*, 31(2), 108–111.

Lange, K., Müller-Seitz, G., Sydow, J., & Windeler, A. (2013). Financing innovations in uncertain networks—Filling in roadmap gaps in the semiconductor industry. *Research Policy*, 42(3), 647–661.

Laursen, K., & Salter, A. (2006). Open for Innovation: The role of openness in explaining innovation performance among U.K. manufacturing firms. *Strategic Management Journal*, 27(2), 131–150.

Laursen, K., & Salter, A. (2014). The paradox of openness: Appropriability, external search and collaboration. *Research Policy*, 43(5), 867–878.

Levin, D. Z., & Cross, R. (2004). The strength of weak ties you can trust: The mediating role of trust in effective knowledge transfer. *Management Science*, 50(11), 1477–1490.

Liebeskind, J. P., & Oliver, A. L. (2000). *From handshake to contract: Trust, intellectual property and the social structure of academic research*. Oxford, UK: Oxford University Press.

Liebeskind, J. P., Oliver, A. L., Zucker, L., & Brewer, M. (1996). Social networks, learning, and flexibility: Sourcing scientific knowledge in new biotechnology firms. *Organization Science*, 7(4), 428–443.

Lorenzoni, G., & Lipparini, A. (1999). The leveraging of interfirm relationships as a distinctive organizational capability: A longitudinal study. *Strategic Management Journal*, 20(4), 317–338.

Lundvall, B.-Å. (1992). *National systems of innovation: Towards a theory of innovation and interactive learning*. London, UK: Pinter.

Matutes, C., & Regibeau, P. (1988). "Mix and match": Product compatibility without network externalities. *The RAND Journal of Economics*, 19(2), 221–234.

Maurer, I., & Ebers, M. (2006). Dynamics of social capital and their performance implications: Lessons from biotechnology start-ups. *Administrative Science Quarterly*, 51(2), 262–292.

Müller-Seitz, G. (2012). Leadership in interorganizational networks: A literature review and suggestions for future research. *International Journal of Management Reviews*, 14(4), 428–443.

Müller-Seitz, G., & Sydow, J. (2012). Maneuvering between networks to lead—A longitudinal case study in the semiconductor industry. *Long Range Planning*, 45(2-3), 105–135.

Muthusamy, S. K., & White, M. A. (2006). Learning and knowledge transfer in strategic alliances: A social exchange view. *Organization Studies*, 26(3), 415–441.

Nielsen, B. B. (2002). Synergies in strategic alliances: Motivation and outcomes of complementary and synergistic knowledge networks. *Journal of Knowledge Management Practice*, *3*(2), 1–15.

Nieto, M. J., & Santamaría, L. (2007). The importance of diverse collaborative networks for the novelty of product innovation. *Technovation*, *27*(6), 367–377.

Nooteboom, B. (2004). *Inter-firm collaboration, learning and networks*. London, UK: Routledge.

Oliver, A. L. (1997). On the nexus of organizations and professions: Networking through trust. *Sociological Inquiry*, *67*(2), 227–245.

Oliver, A. L. (2001). Strategic alliances and the learning life-cycle of biotechnology firms. *Organization Studies*, *22*(3), 467–489.

Oliver, A. L. (2004). On the duality of competition and collaboration: Network-based knowledge relations in the biotechnology industry. *Scandinavian Journal of Management*, *20*(1), 151–171.

Oliver, A. L. (2009). *Networks for learning and knowledge-creation in biotechnology*. Cambridge, UK: Cambridge University Press.

Oliver, A. L, & Ebers, M. (1998). Networking network studies: An analysis of conceptual configurations in the study of inter-organizational relationships. *Organization Studies*, *19*(4), 549–583.

Oliver, A. L., & Kalish, Y. (2011). Interorganizational learning in alliances and networks. In T. K. Das (Ed.), *Strategic alliances for value creation* (pp. 101–118). Charlotte, NC: Information Age Publishing

Oliver, A. L., & Liebeskind, J. P. (1997). Three levels of networking for sourcing intellectual capital in biotechnology: Implications for studying interorganizational networks. International Studies of Management & *Organization*, *27*(4), 76–103.

Oxford. (2021). *Clique*. https://www.oxfordlearnersdictionaries.com/definition/english/clique. (accessed October 10, 2021).

Paredes-Frigolett, H., & Pyka, A. (2017). A model of innovation network formation. *Innovation*, *19*(2), 245–269.

Parkhe, A., Wasserman, S., & Ralston, D. A. (2006). New frontiers in network theory development. *Academy of Management Review*, *31*(3), 560–568.

Paruchuri, S. (2010). Intraorganizational networks, interorganizational networks, and the impact of central inventors: A longitudinal study of pharmaceutical firms. *Organization Science*, *21*(1), 63–80.

Perkmann, M., & Walsh, K. (2007). University–industry relationships and open innovation: Towards a research agenda. *International Journal of Management Review*, *9*(4), 259–280.

Perrons, R. K. (2009). The open kimono: How Intel balances trust and power to maintain platform leadership. *Research Policy*, *38*(8), 1300–1312.

Phelps, C. C. (2010). A longitudinal study of the influence of alliance network structure and composition on firm exploratory innovation. *Academy of Management Journal*, *53*(4), 890–913.

Poot, T., & Faems, D. (2009). Toward a dynamic perspective on open innovation: A longitudinal assessment of the adoption of internal and external innovation strategies in the Netherlands. *International Journal of Innovation Management*, *13*(2), 1–24.

Powell, W. W. (1990). Neither market nor hierarchy: Network forms of organization. *Research in Organizational Behavior*, *12*(-), 295–336.

Powell, W. W., & Grodal, S. (2005). Networks of innovators. In J. Fagerberg, D. C. Movery, & R. R. Nelson (Eds.), *The Oxford handbook of innovation* (pp. 56–85). New York, NY: Oxford University Press.

Powell, W. W., Koput, K. W., & Smith-Doerr, L. (1996). Interorganizational collaboration and the locus of innovation: Networks of learning in biotechnology. *Administrative Science Quarterly*, *41*(1), 116–145.

Powell, W. W., White, D. R., Koput, K. W., & Owen-Smith, J. (2005). Network dynamics and field evolution: The growth of interorganizational collaboration in the life sciences. *American Journal of Sociology*, *110*(4), 1132–1205.

Provan, K. G., Fish, A., & Sydow, J. (2007). Interorganizational networks at the network level: A review of the empirical literature on whole networks. *Journal of Management*, *33*(3), 479–516.

Provan, K., & Kenis, P. (2008). Modes of network governance: Structure, management, and effectiveness. *Journal of Public Administration Research & Theory*, *18*(2), 229–252.

Randhawa, K., Wilden, R., & Hohberger, J. (2016). A bibliometric review of open innovation: Setting a research agenda. *Journal of Product Innovation Management*, *33*(6), 750–772.

Reagans, R., & McEvily, B. (2003). Network structure and knowledge transfer: The effects of cohesion and range. *Administrative Science Quarterly*, *48*(2), 240–267.

Richardson, G. B. (1972). The organization of industry. *Economic Journal*, *82*(327), 883–896.

Rodan, S., & Galunic, C. (2004). More than network structure: How knowledge heterogeneity influences managerial performance and innovativeness. *Strategic Management Journal*, *25*(6), 541–562.

Roelofsen, A., Boon, W., P. C., Kloet, R. R., & Broerse, J., E. W. (2011). Stakeholder interaction within research consortia on emerging technologies: Learning how and what? *Research Policy*, *40*(3), 341–354.

Sammarra, A., & Biggiero, L. (2008). Heterogeneity and specificity of Inter-Firm knowledge flows in innovation networks. *Journal of Management Studies*, *45*(4), 800–829.

Savino, T., Messeni Petruzzelli, A., & Albino, V. (2017). Search and recombination process to innovate: A review of the empirical evidence and a research agenda. *International Journal of Management Reviews*, *19*(1), 54–75.

Schilling, M. A., & Phelps, C. C. (2007). Interfirm collaboration networks: The impact of large-scale network structure on firm innovation. *Management Science*, *53*(7), 1113–1126.

Scott, W. R., & Davis, G. F. (2015). *Organizations and organizing: Rational, natural and open systems perspectives*. London, UK: Routledge.

Spieth, P., Laudien, S. M., & Meissner, S. (2020). Business model innovation in strategic alliances: A multi-layer perspective. *R&D Management*, *51*(1), 24–39.

Spithoven, A., Clarysse, B., & Knockaert, M. (2011). Building absorptive capacity to organise inbound open innovation in traditional industries. *Technovation*, *31*(1), 10–21.

Swan, J., Bresnen, M., Mendes, M., Newell, S., Perkmann, M., & Roberston, M. (2005). Exploring interactivity in biomedical innovation: A framework and case study analysis. *Proceedings of the 5th European conference on organizational knowledge, learning and capabilities*, Boston, MA.

Sydow, J., Schüßler, E., & Müller-Seitz, G. (2016). *Managing inter-organizational relations—Debates and cases*. London, UK: Palgrave/Macmillan Publishers.

Sydow, J., & Windeler, A. (2003). Knowledge, trust, and control: Managing tensions and contradictions in a regional network of service firms. *International Studies of Management and Organization*, *33*(2), 69–100.

Tortoriello, M., Reagans, R., & McEvily, B. (2012). Bridging the knowledge gap: The influence of strong ties, network cohesion, and network range on the transfer of knowledge between organizational units. *Organization Science*, *23*(4), 1024–1039.

Van de Vrande, V., De Jong, J. P., Vanhaverbeke, W., & de Rochemont, M. (2009). Open innovation in SMEs: Trends, motives and management challenges. *Technovation*, *29*(6), 423–437.

Von Hippel, E. (1986). Lead users: A source of novel product concepts. *Management Science*, *32*(7), 791–805.

Von Hippel, E. (1995). *The source of innovation*. Oxford, UK: Oxford University Press.

Vörös, A., & Snijders, T.A. (2017). Cluster analysis of multiplex networks: Defining composite network measures. *Social Networks*, *49*(-), 93–112.

Wasserman, S., & Faust, K. (1994). *Social network analysis: Methods and applications*. Cambridge, UK: Cambridge University Press.

West, J., & Bogers, M. (2014). Leveraging external sources of innovation: A review of research on open innovation. *Journal of Product Innovation Management*, *31*(4), 814–831.

West, J., Salter, A., Vanhaverbeke, W., & Chesbrough, H. (2014). Open innovation: The next decade. *Research Policy*, *43*(5), 805–811.

Whittington, K. B., Owen-Smith, J., & Powell, W. W. (2009). Networks, propinquity, and innovation in knowledge-intensive industries. *Administrative Science Quarterly*, *54*(1), 90–122.

Xue, J. (2018). Understanding knowledge networks and knowledge flows in high technology clusters: The role of heterogeneity of knowledge contents. *Innovation*, *20*(2), 139–163.

Zaheer, A., Gözübüyük, R., & Milanov, H. (2010). It's connections: The network perspective in interorganizational research. *Academy of Management Perspectives*, *24*(1), 62–77.

Zeithaml, V., Berry, L., & Parasuraman, A. (1996). The behavioral consequences of service quality. *Journal of Marketing*, *60*(2), 31–46.

Zeng, S. X., Xie, X. M., & Tam, C. M. (2010). Relationship between cooperation networks and innovation performance of SMEs. *Technovation*, *30*(3), 181–194.

.

CHAPTER 10

SOCIAL TECHNOLOGY AND STABILITY/TRANSFORMATION OF ALLIANCE NETWORKS

Dilemmas and Paradoxes of Cooperation

Sof Thrane and Jan Mouritsen

ABSTRACT

This chapter analyzes and develops the concept of social technologies in alliance networks. The literature has pointed to the importance of several elements of social technologies such as shared values, trust and cooperative behavior in sustaining and developing networks. The chapter adds to the literature through showing how the mobilization of the social technology of cooperative behavior is a non-linear and fragile accomplishment. The mobilization of social technologies is uncertain because alliance networks are formed to exploit complementarity and diversity. Diversity, however, separates the network into groups around faultlines demarcating contradictory social structures. The utilization and mobilization of social technologies in alliance networks are therefore paradoxical. On the one hand, alliances and networks thrive on diversity and, on the other hand, diversity and faultlines make collective decision-making difficult. Alliance networks are therefore highly unstable and complex since conformity is necessary for social technology to work, yet diversity is necessary to make complementarity productive. The chapter suggests that alliances are especially prone to conflict and disintegration when collective decisions are made in the alliance, whereas bilateral

Managing Interpartner Cooperation in Strategic Alliances, pp. 275–304
Copyright © 2022 by Information Age Publishing
www.infoagepub.com
275

or dyad interactions flow more smoothly. These findings are based on a longitudinal study of two alliance networks. The alliance networks consist of potential competitors who ally in order to exploit complementarities based on differences in technological competencies and geographic scope as well as to enhance credibility to efforts at diversification their businesses and winning large contracts.

INTRODUCTION

Research on inter-organizational networks identifies the importance of social technologies such as trust and shared valued in sustaining, developing, and controlling inter-firm networks and alliances. Shared values and trust can replace formal types of controls and safeguards as these are more effective in building relational advantages. Dyer and Singh hypothesize that: "The greater the alliance partners' ability is to employ *informal* self-enforcing safeguards (e.g., trust) rather than *formal* self-enforcing safeguards (e.g., financial hostages), the greater the potential will be for relational rent, owing to (1) lower marginal costs and (2) difficulty of imitation" (Dyer & Singh, 1998, p. 671; emphasis in original).

Shared values and trust are thus control mechanisms. They are a governance structure capable of increasing rents to interfirm cooperation. Social control is portrayed as increasing with time: "Several theories suggest that cooperative behavior between firms increases with the length of the relationship" (Inkpen & Currall, 2004, p. 593; Tomkins, 2001). Trust is said to be part of a virtuous circle in which initial trust lowers cost and feeds into a greater reliance on social controls: "The greater the initial level of trust between joint venture partners, the lower the initial joint venture monitoring and control costs by the partners and the greater the initial reliance on social controls." (Inkpen & Currall, 2004, p. 590). Faems, Janssens, Madhok, and van Looy (2008) study the relationship between structural (contracts) and relational (trust) perspectives arguing that contractual flexibility feeds into alliance dynamics with increasing trust and returns to the relationship. Cooperative behavior and trust are thus a potentially powerful social technology capable of lowering cost and developing the relationship. Trust is "the magic in alliance success" (Koza, as cited in Young-Ybarra, & Wiersema, 1999, p. 439).

Despite the promises of social technologies in developing a network or relationship, it has been suggested that the effects of social technologies diminish over time. If a joint venture leads to the transfer of skills, the relative bargaining power of each party may change and provide incentives for opportunistic behavior leading to an increase in formal controls (Inkpen & Currall, 2004; Khanna, Gulati & Nohria, 1998). Yet the literature generally lacks longitudinal studies of the ways in which social technologies emerge and develop (Adler & Kwon, 2002; Ariño & de la Torre, 1998; Koza & Lewin, 1999). Furthermore, withdrawal from alliances is a neglected subject within the literature (Greve, Baum, Mitsuhashi, & Rowley, 2010).

The chapter employs longitudinal analysis to study two alliance networks, which are "multiparty alliances, in which multilateral transactions among the network members are facilitated by the network … network members are co-specialized, bringing a unique value adding capability, such as knowledge resources or market access, to the network" (Koza & Lewin, 1999, p. 639). Such alliances are instable (Das & Teng, 2000), operating far from equilibrium. This is why it is interesting to study the complexities and emergence of social structures and technologies. The chapter draws on structuration theory (Giddens, 1984) and research on group dynamics (Pelled, Eisenhardt, & Xin, 1999) and argues that social technologies are paradoxical in a collective network mode—such as when joint decisions are made—where they may actualize contradictions and transform them into conflicts.

DEVELOPMENT OF THEORY

The Social Technology of Networks

The literature on inter-firm alliances and networks indicates that formal governance mechanisms such as contracts and hostages should be supplanted by informal social mechanisms such as trust and norms of cooperative behavior (Dyer & Chu, 2003; Dyer & Singh, 1998; Husted & Folger, 2004; Inkpen & Currall, 2004; Zollo, Reuer & Singh, 2002; Young-Ybarra & Wiersema, 1999). Social technologies are said to be more effective than formal governance mechanisms in generating relational advantages and capabilities (Dyer & Chu, 2003; Dyer & Singh, 1998) and in minimizing transaction and production cost. Dyer and Chu found that trust lowered ex-post transaction cost (negotiation cost) and concluded that "trust [is] unique as a governance mechanism because the investments that trading partners make to build trust often simultaneously create economic value (beyond minimizing transaction costs) in the exchange relationship" (Dyer & Chu, 2003, p. 66).

The social technology of networks has been proposed to stand for many elements such as justice (Husted & Folger, 2004), social capital (Bolino, 2002; Frank & Yasumoto, 1998; Gargiulo & Benassi, 2000; Leenders & Gabbay, 1999; Nahapiet & Ghoshal, 1998; Walker, Kogut & Chan, 1997; Portes, 1998; Tsai, 2000; Yli-Renko, Autio & Sapienza, 2001), trust (Inkpen & Currall, 2004; Young-Ybarra & Wiersema, 1999), inter-organizational routines (Zollo et al., 2002), cooperation versus competition (Das & Teng,

2000), short-term versus long-term orientation (Das & Teng, 2000), shared values (Young-Ybarra & Wiersema, 1999), and network identity and learning routines (Dyer & Nobeoka, 2000).

Despite these different emphases, social technologies are generally understood as generalized factors that shape practices and improve performance linearly and directly (see Das & Teng, 2000, for an exception). Social technology has been defined as concerned "with what exists as a revelation of what ought to be, and of the method of realizing what ought to be" (Henderson, 1901, p. 468). They identify an ideal and methods of reaching these ideals. Social technologies reflect "a system or mechanism adapted to further in the best possible way all the interests ... of the entire community; (Henderson, 1901, p. 471). The social technology of networks thus entails a vision of how the network should function, what the goals of the network should be and methods of realizing its intended functioning, and it is supposed to further the interest of all the members of the network. A network "must agree on a policy because they must live together, and must find a practicable method of realizing the covenanted end. Thus they are social technologist" (Henderson, 1912, p. 216).

Social technologies are mobilized in concrete settings by actors in a network. The social technology of networks entails, as stated above, elements such as shared values, trust, common identity and learning and inter-organizational routines, which participants must agree on in order to further the goals of the network. Yet this position seems to neglect a fundamental feature of social life—social systems are differentiated in terms of values, trust, and acceptance of the use of power (Giddens, 1984).

The evolution and change of social technology is, furthermore, a process. Whether this evolution is effective is a much more difficult question, since it is an open question if shared values are always beneficial (Young-Ybarra & Wiersema, 1999). If network partners have less-than-fully-common interests and values, it may not be likely that common goals evolve without problems.

In an alliance network which consists of multiple partners and focuses on the exploitation of complementary resources, homogeneity in firm values is unlikely. Diversity, which is understood as differences in firms' or partners' normative orientations (e.g., risk aversion, view of what effective network structures are), and which may be related to demographic variables (e.g., firm size and technology) is a basis for complementarity and can, as such, create positive economic effects, but also ambiguities and contradictions (Dyer & Singh, 1998; Pelled 1996).[1] Diversity may create faultlines (Lau & Murnighan, 1998) along dimensions such as race, sex, and age (Pelled, 1996), functional background, education and tenure (Pelled, Eisenhardt, & Xin, 1999; Peters & Karen, 2009), and personal diversity (Harrison, Price, & Myrtle, 1998), which may challenge social technologies. Hence contradictions and conflicts related to diversity and faultlines (Brickson, 2000; Chatman & Flynn, 2001; Watson, Kumar & Michaelsen, 1993) may hamper the use of the social technology. The proposed effects of implementation of social technologies may not materialize because interaction and alliance dynamics may impede such a linear relationship.

Mobilization of Social Technologies and Structuration Theory

Giddens' (1984) structuration theory proposes that structure—which social technologies seek to change—both enable and constrain behavior in an alliance network. The relationship between the social technology and behavior form a duality: "According to the notion of duality of structure, the structural properties of social systems are both medium and outcome of the practices they recursively organize" (Giddens, 1984, p. 25). Structure consists of the "rules and resources, recursively implicated in the reproduction of social systems" (Giddens, 1984, p. 377). In this perspective, social elements such as trust, norms of cooperative behavior and shared values are fragile and social structures can be *drawn on* in specific episodes to condition outcomes, but they are not reified as social structures that lay firm foundations for social practices.

Structuration theory is a complex body of propositions that has been debated elsewhere (e.g., Held & Thompson, 1989). For our purposes, it suffices to point out the three central elements of the duality of structure: Signification (language), domination (power) and legitimation (norms and sanctions) (Giddens, 1984, p. 29). Signification allows actors to make sense of the world and to uphold communication through commonly understood interpretative schemes, which are the "modes of typification incorporated within actors' stocks of knowledge, applied reflexively in the sustaining of communication" (Giddens, 1984, p. 29). Social technologies promote certain discourses and sense making patterns, which may motivate but not determine interactions. Domination is related to power over people or nature through the use of various kinds of facilities that help to command people or objects (Giddens, 1984, p. 33). Domination and power are related to (control) mechanisms that make certain kinds of social practices strong and other forms weak. Last, legitimation informs sanctions through norms, which "centre upon relations between the rights and obligations expected of those participating in a range of interaction contexts" (Giddens, 1984, p. 30). These analytical distinctions help us to understand how social technologies are involved in inter-organizational processes, specifically how social technologies evolve and disintegrate. Such studies are lacking (Ariño & de la Torre, 1998; Koza & Lewin, 1998).

There is active mobilization of social technologies because in principle, all actors could decide to "act otherwise," reject them and make them superfluous. This makes the actual use and emergence of social technologies important. Structuration theory also helps to understand change through contradiction and conflict: "A structurationist perspective, rather than defining relationships in networks as trusted, fair, reciprocal, and mutually committed, it would be more fruitful to conceptualize social processes in general and network processes in particular as full of tension and contradiction" (Sydow & Windeler, 1998, p. 280).

Contradiction—disjunction of principles of system organization—may lead to conflict because it supplies faultlines (Giddens, 1981, p. 237). Hence "conflict and contradiction tend to coincide because contradiction expresses the main faultlines in the structural constitution of societal systems. The reason for this coincidence is that contradiction tends to involve divisions of interest between different groupings or categories of people" (Giddens, 1984, p. 198). Contradiction is based on differences, and it may (or may not) translate into active conflict, for example, via tensions around shared goals and shared culture (Inkpen & Tsang, 2005; Tsai & Ghoshal, 1998). Through these lenses it is possible to analyze carefully how social technologies are constructed, developed, and mobilized in action.

METHOD

Drawing on structuration theory, the study is grounded in theoretical assumptions that allowed us to develop categories and concepts through the empirical investigation. The approach is "interpretative with a critical flavor" (Gephardt, 2004, p. 456; Weber, 1922/1980). Figure 10.1 shows our research model.

Research Object and Selection of Cases

Structuration theory guided our reflections on how to study social technologies as a dynamic, non-fixed phenomenon (Lee, 1999) in a "real-life" context (Yin, 1994, p. 6). The case study approach can help to theorize the multiplicity of linkages and relations between existing, potential and abandoned entities in the network.

Two commercial networks that wished to cooperate about branding, knowledge development, and sharing of customers were enrolled in the study. They were formalized alliance networks rather than value chains (Ahuja, 2000, p. 318; Inkpen & Tsang, 2005; Koza & Lewin, 1999) with explicit membership rules, decision rules, common IT systems, as well as

Figure 10.1

The Research Model

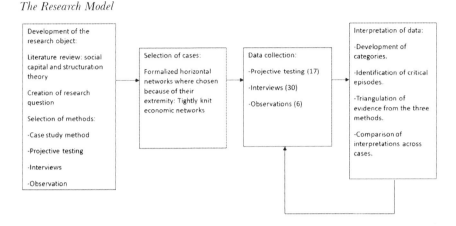

quality controls. This type of network is interesting because it has sufficient closure to enable the formation of shared values (Coleman, 1988), trust and norms of justice. Cases were thus chosen based on their extremity as tightly knit formalized networks (Pratt & Rose, 2003) and theoretical relevance (Dutton & Dukerich, 1991; Eisenhardt, 1989).

Data Collection

First, we applied what Alvesson (2003) calls reflexive interviewing and developed a dialogue with respondents. We explored their concerns and preoccupations by continually following their lines of reasoning rather than merely keeping to our predetermined interview guide. The interview situation was an exploration of respondents' perspectives on their participation in the network.

Second, the interview explored the following themes and questions: (1) What is the business idea of the network? (2) What are the valued characteristics of network partners? (3) How is cooperation within the network organized? (4) What is management in and of the network? (5) What is leadership in the network? (6) How is knowledge managed in the network?

Our interest in social technologies and structuration theory motivated these questions (see also Koza & Lewin, 1999, p. 639) The first item of the interview guide concerned motives for entering the network and expected social and economic benefits from network participation and it addressed signification through attention to perceived effects and logic of the network. The second item covered legitimate behaviors and practices in the network. The third fourth, fifth and sixth items concerned power and domination in various ways: partners' relations, facilities, technologies, and tools.

The categories of the interview guide were complemented with case specific issues. Like Dutton and Dukerich (1991) and (Ariño & de la Torre, 1998) we focused on key events, issues and themes such as, for example, the attempt to set up a sales function in one of the networks. This issue emerged in the interviews just before the decision was taken and was fiercely discussed in the network. These events were moments during which social technologies should prove their worth and they were incorporated into the interview guide. The guide thus developed over time although the structure of six items was kept intact. In total 30 interviews were conducted, and they were transcribed verbatim.

We also employed *projective interview techniques*[2] in order to investigate interpretive schemes (signification) and norms (legitimation) more carefully because by making the respondent talk about another person, he or she presents arguments about what is important for the network (signification) and what legitimate behavior is (legitimation). The projective interview technique identifies values and norms unobtrusively (Hechter, 1992, p. 215). This data collection method complies with the demand that "the crucial point is that the relevant deep-level variables in any situation are those that bear directly on the fundamental purposes of the group" (Harrison et al., 1998, p. 105). The use of implicit interview techniques enabled categorization of norms and interpretive schemes in the network. Concepts and elements of the social technology like "cooperative behavior" were developed in the analysis phase. An example of how this has been written up in our research manuals is provided in Table 10.1 from the network that will subsequently be called Elec.net.

Table 10.1 shows what respondents consider good and bad norms and behavior and it shows our notes about the encounters reported in the projective interview. It will be used in the empirical section of the chapter. In addition to interviewing and projective testing, network interactions at board meetings and general assemblies were observed on six occasions. In two instances, we were allowed to tape-record the meeting and twice we were not allowed to do so. At two other occasions we deemed it inappropriate. Observation of the network was important because we could experience interaction around issues discussed in interviews and projective testing. Also, observing network interaction gave rise to new questions in the interviews. This additional information allowed us to create a nuanced account of network interaction.

Table 10.1

Projective Interview Data From Elec.net (Abbreviated Examples)

Respondent number	Quotations about the perfect member	Quotations about the inadequate member	Comments/ interpretation
1	"He is thoughtful and has an eye for the financial side, he has got control of his organization and if you control your organization, then you are also a good partner that keeps appointments and makes sure that his employees have the competence that they need."	"He is eerie. He looks to the side. He is not trustworthy."	Thoughtfulness develops control or command of own operations, and competence. This is related to trustworthiness.
2	"Dynamism, sporty, power. He will not be stopped by the first hindrance and if he was a salesman, then if he is thrown out of the front door, he crawls in by the back door."	"A stupid grinning and laidback, withdrawn. It is good to be visionary and he is not. We should drive fast forward."	Movement is positive; the business should be driven fast forward.
3	"Fresh, open, not afraid to use himself to go forward, he has got drive."	None	Openness and drive are important; the network should progress.
4	"Trustworthy and in control of things of the things that he works with as well as in relation to the people that he works with."	"He is not open; he looks distant, maybe calculating. He is type that says 'first my own gain and then I will contribute."	Trustworthiness is positive and free-riding is negative.
5	"He has got the open trustful face. Honest. Honesty is important".	"Hides himself, one who has no opinion."	Someone closed is valued negatively.
6	"Looks open and honest."	"This guy might be speculating how I can get something out of it."	The distinction is between open and honest people and people inclined to free ride.

(Table continued on next page)

Table 10.1 (Continued)

Projective Interview Data From Elec.net (Abbreviated Examples

Respondent number	Quotations about the perfect member	Quotations about the inadequate member	Comments/ interpretation
7	"Serious and is able to cut through the crap. He signals that he is in control and he is calm An active person in control. Calm. The other person is positive and has energy, and that is important. Everybody likes that. It drives things, it is important to have somebody who talks like waterfall, who can pull things with him, where the other guy might be holding things back."	"Don Juan. Not trustworthy, he is distant. He is spoiled. Things are not moving fast enough, he is probably more into selling clothes and stuff like that, cars where you do not have to go into details."	The serious person is in control and creates trust with the customer.
8	"He looks trustworthy; if you make a deal with him, then he keeps it. He would not run away with your customers."	"Some only think about themselves."	A good partner is trustworthy and does not steal your customers.

Interpretation

Interviews were transcribed and analyzed throughout the research period. Interpretation followed a three-stage process. First, each interview was interpreted to gain an understanding of the respondent's views generally. Second, key categories, events and issues were developed through open coding (Strauss & Corbin, 1998). Third, interviews were reread and comments and quotations pertaining to explanations of key issues (e.g., the central sales mentioned above) were then gathered in separate documents, that is, axial coding. Fourth, the case study was written around events and issues. Finally, two types of control were employed.

The first control was triangulation (Yin, 1994, p. 92). Two researchers were involved in collecting data and several methods and data sources were used (interviews, projective testing, and direct observation). This approach may augment construct validity and the accuracy of the study. Triangulation may also enhance validity because it allows data collection to be reflexive. Generally, the different data sources corroborated each other. The set-up of central sales in one of the networks may serve as an example.

Respondents in the implicit interviews distinguished between two types of partners—for example, progressives and skeptics—and these categories were corroborated by interviews and observation, for example, skeptical partners were opposed to central sales also in interviews and at a general assembly, we observed that the group of "skeptics" acted to oust a "progressive" on formal grounds rather than follow the custom of accommodating breaches of formalities. Triangulation of empirical evidence developed interpretations because it was possible to see the tensions in accounts since they could be checked against other materials. This was for example the case in which some respondents in interviews smoothed over conflicts and painted a brighter picture than observations produced.

A second control was to obtain feedback from respondents through workshops with network partners based on our findings. The purpose was to ensure validity of concepts through debating preliminary propositions, conclusions and perspectives developed in the research.

EMPIRICAL FINDINGS:
PATTERNS OF NETWORK INTERACTION

The empirical findings about the two cases are structured according to our research problem. We start with a short introduction, which is followed by a description of the social technology/social structures sought implemented as well as the social structure is defined. Followed by an analysis of how social technologies/structures are mobilized and transformed.

Advice.net

Advice.net was a network of independent consultants who aimed to sell "competencies" in contrast to the "big" consulting firms who were said to sell "systems." Three experienced consultants founded the network two years prior to the research. All partners had previously worked in larger companies in senior positions, but they did not enjoy life in the "big" companies. The partners prided themselves as independent, mature consultants who had worked as senior consultants and managers. The number of partners varied from a peak of 15 to 8 consultants when the research finished.

Advice.net had a *bilateral ownership structure*. First, it was an *egalitarian partnership* with shared liability and second, the three founders owned a firm that had the rights to the *brand name*. These three founders therefore levied a fee on all transactions executed in the name of the network. To the individual consultant, Advice.net was a means to find resources and execute projects that could not be handled individually. It helped them to simultaneously be small and yet exploit the possibilities of a collectivity based on a brand name, and size based on cooperation with partners. The case analysis starts with developing the social technology of Advice.net followed by an analysis of two distinct modes of mobilization—bilateral and collective mobilization.

The Efforts at Implementing Social Technologies in Advice.net

A group around the founders was explicit in the norms and practices that they wanted to govern the network. They sought to implement specific social structures, that is, to implement a social technology and they presented norms as strength (self-confidence and extroversion), a culture of sharing, and flexibility. Strong behavior and self-confidence were mentioned in interviews and deemed necessary to share knowledge and to enable freedom, openness, and learning. The norms aspired to can be explained as follows by a respondent who was also founder:

> If you do not have high self-esteem and reflexivity, then I think you need to protect yourself more than what is otherwise necessary. One of the things that we have worked with in the network—where I think we have accomplished a lot—is to share knowledge and ideas without having to own the knowledge and the ideas and without payment.

These rules encouraged knowledge sharing and defined values, action patterns and learning aspirations accordingly. Another partner had parallel thoughts: "What makes a network exist? It is that we as persons are open, we can use ourselves and each other not just as professional colleagues, but also as persons, as humans." Through its focus on openness, Advice.net had traits of a learning organization:

> We have, for the first time in our lives, such teamwork that you read about. You know how when you read about these fantastic teams, then you say "yeah all right, that's all very well but how do you get it? We have experienced this."

Second, a cooperative attitude by which consultants were willing to share customers and knowledge were deemed necessary for the functioning of the network. One of the partners suggested:

> I have become very aware that networks are based on giving and not primarily on getting. Because a network in itself is nothing, the network exists only through what you give to it.... The network exists because you give as-

signments to it. It is when you bring somebody from the network with you on your projects, which then creates new projects.

Sharing—a cooperative attitude as opposed to a competitive attitude (Das & Teng, 2000; Jorde & Teece, 1989; Zeng & Chen, 2003)—was therefore a crucial norm. Without a cooperative attitude there would be no network since it was carried only by common projects and shared customers. The value of sharing was therefore the main asset and social technology to be implemented.

A third espoused norm was extroversion and independence. Independence was closely related to sharing, because a consultant was only able to give when he had secured projects and could invite others to join. Selling projects involved contact with customers and required extroversion and directness:

> We do not want to get partners that are unable to sell actively. There are many of these consultants that do not sell actively. We are not interested in these persons if they are of no use. You have to be able to get in contact with the customers and you have to be able to acquire projects.

The interviewees argued that introverted consultants could not sell since they could not persuade customers. Therefore, independence, extroversion and sharing were interrelated. A fourth norm concerned creativity and flexibility. Most of the consultants chose to be independent because they were tired of the hierarchies of the modern enterprise. "I don't want to manage or to be managed" was a general slogan. This value had an effect on the structuring of the network as a new partner explained:

> It is funny. These people have fled from hierarchical positions in industry, with all the control and role-playing and a lot of other stuff. They say: Now I want to be creative, I will develop myself, I want to create something on the basis of all the experience I have. Both in relation to all the positive things I have not been able to implement because I have been locked up in the role I was playing. And in relation to all the negative experiences I have had with this bureaucratic inflexibility. We want something that is directly opposite. They are afraid of defining the things (e.g., vision, marketing, strategy, added) that "smell" like a normal business.

Organizational structure, hierarchy and procedures were problematical, and freedom was praised. The founders thus aspired to have low levels of structural rigidity (Das & Teng, 2000; Faems et al., 2008). Networking entailed positive energies and development. A partner who had left the network suggested: "They wanted this uncontrollability because somewhere there is an anxiety that it [referring to procedures] hinders creativity." Creativity and flexibility were norms and values in opposition to hierarchy.

However, the norms (legitimation) and interpretative schemes (signification) were fragile and not uniformly shared. Some partners questioned the practicability of the values of strength and independence because not all were able to attract customers equally well. It was suggested that if the network developed a division of labor under which some consultants were responsible for selling and others, for example, for producing internal services, everybody would be able to participate. This approach was in conflict with the values of independence and flexibility since designated roles would create organizational procedures, which the partners of the network tried to avoid when starting their own firm. A partner who had left the network explained the problem as follows:

> We should have done it much more systematically. I had difficulty convincing the three founders about it. They do not like systems and structures. That does not belong in a network. A network is a symbiosis, an amoeba and stuff like that. That it is all fine, but things do not necessarily happen, if you do not agree how they are to happen. Then things happen unsatisfactorily and some things fall out that did not have to fall out, if we had been a bit more considerate.

A partner agreed: "Network does not mean that everybody has to take care of him or herself. It means that we should help each other". The values of the network were not uniformly shared, because sharing and flexibility often ran contrary to solidarity with partners who were not as strong and independent as others. Two versions of social technology, with differing goals, means and values thus competed in Advice.net (see Table 10.2, which is developed on the basis of projective testing, interviews and observation).

This was problematic because the interpretive schemes and norms were also social technologies which, through a specific mode of functioning for the network as a whole, were supposed to translate network interaction into desirable economic effects. This would preclude tension and conflict. The contradiction between norms of sharing and non-hierarchical attention to each other on the one hand and some partners' hope of a network based on functional specialization on the other was fundamental.

Bilateral and Collective Mobilizing of Social Technologies in Advice.net.

Table 10.2 characterizes the contradiction between the two types of partners in relation to the type of network that they preferred and the means to achieve these goals—their views on social technology. The bilateral

Table 10.2

Social Technologies in Advice.net

	The amorphous network	The hierarchical network
Preferred network type	Loose couplings and strong, open and independent partners.	Functional specialization so all can participate.
Values	Openness and strength, independence, sharing, flexibility	Solidarity, sharing, structured approach to interaction.
Desired node characteristics	High self-esteem, extroversion strength, no role-playing, and altruistic orientation to work.	Specialized consultant who excels in certain roles, altruistic attitude to work life.
Anticipated effects and goals	Amorphous, chaotic, learning network of strong consultants able to generate projects.	Functionally specialized network. A strongly orchestrated network where some sell and others produce.

mobilization was about the joint projects that partners implemented and was when partners were excluded from the network. The introvert and less strong partners could not deliver and increasingly they were not invited to participate in activities. Gradually their activities in the network were reduced and they gradually withdrew; they were silently excluded (domination). One of the partners explained as follows:

> If you do not contribute, but only want to receive, then this network that we are creating is not the right thing for you. You have to find a new network and that's it. I mean to select, to exclude the partners that show no contribution, this is a necessary process.

Participation literally just stopped if a partner did not fit in; no decision had to be made. For example, the network had developed a big contract with a newspaper about joint marketing of seminars for business professionals. The contract was made with the founders and consequently "they (the founders) have the power over the assignment with the newspaper," as the dilemma was presented to us. Also, the telephone number posted in newspaper ads was that one of the founders' secretaries prompting the following speculation:

> On the basis of the campaign in the newspaper there were a lot of calls and I said if they go to one of the founder's numbers, who hands out the requests? Then I was told: "there are no requests on the basis the market-

ing campaign in the newspaper; it is all from somebody that we know," I got the impression that the founders took first and that there was nothing left for the rest of us.

Access to customers created centrality in the network, and this was related to power (domination), even to the point where espoused aspirations were rejected (abandoning legitimation). The perception was that norms were tradable if economic gains were possible, and these perceptions questioned the extent to which members in the network could be trusted. The customer base was "your power base; this is your customers, if you have customers to trade with, then they ask you to participate in projects. If you do not have customers, then you are out," such facilities make a partner powerful and a central person in the network.

Ten partners had left or had been asked to leave the network over the course of the two years of the research. The partners still in the network were the "strong" consultants, who paradoxically did not really "need the network," a partner said. A partner who had left the network explained how it worked:

> They might think that I wanted something else than what I wanted. I just wanted to participate. If just one of them had taken me on an assignment, then it would have been fine for me; this was all I asked for…. They might have thought that I wanted to take over their customers.

The dilemmas of a cooperative attitude (sharing) and the power of external ties (Burt, 1992) conflicted and motivated the transformation of the network toward one with less trust among members.

> In the collective mobilization the network functioned—at times —as the group around the founders envisioned, as trusting cooperation between strong individuals. This showed in partner meetings that were oriented to affirm norms through socializing because they "usually revolve around values and culture." Some partners felt very emotionally attached to the network. A founder explains:

> I experience that Advice.net had become more like a family, an equal family. I think we do have something very special, which I will go a long way to keep. We have a family structure in some way, without there being a mom, dad, or children. It is closely related. Just like, I can be with close friends. This is just a working community, but there is the whole of me in it. I can talk about having pains in my back, that I am sad, I can tell about my kids, my husband, and about my life. It matters to me. (Interview with founder)

Norms and joint decision making were difficult to reconcile, however, which can be illustrated by the episode of signing a required partner agreement:

What I experienced (at this meeting) was that we were looking at the holes in the cheese, instead of trying to see what would be the best for us if we get in this situation. What I experienced here was, that we were devil's advocates for each other, including myself, and I experienced that all the energy was taken out of the room, and then I thought that I don't want to do this—that was not the idea. So when we had tried 2 or 3 times, I said I don't want to do it. And then I went from fear and feeling insecure about not having signed this paper, so that we complied with the legal requirements. And I changed from wanting to sign to saying, "I don't want to sign that paper; because it contained exactly the opposite of the idea behind the network."

The legal contract symbolized governance and hierarchy and was a challenge to the founders' espoused norms and legitimation because it was about power (domination). Others characterized these discussions as "tiring" and "tough" because they contrasted with norms of trust-based behavior and a concern for sharing and flexibility. Instead of focusing on the positive actions the network could take, discussions focused on negative discussions of what could go wrong. Hence, in the collective mobilization the contradictory values and social technologies turned into conflict. This change from "silent" contradiction to open conflict was triggered by discussions which necessitated joint decision-making along the faultlines of the network. For instance, the partnership agreement could both be interpreted from "a trust based" perspective and a "functional specialization" perspective and the joint decision-making regarding the contract therefore transformed contradiction into conflict. The network could function without conflict as long as sensitive issues were avoided.

Elec.net

Elec.net was a network of electrical installation companies that considered ICT an important business option, and it was founded with the aim to develop and exploit the then emerging information and communication technology (ICT) business. Previously, the telecom industry was a government monopoly and the network founders worked here. They formed the network in the aftermath of the liberalization of the industry some 12 years prior to the research.

The network partners were small-and medium-sized companies ranging in size from 10 to 100 employees. At the time of the research, the network had 13 partner firms owning the shares of the network and 20 associated partners who did not own any stock in the network. The expectation was that their number would increase to around 50. The size of Elec.net varied over the years and ranged from 26 to now 13 partner firms. More than *40 partner firms* had entered and left the network.

Elec.net had a formal management apex with a full-time manager (network CEO) that had a database showing what technologies partners could operate and their experience and competence with these technologies. The management apex provided procedures for training and education, and it was a nexus for strategic discussions. It also observed developments in markets and technology, and lastly it carried out network administration and external relations, for example, homepage maintenance. Elec.net was a closed network and partners were *interrelated and interdependent*. Interdependence was underscored by the network brand-name, which discouraged partners from discontinuing their membership. They "are afraid to lose their customers if they cannot use the Elec.net brand name," as it was suggested to us. To step out the network could be very costly. Interdependence was thus based on *shared brand assets* and it was induced by *administrative procedures* and information systems that were part of the infrastructure of the network and the individual firm: "All our systems are constructed around Elec.net; perhaps particularly our competency development systems," a partner explained.

Generally, three reasons to join the network were mentioned by respondents. One was access to markets. The partners were dispersed geographically and depended on each other to deliver the same quality of service to large customers who wanted their installations to work all over the country. They wished to cooperate in relation to customers as several partners would have to coordinate efforts to match the geographical spread of customer's offices. They thus pursued residual referral income (Koza & Lewin, 1999). The second was access to technological resources of partners and network. The network for example made courses in ICT for partner firms. Finally, partners wanted increased trustworthiness of a brand name, which was important because many customers doubted that electrical installation companies could posses the competencies needed in the ICT business.

Social Technology in Elec.net

In Elec.net there were differing views on what should constitute the values and behaviors of the network. Entering the network in itself entailed long-term investments in ICT competencies for each partner and hence, to some extent, a long-term perspective on the cooperation, it further was built on the notion of cooperative behavior—partners were expected to share customers. Despite these basic elements of the social technology in Elec.net, partners disagreed on emphasis in values and orientations:

It will always be so when that many people have gathered who have known each other for so many years. There will always be somebody "with whom you dance better than with others." You clear your opinions with them, in order to see if they are aligned, so that you do not stand alone with opinion on the day. So, it functions like a small parliament.

Social bonds were *not equally distributed* and cliques had formed over the years. According to the words of respondents, Elec.net was divided in two cliques. One group called itself the "progressives" and differentiated itself from the "skeptics." Their traits were different as a "progressive" explained:

The "progressives" are those that in my eyes are competent enough to see the trend in the market and what the customers want. It has something to do with age, company culture and your employees. If you have a firm where all employees are of the type that comes in at 8 am and leaves at 4 pm and who does not think about his job anymore, when he has come home, then it is difficult to be in this market, because it requires another culture than just to be a traditional electrical installation-guy. So you need visionary co-workers that want something more than just that.

The division was also based on personal traits of the partners to which another "progressive" gave details:

If the customer has a need and another partner has the competencies to fulfill that need, then he should get the assignment because the more business we generate in total, the better. The "progressive" sees it like that – as opportunities. The other says, "You cannot come in and work in my geographical area, we will handle it ourselves" then it does not matter if another competitor gets it.

According to this "progressive," the "skeptics" were more self-centered and to some extent did not understand the network culture. For the "progressives," the interpretive scheme (signification) concerned the enhancement of Elec.net through common investments to create growth in the ICT business, while for the "skeptics" the ICT business was not to incur too high investments and risk. It should not replace the traditional electrical installation business, but just be an addition. And the "progressive" norms (legitimation) focused on mastering the future through intervention that would alter the course of affairs, while the "skeptic" norms reflected a conservative continuity between the past and the future. The two groups of skeptics and progressives were based on diversity. The two groups are characterized in Table 10.3 (see Table 10.1 in the methods section for how projective testing was used).

Table 10.3

Social Technologies in Elec.net

	The risk taking network	The conservative network
Preferred type of network	A fast-developing, high-investment and high-risk network "Progressives."	A consolidating network, which develops competencies slowly and systematically. "Skeptics"
Value	Forward-looking approach to developing the network as an entity.	Cautious approach to maintain the past benefits of the existing network focusing on the individuality of the partner firms.
Desired node characteristics.	Speed and risk. Competition through aggressive investment and explicit management of the market beyond the interest of any particular partner firm.	Safety and prudence. Competition through safeguarding money flows and reduced risk, and decentralized relations between partner firms.
Anticipated effects and goals	Efficiency and growth of the network enhanced via sharing of customers and common investments.	Network through voluntary growth of relations between partner firms. Risk reduced and growth manageable by decentralized means.

Mobilization and Construction of Social Technology in Elec.net: Strategy and Organization

The contradiction between the two views (the conservative vs. the risk-taking approach) on the network was silent between meetings and decisions in the network. "Skeptics" would routinely call on "progressives" to carry out jobs in other parts of the country where they were not represented or when they had relevant competencies. So, at times, the differences had no consequences and even the fiercest of "skeptics" used the most progressive firms to carry out assignments. In the bilateral mobilization of network ties, the network had no problems and, unlike the consultancy network, no apparent exclusion of specific types of partners was noticed.

However, as the network partners were interdependent, sometimes decisions had to be coordinated and made collectively, and in the collective mobilization of the network contradictions sometimes turned into conflicts. One example is as follows:

> At a point in time it was decided that we need to have this organized as a real company. It is not good enough to control by meetings in various

parts of the country. Yet, this is a voluntary organization, so it cannot be controlled like a real company. But because of this decision, we appointed managers and what-do-I-know-functions of the network. Then we had to appoint section managers in all partner firms who were to attend section manager meetings. In reality, it was the network-CEO or a board member that made the decisions about adding central sales.... So now we suddenly have to pay a monthly fee of $1.500 for marketing staff without any real discussion of it.

The changes towards more rigid structures (Das & Teng, 2000) enabled the "progressives" to move their agenda of higher levels of investment forward, particularly in relation to the development of a sales function for the entire network. The investment was a challenge to a prior praxis of egalitarian decision-making because the "skeptics" did not think they had approved the decision. One of the "skeptics" explained his feelings as follows:

An example is the "central sales" that was decided without really asking us. It is bad and annoying because I was at that meeting we had in April last year and I think we had the first discussion of it then. But the people present were employed (i.e., managers in a partner firm, not partners) and they were told bluntly that this is how it is.

Many of the partners were unaware of the decision and "just received it in the mailbox." The "skeptics" responded by setting up an unofficial meeting between the owners without the network CEO:

The 15 of August we held an unofficial board meeting in to order determine the frame of mind of the owners and to try and influence the board and we did it without our CEO, not because he was not allowed to be there, but because I think that there are people who do not say much when the CEO is present, because he may intimidate them.

At a later board meeting in August "skeptics" agreed prior to the meeting to use a formal, rarely practiced, internal network rule about financial solidity to exclude a progressive from the meeting in order to enhance their chances of rejecting central sales. At the meeting it was decided to close central sales. However, because of the execution of the decision central—the decision was executed after trial period where it could have been closed within a month—sales was to be closed four months later and not one month later as envisaged by the "skeptics." This gave extra time to secure funding within or outside the network.

These developments increased withdrawal from the network. One "skeptic" explained: "There have been some "progressive" forces on the board that would like things to move faster than the majority of firms in Elec.net."

A consequence was that some "skeptics" left the network and that others were contemplating leaving:

> I had hoped that we could bring Elec.net down to another more reasonable level of ambition, where more of us could join, and where we also could participate in the future, but that is not the way things turned out.

DISCUSSION:
MOBILIZING AND CHANGING SOCIAL STRUCTURES

The detailed empirical material presented above suggests that the social technology of the network is a surprising set of rules and resources. Not only will it reinforce a community held together by values, sympathy, and trust, it also—and more importantly—carves out lines of contradiction and conflict.

Advice.net was intended as a community based on sharing, trust, openness, and flexibility, and it was a platform to team up for temporary projects. Partners had to be strong and self-organized. This norm was contradicted by partners who did not have these qualities and they would gradually become marginalized because they were not assets in project work. The implementation of social technology entailed marginalization and exclusion and a return to a more "pure" network organization.

Elec.net illustrates that conflict arose when joint decisions were made and groups defined themselves by differences in signification and legitimation. Collective decision making was a clash between social structures and the effect was that certain types of partners (the "skeptics") tended to leave the network making it a more "pure" "progressive" one.

Social Technology as Process

Focusing on the details of social interaction, it is possible to theorize social technologies as a fragile set of rules and resources, which can be initiated, transformed and destroyed. Figure 10.2 illustrates how this is done.

Figure 10.2 models networks dynamics with a social technology of shared values and trust. Diversity influences group formation when partners with values and norms join in order to advance their agenda. Diversity is necessary, however, because to survive, a commercial network needs partners with complementary competencies (Dyer & Singh, 1998). It also models how processes develop around this state, and four possible paths can be identified two of which are about continuation and stabilization of network

Figure 10.2

Mobilization and Transformation of Social Technologies

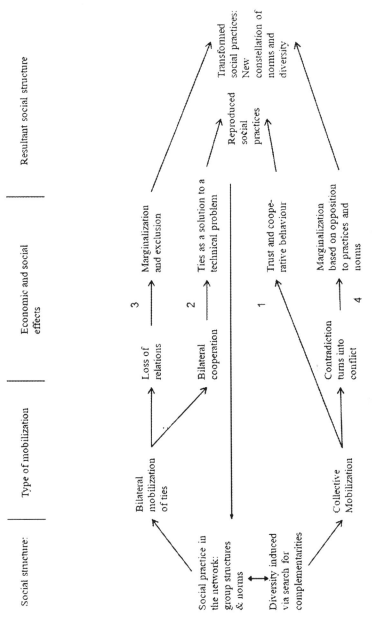

activities (Paths 1 and 2) and the other two ones are about change and transformation (Paths 3 and 4).

Path 1 at the bottom of Figure 10.2 shows how the network works as a collectivity so that heterogeneity is a resource, and the normative aspirations of the collectivity are not disputed. For example, Elec.net worked by integrating different competencies toward the customer, and they advertised their network on homepage illustrating solutions. They got quantity discounts through combining their purchases. Path 2 shows individual ties between actors in the network. In Path 2 individuals draw on each other in specific business ventures by mutual agreement. For example, Elec.net partners located in different parts of the country call on each other to meet the needs of large customers who needed more manpower than they could offer individually. And if a customer having locations at several places in the country needed a job performed in another part of the country far away, the partner could ask a partner in that part of the country to perform the job thereby substantially decreasing transportation cost and enabled through a profit-sharing regime. The purpose is to solve an economic/technical problem rather than a social problem.

Figure 10.2 also shows two types of transformation through conflict. Path 3's conflict marginalizes an actor when a relationship simply stops; no one call on the partner anymore and this partner is then expelled, with the consequence that the network has been transformed by a change in membership. Path 4, in contrast, is dramatic because this is the path by which social technology and structure of the networks are overtly at stake and whose content is articulated. Path 4 shows the network seeking to function as a coherent unit making joint decisions, and this is when contradictions between systems of signification, domination, and legitimation challenge existing practices. The resulting conflict is not about a single tie, but about the system of ties, and the conflict is transpired as one system of rules and resources versus another. This conflict puts pressure on partners, and it is resolved when partners choose to leave or by when partners are ousted because they do not share the rules and resources of the group turning out to be dominant. Conflict expels actors directly or through pressure from collective investments and arrangements that make life difficult for these actors. When the conflict eases again, social practices are more purely informed by the resulting social order and technology.

Contradiction does not necessarily produce conflict. Conflict is actualized only when the network seeks to mobilize social technology acting as coherent unity. It happens when the ambitions of the network as a totality are at stake, for example, in relation to decisions about strategy and structures in the network, when marginalization of members is a collective process.

In Paths 1 and 2 diversity and contradiction are resources for value creation because they allow complementarity to develop. Paths 2 and 3 show continuity and change without strong mobilization of social technology apart from norms about sharing customers. These findings contrast with and yet extend Gargiulo and Bernassi's (2000) conclusion that a network is either closed and cohesive, or sparsely connected through multiple structural holes. Their cross-sectional approach can be transcended by our longitudinal and process approach so that the network and its social technologies are potentialities that need to be mobilized in order to have effects. In this mobilization process it is always possible to marginalize a member or to include another member. Social technologies can be mobilized in a variety of ways through Paths 3 and 4.

The Paradox and Dilemma of Inter-Firm Networks

Commercial networks require diversity. Competencies, personality traits and strategic hopes and aspirations are complementarities potentially important for relational advantages (Dyer & Singh, 1998). Complementarities require differences and diversity between partners. In Advice.net degrees of strength, extroversion and personal flexibility separated participants and created distinctions. In Elec.net diversity in age, business focus and perspectives regarding cooperation differed between "skeptics" and "progressives." Such diversity influenced the structuring of the network; it mobilized differing interpretive schemes (signification) and norms (legitimation).

Inkpen and Tsang (2005, p. 158) argue that "the overall effect of cultural diversity should be beneficial to knowledge transfer." However this view misses the point that social structures are then heterogeneous because of different accounts of effective behavior, it mobilizes normative questions about what the network should accomplish, and it expresses contradictions and faultlines. These contradictions and faultlines are not operative in the network continuously, but are mobilized in relation to situations in which the network is compelled to act strategically as a coherent unit or in which members begin to informally and bilaterally exclude partners. In the Elec. net case, for example, we saw how the division between "progressives" and "skeptics" was mobilized when the network discussed adding a central sales unit to the network. In other situations, "progressives" and "skeptics" were able to work together without any overt problems.

This dual functioning of the network points to a paradox in the management of alliance networks. They are formed in order to help orchestration and management of a diverse collection of partners acting in unity. They develop joint marketing, technology, strategy, and so forth, but exactly in situations where the alliance network seeks to function as a unity—as a community—contradictions can be transformed into conflicts. When striving to act as a unit with strategies and joint goals, conflicts can emerge transforming the network and destroying, or changing the intended functioning of the social technology.

This paradox has three implications. First, cultural and technological diversity are related to fragmentation that inhibits the mobilization and stabilization of social technologies (Pelled, 1996; Pelled et al., 1999). Second, network economics require competencies/technologies to be non-redundant and thereby require diversity, but this also creates interdependencies and increases contradiction. Thirdly, when diversity and complementarity are maximal, alliance networks may have to avoid or postpone joint decision-making and mobilization of the entire network, or they may engage in strong coordination primarily when diversity is minimal. Otherwise, conflict may rip them apart.

Koza and Lewin (1999) suggest that alliance networks over time evolve into being more rationalized as well as utilizing more formalized modes of functioning. Institutional pressures direct isomorphic processes especially in stable industries. Our findings seem to question this finding. Elec.net was a 14-year-old network and despite the possibility of a slightly increasing formalization, the network did not evolve into more a rationalized and uniform mode of functioning. Rather the steady influx of new partners (45 over the past 14 years) enabled the network to maintain its fragile balance between different groups of partners poised at edge of chaos (Prigogine & Stengers, 1984). This complex, unstable functioning of the network may be the only way that a network can both build relational advantages through complementarities and achieve joint goals through the implementation of social technologies. The social order, instabilities and contradictions should be upheld by an influx of new partners that maintains diversity and the balance between different groups. An alliance network achieving order, stability and equilibrium through social technologies may effectively be undermining its justification—its business model.

CONCLUSION

Drawing on longitudinal evidence about the operation of two small commercial networks, this chapter has analyzed the way in which social technologies impact alliance networks. Trust and shared values are not the magic ingredients that would ensure effective cooperation. When social technologies are analyzed and studied as processes, it becomes clear that they are fragile accomplishments, because they can be changed in any interaction and because diversity and faultlines separate groups with contradictory norms and interpretative schemes. Social technologies are constantly mobilized in interaction and therefore are potentially questioned and transformed all the time.

When social technology is related to a set of bilateral ties, it is substituted by economic and technical affairs in ongoing business relations. Ties can be developed by merely adding or dropping interactions as can be done by any individual. This changes the constellation of ties and thereby of the social technology as an effect of the structure of participants. When social technology is related to the collectivity, it works differently. In networks, differences in competences are necessary because otherwise there would be no complementarity. But complementarity also produces differences in outlook between groups regarding the business of the network. Faultlines thus accumulate and when they are problematized, they create conflict associated with differences in social technology. Often the network membership is changed through such processes and the result is a re-constitution of the social technology of the network; it has become more "pure" and less differentiated. Such a network undermines its own business proposition, and it therefore needs an influx of new members in order to maintain its complex, fragile order.

NOTES

1. Here, diversity focuses first on firm diversity as opposed to personal diversity. Secondly, diversity is measured as the values of owners view on corporation (Harrison et al., 1998, p. 105) rather than on their demographic variables such as firm size and technological specialization. These are interrelated but not directly and automatically.

2. The implicit system IMP-SYS has been developed by Heylen and licensed by NFO (www.nfoeurope.com) and is usually used for testing brand names. One of the researchers has been formally trained in the method. The projective technique consists of a photo set of 8 men and woman displaying 8 validated, behavioral positions. We showed the respondents the photos and asked them to choose one or more that typified a person with whom they would like to cooperate.

ACKNOWLEDGMENT

This chapter, save some minor changes, was earlier published as Thrane, Sof, & Mouritsen, Jan (2012). Social technology and stability/transformation of alliance networks: Dilemmas and paradoxes of cooperation. In T. K. Das (Ed.), *Management dynamics in strategic alliances* (pp. 237–266). Charlotte, NC: Information Age Publishing.

REFERENCES

Adler, P. S., & Kwon, S. W. (2002). Social capital: Prospects for a new concept. *Academy of Management* Review, *27*, 17–40.

Ahuja, G. (2000). The duality of collaboration: Inducements and opportunities in the formation of interfirm linkages. *Strategic Management Journal, 21*, 317–343.

Alvesson, M. (2003). Beyond neopositivists, romantics, and localists: A reflexive approach to interviews in organizational research. *Academy of Management Review, 28*, 13–33.

Ariño, A., & de la Torre, J. (1998). Learning from failure: Toward an evolutionary model of collaborative venture. *Organization Science, 9*, 306–325.

Bolino, M. C. (2002). Citizenship behavior and the creation of social capital in organizations. *Academy of Management Review, 27*, 505–523.

Brickson, S. (2000). The impact of identity orientation on individual and organizational outcomes in demographically diverse settings. *Academy of Management Review, 25*, 82–102.

Burt, R. S. (1992). *Structural holes: The social structure of competition.* Cambridge, MA: Harvard University Press.

Chatman, J., & Flynn, F. J. (2001). The influence of demographic heterogeneity on the emergence and consequences of cooperative norms in teams. *Academy of Management Journal, 44*, 956–975.

Coleman, J. S. (1988). Social capital in the creation of human capital. *American Journal of Sociology, 94*, 95–120.

Das, T. K., & Teng, B. (2000). Instabilities of strategic alliances: An internal tensions perspective. *Organization Science, 11*, 77–101.

Dutton, J. E., & Dukerich, J. M. (1991). Keeping an eye on the mirror: Image and identity in organizational adaptation. *Academy of Management Journal, 34*, 517–554.

Dyer, H., & Chu, W. (2003). The role of trustworthiness in reducing transaction cost and improving performance: Empirical evidence from the United States, Japan, and Korea. *Organization Science, 14*, 57–68.

Dyer, J. H., & Nobeoka, K. (2000). Creating and managing a high performance knowledge-sharing network: The Toyota case. *Strategic Management Journal, 21*, 345–367.

Dyer, J. H., & Singh, H. (1998). The relational view: Cooperative strategy and sources of interorganizational competitive advantage. *Academy of Management Review, 23*, 660–679.

Eisenhardt, K. M. (1989). Building theories from case study research. *Academy of Management Review, 14*, 532–550.

Faems, D., Janssens, M., Madhok, A., & van Looy, B. (2008). Toward an integrative perspective on alliance governance: Connecting contract design, trust dynamics, and contract application. *Academy of Management Journal, 51*, 1053–1078.

Frank, K. A., & Yasumoto, J. Y. (1998). Linking action to social structure within a system: Social capital within and between groups. *The American Journal of Sociology, 104*, 642–686.

Gargiulo, M., & Bernassi, M. (2000). Trapped in your own net? Network cohesion, structural holes, and the adaptation of social capital. *Organization Science, 11,* 183–196.

Gephardt, R. P., Jr. (2004). From the editors. *Academy of Management Journal, 47,* 454–463.

Giddens, A. G. (1984). *The constitution of society.* Cambridge, UK: Polity Press.

Giddens, A. G. (1981). *A contemporary critique of historical materialism.* London, UK: Macmillan Press.

Greve, H. R., Baum, J. A. C., Mitsuhashi, H., & Rowley, T. J. (2010). Built to last but falling apart: Cohesion, friction, and withdrawal from interfirm alliances. *Academy of Management Journal, 53,* 302–322.

Harrison, D. A., Price, K. H., & Myrtle P. B. (1998). Beyond relational demography: Time and the effects of surface- and deep level diversity on work group cohesion. *Academy of Management Journal, 41,* 96–107.

Hechter, M. (1992). Should values be written out of the social scientist's lexicon? *Sociological Theory. 10,* 214–230.

Held, D., & Thompson, J. B. (1989). *Social theory of modern societies—Anthony Giddens and his critics.* Cambridge, UK: Cambridge University Press.

Henderson, C. R. (1901). The scope of social technology. *American Journal of Sociology, 6,* 465–486.

Henderson, C. R. (1912). Applied sociology (or social technology). *American Journal of Sociology, 18,* 215–221.

Husted, B. W., & Folger, R. (2004). Fairness and transaction costs: The contribution of organizational justice theory to an integrative model of economic organization. *Organization Science, 15,* 719–729.

Inkpen, A. C., & Currall, S. C. (2004). The coevolution of trust, control, and learning in joint ventures. *Organization Science, 15,* 586–599.

Inkpen, A. C., & Tsang, E. W. K. (2005). Social capital, networks, and knowledge transfer. *Academy of Management Review, 30,* 146–165.

Jorde, T. M., & Teece, D. J (1989). Competition and cooperation: Striking the right balance. *California Management Review, (Spring),* 25–37.

Khanna, T., Gulati, R., & Nohria, N. (1998). The dynamics of learning alliances: Competition, cooperation, and relative scope. *Strategic Management Journal, 19,* 193–210.

Koza, M. P., & Lewin, A. Y. (1999). The coevolution of network alliances: A longitudinal analysis of an international professional service network. *Organization Science, 10,* 638–653.

Lau, C. D., & Murnighan, J. K. (1998). Demographic diversity and faultlines: The compositional dynamics of organizational groups. *Academy of Management Review, 23,* 325–340.

Lee, T. (1999). *Using qualitative methods in organizational research.* Thousand Oaks, CA: SAGE.

Leenders, R. T. A. J., & Gabbay, S. M. (1999). *Corporate social capital and liability.* Norwell MA: Kluwer Academic.

Nahapiet, J., & Ghoshal, S. (1998). Social capital, intellectual capital, and the organizational advantage. *Academy of Management Review, 23,* 242–266.

Pelled, L. H. (1996). Demographic diversity, conflict and work group outcomes: An intervening process theory. *Organization Science, 7*, 615–632.

Pelled L. H., Eisenhardt, K. M., & Xin, K. R. (1999). Exploring the black box: An analysis of work group diversity, conflict, and performance. *Administrative Science Quarterly, 44*, 1–29.

Peters, L., & Karren, R. J. (2009). An examination of the roles of trust and functional diversity on virtual team performance ratings. *Group & Organization Management, 34*, 479–504.

Portes, A. (1998). Social capital: Its origins and applications in modern sociology. *Annual Review of Sociology, 24*, 1–24.

Prigogine, I., & Stengers, I. (1984). *Order out of chaos.* New York, NY: Bantam Books.

Pratt, M. G., & Rose, J. A. (2003). Transforming work-family conflict into commitment in network marketing organizations. *Academy of Management Journal, 46*, 395–418.

Strauss, A., & Corbin, J. (1998). *Basics of qualitative research – techniques and procedures for developing grounded theory* (2nd ed.). London, UK: SAGE.

Sydow, J., & Windeler, A. (1998). Organizing and evaluating interfirm networks: A structurationist perspective on network processes and effectiveness. *Organization Science, 9*, 265–284.

Tomkins, C. (2001). Interdependencies, trust and information in relationships, alliances and networks. *Accounting, Organizations and Society, 26*, 161–191.

Tsai, W. (2000). Social capital, strategic relatedness, and the formation of intraorganizational linkages. *Strategic Management Journal, 21*, 925–939.

Tsai, W., & Ghoshal, S. (1998). Social capital and value creation: The role of interfirm networks. *Academy of Management Journal, 41*, 464–476.

Walker, G., Kogut, B., & Shan, W. (1997). Social capital, structural holes and the formation of an industry network. *Organization Science, 8*, 109–125.

Watson, W. E., Kumar, K., & Michaelsen, L. K. (1993). Cultural diversity's impact on interaction process and performance: Comparing homogenous and diverse task groups. *Academy of Management Journal, 36*, 590–603.

Weber, M. (1980). *Wirtschaft und Gesellschaft.* Tübingen, Germany: Mohr. (Original work published 1922)

Yin, R. K. (1994). *Case study research: Design and methods* (2nd ed.). Thousand Oaks, CA: SAGE.

Yli-Renko, H., Autio, E., & Sapienza, H. J. (2001). Social capital, knowledge capital, knowledge acquisition and knowledge exploitation in young technology-based firms. *Strategic Management Journal, 22*, 587–613.

Young-Ybarra, C., & Wiersema, M. (1999). Strategic flexibility in information technology alliances: The influence of transaction cost economics and social exchange theory. *Organization Science, 10*, 439–459.

Zeng, M., & Chen, X. (2003). Achieving cooperation in multiparty alliances: A social dilemma approach to partnership management. *Academy of Management Review, 28*, 587–605.

Zollo, M., Reuer, J. J., & Singh, H. (2002). Interorganizational routines and performance in strategic alliances. *Organization Science, 13*, 701–713.

CHAPTER 11

HOW MUCH DOES ALLIANCE PARTNER DIVERSITY MATTER IN INTERPARTNER COOPERATION, REALLY?

A Meta-Analysis

Giulio Ferrigno and Angelo M. Solarino

ABSTRACT

A considerable number of studies argue that partner diversity is important for managing interpartner cooperation in strategic alliances. Alliance partner diversity has been examined across various dimensions and disciplines, and its implications for alliance performance are neither theoretically clear nor empirically consistent. Drawing on a meta-analytic approach, we first provide a systematic analysis of alliance partner diversity-alliance performance relationship. Then, we assess whether each alliance partner's diversity type mediates the relationship between the other diversity types and alliance performance. Our meta-analysis findings advance alliance inquiry by revealing that only some types of alliance partner diversity matter for firm performance and that only some mediate the alliance partner diversity-performance relationship, thereby providing a more fine-grained understanding of the effects of alliance partner diversity on alliance performance.

Managing Interpartner Cooperation in Strategic Alliances, pp. 305–328
Copyright © 2022 by Information Age Publishing
www.infoagepub.com
305

INTRODUCTION

It is a widespread belief in corporate strategy literature that alliance partner diversity affects alliance performance (Jiang, Tao, & Santoro, 2010; Yasuda, 2021). Drawing upon this belief, extant alliance research has examined the performance implications of various dimensions of alliance diversity, including size (Ferrigno, Dagnino, & Di Paola, 2021; Schilke & Lumineau, 2018), cultural (Kwon, Haleblian, & Hagedoorn, 2016), industrial (Bakker, 2016) and technological diversity (Ferrigno et al. 2021; Joshi & Lahiri, 2015). However, a lack of consensus exists with regard to the influence of alliance diversity on alliance performance. More precisely, alliance literature presents mixed findings, ranging from positive (Nieto & Santamaria, 2007; Srivastava & Gnyawali, 2011) to negative implications (Cui & O'Connor, 2012), to inverted U-shaped (De Leeuw, Lokshin, & Duysters, 2014; Oerlemans, Knoben, & Pretorius, 2013) or even U-shaped relationships (Wuyts & Dutta, 2014). Taken together, previous findings suggest that such empirical inconsistencies imply a need for a better understanding of alliance diversity's implications for alliance performance (Ferrigno, 2020). In this regard, Lee, Kirkpatrick-Husk, and Madhavan (2017) have joined the debate by adopting a meta-analytic approach to investigate alliance diversity and its impact on firm performance. The authors provided a quantitative synthesis of the relationship between alliance portfolio diversity and firm performance and examined whether different types of portfolio diversity influenced focal firm performance. In this study, we build on their findings to develop our contributions in two directions. First, we complement the research by taking into consideration a broader relationship, that is, the relationship between alliance partner diversity (APD) and alliance performance. More specifically, we use a meta-analysis for providing a systematic synthesis of APD implications for alliance performance.

Second, Lee et al. (2017) have not taken into consideration the relationships among the different types of APD. In this chapter, we contribute to the literature on APD by assessing whether the mediations among the diversity measures affect the relationship between APD and alliance performance. Indeed, some forms of APD reinforce the benefits or the costs associated with the other types of APDs. To the best of our knowledge, this is the first study to assess how different types of APD mutually strengthen or weaken their relationship with alliance performance.

The chapter is structured as follows. First, we review the theoretical background that informs interpartner cooperation by focusing on alliance partner diversity. Second, we develop a set of hypotheses between each dimension of alliance partner diversity and alliance performance. Third, we present the method, the collection of sample studies analyzed, and the meta-analytic procedures used. Fourth, we show and discuss the findings of the study. Finally, we submit conclusions, assess limitations, and provide a few directions for future research.

MANAGING DIVERSITY IN INTERPARTNER COOPERATION

Constructs of Alliance Partner Diversity

Alliance partner diversity has been considered as an important factor influencing partner selection or alliance outcomes (e.g., Cui & O'Connor, 2012; Goerzen & Beamish, 2005; Jiang et al., 2010; Kim & Parkhe, 2009; Yasuda, 2013). Despite a growing consensus on the importance of alliance diversity for alliance outcomes, there is no single, overarching explanation of its consequences. Most frequently, however, studies have highlighted four constructs of partner diversity among alliance members and its variants. Table 11.1 reports the split between hypothesized and found relationship in 54 articles published in top management journals between 2000 and 2015.

Table 11.1

Summary of Existing Knowledge on Predictions and Significance of the "Diversity-Alliance Performance" Relationship

Panel a) Predictions and significance of the "diversity-alliance performance" analyses

Alliance Partners' Diversity Dimension	Hypothesized effect	# Tests	Results of the analysis			Correctly supported
			Positive	Non-significant	Negative	
Size Diversity	Positive	5	·	4	1	0%
Size Diversity	Not hypothesized	5	4	1	·	n.a.
Size Diversity	Negative	6	·	6	·	0%
Cultural Diversity	Positive	2	·	2	·	n.a.
Cultural Diversity	Not hypothesized	6	1	4	1	n.a.
Cultural Diversity	Negative	38	7	19	12	32%
Industry Diversity	Positive	·	·	·	·	n.a.
Industry Diversity	Not hypothesized	2	·	1	1	50%
Industry Diversity	Negative	·	·	·	·	n.a.

(Table continued on next page)

Table 11.1 (Continued)

Summary of Existing Knowledge on Predictions and Significance of the "Diversity-Alliance Performance" Relationship

Panel a) Predictions and significance of the "diversity-alliance performance" analyses

Alliance Partners' Diversity Dimension	Hypothesized effect	Results of the analysis				
		# Tests	Positive	Non-significant	Negative	Correctly supported
Technological Diversity	Not hypothesized	2	1	1	·	n.a.
Technologica Diversity	Negative	1	·	1	·	0%
Total		75	17	42	17	15%

^ one study theorized the relationship as U–shaped, it has been counted twice.

Panel B1) Model Choice

Model	Effect size and 95% interval				Test of null (2–Tail)		Heterogeneity			
	Number Studies	Point estimate	Lower limit	Upper limit	Z–value	P–value	Q–value	df (Q)	P–value	I–squared
Fixed	212	0.12	0.11	0.12	151.40	0.00	24320.79	211.00	0.00	99.13
Random effects	212	0.03	0.01	0.05	2.67	0.01				

Panel B2) Individual APD effects (Random effects)

Size diversity	21	–0.06	–0.17	0.05	–1.02	0.31
Industry diversity	67	0.00	–0.04	0.03	–0.19	0.85
Cultural diversity	71	0.05	0.00	0.11	1.92	0.05
Tech Diversity	53	0.08	0.02	0.14	2.57	0.01

Panel B3) MASEM of alliance partner diversity on alliance performance

	Estimate	S.E.	Est./S.E.	P–Value
Size diversity	–0.089	0.022	–3.979	$p < 0.001$
Industry diversity	–0.015	0.022	–0.677	0.499
Cultural diversity	0.045	0.022	2.034	0.042
Tech diversity	0.062	0.022	2.8	0.005
Equity ties	0.092	0.022	4.214	$p < 0.001$
R–square	0.023			

Perf. = Alliance performance; all analyses are two–tailed. $N = 2,044$

The first construct of partner diversity deals with the dissimilarities of size between alliance partners. Strategy and innovation scholars have indeed dedicated extensive attention to the construct of *size diversity*. Size dissimilarities between alliance partners can give rise to complementary abilities which can fuel better performance (Millington & Bayliss, 1997; Yeheskel, Zeira, Shenkar, & Newburry, 2001). The smaller partner, being more adaptable and flexible is better suited to accommodate the needs of the larger partner (Diestre & Rajagopalan, 2012; Ferrigno, Piccaluga, & Dagnino, 2021) as well as it can respond quickly to the needs of the larger partner.

The second construct of partner diversity concerning *cultural diversity* has been the subject of much scholarly debate. Cultural diversity generally refers to dissimilarities in beliefs, values, practices, and behaviors shared by members of a nation (Hofstede, 1980). Some researchers agree that the cultural distance between alliance members is negatively related to performance, because of the increased risks of mistrust, misunderstandings, miscommunication, and managerial conflicts, which hamper the efficient alliance management (e.g., Glaister & Buckley 1999; Kim & Parkhe 2009; Makino, Chan, Isobe, & Beamish, 2007).

The third construct of partner diversity deals with concerns about *industry diversity*. Similarities in business activities, products, and industries of the organizations involved have been argued to have a positive effect on alliance performance. It creates the potential for economies of scale, and for facilitating the transfer of knowledge and resources (Merchant & Schendel, 2000). Likewise, because of the ease of understanding of each other businesses, industry relatedness has been argued to be useful to detect and thus deter opportunistic behaviors (Luo, 1997; Merchant & Schendel, 2000). In presence of industry diversities between alliance partners, these benefits disappear. Furthermore, the different "industry speed," competitive dynamics, and customers' needs will give rise to tensions among the alliance partners. If on one hand, the alliance partners can access new know-how, the industry diversity will make it more costly to absorb, integrate, and implement the new knowledge (Jiang et al., 2010), resulting in decreased alliance performances.

The fourth construct of partner diversity is related to *technological diversity*. Several researchers found that the more diverse the partners in the alliance are, the more they can generate innovation and sustain the alliance's competitive advantage (Levinthal, 1995; Subramaniam & Youndt, 2005). Firms partnering with dissimilar companies are aware of the challenges ahead (Dagnino & Ferrigno, 2015) therefore they can adapt their structure to accommodate these differences. Being the firm ready to deal with partners that speak different technological jargon, have different mindsets, and so forth, they are also better suited to handle the other differences with their alliance partner (Ferrigno, 2017).

Taken together, the four constructs of alliance partner diversity hint at mediations among the diversity measures on the relationship between APD and alliance performance. Indeed, some forms of APD reinforce the benefits or the costs associated with the other types of APDs.

The overall objective of mediation analysis is to make inferences about mechanisms. Investigating paths among each construct of alliance partner diversity and alliance performance can provide a more complete understanding of the overall relationship between APD and alliance performance. In the following sections, we examine whether the hypothesized mediations are sustained by empirical evidence through a quantitative summary and cumulative tests of alliance findings.

HYPOTHESES

The Mediating Effect of Size Diversity

In the extant alliance literature, it has been shown that cultural differences between alliance partners are negatively related to performance. This is because of the increased risks of mistrust, misunderstandings, miscommunication, and managerial conflicts, which hamper efficient alliance management (e.g., Glaister & Buckley 1999; Kim & Parkhe 2009; Makino et al., 2007). Seen from this perspective, we expect that the diversity of size between the allied partners can be critical in enhancing such an effect. In fact, research shows that smaller partners develop different procedures and routines from larger partners in approaching the alliance. Smaller partners are more flexible and adaptable than larger partners (Diestre & Rajagopalan, 2012). Following this logic, the negative performance outcomes of cultural diversity could be enhanced when alliance partners' size is variegated.

In addition, we expect that partner size could positively mediate the relationship between industry diversity and alliance performance. It has been demonstrated that, in presence of industry diversities between alliance partners, opportunistic behaviors (Luo, 1997; Merchant & Schendel, 2000) and tensions among alliance partners emerge. Moreover, such alliances are prone to resource misfits and/or lack of synergies, causing alliances to underperform.

This, in turn, makes it more costly to integrate and implement the new knowledge (Jiang et al., 2010), resulting in decreased alliance performances. Given these conflicts, we expect that dissimilarities in size among alliance partners could influence the negative effect of industry diversity on alliance performance. In fact, larger partners usually can leverage bargaining power, especially in the negotiation phase, which leads to opportunistic behaviors and tensions among alliance partners.

Finally, we propose that size diversity could enhance the effect between technological diversity and alliance performance. In the alliance literature, it is a widespread belief that that technologically unrelated partners can access diverse information, competencies, and capabilities, resulting in the creation of alliance competitive advantage (Ferrigno et al., 2021; Levinthal, 1995; Subramaniam & Youndt, 2005). In this vein, we argue that size diversity could augment this positive outcome. As a matter of fact, the research found that size dissimilarities between alliance partners can give rise to complementary abilities which can fuel better performance (Millington & Bayliss, 1997; Yeheskel et al., 2001). This, in turn, inevitably allow the allied partners to integrate and absorb the diverse knowledge accessed when partners are dissimilar in technology. Drawing on these arguments, we hypothesize that partner size diversity can positively mediate the relationship between the other APDs (industry, cultural and technological diversity) and firm performance. Therefore, we propose the following:

Hypothesis 1: *Partners' size diversity positively mediates the relationship between the other types of alliance diversity and firm performance*

The Mediating Effect of Cultural Diversity

Alliance literature found that dissimilarities in size positively affect alliance performance. In fact, several scholars have shown that size diversity provides complementary capabilities, knowledge, and competencies that ultimately impact innovation performance (Millington & Bayliss, 1997; Yeheskel et al., 2001). From this perspective, we argue that cultural diversity can negatively mediate such relationships. In fact, the benefits associated with size diversity can be limited by the presence of cultural differences among alliance partners. As an example, some scholars found that dissimilarities in beliefs, values, practices, and behaviors shared by alliance members can generate mistrust, misunderstandings, miscommunication, and managerial conflicts (Bai, Du, & Solarino, 2018), which hamper the exploitation of the capabilities provided by small and large partners (Glaister & Buckley, 1999; Kim & Parkhe, 2009; Makino et al., 2007).

Moreover, we further argue that cultural diversity negatively mediates the impact of industry diversity on alliance performance. Alliances with firms from different industries bring a host of benefits that facilitate entry into new markets (Kogut, 1988) or stimulate technological innovations. However, such alliances are also characterized by some costs such as resource misfit and/or lack of synergies (Goerzen & Beamish, 2005), causing alliances to underperform (Jiang et al., 2010). Partners from different industries may also have very different routines and processes that can make collaboration challenging. In this context, difficulties in the interaction/acculturation process involving nationals from different countries (Tung, 1993) hamper the benefits associated with partner industry diversity.

Finally, we argue that cultural differences regarding business practices or communication limit the benefits that arise from technological diversity. Researchers agree that when alliance partners are technologically diverse, innovation outcomes are positively related to the diversity of knowledge accessed by alliance partners. However, once a new relationship is established, the nascent organizational routines require higher monitoring costs given the partners' unfamiliarity with each other's business practices or communication processes, systems, and routines. This escalating dispersion would greatly augment managerial information-processing demands (Hitt, Hoskisson, & Ireland, 1994), making the access to the diversity of knowledge much more complex and difficult to manage (Roth, Schweiger, & Morrison, 1991) and resulting in a decreased alliance performance (Hofstede, 1980).

Drawing on these arguments, we hypothesize that partner cultural diversity can negatively mediate the relationship between the other APDs (size, industry, and technological diversity) and firm performance. Accordingly, we propose the following:

Hypothesis 2: *Partners' cultural diversity negatively mediates the relationship between the other types of alliance diversity and firm performance*

The Mediating Effect of Industry Diversity

Various alliance scholars have provided clear evidence of the impact of size diversity on firm performance. The majority of these studies show a positive relationship between size diversity and performance, suggesting size diversity as one of the main constructs explaining APD effects on performance. Different types of organizations provide various pools of resources and capabilities (Harrison, Hitt, Hoskisson, & Ireland, 2001). For instance, large pharmaceutical firms often ally with small biotech firms to access proprietary technologies or specific technological expertise while smaller biotechnology firms gain access to financial, marketing, and/or managerial resources and capabilities (Santoro & McGill, 2005). However, we expect that industry diversity could hamper these benefits. The lack of synergy with partners in unrelated industries can make access to resources and capabilities more difficult to exploit, thereby resulting in decreased positive outcomes (Goerzen & Beamish, 2005; Jiang et al., 2010).

Additionally, we expect that industry diversity could negatively affect cultural diversity's effect on firm performance. Several researchers agree that the cultural distance between alliance members is negatively related to performance, because of the increased risks of mistrust, misunderstandings, miscommunication, and managerial conflicts, which hamper the efficient alliance management (e.g., Glaister & Buckley 1999; Kim & Parkhe, 2009; Makino et al., 2007). Given the disadvantages derived from culturally diverse partners, we expect the mediating function of industry diversity on the performance impact of cultural diversity. Such mediation occurs as partners from different industries may have very different routines and processes that can make the interaction/acculturation process even more difficult to manage (Parkhe, 1991, 1993; Tung, 1993), thereby resulting in a decreasing firm performance.

Last but not least, the influence of technological diversity on firm performance could be mediated by dissimilarities emerging from partners operating in unrelated industries. While it is unquestionable that technological diversity can bring several benefits, such as access to diverse information, competencies, and capabilities, resulting in the creation of alliance competitive advantage (Levinthal, 1995; Subramaniam & Youndt, 2005) for allied partners, we propose that partners from different industries have developed different routines and procedures that make difficult handling such access to diverse knowledge. Drawing on these arguments, we hypothesize that partner industry diversity can negatively mediate the relationship between the other APDs (size, cultural, and technological diversity) and firm performance. Formally, we propose the following:

Hypothesis 3: *Partners' industry diversity negatively mediates the relationship between the other types of alliance diversity and firm performance*

The Mediating Effect of Technological Diversity

Researchers have long investigated the impact of partner size on firm performance. Most of these studies found that dissimilarities in size clearly influence firm performance because of complementarity abilities that can stem from dissimilar organizations (Millington & Bayliss, 1997; Yeheskel et al., 2001). Small partners have been shown to be better suited to accommodate the needs of larger partners as they are more flexible and adaptable (Diestre & Rajagopalan, 2012). On the other hand, large partners allow small partners to gain access to financial, marketing, and/or managerial resources and capabilities (Santoro & McGill, 2005). In line with this reasoning, we argue that technologically unrelated partners can enhance these benefits. In fact, in presence of technological diversity, the likelihood of new external information being associated with knowledge accessed and assimilated in the past increases (Cohen & Levinthal, 1990; Wuts & Dutta, 2014).

Furthermore, we propose a mediation function of technological diversity on cultural diversity. Most of the research exploring cultural diversity suggests that dissimilarities in beliefs and business practices make alliance management more complex, ending with decreased firm performance. Following this logic, we posit that technological diversity could cause the generation of these disadvantages more critical, as technological diversity makes knowledge transfer more difficult between the allied firms (Sampson, 2007).

Finally, we argue that technological diversity positively mediates industry diversity's effects on firm performance. Several management scholars have advocated that partners in unrelated industries can facilitate entry into new markets (Kogut, 1988) or stimulate technological innovations. In this perspective, we argue that technological diversity can augment these benefits. Technological diversity, in fact, stimulates breadth of perspective and creative thinking as innovation often results from recombination across diverse technological fields (Goerzen & Beamish, 2005; Hargadon & Sutton, 1997; Henderson & Clark, 1990; Nelson & Winter, 1982; Schumpeter, 1939).

Drawing on these arguments, we hypothesize that partner technological diversity can positively mediate the relationship between the other APDs (size, cultural, and industry diversity) and firm performance. Accordingly, we propose the following:

Hypothesis 4: *Partners' technological diversity positively mediates the relationship between the other types of alliance diversity and firm performance.*

Given the above hypotheses, it is not surprising that a narrative literature review suggested that more studies are needed (Christoffersen, 2013, Wassmer, 2010). Schmidt and Hunter (2015) observe that divergent findings are quite common in the behavioral and social sciences, indicating that varying patterns of positive, null, and negative results are a problem that is not unique to alliance research. These authors also noted that the application of meta-analysis has a strong potential both to synthesize discordant findings and to advance theory. This chapter will use meta-analysis to better understand the relative effects of the diversities across alliance partners.

RESEARCH DATA AND METHOD

We did a manual search in a sample of representative journals between the years 2000 and 2016 looking for articles that address the role of APD and alliance performance. We searched the keywords "alliance diversity," "alliance and size," "alliance and industry," "international alliance," "cross country alliance," "resource diversity," "alliance partners," "complementar* partners," "complementar* alliance," "alliance performance" on a set of prominent journals in management, international business, accounting, and finance. We then focus on empirical articles that report the relevant statistics (correlations or t-tests) for computing meta-analytic effect sizes. Among the articles screened only 155 articles reported the necessary information for conducting a meta-analysis, for a total of 947 effect sizes.[1] The description of the variables is reported in Table 11.2. We excluded unpublished papers, as the 'file drawer problem' has been found to have minimal influence on the outcome of meta-analyses (Dalton, Aguinis, Dalton, Bosco, & Pierce, 2012).

Table 11.2

Variables Data Collected

Variable	Measure	Representative Publication
Performance	Accounting indicators Financial indicators Sales growth Satisfaction with performance Survival	Bruyaka & Durand, 2012; Chung & Beamish, 2012; Klijn, Reuer, Van den Boshc, & Volberda, 2013; Maurer, Bartsch & Ebers, 2011; Meschi & Riccio, 2008; Mohr, Wang, & Goerzen, 2016
Size Diversity	Dissimilarity in size, size difference in absolute or log scale, measured as both in terms of accounting indicators (e.g., asset size) and the number of employees. Small partner	Arino, Ragozzino, & Reuer, 2008; Dussauge, Garrette, & Mitchell. 2004; Li, Eden, Hitt, Ireland, & Garrett, 2012; Lui & Ngo, 2004; Schilke & Lumineau, 2016

(Table continued on next page)

Table 11.2 (Continued)

Variables Data Collected

Variable	Measure	Representative Publication
Cultural Diversity	Cultural distance	Dussauge, Garrette, & Mitchell, 2004; Hwee, Ang, & Michailova, 2008; Isidor, Schwens, Hornung, & Kabst, 2015; Kwon, Haleblian, & Hagedoorn, 2016; Lavie & Miller 2008; Richards & De Carolis, 2003
	Institutional distance	
	Same-continent alliance	
	Normative distance	
	Same–continent alliance*	
	Cultural similarity*	
	Cross-border	
	Geographic distance	
	Partner country diversity	
	Religious similarity*	
	Common language*	
Industry Diversity	SIC relatedness* / distance	Ahuja, Polidoro jr, & Mitchell, 2009; Bakker, 2016; Beugelsdijk, Koen, & Noorderhaven, 2006; Bruyaka & Durand, 2012; Chung & Beamish, 2012; García Canal, Valdés-Llaneza, & Ariño, 2003
	Alliance in the same industry*	
	Diversification	
	Business relatedness*	
	Competitive overlap*	
	Product–market similarity*	
	Competitors (dummy)*	
	Upstream alliances (ln)	
	Downstream alliances (ln)	
	Client	
	Supplier	
Technological Diversity	Diversity of technology	Ahlstrom, Levitas, Hitt, Dacin, & Zhu, 2014; Anand, Oriani, & Vassolo, 2010; Chung & Beamish, 2012; Feller, Parhankangas, Smeds, & Jaatinen, 2013; Joshi & Lahiri, 2015; Lu & Xu, 2006; Porrini, 2004; Rothaermel & Deeds, 2004; Sampson, 2005
	Technological Distance / diversity /	
	overlap*/ similarity*	
	Complementary capabilities*	
	Knowledge diversity / similarity*	

(Table continued on next page)

Table 11.2 (Continued)

Variables Data Collected

Variable	Measure	Representative Publication
Equity Ties (Control Variable)	Foreign ownership	Bruyaka & Durand, 2012; van Kranenburg, Hagedoorn, & Lorenz-Orlean, 2014; Lee, Hoetker, & Qualls, 2015
	Percentage of ownership	
	International Joint Venture (dummy)	
	The alliance involves equity (dummy)	

(*) inversely coded

Although meta-analyses can be affected by sample dependence across individual studies, this potential concern is mitigated by three aspects of our sample: our use of a 30-year time horizon, sampling across three disciplines, and the broad range of nations sampled. Two graduate students performed the coding independently of all the diversity-performance relationships. A more senior scholar verified the quality of the output. No differences were found in the coding results.

Meta-Analysis

To assess whether a relationship between APD and alliance performance exists, and to generate the effect size matrix for the MASEM, we performed several meta-analyses. Meta-analyses are statistical techniques that allow the estimation of the true relationship between two variables in the population through the aggregation of results across independent studies. We computed meta-analytic effect sizes using relevant statistics (correlations or t-tests) and converted them into Fisher-Z.

MASEM Procedures

We follow the standard two-stage approach (e.g., Cheung & Chan, 2005) for a meta-analytic structural equation modeling (MASEM), including the best practice guidelines for this methodology (Bergh et al., 2016). The first step is to create a weighted correlation matrix for the constructs of interest identified in our 155 articles. Researchers have the choice of focusing their meta-analysis on articles or effect sizes as the unit of analysis. Following recent guidelines, we conduct our analysis based on effect size (e.g., Aguinis, Beaty, Boik, & Pierce, 2005; Aguinis, Pierce, Bosco, Dalton, & Dalton, 2011; Bergh et al., 2016), as it captures both the heterogeneity of the effect-size estimates and the unique information for each relationship that otherwise would be missing (van Mierlo, Vermunt, & Rutte, 2009). We used the Comprehensive Meta-Analysis (Borenstein, Hedges, Higgins, & Rothstein, 2005) software package. To provide more conservative estimates, we did not include any adjustments for measurement error.

The second step in MASEM is to test the theory by using the correlation matrix as input into a structural-equation model. As recommended by previous studies (e.g., Bergh et al., 2016), we use the harmonic mean across the meta-analyses as the sample size for our analysis. Our sample is composed of 2,044 observations. Consistent with other studies and best practice recommendations, we evaluated all models using a combination of global and local fit indices and also considered alternate causal structures to validate the robustness of our hypothesized effects. The structural models were evaluated using MPlus 8. In the MASEM analysis, we use a conservative 0.80 reliability estimate (Aguinis et al., 2011; Bergh et al., 2016; Solarino & Boyd, 2020).[2]

RESULTS

First, we tested which model was the most appropriate. Random effects model results to be the appropriate one (Table 11.1-Panel B1). Then, we run separate meta-analyses between APD and alliance performance (Table 11.1-Panel B2). It emerges that only two types of APD are positively and significantly related to alliance performance: cultural (0.05, $p = 0.05$) and technological diversity (.08, $p = 0.01$). We re-run the analysis using the MASEM procedure that allows for the inclusion of our control variable equity ties (Table 11.1- Panel B3). The results confirm the positive effect of AP cultural and technological diversities on alliance performance but also evidenced that size diversity has a negative effect on alliance performance, and its effect appears to be the largest one across the different types of APD ($-0.09, p < 0.001$)—once controlling for the presence of equity ties. We now discuss the results of our hypotheses. The results are reported in Table 11.3.

H1 proposes that AP size diversity will positively mediate the effect between all other APD and alliance performance. The hypothesis is supported with regards to cultural and industry diversity, but the effect is opposite and significant for technological diversity. H2 proposes that AP cultural diversity will negatively mediate the effect between all other APD and alliance performance. The results partially support the hypothesis. The effect is significant and in the expected direction for size diversity, but not significant for the other forms of APD. H3 proposes that the AP industry

Table 11.3

MASEM Results

Size Diversity as Mediator

Path	Estimate	S.E.	Z-value	P-Value
Size D.—> Perf.	-0.085	0.022	-3.9	p <0.001
Equity Ties —> Perf.	0.096	0.022	4.386	p <0.001
Tech. D.—> Size D.	0.128	0.022	5.92	p <0.001
Cultural D.—> Size D.	-0.119	0.022	-5.51	<0.001
Industry D.—> Size D.	-0.113	0.022	-5.213	p <0.001
Indirect effects				
Tech. D.—> Size D.—> Perf.	-0.011	0.003	-3.249	0.001
Cultural D.—> Size D.—> Perf.	0.01	0.003	3.176	0.001
Industry D.—> Size D.—> Perf.	0.01	0.003	3.116	0.002
Model FIT				
RMSEA	0.038			
CFI	0.906			

Cultural diversity as Mediator

Path	Estimate	S.E.	Z-value	P-Value
Cultural D.—> Perf.	0.054	0.022	2.469	0.014
Equity Ties —> Perf.	0.097	0.022	4.423	p <0.001
Size D.—> Cultural D.	-0.122	0.022	-5.513	p <0.001
Industry D.—> Cultural D.	-0.022	0.022	-0.986	0.324
Technological D.—> Cultural D.	-0.003	0.022	-0.155	0.877
Indirect effects				
Tech. D.—> Cultural D.—> Perf.	0	0.001	-0.154	0.877
Size D.—> Cultural D.—> Perf.	-0.007	0.003	-2.248	0.025
Industry D.—> Cultural D.—> Perf.	-0.001	0.001	-0.915	0.36
Model FIT				
RMSEA	0.053			
CFI	0.693			

(Table continued on next page)

Table 11.3 (Continued)

MASEM Results

Size Diversity as Mediator

Path	Estimate	S.E.	Z-value	P-Value
Chi-Square	16.047			
Df (4)				

Industry Diversity as Mediator

Path	Estimate	S.E.	Z-value	P-Value
Industry D.—> Perf.	-0.001	0.022	-0.045	0.964
Equity Ties —> Perf.	0.1	0.022	4.344	$p < 0.001$
Tech. D.—> Industry D.	0.103	0.022	4.689	$p < 0.001$
Cultural D.—> Industry D.	-0.022	0.022	-0.986	0.324
Size D.—> Industry D.	-0.115	0.022	-5.18	$p < 0.001$

Indirect effects

Path	Estimate	S.E.	Z-value	P-Value
Tech. D.—> Industry D.—> Perf.	0	0.002	-0.045	0.964
Cultural D.—> Industry D.—> Perf.	0	0	0.045	0.964

Cultural diversity as Mediator

Path	Estimate	S.E.	Z-value	P-Value
Chi-Square	27.153			
Df (4)				

Technological diversity as Mediator

Path	Estimate	S.E.	Z-value	P-Value
Tech. D.—> Perf.	0.049	0.022	2.23	0.026
Equity Ties —> Perf.	0.1	0.022	4.527	p<0.001
Size D.—> Tech. D.	0.13	0.022	5.872	p<0.001
Industry D.—> Tech. D.	0.103	0.022	4.69	p<0.001
Cultural D.—> Tech. D.	-0.003	0.022	-0.153	0.878

Indirect effects

Path	Estimate	S.E.	Z-value	P-Value
Size D.—> Tech. D.—> Perf.	0.006	0.003	2.084	0.037
Cultural D.—> Tech. D.—> Perf.	0	0.001	-0.153	0.879

(Table continued on next page)

Table 11.3 (Continued)

MASEM Results

Indirect effects					Indirect effects				
Size D.—> Industry D.—> Perf.	0	0.003	0.045	0.964	Industry D.—> Tech. D.—> Perf.	0.005	0.003	2.014	0.044
Model FIT					Model FIT				
RMSEA	0.053				RMSEA	0.048			
CFI	0.718				CFI	0.795			
Chi–Square	27.132				Chi–Square	22.645			
Df (4)					Df (4)				

Perf. = Alliance performance; Tech. D. = technological diversity; all analyses are two-tailed. $N = 2,044$

diversity will negatively mediate the effect between all other APD and alliance performance. All mediation effects are non-significant, thereby we did not find any support for our hypothesis. H4 proposes that AP technological diversity will positively mediate the effect between all other APD and alliance performance. The hypothesis found support for size and industry diversity, but not for cultural diversity. The fit index of the models spans from very good to acceptable.

DISCUSSION AND CONCLUSIONS

The first contribution of this chapter is that we contribute to the alliance diversity literature by consolidating what we know about the APD-alliance performance relationship. By taking advantage of the benefits that can be achieved through a meta-analytic approach, we provide a systematic synthesis of APD implications for alliance performance. More specifically, we found that some diversity measures, namely size, cultural, technological, and industry diversity, are well-studied variables for alliance performance. Taken together, these findings suggest that the importance of these alliance diversity measures remains when we extend our angle from the portfolio (Lee et al., 2017) to partner diversity implications for alliance performance.

The second contribution of this chapter is that the typologies of alliance partner diversity matter to some extent for alliance performance. More specifically, our meta-analysis shows that some forms of APD reinforce the benefits, or the costs associated with the other types of APDs, thereby suggesting the importance of their relatedness for alliance performance. The APD–alliance performance relationship in prior studies is to a large extent mediated by size diversity, cultural diversity, and technological diversity. Size diversity appears to have the strongest and negative mediation effect on the relationships between APD and alliance performance. These results, somewhat surprising, can be attributed to partners' lack of adequate expectations in terms of bureaucratization of policies (e.g., Merchant & Schendel, 2000) which led to difficulties in partners' mutual understanding and increased risk for opportunistic rather co-operative behaviors (Beamish & Jung 2005). Interestingly, industry diversity does not mediate the APD-alliance performance relationship, while it has a direct effect. Could be that the potential for economies of scale, and for facilitating the transfer of knowledge and resources (Merchant & Schendel, 2000) is not recognized by the firms for the other dimensions. Our study has important implications for the alliance partner selection because it suggests that firms must pay particular attention to a not-so-studied dimension of the APD: size differences between the partners, which appears to be a source of risk firms do not take properly into account.

Finally, our results suggest that a complex nexus of relationships between diversity measures certainly exists and needs to be further investigated. Future scholars may, for example, take benefits of fuzzy set analyses (Del Sarto, Di Minin, Ferrigno, & Piccaluga, 2019; Ferrigno et al., 2021; Ragin, 2008) to deepen the mechanisms underlying the findings of our study. Future studies could also assess the causal mechanisms using qualitative interviews (Solarino & Aguinis, 2021) and the role of context in the governance of the APD and the alliance more in general (Boyd, Gove, & Solarino, 2017). As a side note, our study reveals the importance of the equity ties in alliances. Future research should also assess the role of ownership types and how the different types of owners (Boyd & Solarino, 2016) shape the effectiveness of the APD.

NOTES

1. Journals included in the manual search: *Academy of Management Journal, Asia Pacific Journal of Management, British Journal of Management, Global Strategy Journal, International Business Review, Journal of International Business Studies, Journal of International Management, Journal of Management Studies, Journal of Management, Journal of World Business, Management International Review, Organization Science, Organization Studies, Strategic Management Journal,* and *Strategic Organization.*
2. We also re–ran the analysis using a reliability of 1.0. The results of the hypothesis tests were unaffected.

REFERENCES

Aguinis, H., Beaty, J. C., Boik, R. J., & Pierce, C. A. (2005). Effect size using power in assessing moderating effects of categorical variables using multiple regression: A 30–year review. *Journal of Applied Psychology, 90,* 94–107.

Aguinis, H., Pierce, C. A., Bosco, F. A., Dalton, D. R., & Dalton, C. M. (2011). Debunking myths and urban legends about meta-analysis. *Organizational Research Methods, 14,* 306–331.

Ahlstrom, D., Levitas, E., Hitt, M. A., Dacin, M. T., & Zhu, H. (2014). The three faces of China: Strategic alliance partner selection in three ethnic Chinese economies. *Journal of World Business, 49*(4), 572–585.

Ahuja, G., Polidoro Jr, F., & Mitchell, W. (2009). Structural homophily or social asymmetry? The formation of alliances by poorly embedded firms. *Strategic Management Journal, 30*(9), 941–958.

Anand, J., Oriani, R., & Vassolo, R. S. (2010). Alliance activity as a dynamic capability in the face of a discontinuous technological change. *Organization Science, 21*(6), 1213–1232.

Arino, A., Ragozzino, R., & Reuer, J. J. (2008). Alliance dynamics for entrepreneurial firms. *Journal of Management Studies*, *45*(1), 147–168.

Bai, T., Du, J., & Solarino, A. M. (2018). Performance of foreign subsidiaries "in" and "from" Asia: A review, synthesis and research agenda. *Asia Pacific Journal of Management*, *35*(3), 607–638.

Bakker, R. M. (2016). Stepping in and stepping out: Strategic alliance partner reconfiguration and the unplanned termination of complex projects. *Strategic Management Journal*, *37*(9), 1919–1941.

Beamish, P. W., & Jung, J. C. (2005). The performance and survival of joint ventures with parents of asymmetric size. *Management International*, *10*(1), 19–30.

Bergh, D. D., Aguinis, H., Heavey, C., Ketchen, D. J., Boyd, B. K., Su, P., & Joo, H. (2016). Using meta-analytic structural equation modeling to advance strategic management research: Guidelines and an empirical illustration via the strategic leadership-performance relationship. *Strategic Management Journal*, *37*(3), 477–497.

Beugelsdijk, S., Koen, C. I., & Noorderhaven, N. G. (2006). Organizational culture and relationship skills. *Organization Studies*, *27*(6), 833–854.

Borenstein, M., Hedges, L., Higgins, J., & Rothstein, H. (2005). *Comprehensive meta-analysis*. Englewood, NJ: Biostat.

Boyd, B. K., Gove, S., & Solarino, A. M. (2017). Methodological rigor of corporate governance studies: A review and recommendations for future studies. *Corporate Governance: An International Review*, 25(6), 384–396.

Boyd, B. K., & Solarino, A. M. (2016). Ownership of corporations: A review, synthesis, and research agenda. *Journal of Management*, 42(5), 1282–1314.

Bruyaka, O., & Durand, R. (2012). Sell–off or shut–down? Alliance portfolio diversity and two types of high-tech firms' exit. *Strategic Organization*, *10*(1), 7–30.

Cheung, M. W. L., & Chan, W. (2005). Meta–analytic structural equation modeling: A two–stage approach. *Psychological Methods*, *10*(1), 40–64.

Christoffersen, J. (2013). A review of antecedents of international strategic alliance performance: Synthesized evidence and new directions for core constructs. *International Journal of Management Reviews*, *15*(1), 66–85.

Chung, C. C., & Beamish, P. W. (2012). Multi-party international joint ventures: Multiple post-formation change processes. *Journal of World Business*, *47*(4), 648–663.

Cohen, W. M., & Levinthal, D. A. (1990). Absorptive capacity: A new perspective on learning and innovation. *Administrative Science Quarterly*, *35*(1), 128–152.

Cui, A. S., & O' Connor, G. (2012). Alliance portfolio resource diversity and firm innovation. *Journal of Marketing*, *76*(4), 24–43.

Dagnino, G. B., & Ferrigno, G. (2015). The strategic management of multipartner alliances: Uncovering the triadic alliance problem. In T. K. Das (Ed.), *Managing multipartner strategic alliances* (pp. 135–169). Charlotte, NC: Information Age Publishing.

Dalton, D. R., Aguinis, H., Dalton, C. M., Bosco, F. A., & Pierce, C. A. (2012). Revisiting the file drawer problem in meta-analysis: An assessment of published and nonpublished correlation matrices. *Personnel Psychology*, *65*(2), 221–249.

de Leeuw, T., Lokshin, B., & Duysters, G. (2014). Returns to alliance portfolio diversity: The relative effects of partner diversity on firm's innovative performance and productivity. *Journal of Business Research*, 67(9), 1839–1849.

Del Sarto, N., Di Minin, A., Ferrigno, G., & Piccaluga, A. (2019). Born global and well educated: Start-up survival through fuzzy set analysis. *Small Business Economics*, 56, 1405–1423.

Diestre, L., & Rajagopalan, N. (2012). Are all 'sharks' dangerous? New biotechnology ventures and partner selection in R&D alliances. *Strategic Management Journal*, 33(10), 1115–1134.

Dussauge, P., Garrette, B., & Mitchell, W. (2004). Asymmetric performance: the market share impact of scale and link alliances in the global auto industry. *Strategic Management Journal*, 25(7), 701–711.

Feller, J., Parhankangas, A., Smeds, R., & Jaatinen, M. (2013). How companies learn to collaborate: Emergence of improved inter–organizational processes in R&D alliances. *Organization Studies*, 34(3), 313–343.

Ferrigno, G. (2017). Looking for alliance portfolio characteristics: The case of telecom industry. In T. K. Das (Ed.), *Managing alliance portfolios and networks* (pp. 177–201). Charlotte, NC: Information Age Publishing.

Ferrigno, G. (2020). *Alleanze strategiche e performance d'impresa. Un approccio strategico-manageriale* [Strategic alliances and firm's performance. A strategic–managerial approach]. Rome, Italy: Aracne Editrice.

Ferrigno, G., Dagnino, G. B., & Di Paola, N. (2021). R&D alliance partner attributes and innovation performance: A fuzzy set qualitative comparative analysis. *Journal of Business and Industrial Marketing*, 36(13), 54–65.

Ferrigno, G., Piccaluga A., & Dagnino G. B. (2021). Managing alliance partner attributes: Lessons from the Ericsson case study. In T. K. Das (Ed.), *Managing the partners in strategic alliances*. Charlotte, NC: Information Age Publishing.

García-Canal, E., Valdés-Llaneza, A., & Ariño, A. (2003). Effectiveness of dyadic and multi–party joint ventures. *Organization Studies*, 24(5), 743–770.

Glaister, K. W., & Buckley, P. J. (1999). Performance relationships in UK international alliances. *Management International Review*, 123–147.

Goerzen, A., & Beamish, P. W. (2005). The effect of alliance network diversity on multinational enterprise performance. *Strategic Management Journal*, 26(4), 333–354.

Hargadon, A., & Sutton, R. I. (1997). Technology brokering and innovation in a product development firm. *Administrative Science Quarterly*, 42(4), 716–749.

Harrison, J. S., Hitt, M. A., Hoskisson, R. E., & Ireland, R. D. (2001). Resource complementarity in business combinations: Extending the logic to organizational alliances. *Journal of Management*, 27(6), 679–690.

Henderson, R. M., & Clark, K. B. (1990). Architectural innovation: The reconfiguration of existing product technologies and the failure of established firms. *Administrative Science Quarterly*, 35(1), 9–30.

Hitt, M. A., Hoskisson, R. E., & Ireland, R. D. (1994). A mid-range theory of the interactive effects of international and product diversification on innovation and performance. *Journal of Management*, 20(2), 297–326.

Hofstede, G. (1980). Culture and organizations. *International Studies of Management & Organization*, 10(4), 15–41.

Isidor, R., Schwens, C., Hornung, F., & Kabst, R. (2015). The impact of structural and attitudinal antecedents on the instability of international joint ventures: The mediating role of asymmetrical changes in commitment. *International Business Review*, *24*(2), 298–310.

Jiang, R. J., Tao, Q. T., & Santoro, M. D. (2010). Alliance portfolio diversity and firm performance. *Strategic Management Journal*, *31*(10), 1136–1144.

Joshi, A. M., & Lahiri, N. (2015). Language friction and partner selection in cross-border R&D alliance formation. *Journal of International Business Studies*, *46*(2), 123–152.

Kim, J., & Parkhe, A. (2009). Competing and cooperating similarity in global strategic alliances: an exploratory examination. *British Journal of Management*, *20*(3), 363–376.

Klijn, E., Reuer, J. J., Van den Bosch, F. A., & Volberda, H. W. (2013). Performance implications of IJV boards: A contingency perspective. *Journal of Management Studies*, *50*(7), 1245–1266.

Kogut, B. (1988). Joint ventures: Theoretical and empirical perspectives. *Strategic Management Journal*, *9*(4), 319–332.

Kwon, S. W., Haleblian, J., & Hagedoorn, J. (2016). In country we trust? National trust and the governance of international R&D alliances. *Journal of International Business Studies*, *47*(7), 807–829.

Lavie, D., & Miller, S. R. (2008). Alliance portfolio internationalization and firm performance. *Organization Science*, *19*(4), 623–646.

Lee, D., Kirkpatrick-Husk, K., & Madhavan, R. (2017). Alliance diversity and firm performance: A meta-analysis. *Journal of Management*, *43*(5), 1472–1497.

Lee, J., Hoetker, G., & Qualls, W. (2015). Alliance experience and governance flexibility. *Organization Science*, *26*(5), 1536–1551.

Levinthal, D. A. (1995). Strategic management and the exploration of diversity. In C. A. Montgomery (Ed.), *Resource-based and evolutionary theories of the firm: Towards a synthesis* (pp. 19–42). Boston, MA: Springer.

Li, D., Eden, L., Hitt, M. A., Ireland, R. D., & Garrett, R. P. (2012). Governance in multilateral R&D alliances. *Organization Science*, *23*(4), 1191–1210.

Lui, S. S., & Ngo, H. Y. (2004). The role of trust and contractual safeguards on cooperation in non-equity alliances. *Journal of Management*, *30*(4), 471–485.

Luo, Y. (1997). Partner selection and venturing success: The case of joint ventures with firms in the People's Republic of China. *Organization Science*, *8*(6), 648–662.

Makino, S., Chan, C. M., Isobe, T., & Beamish, P. W. (2007). Intended and unintended termination of international joint ventures. *Strategic Management Journal*, *28*(11), 1113–1132.

Maurer, I., Bartsch, V., & Ebers, M. (2011). The value of intra-organizational social capital: How it fosters knowledge transfer, innovation performance, and growth. *Organization Studies*, *32*(2), 157–185.

Merchant, H., & Schendel, D. (2000). How do international joint ventures create shareholder value? *Strategic Management Journal*, *21*(7), 723–737.

Meschi, P. X., & Riccio, E. L. (2008). Country risk, national cultural differences between partners and survival of international joint ventures in Brazil. *International Business Review*, *17*(3), 250–266.

Michailova, S., & Hwee Ang, S. (2008). Institutional explanations of cross-border alliance modes: The case of emerging economies firms. *Management International Review*, *48*(5), 551–576.

Millington, A. I., & Bayliss, B. T. (1997). Instability of market penetration joint ventures: A study of UK joint ventures in the European Union. *International Business Review*, *6*(1), 1–17.

Mohr, A., Wang, C., & Goerzen, A. (2016). The impact of partner diversity within multiparty international joint ventures. *International Business Review*, *25*(4), 883–894.

Nelson, R. R., & Winter, S. G. (1982). The Schumpeterian tradeoff revisited. *The American Economic Review*, *72*(1), 114–132.

Nieto, M. J., & Santamaría, L. (2007). The importance of diverse collaborative networks for the novelty of product innovation. *Technovation*, *27*(6), 367–377.

Oerlemans, L. A., Knoben, J., & Pretorius, M. W. (2013). Alliance portfolio diversity, radical and incremental innovation: The moderating role of technology management. *Technovation*, *33*(6), 234–246.

Parkhe, A. (1991). Interfirm diversity, organizational learning, and longevity in global strategic alliances. *Journal of International Business Studies*, *22*(4), 579–601.

Parkhe, A. (1993). Strategic alliance structuring: A game theoretic and transaction cost examination of interfirm cooperation. *Academy of Management Journal*, *36*(4), 794–829.

Porrini, P. (2004). Can a previous alliance between an acquirer and a target affect acquisition performance? *Journal of Management*, *30*(4), 545–562.

Ragin, C. C. (2009). Qualitative comparative analysis using fuzzy sets (fsQCA). In B. Rihoux & C. C. Ragin (Eds.), *Configurational comparative methods: Qualitative comparative analysis (QCA) and related techniques* (pp. 87–121). Thousand Oaks, CA: SAGE.

Richards, M., & De Carolis, D. M. (2003). Joint venture research and development activity: An analysis of the international biotechnology industry. *Journal of International Management*, *9*(1), 33–49.

Roth, K., Schweiger, D. M., & Morrison, A. J. (1991). Global strategy implementation at the business unit level: Operational capabilities and administrative mechanisms. *Journal of International Business Studies*, *22*(3), 369–402.

Rothaermel, F. T., & Deeds, D. L. (2004). Exploration and exploitation alliances in biotechnology: A system of new product development. *Strategic Management Journal*, *25*(3), 201–221.

Sampson, R. C. (2005). Experience effects and collaborative returns in R&D alliances. *Strategic Management Journal*, *26*(11), 1009–1031.

Sampson, R. C. (2007). R&D alliances and firm performance: The impact of technological diversity and alliance organization on innovation. *Academy of Management Journal*, *50*(2), 364–386.

Santoro, M. D., & McGill, J. P. (2005). The effect of uncertainty and asset co-specialization on governance in biotechnology alliances. *Strategic Management Journal*, *26*(13), 1261–1269.

Schilke, O., & Lumineau, F. (2018). The double-edged effect of contracts on alliance performance. *Journal of Management*, *44*(7), 2827–2858.

Schmidt, F. L. & Hunter, J. E. (2015). *Methods of meta-analysis: Correcting error and bias in research findings*, Thousand Oaks, CA: SAGE.

Schumpeter, J. A. (1939). *Business cycles*. New York, NY: McGraw-Hill.

Solarino, A. M., & Aguinis, H. (2021). Challenges and best-practice recommendations for designing and conducting interviews with elite informants. *Journal of Management Studies, 58*(3), 649–672.

Solarino, A. M., & Boyd, B. K. (2020). Are all forms of ownership prone to tunnelling? A meta-analysis. *Corporate Governance: An International Review, 28*(6), 488–501.

Srivastava, M. K., & Gnyawali, D. R. (2011). When do relational resources matter? Leveraging portfolio technological resources for breakthrough innovation. *Academy of Management Journal, 54*(4), 797–810.

Subramaniam, M., & Youndt, M. A. (2005). The influence of intellectual capital on the types of innovative capabilities. *Academy of Management Journal, 48*(3), 450–463.

Tung, R. L. (1993). Managing cross-national and intra-national diversity. *Human Resource Management, 32*(4), 461–477.

van Kranenburg, H., Hagedoorn, J., & Lorenz-Orlean, S. (2014). Distance costs and the degree of inter-partner involvement in international relational-based technology alliances. *Global Strategy Journal, 4*(4), 280–291.

Van Mierlo, H., Vermunt, J. K., & Rutte, C. G. (2009). Composing group-level constructs from individual-level survey data. *Organizational Research Methods, 12*(2), 368–392.

Wassmer, U. (2010). Alliance portfolios: A review and research agenda. *Journal of Management, 36*(1), 141–171.

Wuyts, S., & Dutta, S. (2014). Benefiting from alliance portfolio diversity: The role of past internal knowledge creation strategy. *Journal of Management, 40*(6), 1653–1674.

Yasuda, H. (2013). Impact of interpartner diversity on the performance of global strategic alliances. In. T. K. Das (Ed.), *Interpartner dynamics in strategic alliances*. Charlotte, NC: Information Age Publishing.

Yasuda, H. (2021). Managing interpartner diversities for alliance performance. In T. K. Das, (Ed.), *Managing the partners in strategic alliances*. Charlotte, NC: Information Age Publishing.

Yeheskel, O., Zeira, Y., Shenkar, O., & Newburry, W. (2001). Parent company dissimilarity and equity international joint venture effectiveness. *Journal of International Management, 7*(2), 81–104.

CHAPTER 12

TO COOPERATE OR NOT TO COOPERATE?

The Dilemma Faced by Inexperienced Firms in R&D Consortia

Isabel Estrada, Natalia Martín-Cruz,
and Victor M. Martín-Pérez

ABSTRACT

This chapter examines a phenomenon we observed in a real–life consortium and for which a proper academic explanation is still lacking: under the same challenging conditions, why do only a few inexperienced partners behave cooperatively in the formation process of R&D consortia? Drawing on a multicase study on several consortium partners, we conclude that the reaction of inexperienced firms to the social dilemma inherent to R&D consortia depends on their individual value-creation expectations, which in turn are forged by combinations of incentives of diverse nature. In particular, in the formation of R&D consortia, inexperienced firms are likely to behave cooperatively if they perceive that the consortium entails high strategic potential and brings learning opportunities to realize such potential. At the same time, inexperienced firms facing coopetition tensions are likely to behave noncooperatively, even if they expect important learning and strategic benefits from the consortium. Our evidence, therefore, indicates that the "to cooperate or not to cooperate" dilemma faced by inexperienced partners in multipartner alliances might be better understood as a trade-off between perceived benefits and threats from close interaction with alliance partners.

Managing Interpartner Cooperation in Strategic Alliances, pp. 329–353
Copyright © 2022 by Information Age Publishing
www.infoagepub.com

INTRODUCTION

Research and development (R&D) consortia (i.e., collaborative agreements among multiple partners to jointly conduct a R&D project) bring together many different resources and perspectives and thus afford high potential for synergies and innovation (Doz, Olk, & Ring, 2000). Seeking to seize such potential, public innovation policies across the world are supporting the creation of this particular type of consortia. The Strategic Growth Technologies Program in Denmark, the Multidisciplinary Research Consortia Program in UK, or the National Strategic Consortia for Technical Research Program in Spain can serve as examples. Although large, well-endowed companies have traditionally been the recipients of such public funds, policy makers are increasingly emphasizing the participation of firms with limited experience in R&D collaborative settings, for instance, small firms that operate in low-tech industries. Lack of experience may make the formation of R&D consortia, which is *per se* a complex process (Doz et al., 2000), even more challenging.

R&D consortia, as a particular type of multipartner alliance, entail ambiguous patterns of exchange and reciprocity among the partners (Das & Teng, 2002). Therefore, once a firm has decided to join a R&D consortium, it faces a social dilemma (Zeng & Cheng, 2003): the partner must make a choice between (a) to behave cooperatively and thus contribute to maximizing potential collective gains from the consortium under uncertain conditions of reciprocity *or* (b) not to behave cooperatively, reducing potential collective gains whilst protecting its own resources from unintended leakages and other partners' opportunism. Such a dilemma is inherently overwhelming for inexperienced firms which, not knowing how to capture collective gains whilst protecting their own resources (Sampson, 2005; Reuer, Zollo, & Singh, 2002), may find the "not to cooperate" option as the best strategy.

With these basic premises, we started studying the formation process of a government-sponsored consortium formed by inexperienced partners in the Spanish aquaculture industry (i.e., Acuisost Consortium). We observed that different partners, under the same challenging conditions, reacted to the "to cooperate or not to cooperate" dilemma in different ways. In particular, whereas most of the partners displayed non–cooperative behaviors, a few partners cooperated actively in pushing the consortium ahead, triggering a cooperative disequilibrium.

Existing research on cooperation in multipartner settings (e.g., Doz et al., 2000; Lavie, Lechner, & Singh, 2007; Thorgren, Wincent, & Eriksson, 2010), while providing important insights, has yet to fully unearth this cooperative phenomenon. Understanding how inexperienced partners react to the R&D consortia social dilemma may bring important implications for theory and for managerial and policy practice as well. Based on the longitudinal study on the Acuisost Consortium, we therefore seek to examine why some inexperienced partners behave cooperatively while others do not during the formation stage of R&D consortia.

We find strong evidence that the reaction of inexperienced partners to the "to cooperate or not to cooperate" dilemma likely depends on their value–creation expectations with the consortium, which in turn are forged by combinations of incentives of diverse nature. In particular, our findings contribute to a richer theoretical understanding on the phenomenon of cooperation in multipartner alliances in two main ways. First, whereas prior research has suggested different but independent effects of several sources of expectations on cooperation, our study offers a more integrative explanation, showing the existence of reinforcing links and tensions between them. In the absence of collaborative experience, a partner is likely to behave cooperatively if it expects strong learning and strategy-related benefits from the consortium and, at the same time, does not perceive significant risk of knowledge leakages inside the consortium. In contrast, inexperienced partners facing coopetition situations in the consortium are likely to behave in a non-cooperative fashion: the associated risk of knowledge leakages may even eclipse other learning and strategic expectations, triggering negative reactions to the social dilemma. Second, our study provides some new insights on the relationship between cooperation and reciprocity in the multipartner setting. Relying on social exchange theory (Das & Teng, 2002), scholars have traditionally argued that lack of generalized reciprocity may hinder the sustainability of cooperation in multipartner alliances. Our data nevertheless seem to indicate that, in situations where generalized reciprocity is lacking, direct reciprocity with key actors in the consortium may motivate some inexperienced partners to continue cooperating.

In the following pages of this chapter, we first present the social dilemma that inexperienced firms face when they enter a R&D consortium. After presenting the methodology, we provide the case-based evidence. Subsequently, we discuss the main findings of the study on the Acuisost Consortium. The chapter concludes with the main implications and limitations, as well as some lines for further work.

CONCEPTUAL BACKGROUND

The formation stage of any alliance is critical in the value-creation process: initial conditions are defined (Doz, 1996; Doz et al., 2000) and partners test their compatibility and trustworthiness (Zajac & Olsen, 1993). During this process, cooperation—that is, the relational norm entailing partners' coordinated actions to attain mutual benefits (Anderson & Narus, 1990)—facilitates key activities such as the alignment of goals and expectations and the establishment of legitimacy between the partners (Doz et al., 2000; Mahnke & Overby, 2008).

R&D consortia, and multipartner alliances in general, imply multilateral interaction among multiple partners (Lavie et al., 2007). Given these unique logics of collaboration, the formation process of R&D consortia is likely to be particularly complex (Doz et al., 2000) and cooperation herein is likely to prove even more relevant (Hwang & Burgers, 1997; Zeng & Chen, 2003). At the same time, however, achieving cooperation is far from straightforward, since the generalized nature of reciprocity governing exchanges in R&D consortia (Das & Teng, 2002) triggers a social dilemma for partners (Zeng & Cheng, 2003). In the following, we briefly describe such a dilemma, eventually explaining how partners are expected to react when they lack prior collaborative experience.

The Social Dilemma in R&D Consortia

According to social exchange theory scholars (Blau, 1964; Das & Teng, 2002), the main difference between multipartner and dyadic alliances resides in the patterns of exchange between partners (and the associated patterns of reciprocity). Dyadic alliances entail direct exchange and reciprocity between two partners, whereas multipartner alliances entail also generalized patterns of exchange and reciprocity among multiple partners (Das & Teng, 2002). In generalized exchanges, partners make individual contributions to the alliance (which could benefit one or more partners), expecting something in return from the alliance (but not necessarily from a specific partner). Reciprocity obligations among the multiple partners are therefore ambiguous (Thorgren et al., 2010).

Given these conditions, partners face a social dilemma in the formation process of multipartner alliances (Zeng & Chen, 2003) which, due to the nature of the exchange resources, may be particularly pronounced in the setting of R&D consortia. Once a firm has decided to enter a multipartner alliance, it must make an important choice: to cooperate or not to cooperate. R&D consortia entail high potential for collective learning and innovation (Doz et al., 2000) but also high levels of relational risk (Das & Teng, 2000; Sampson, 2005). Partners therefore need to interact closely in order to combine their knowledge and technological resources (Doz et al., 2000; Mothe & Quelin, 2001) and, at the same time, they have to protect such resources from undesirable leakages that may happen through multiple points (Hwang &Burgers, 1997; Oxley &Sampson, 2004). In R&D

consortia, both the "to cooperate" and "not to cooperate" positions entail therefore relative advantages and disadvantages.

On the one hand, a partner that behaves cooperatively (i.e. complying with the spirit of cooperation) contributes to making the agreement work and therefore to enhancing the potential collective gains of the alliance (Ariño, 2001; Kumar & Nti, 1998). At the same time, a cooperative partner assumes a vulnerable position in the consortium (Das & Teng, 2002; Thorgren et al., 2010). Since mutual obligations are unclear, cooperating means making blind contributions of resources, not knowing whether, how and by whom such efforts will be reciprocated. On the other hand, a partner that behaves non-cooperatively reduces the overall potential of the alliance to generate collective gains but also limits its exposure and vulnerability to partners' opportunism.

How do Partners React to the Social Dilemma in R&D Consortia?

Reviewing the existing literature on strategic alliances, we identify two main groups of studies providing useful insights to address this question. The first group assumes that the degree of cooperation of individual partners depends on their individual value-creation expectations with the exchange relationship (e.g., García-Canal, Valdés-Llaneza, & Ariño, 2003; Mothe & Quelin, 2001; Olk & Young, 1997). Based on this premise, these studies suggest several factors triggering positive or negative reactions to the dilemma in R&D consortia. For example, a number of studies have focused on the phenomenon of coopetition in innovation settings (i.e., firms that compete in the marketplace team up to jointly conduct innovation activities). Collaboration with direct competitors, which is quite common in R&D consortia, may lead to either positive or negative reactions to the social dilemma. On the one hand, competitors often share market interests and have similar knowledge bases, making the creation of mutual benefits possible (Doz et al., 2000), which in turn fosters cooperation. At the same time, however, rivalry among partners may trigger mutual suspicious and mistrust in the consortium (García-Canal et al., 2003; Oxley & Sampson, 2004). In these cases, knowledge sharing, and close interaction may be perceived as extremely risky, and partners may thus adopt "not to cooperate" positions to protect themselves vis-à-vis competitors. Other scholars have pointed to the potential of R&D consortia to generate learning and other strategic benefits. Since learning requires frequent and intense interaction and knowledge exchange, strong learning orientation of partners (Hamel, 1991) is likely to promote positive reactions to the dilemma in R&D consortia (e.g., Mothe & Quelin, 2001; Olk

& Young, 1997). Likewise, partners are expected to cooperate when the purpose and scope of the R&D consortium are clearly linked to their core strategic activities: the higher the strategic importance of the consortium to the partner, the lower the distance between collective and private gains for that partner (e.g. Lunnan & Haughland, 2008; Mothe & Quelin, 2001).

A second group of studies sheds light on how partners react to the "to cooperate or not to cooperate dilemma" by linking such a dilemma to the alliance experience phenomenon. Existing research has widely demonstrated that firms learn to successfully manage alliances as they accumulate collaborative experience and build collaborative routines (Anand & Khanna, 2000; Simonin, 1997). In R&D consortia, experienced partners, therefore, may be more able to contribute to generating collective gains and to actually capture a greater portion of such gains. In contrast, lack of alliance experience may entail huge challenges for partners (Sampson, 2005). In particular, inexperienced partners lack routines (Zollo & Winter, 2002) to share and, simultaneously, protect valuable resources in R&D consortia. Therefore, existing theory suggests that inexperienced partners may find the "not to cooperate" option as the most rational strategy. After all, it is complex to detect and sanction individual non–cooperative behaviors in R&D consortia and partners may feel not particularly guilty for not cooperating (Mahnke & Overby, 2008; Zeng & Chen, 2003).

Both groups of studies have significantly contributed to explaining cooperation dynamics in multipartner settings like R&D consortia. However, we still do not know how different sources of expectations (e.g., coopetition situations, learning orientation and strategic importance) play out when the partner lacks alliance experience and jointly impact the "to cooperate or not to cooperate" decision. This lack of evidence gives meaning to the case study on the Acuisost Consortium.

METHODS

In order to examine why some inexperienced partners behave cooperatively during the formation stage of R&D consortia, we conducted a longitudinal study on the Acuisost Consortium. Our study takes the partner firm as the main unit of analysis and therefore can be described as a "nested" case study (Gibbert, Ruigrok, & Wicki, 2008): focusing on one single setting (i.e., the *Acuisost Consortium*), we study and compare data across multiple cases (i.e., the *partners* of the Acuisost Consortium) that are embedded in this setting. The main advantage of this kind of case study design resides on the opportunity to conduct robust cross-case comparison while minimizing the risk of extraneous variation (Eisenhardt, 1989; Yin, 2003). Below, we present an overview of the research setting and explain how data were collected and analyzed in this study.

Research Setting

The Acuisost Consortium was a R&D consortium aimed to foster sustainable development of Spanish fish aquaculture through four main subprojects (Nutrition, Biosecurity, Waste Management, and Ready Meals). The formation process of the consortium covered the period from January 2006 to March 2009. In January 2006, Aqua-Environ Consulting, a start-up consulting firm, sensed the opportunity to create the Acuisost Consortium (due to confidentiality reasons, the names of the firms used in the chapter are pseudonyms). Spanish aquaculture industry was experiencing a period of great expansion. However, experts were emphasizing the need for innovation efforts to enhance the environmental sustainability of the field. At the same time, sustainability was one of the priorities of the Spanish National Innovation Plan and its several measures, such as the Program of National Strategic Consortia for Technical Research (CENIT Program). Therefore, a collaborative R&D initiative such as the Acuisost Consortium was likely to receive a CENIT grant. Guided by such expectations, Aqua-Environ Consulting started orchestrating the formation of the consortium.

Eventually, eighteen firms (i.e., the consortium lead firm and seventeen consortium partners) founded the Acuisost Consortium. In CENIT consortia, there are two categories of firms: the lead firm of the consortium (i.e., a partner which assumes coordination and governance responsibilities and holds a higher economic participation in the consortium's budget) and the consortium partners (i.e., firms that play the role of ordinary partners of the consortium). Since participation conditions and expectations of the lead firm and the ordinary partners are inherently different, our analysis focuses on the group of consortium partners. In order to ensure reliable comparison of data across cases, we selected twelve consortium partners following theoretical sampling criteria (Yin, 2003). First, we did not include in the analysis two of the seventeen founding partners that left the Acuisost Consortium during the studied period. Second, according to the criterion of "polar cases" (Eisenhardt, 1989), we concentrated on those partners displaying clear reactions (either positive or negative) to the social dilemma in the Acuisost Consortium. From the fifteen partners that remained involved during the whole studied period, we excluded three partners displaying ambiguous reactions (e.g., behaving cooperatively sometimes and non-cooperatively at other times). Table 12.1 displays general information on the selected partners.

Table 12.1

Selected Partners of the Acuisost Consortium

Partner firms	Industry	Size	Age	Consortium subprojects
BioMilk	Biotechnology	Micro-enterprise	Incumbent	Nutrition
Chemics&Proteins	Chemical	SME	Incumbent	Nutrition
Fish&Meals	Food	SME	Start–up	Nutrition Ready Meals
Green Solutions	Chemical	SME	Incumbent	Biosecurity
Iberian Eels	Aquaculture	SME	Incumbent	Nutrition Wastes
Industrial Packages Co.	Industrial packing	Large	Incumbent	Ready Meals
Mediterranean Aquaculture	Aquaculture	SME	Incumbent	Nutrition Ready Meals
MngProjects	Technology consulting	SME	Incumbent	Nutrition Biosecurity
Northern Trouts Co.	Aquaculture	SME	Incumbent	Biosecurity
Southern Trouts Co.	Aquaculture	SME	Incumbent	Biosecurity Wastes
The Biscuits Co.	Food	Large	Incumbent	Nutrition
WasteMng Co.	Waste management	SME	Start-up	Wastes

Selected partners differed in terms of organizational characteristics such as industry affiliation (e.g., aquaculture, food, biotechnology, chemical industry, etc.), but shared an important feature: all these partners had little prior experience in collaborative R&D (mostly with research centers) and none in R&D consortia. Between January 2007 and March 2009, the partners had to allocate resources, first to structure the consortium and, once public funding was confirmed (in January 2008), to starting up the research project (until March 2009). However, as already mentioned, not all the involved partners contributed equally to the formation of the consortium.

Data Collection and Analysis Procedures

We collected data in the period April 2008 to June 2009, moving from exploratory to more focused actions (Faems, Janssens, Madhok, & Van

Looy, 2008; Pettigrew, 1990). This longitudinal approach enhanced the quality of data collection by allowing us to gradually get immersed into the research context and build trust with key informants (Miles & Huberman, 1994), as well as to update our data records on an ongoing basis with real-time information (Langley, 1999). Since the formation process of the Acuisost Consortium covered the period from January 2006 to March 2009, we partially relied on a retrospective approach. Although retrospective approaches are usually associated with efficiency in data collection, reconstruction of past events may be biased (Leonard-Barton, 1990). In order to mitigate these potential problems, we applied several strategies: we conducted structured interviews based on interview protocols, interviewed multiple informants, and triangulated interview data with information from other data sources whenever possible (Faems et al., 2008; Yin, 2003). In all, we conducted 26 interviews (twenty four face-to-face interviews and two phone interviews) with twenty different informants. Interviewees included representatives of (i) the lead firm (CEO, Aquaculture Division Manager, and R&D Manager), (ii) Aqua-Environ Consulting (Project Manager), (iii) 10 partner firms (including six members of the Scientific Committee of the consortium), and (iv) five research centers involved in the consortium. In addition, we interviewed the manager of a non-profit association for innovation in aquaculture, who provided detailed information on the context of the consortium. Furthermore, we collected publicly available information about the consortium, its legal and industrial framework, and its partners (i.e. press releases, policy and corporate reports), analyzed private consortium documents (i.e., consortium reports, consortium agreement, minutes of meetings), collected general survey data on partners (e.g., organizational characteristics, expectations with the consortium), and conducted direct observation in three consortium committees and a consortium annual meeting. Direct observation provided useful data on the partners reactions to the "to cooperate or not to cooperate dilemma" in the studied period. For example, we observed how Scientific Committee members discussed about knowledge exchange and interaction within the different subprojects of the consortium and collected first-hand information on partners' presence/absence in those consortium meetings.

As common in case study research, we analyzed data on the selected cases through an iterative process, moving from description to explanation (Pentland, 1999) and combining within–case analysis with comparison of data across cases (Eisenhardt, 1989). We started by systematically coding collected data. Based on existing literature, we designed a schema for explicit conversion of raw data from multiple sources into theoretical constructs (Larson, 1993). Emerging findings however triggered some adjustments in the initial schema. For example, we realized that the individual degree of financial involvement in the consortium did not reflect the actual cooperation of all partners, in contrast to what prior studies suggest (e.g., Lavie et al., 2007; Mothe & Quelin, 2001). Given the government–sponsored nature of the Acuisost Consortium, some partners could have economic incentives to increase their participation in the consortium's budget, regardless of their subsequent behavior. This coding process yielded two main outputs, displayed in Table 12.2.

Table 12.2

Coding Process: Main Outputs

Partner firms	Reaction to the Social Dilemma	Coopetition	Learning Orientation	Strategic Importance
BioMilk	(+) Cooperative behavior	No	High	Medium
Chemics&Proteins	(+) Cooperative behavior	No	High	Medium
Fish&Meals	(−) Non-cooperative behavior	No	Low	Medium
Green Solutions	(−) Non-cooperative behavior	No	Medium	Low
Iberian Eels	(+) Cooperative behavior	No	High	High
Industrial Packages Co.	(−) Non-cooperative behavior	No	Low	Medium
Mediterranean Aquaculture	(−) Non-cooperative behavior	Yes	High	High
MngProjects	(−) Non-cooperative behavior	No	Low	Medium
Northern Trouts Co.	(−) Non-cooperative behavior	Yes	High	High
Southern Trouts Co.	(−) Non-cooperative behavior	Yes	Medium	High
The Biscuits Co.	(+) Cooperative behavior	No	High	Medium
WasteMng Co.	(+) Cooperative behavior	No	High	High

First, based on the two-dimension conceptualization of cooperative behavior (i.e., veracity and commitment) offered by Arino (2001), we identified two main categories of partners: cooperative and non-cooperative partners. Our data clearly indicated a cooperative disequilibrium: only five partners were contributing actively to the formation of the consortium, whereas the involvement of the remaining seven partners in the process turned out to be rather low. Second, the coding process shed light on the main sources of partners' expectations in the consortium, potentially determining their individual reactions to the "to cooperate or not to cooperate dilemma." In particular, we identified those partners facing coopetition in the consortium (e.g., Oxley & Sampson, 2004) and, for each partner, the degree of strategic importance of the consortium (e.g., Mothe & Quelin, 2001) and the level of learning orientation with the consortium (e.g., Hamel, 1991). In several interviews, the R&D Manager of the consortium lead firm, who had detailed information on the research setting and the particular cases, provided insightful feedback on coding process results (Larsson, 1993).

Subsequently, we systematically compared coded data across cases, seeking to identify patterns that could explain why some partners behaved cooperatively during the studied period whilst other did not. In order to do so, we juxtaposed partners' reactions to the "to cooperate or not to cooperate" dilemma during the studied period against the other variables reflecting sources of expectations (coopetition, learning orientation, and strategic importance). This coding strategy allowed us to reduce all the available information to operationalized variables, which in turn facilitated systematic sensemaking and rigorous comparison of data across cases (Eisenhardt, 1991). However, operationalization of case data into formalized constructs may be at the expense of qualitative richness (Dyer & Wilkins, 1991). In order to mitigate this problem, as the last step of the analysis, we came back to insights from individual cases to explain the logic behind the identified patterns (Leonard-Barton, 1990).

REACTIONS TO THE SOCIAL DILMEMMA IN THE ACUISOST CONSORTIUM

In this section, we first provide an overview of the patterns identified from the systematic comparison of data across cases (see Table 12.3). Subsequently, we provide narrative descriptions of four different cases (two cooperative and two non-cooperative partners), focusing on (i) the individual membership conditions of the partners in the consortium, (ii) their reactions to the "to cooperate or not to cooperate" dilemma during the studied period, and (iii) the impact of the studied sources of expectations on such reactions.

Table 12.3

Positive and Negative Reactions to the Social Dilemma: Identified Patterns

Reaction to the Social Dilemma	Partner firms	Patterns
(+) Cooperative behavior	BioMilk The Biscuits Co. Chemics&Proteins Iberian Eels WasteMng Co.	• No coopetition in the consortium • High learning orientation with the consortium • High/medium strategic importance of the consortium
(−) Non-cooperative behavior	Mediterranean Aquaculture Northern Trouts Co. Southern Trouts Co.	• Coopetition in the consortium • Medium/high learning orientation with the consortium • High strategic importance of the consortium
	Fish&Meals Green Solutions Industrial Packages Co. MngProjects	• No coopetition in the consortium • Medium/low learning orientation with the consortium • Medium/low strategic importance of the consortium

Since the purpose of these narratives is to illustrate the logic behind the identified patterns, the four cases were selected according to two main criteria (Eisenhardt, 1989). First, in each selected case, the process of interest (i.e., how partners' expectations shaped their reactions to the social dilemma) was transparently observable. Second, each case represents a pattern within its category.

Comparing data across the five cases included in the category of cooperative partners (BioMilk, The Biscuits Co., Chemics & Proteins, Iberian Eels, and WasteMng Co.), we identified a single pattern. None of these partners faced coopetition inside the consortium. Further, they had a high learning orientation with the consortium and attached medium to high levels of strategic importance to the consortium. In contrast, the systematic comparison of the seven non-cooperative partners allowed us to identify two different patterns. In the first pattern, the three partners (Mediterranean Aquaculture, Northern Trouts Co., and Southern Trouts Co.) were active in the field of aquaculture and collaborated with direct competitors in the consortium. At the same time, these three partners considered the consortium to be of high strategic importance and held important learning expectations with the consortium. In the second pattern, the four partners (Fish&Meals, Green Solutions, Industrial Packages Co., and MngProjects)

were active in industries other than aquaculture and did not face coopetition inside the consortium. They however lacked strong incentives in
terms of perceived strategic importance of the Acuisost Consortium and/
or expected learning benefits. The following narratives illustrate how the
identified patterns led to different reactions to the social dilemma in the
Acuisost Consortium.

Positive Reactions to the Social Dilemma in the Acuisost Consortium

Iberian Eels

Iberian Eels, a SME leading the eel niche market in Spain, was involved
in the subprojects of Nutrition and Waste Management, which the firm
considered to be critical for its core business areas. The section of the consortium's report devoted to Iberian Eel's strategy illustrates these ideas:

> The strategy of the firm with the consortium entails the development of
> a new diet for its main product, the eel, that could allow high-quality and
> more sustainable nutrition and, at the same time, could provide a distinc-
> tive sign in the marketplace. (Consortium's report)

In addition, Iberian Eels sought to acquire, during its participation in
the consortium, the required knowledge to develop "an integrative system"
for managing and transforming organic wastes generated in the day-to-day
activities of the company.

Our data indicate that the above perceived strategic and learning benefits led Iberian Eels to be one of the most cooperative partners in the
Acuisost Consortium during the period under study. For example, the
coordinator of the Waste Management subproject explicitly recognized the
strong cooperative efforts of Iberian Eels, which contrasted strongly with
the behavior of other partners in the subproject:

> Other firms involved in this subproject are showing their lack of commit-
> ment. In contrast, Iberian Eels is playing its role properly [...] taking the
> research project really seriously ... always willing to attend meetings and
> showing a positive attitude in them. (General Manager of WasteMng)

Similar observations were made about the behavior of Iberian Eels in the
Nutrition subproject, where the firm's tasks would be developed in close
interaction with the consortium lead firm. As the General Manager of Iberian Eels explained, whereas the Waste Management subproject could offer

"higher future potential" than the Nutrition subproject, the technologies to be developed in the latter subproject were part of the commitments made to support the leader in the process of "reinventing aquaculture."

BioMilk

BioMilk, an established biotech microenterprise, perceived important synergies between its core business activities and the aquaculture nutrition field. In particular, the involvement of BioMilk in the Nutrition subproject of the consortium entailed a huge opportunity to explore aquaculture applications of the firm's core products (i.e., probiotics). As stated in the consortium's report, probiotics are "effective tools to inhibit fish pathogens" and, at the same time, "stimulate fish appetite and facilitate digestibility." Collected data also indicated that BioMilk expected to develop new knowledge on both technical and market aspects of the aquaculture nutrition field, since the firm's products had been traditionally applied into human nutrition products:

> New production processes require new technologies and new knowledge ... close collaboration with industry agents may enable the firm to acquire detailed knowledge on the new processes ... to find the most appropriate solutions to apply our products and to get familiar with the new market. (Consortium's report)

As observed in the previous case, strategic and learning expectations motivated BioMilk to be one of the most cooperative partners of the Acuisost Consortium during the studied period. From the very beginning, BioMilk showed its willingness to actively exchange knowledge and to maintain close, frequent, and multilateral interaction with other partners. For example, BioMilk's R&D manager, as a member of the Scientific Committee of the consortium contributed, in the words of the lead firm's R&D Manager, to generating "a mini-consortium within the consortium."

The R&D Manager of BioMilk explicitly complained that some partners were not acting "according to the sharing spirit of CENIT consortia," which was causing "unfair situations." She however emphasized that behaving in such a cooperative way was a win-win strategy with regard to the lead firm of the consortium. BioMilk sought to develop high innovative aquaculture products that could enhance the product portfolio of the lead firm, as a leading nutrition company. In addition, she stressed that the lead firm was providing significant technical support to BioMilk. Developing the knowledge required to explore an important business opportunity in close connection with an important potential client was therefore compensating the cooperative efforts of the firm.

Negative Reactions to the Social Dilemma in the Acuisost Consortium

Mediterranean Aquaculture

Mediterranean Aquaculture, a large fish–farming firm, became involved in the Nutrition and Ready Meals subprojects of the consortium. These two subprojects addressed two of what experts termed as the main challenges of Spanish aquaculture: improving the quality and efficiency of fish nutrition and extending the range of products offered to the market (e.g., introducing new high value-added products like filleted fish). Therefore, the Acuisost Consortium afforded huge strategic opportunities for the development of the core business areas of Mediterranean Aquaculture:

> In recent years, the mass entrance of imported low-cost fish and the reduction in the growth rates of the domestic market are challenging the survival of aquaculture in our country ... the firm seeks to take advantage of the great opportunities offered by the Acuisost Consortium to improve its current competitive position vis-à-vis rivals. (General Manager of Mediterranean Aquaculture)

In addition, Mediterranean Aquaculture conceived its participation in the Acuisost Consortium as an opportunity to develop new technological knowledge. Mediterranean Aquaculture, as many other large firms in the field, had strong production capacities but underdeveloped technological capabilities. For example, our data indicate that the firm lacked specialized staff and lab facilities. The Acuisost Consortium could provide the firm with "the basic technological infrastructure" required to survive in the medium term, since the traditional market of aquaculture was becoming saturated.

Contrary to what might be expected in light of the above observations, Mediterranean Aquaculture did not allocate cooperative efforts during the studied period. Our data point to coopetition tensions as the main cause. In both the Nutrition and Ready Meals subprojects, Mediterranean Aquaculture collaborated directly with one of its major competitors in the marketplace. During our interviews, it became clear that the presence of a direct competitor in the consortium led Mediterranean Aquaculture to be more concerned with protecting its core knowledge resources than with actual collaboration, thus preventing the emergence of cooperation:

> We are highly cautious in disseminating relevant information. Let's say that
> the enemy is at home … I think this is a mutual feeling. In this subproject
> we have had no meetings to date and nobody has complained about it.
> (General Manager of Mediterranean Aquaculture)

Based on his global vision of the consortium, the R&D Manager of the
lead firm confirmed that Mediterranean Aquaculture was reluctant to disclose technical aspects such as "the level of progress made in the project,
emerging obstacles, and the solutions applied" in order to "prevent competitors from finding out this information."

Fish&Meals

Fish&Meals, a SME producing fish-based prepared meals, participated
in the Nutrition and Ready Meals subprojects of the Acuisost Consortium,
identifying a twofold opportunity which entailed important strategic implications for the firm:

> On the one hand, exploring the possibilities of revaluing a high-protein
> by-product from our production process that we still fail to take advan-
> tage of.… On the other, developing new ready-to-eat products made from
> aquaculture fish that could enhance our position in the national market.
> (Consortium's report)

Despite these expectations, Fish&Meals was one of the least cooperative partners of the Acuisost Consortium during the period studied. For
example, Fish&Meals' technical reports were highly generic and did not
provide details on the firm's alliance strategy or the technical state of its
projects in the consortium, and the firm systematically missed consortium meetings and committees. Our data clearly indicate that the reason
for which Fish&Meals lacked motivation to engage in cooperation had
to do with its particular view of R&D consortia. The R&D Manager of
Fish&Meals described these settings as "shared spaces" in which each
partner firm could individually develop its research project, disregard-
ing the importance of close collaboration with other partners to achieve
individual objectives. As such, Fish&Meals did not expect to acquire new
knowledge from the consortium, neither about technology nor about aquaculture market, that could be essential to capture the abovementioned
opportunities. For example, the R&D Manager of Fish&Meals justified
her absences in consortium meetings by arguing that these meetings were
actually "a waste of time" and that coordination could be perfectly achieved
"by email or phone," neglecting the learning potential from interpartner
interaction.

DISCUSSION OF FINDINGS

In this section, we discuss our observations on the Acuisost Consortium and link them to existing literature. We subsequently formulate theoretical propositions explaining why only some inexperienced partners behave cooperatively during the formation stage of R&D consortia.

First, we observed that many of the partners that expected important learning and strategic benefits from the consortium behaved cooperatively during the studied period. Therefore, our evidence supports the findings from prior studies that high perceived levels of learning and strategic potential generate incentives for cooperation. For example, Mothe and Quelin (2001) and Olk and Young (1997) point to strategic importance and learning orientation as two key antecedents, respectively, of resource creation and membership continuity in R&D consortia. At the same time, however, our data on the Acuisost Consortium lead us to deviate from the assumption that the effects of these two factors, when present, are *per se* additive, triggering automatically positive reactions to the "to cooperate or not to cooperate" dilemma. Our comparative analysis suggests that, in the absence of alliance experience, partners that perceive high strategic potential of the consortium are only motivated to cooperate if they expected to acquire from the consortium the knowledge required to realize such potential. For example, informants of BioMilk and The Biscuits Company emphasized that the consortium provided their respective firms with the opportunity to enter into the aquaculture market, which in turn required the acquisition of new knowledge by collaborating closely with other partners of the consortium. In contrast, other non-cooperative partners such as Fish&Meals or Industrial Packages Co. perceived significant strategic opportunities from the consortium but neglected the importance of inter-partner learning to pursue such opportunities. Therefore, inexperienced partners, even if convinced of the strategic potential of the consortium, may fail to recognize the importance of close interaction and knowledge exchange with other partners, thus lacking motivation to engage in cooperative behavior.

Second, we observed that those partners experiencing coopetition tensions inside the consortium behave non-cooperatively during the studied period, whereas none of the cooperative partners faced such tensions. In this regard, our data strongly indicate that coopetition leads inexperienced partners to adopt negative reactions to the social dilemma. This finding concurs closely with existing research linking competition and instability in alliances (e.g., García-Canal et al., 2003; Park & Russo, 1996). At the same time, our data on the Acuisost Consortium question the idea that competitors are willing to mutually cooperate in pursuit of strategic interests. In particular, we observed that, paraphrasing Park and Russo

(1996), *competition eclipsed cooperation* between aquaculture partners. Several informants indicated that aquaculture partners overemphasized the protection of their own knowledge and position vis-à-vis rivals, giving up important strategic opportunities afforded by the Acuisost Consortium, such as solving structural technology problems of Spanish aquaculture or establishing barriers for international competition. Therefore, our data show that, when partners lack alliance experience, perceived risks of knowledge leakages associated to direct competition likely eliminate other cooperative incentives (derived from strategic importance and learning orientation). This evidence parallels competition tensions in intra–organizational settings. Tsai (2002), for example, argues that, in multi-unit organizations, competition for obtaining resources between units pursuing common strategic projects discourages knowledge-sharing behaviors. The perception of competitors as "enemies" may be stronger in R&D consortia formed between inexperienced partners than in other coopetition settings described in prior studies (e.g., Gimeno, 2004; Gomes-Casseres, 1996) in which partners, well-endowed with alliance experience, know how to interact in pursuit of common strategic interests without putting at risk their own competitive position.

In sum, factors like learning orientation, strategic importance, and coopetition are important sources of expectations, shaping partners' reactions to the social dilemma in R&D consortia. However, our data strongly indicate that these factors, when considered individually, fail to explain how inexperienced partners react to such a dilemma. In particular, we observed that strategic and learning expectations must be mutually reinforcing to actually prompt inexperienced partners to react positively to the "to cooperate or not to cooperate" dilemma. At the same time, perceived threats of knowledge leakages associated with coopetition are likely to crowd out such cooperative incentives, encouraging inexperienced partners to adopt the "not to cooperate" position. This discussion gives rise to the following propositions:

Proposition 1a: *In the formation of R&D consortia, inexperienced firms are likely to behave cooperatively if they perceive that the consortium (a) entails high strategic potential and (b) brings learning opportunities to realize such potential.*

Proposition 1b: *In the formation of R&D consortia, inexperienced firms facing coopetition tensions are likely to behave non-cooperatively, even if they expect important learning and strategic benefits from the consortium.*

The above discussion raises the question of whether the above combination of learning and strategic benefits, when coopetition tensions are lacking, fully explains how cooperative partners frame and react to the social dilemma. Put differently, which role did the reciprocity-cooperation link play in the Acuisost Consortium? Social exchange scholars have suggested that reciprocity sustains cooperation over time (Anderson & Narus, 1990; Lado, Boyd, & Hanlon, 1997). In contrast, when generalized reciprocity is lacking in a multipartner alliance (as occurred in the Acuisost Consortium), incentives for cooperation may disappear (Das & Teng, 2002; Zeng & Chen, 2003). Our observations seem to suggest that bilateral or direct reciprocity with key actors in the consortium (lead firm), as long as coopetition tensions are lacking, may be strong enough to sustain cooperation during the formation stage. In the Acuisost Consortium, a sense of direct reciprocity emerged between some of the cooperative partners (those working on new aquaculture nutrition products) and the lead firm of the consortium (a leading company in aquaculture nutrition). Informants of these partners complained about "the imbalance in partners' contributions" but emphasized that the support they were receiving from the lead firm, with which they envisioned future commercial agreements, compensated for their cooperative efforts.

CONCLUSION AND IMPLICATIONS

Based on a longitudinal multiple case study, we have examined why only some inexperienced partners behave cooperatively during the formation stage of R&D consortia. Below, we discuss the main implications of the study, for research and practice, as well as the main limitations and some interesting ideas for future work.

Implications for Research

Whereas the positive effects of strong alliance experience have been widely discussed (e.g., Sampson, 2005; Zollo & Winter, 2002), existing alliance research rarely looks at firms lacking collaborative experience. Our study focuses on the social dilemma of multipartner alliances for partners that do lack collaborative experience. In doing so, we present an integrative view on the factors shaping partners' expectations and their impact on the reactions to the "to cooperate or not to cooperate" dilemma. Existing studies seem to suggest that factors like coopetition (García-Canal et al., 2003), learning orientation (Hamel, 1991), or strategic importance (Mothe & Quelin, 2001) trigger different but somewhat independent effects on cooperation. Our data, however, indicate that the effects of these factors are intertwined. In R&D consortia created by inexperienced partners, positive reactions to the social dilemma are likely associated with two simultaneous conditions: (a) partners perceive that the consortium entails high strategic potential and brings learning opportunities to realize such potential, and (b) partners do not perceive threats of unintended knowledge spillovers inside the consortium. In contrast, coopetition situations among inexperienced partners are likely to trigger negative reactions to the social dilemma. Under situations of coopetition, inexperienced partners are likely to perceive that potential losses from knowledge leakages outweigh potential learning and strategic benefits.

Overall, our findings provide a more comprehensive understanding on how inexperienced partners frame and react to the overwhelming dilemma of multipartner collaborative settings such as R&D consortia (Zeng & Chen, 2003). By identifying interactions between several antecedents of alliance behavior, our study shows that the reactions of partners to the social dilemma are contingent on their individual value–creation expectations with the consortium, which in turn reflect a trade-off between the expected benefits and costs from interaction with alliance partners. Our observations suggest therefore an analogy between the social dilemma of "to cooperate or not to cooperate" faced by inexperienced partners in R&D consortia and the broader strategic dilemma of "to invest or not to invest" in new projects under uncertainty (McGrath & Nerkar, 2004). In addition, we offer some novel insights on the cooperation–reciprocity relationship in such complex collaborative settings. Our findings seem to indicate that cooperation may be possible in specific parts of the consortium where direct reciprocity prevails, even when partners perceive a lack of generalized reciprocity in the consortium that would make it difficult for members to cooperate in a sustained manner (Das & Teng, 2002; Thorgren et al., 2010). In particular, perceived bilateral reciprocity with key actors in the consortium could be strong enough to motivate some partners with high value-creation expectations to continue cooperating.

Implications for Managerial and Policy Practice

Based on the case study on the Acuisost Consortium, we offer some recommendations for the management of R&D consortia formed by inexperienced partners and for public policies funding this kind of collaborative initiatives. First, in order to promote positive reactions to the social dilemma, selection of potential partners must take into account not only theoretical synergies that may emerge among the partners, but also the compatibility of their multiple value-creation expectations. Furthermore, when approaching potential partners, triggering entities must convey the spirit of multilateral cooperation and emphasize that the potential strategic benefits the consortium affords requires interactive learning, making clear the commitments that partners will be expected to undertake in this regard. In addition, establishing several subprojects may improve efficiency and coordination in R&D consortia (Dyer & Nobeoka, 2000), but the composition of each subproject should be carefully defined. In particular, our findings suggest preventing coopetition tensions in order to support knowledge sharing within each consortium subproject.

Public funds may bring otherwise unattainable R&D opportunities to inexperienced firms, often SMEs in non-high-tech industries. Many informants of the Acuisost Consortium emphasized this point during interviews. However, public policies should help those firms to learn how to cooperate in such complex settings. For example, government agencies may act as triggering entities of micro-constellations formed by competitors in industries like Spanish aquaculture facing global competitive challenges. As learning is a matter of experience accumulation, these initiatives may favor the long-term performance of macro-constellations such as R&D consortia. Likewise, in deciding allocation of funds, public agencies should assess the relational potential of each applicant consortium. Based on our observations, we suggest paying special attention to (a) whether partners are convinced that the consortium could bring important opportunities for strategic development and, at the same time, the required knowledge to seize such opportunities, and (b) whether coopetition tensions could make even more complex the formation process of the consortium by hindering the emergence of cooperation.

Limitations and Future Research

While this study provides interesting insights, some important limitations should be noted. Taken together, these insights and limitations suggest some promising avenues for future research. First, the reduced risk of extraneous variation inherent to "nested" case study approaches allows rigorous analytical generalization of findings (Eisenhardt, 1989), but may reduce theoretical richness (Gibbert et al., 2008). Our findings are clearly contextualized in the setting of the Acuisost Consortium and thus prevent broader replication. Future research should explore how inexperienced partners react to the social dilemma in other R&D consortia, accounting for different industrial and institutional settings. Furthermore, in order to ensure rigor in comparative analysis, we did not study some partners displaying ambiguous reactions to the "to cooperate or not to cooperate" dilemma. To some extent, our framework offers a simplistic picture focused on what existing research (e.g., Ariño, 2001; Kumar & Nti, 1998) considers the typical modes of alliance behavior (cooperative and non-cooperative behavior). Examining why some partners adopt *atypical* modes of alliance behavior in R&D consortia could be an interesting line for further work.

In addition, our findings raise the question of under which conditions inexperienced partners start building their alliance capabilities (De Man, Duysters, & Saebi, 2010). Cooperation entails investments of resources that, together with other initiatives, may lead to the creation of collaborative routines (Dyer & Singh, 1998). Cooperative behavior may thus reflect part of the initial alliance capability-building investments of inexperienced firms. Given the relational dimension of alliance capabilities (e.g., Sarkar, Aulakh, & Madhok, 2009), the decision of a firm to start creating alliance capabilities or not to do so is likely related to its reciprocity perceptions. For example, regarding partners' reciprocity perceptions, our findings indicate a potential tension between the presence of coopetition and the presence of a strong relationship with the consortium leader.

Finally, the Acuisost Consortium case provides indications that key actors in alliances could use governance mechanisms to foster cooperation, for example by reinforcing partners' initial cooperative frames (Dyer & Singh, 1998; Sarkar et al., 2009). Yet much remains unknown about the role played by lead firms and/or triggering entities in R&D consortia from a relational governance perspective (Doz et al., 2000; Faems et al., 2008). Further exploration of these questions could contribute to a better understanding of the unique dynamics of cooperation in multipartner collaborative settings.

ACKNOWLEDGMENTS

This chapter, save some minor changes, was earlier published as Estrada, Isabel, Martín–Cruz, Natalia, & Martín–Pérez, Victor M. (2014). To cooperate or not to cooperate? The dilemma faced by inexperienced firms in R&D consortia. In T. K. Das (Ed.), *Strategic alliances for innovation and R&D* (pp. 159–183). Charlotte, NC: Information Age Publishing. The study reported in this chapter is part of a broader research project on the Acuisost Consortium, which received financial support from the European Social Fund and the Junta de Castilla y León [Contract for Novel Researchers 2008–2012], from the Ministerio de Economía y Competitividad (Plan Nacional de I+D+i) of Spain [ECO2012-32075], and the 10th Juan José Renau Piqueras Award in Economic Research of the Vall d'Albaida University Foundation (University of Valencia).

REFERENCES

Anand, B. N., & Khanna, T. (2000). Do firms learn to create value? The case of alliances. *Strategic Management Journal, 21*, 295–315.

Anderson, J. C., & Narus, J. A. (1990). A model of distributor firm and manufacturer firm working partnerships. *Journal of Marketing, 54*(1), 42–58.

Ariño, A. (2001). To do or not to do? Noncooperative behavior by commission and omission in interfirm ventures. *Group & Organization Management, 26*(1), 4–23.

Blau, P. M. (1964). *Exchange and power in social life*. New York, NY: Wiley.

Das, T. K., & Teng, B. (2000). Instabilities of strategic alliances: An internal tensions perspective. *Organization Science, 11*, 77–101.

Das, T. K., & Teng, B. (2002). Alliance constellations: A social exchange perspective. *Academy of Management Review, 27*, 445–456.

De Man, A. P., Duysters, G., & Saebi, T. (2010). Alliance capability as an emergent theme: Past, present, future. In T. K. Das (Ed.), *Researching strategic alliances: Emerging perspectives*. Charlotte, NC: Information Age Publishing.

Doz, Y. L. (1996). The evolution of cooperation in strategic alliances: Initial conditions or learning processes? *Strategic Management Journal, 17*(Summer special issue), 55–83.

Doz, Y. L., Olk, P. M., & Ring, P. S. (2000). Formation processes of R&D consortia: Which path to take? Where does it lead? *Strategic Management Journal, 21*, 239–266.

Dyer, J. H., & Singh, H. (1998). The relational view: Cooperative strategy and sources of interorganizational competitive advantage. *Academy of Management Review, 23*, 660–679.

Dyer, J. H., & Nobeoka, K. (2000). Creating and managing a high-performance knowledge-sharing network: The Toyota case. *Strategic Management Journal, 21*, 345–367.

Dyer, W. G., & Wilkins, A. L. (1991). Better stories, not better constructs, to generate better theory: A rejoinder to Eisenhardt. *Academy of Management Review, 16*, 613–619.

Eisenhardt, K. M. (1989). Building theories from case study research. *Academy of Management Review, 14*, 532–550.

Eisenhardt, K. M. (1991). Better stories and better constructs: The case for rigor and comparative logic. *Academy of Management Review, 16*, 620–627.

Faems, D., Janssens, M., Madhok, A., & Van Looy, B. (2008). Toward an integrative perspective on alliance governance: Connecting contract design, trust dynamics, and contract application. *Academy of Management Journal, 51*, 1053–1078.

García-Canal, E., Valdés-Llaneza, A., & Ariño, A. (2003). Effectiveness of dyadic and multi–party joint ventures. *Organization Studies, 24*, 743–770.

Gibbert, M., Ruigrok, W., & Wicki, B. (2008). What passes as a rigorous case study? *Strategic Management Journal, 29*, 1465–1474.

Gimeno, J. (2004). Competition within and between networks: The contingent effect of competitive embeddedness on alliance formation. *Academy of Management Journal 47*, 820–842.

Gomes–Casseres, B. (1996). *The alliance revolution: The new shape of business rivalry*. Cambridge, MA: Harvard University Press.

Hamel, G. (1991). Competition for competence and interpartner learning within international strategic alliances. *Strategic Management Journal, 12*(Special issue on global strategy), 83–103.

Hwang, P., & Burgers, W. P. (1997). The many faces of multi–firm alliances: Lessons for managers. *California Management Review, 39*(3), 101–117.

Kumar, R., & Nti, K. O. (1998). Differential learning and interaction in alliance dynamics: A process and outcome discrepancy model. *Organization Science, 9*, 356–367.

Lado, A. A., Boyd, N. G., & Hanlon, S. C. (1997). Competition, cooperation, and the search for economic rents: A syncretic model. *Academy of Management Review, 22*, 110–141.

Langley, A. (1999). Strategies for theorizing from process data. *Academy of Management Review, 24*, 691–710.

Larsson, R. (1993). Case survey methodology: Quantitative analysis of patterns across case studies. *Academy of Management Journal, 36*, 1515–1546.

Lavie, D., Lechner, C., & Singh, H. (2007). The performance implications of timing of entry and involvement in multipartner alliances. *Academy of Management Journal, 50*, 578–604.

Leonard–Barton, D. (1990). A dual methodology for case studies: Synergistic use of a longitudinal single site with replicated multiple sites. *Organization Science, 1*, 248–266.

Lunnan, R., & Haugland, S. A. (2008). Predicting and measuring alliance performance: A multidimensional analysis. *Strategic Management Journal, 29*, 545–556.

Mahnke, V., & Overby, M. L. (2008). Failure sources in R&D consortia: The case of mobile service development. *International Journal of Technology Management, 44*(1), 160–178.

McGrath, R., & Nerkar, A. (2004). Real options reasoning and a new look at the R&D investment strategies of pharmaceutical firms. *Strategic Management Journal, 25*, 1–21.

Miles, M. B., & Huberman, A. M. (1994). *An expanded sourcebook of qualitative data analysis*. Thousand Oaks, CA: SAGE.

Mothe, C., & Quelin, B. V. (2001). Resource creation and partnership in R&D consortia. *Journal of High Technology Management Research, 12*(1), 113–138.

Olk, P., & Young, C. (1997). Why members stay in or leave an R&D consortium: Performance and conditions of membership as determinants of continuity. *Strategic Management Journal, 18*, 855–877.

Oxley, J. E., & Sampson, R. C. (2004). The scope and governance of international R&D alliances. *Strategic Management Journal, 25*, 723–749.

Park, S. H., & Russo, M. V. (1996). When competition eclipses cooperation: An event history analysis of joint venture failure. *Management Science, 42*, 875–890.

Pentland, B. T. (1999). Building process theory with narrative: From description to explanation. *Academy of Management Review, 24*, 711–724.

Pettigrew, A. M. (1990). Longitudinal field research on change: Theory and practice. *Organization Science, 1*, 267–292.

Reuer, J. J., Zollo, M., & Singh, H. (2002). Post-formation dynamics in strategic alliances. *Strategic Management Journal, 23*, 135–151.

Sampson, R. C. (2005). Experience effects and collaborative returns in R&D alliances. *Strategic Management Journal, 26*, 1009–1031.

Sarkar, M. B., Aulakh, P. S., & Madhok, A. (2009). Process capabilities and value generation in alliance portfolios. *Organization Science, 20*, 583–600.

Simonin, B. L. (1997). The importance of collaborative know-how: An empirical test of the learning organization. *Academy of Management Journal, 40*, 1150–1174.

Thorgren, S., Wincent, J., & Eriksson, J. (2010). Too small or too large to trust your partners in multipartner alliances? The role of effort in initiating generalized exchanges. *Scandinavian Journal of Management, 27*, 99–112.

Tsai, W. (2002). Social structure of "coopetition" within a multiunit organization: Coordination, competition, and intraorganizational knowledge sharing. *Organization Science, 13*, 179–190.

Yin, R. K. (2003). *Case study research, design and methods*. Thousand Oaks, CA: SAGE.

Zajac, E. J., & Olsen, C. P. (1993). From transaction cost to transactional value analysis: Implications for the study of interorganizational strategies. *Journal of Management Studies, 30*, 131–145.

Zeng, M., & Chen, X. P. (2003). Achieving cooperation in multiparty alliances: A social dilemma approach to partnership management. *Academy of Management Review, 28*, 587–605.

Zollo, M., & Winter, S. G. (2002). Deliberate learning and the evolution of dynamic capabilities. *Organization Science, 13*, 339–351.

ABOUT THE CONTRIBUTORS

Preet S. Aulakh is Professor of Strategy and the Pierre Lassonde Chair in International Business at the Schulich School of Business, York University, Canada. He holds PhD degrees in Law (Osgoode Hall Law School at York University) and Business (University of Texas at Austin, TX), and BS (Mathematics) and MA (History) degrees from Panjab University, Chandigarh, India. Prior to joining Schulich, he taught for several years in the US, and has held visiting positions at the Indian School of Business, Hyderabad, India, and Indian Institute of Management Calcutta, India. He has published numerous articles on international alliances, technology licensing, and cross-border knowledge transfers. His recent research focuses on firms from emerging economies and explores how institutional factors influence their internationalization paths. His research on these topics has been published in journals such as the *Academy of Management Journal, Journal of Marketing, Journal of International Business Studies, Organization Science, Global Strategy Journal, Journal of International Management, Journal of Management Studies, Journal of World Business,* and *Academy of Marketing Science Journal.* His books include *Rethinking Globalization(s)* (Macmillan, 1999), *Mobilities of Labour and Capital in Asia* (Cambridge University Press, 2020), and *Coping with Global Institutional Change* (Cambridge University Press, 2022). Email: paulakh@schulich.yorku.ca

Kaouther Ben Jemaa-Boubaya is a lecturer and researcher in management sciences at Sorbonne Paris Nord University, Paris, France. Her research focuses on international strategic management. She has published in *International Management* and *Management & Avenir.* Her current research interests are in the process of cultural adaptation within international strategic alliances and trust building process through the strategic alliance life cycle. Email: Kaouther_benjemaa@yahoo.fr

Managing Interpartner Cooperation in Strategic Alliances, pp. 355–366
Copyright © 2022 by Information Age Publishing
www.infoagepub.com
355

Foued Cheriet is an assistant professor in agrifood strategy and international marketing at MOISA research unit of the Institut Agro de Montpellier (SupAgro), Montpellier, France. He has a PhD in international business from Institut National d'Etudes Supérieures Agronomiques de Montpellier, France. His research focuses on the agrifood sector in the Mediterranean, and more particularly on interfirm cooperation, the strategies of multinational firms, the analysis of agrifood chains and foreign direct investments. He has published numerous academic articles on asymmetric strategic alliance issues, organizational conflicts, and large firms' internationalization process. Email: foued.cheriet@supagro.fr

T. K. Das is Professor Emeritus of Strategic Management at the City University of New York, New York, NY, where he taught for over three decades and served concurrently as a member of the University's Doctoral Faculty. Prior to entering the academic life, Professor Das had extensive experience as a senior business executive. Professor Das received his PhD in Organization and Strategic Studies from the Anderson Graduate School of Management, University of California at Los Angeles, Los Angeles, CA (UCLA). He has a bachelor's degree in Physics (St. Xavier's College, University of Calcutta, Kolkata, India), a master's degree in Mathematics (Jadavpur University, Kolkata, India), a master's degree in Management (Asian Institute of Management, Manila, Philippines) and a Professional Certification in Banking (C.A.I.I.B., Certified Associate of the Indian Institute of Banking and Finance, Mumbai, India). His research interests are in strategic alliances, strategy making, organization studies, temporal studies, and executive development. Professor Das is the author or editor of 29 academic research books, mainly on strategy, organization, and management, and also 6 booklets on bank management for practicing executives. His research articles have appeared in over 45 journals, of which some of the later ones include *Academy of Management Executive*, *Academy of Management Review*, *Accounting, Organizations and Society*, *British Journal of Management*, *Cross Cultural Management: An International Journal*, *Entrepreneurship Theory and Practice*, *International Journal of Entrepreneurial Behaviour & Research*, *International Journal of Organizational Analysis*, *International Journal of Strategic Business Alliances*, *International Journal of Strategic Change Management*, *Journal of Business and Psychology*, *Journal of Business Ethics*, *Journal of General Management*, *Journal of International Management*, *Journal of Management*, *Journal of Management Development*, *Journal of Management Studies*, *Journal of Managerial Psychology*, *Long Range Planning*, *Management Decision*, *Management International Review*, *Organization Science*, *Organization Studies*, *Scandinavian Journal of Management*, *Strategic Management Journal*, and *Time & Society*. Also, by invitation, he has contributed book reviews in *Administrative Science Quarterly*, *Contemporary Psychology*, and *Journal of*

Management, and authored the entry on "Strategic Alliances" in *Oxford Bib-liographies in Management*. His work has been cited in nearly 1,600 journals published in a wide variety of disciplines. For a number of years now, he has been consistently ranked in the top 2% of scholars in his field of Busi-ness & Management in terms of research impact. Most recently, a Stan-ford University professor led a comprehensive study of the career-long research impact of more than 8 million researchers worldwide across 174 fields during the 60-year period 1960–2019, based on the article citations included in the well-known multidisciplinary citation database *SCOPUS*, and this study has ranked Professor Das among the top 1 percent of schol-ars (complete list published in the journal *PLOS Biology*). Professor Das is a former Senior Editor of *Organization Studies* and has previously served, or is serving, on the editorial boards of a number of other academic jour-nals, and has been an *ad hoc* editorial reviewer for over 70 journals. He is the founding (and current) Series Editor of the three book series, *Research in Strategic Alliances, Research in Behavioral Strategy*, and *Research in Strategy Science* (all published by Information Age Publishing). Email: TK.Das@baruch.cuny.edu

Laure Dikmen is an assistant professor in international strategy and re-search methodology at the University of Poitiers, Poitiers, France. Her research focuses on strategic alliances in emerging countries. She has conducted field studies in Turkey, Algeria, and Madagascar. She co-leads the track "Strategic Alliances, Mergers and Acquisitions and International Networks" for the Atlas AFMI conference. She has published her research results in *Management International, Revue Française de Gestion, Revue des Sciences de Gestion*, and *Harvard Business Review Arabic*. Email: ldikmen@poitiers.iae-france.fr

Isabel Estrada is Associate Professor in the Department of Innovation Management and Strategy at the University of Groningen, Netherlands, where she currently teaches in the area of Organizational Innovation. She received her PhD in 2012 from the University of Valladolid, Spain, with a dissertation titled "Collaboration and value creation in multi-partner R&D alliances: A longitudinal case study on the Acuisost Consortium". Her research focuses on the processes of exchange in interorganizational collaboration, with a particular interest in multipartner settings. Earlier, she enjoyed a Contract for Novel Researchers (2008–2012) at the Uni-versity of Valladolid, Spain, co-funded by the "Junta de Castilla y León" and the UE Social Fund. She has published in *Research Policy, Long Range Planning, British Journal of Management, Industrial Marketing Management, Journal of Small Business Management, Journal of Knowledge Management, and*

Innovation: Management, Policy and Practice, as well as several book chapters. Email: I.Estrada.Vaquero@rug.nl

Giulio Ferrigno is assistant professor at the Catholic University of the Sacred Heart, Milan, Italy. He was a Postdoctoral Scholar at Sant'Anna School of Advanced Studies, Pisa, Italy. He received his PhD in Economics and Management from the University of Catania, Italy. He has held visiting positions at Tilburg University, Netherlands, and University of Umea, Sweden. He received the Best paper award of Academy of Management's Management History Division (2019), the Outstanding Reviewer award of AOM's Strategic Management Division (2015 and 2016), the JMS and SMS Doctoral Workshop Scholarship (respectively in 2015 and 2016). His research interests include strategic alliances, value creation and appropriation, and open innovation. He has published in journals such as *International Journal of Management Reviews*, *Small Business Economics*, *Technological Forecasting and Social Change*, *R&D Management*, *Journal of Business and Industrial Marketing*, and chapters in volumes such as *Managing Multipartner Strategic Alliances* (IAP, 2015) and *Managing Alliance Portfolios and Networks* (IAP, 2018). Email: giulio.ferrigno@unicatt.it.

Olivier Furrer is Chaired Professor of Marketing at the University of Fribourg, Switzerland. Previously, he held positions at the Radboud University Nijmegen, Netherlands, the University of Birmingham (UK), and the University of Illinois at Urbana-Champaign, Champaign, IL. He holds a PhD from the University of Neuchâtel, Switzerland. One of his main research interests is in the area of response strategies in strategic alliances. He has published research articles in such journals as *Journal of International Business Studies*, *Management International Review*, *Journal of International Management*, and *Journal of Business Ethics*. Email: olivier.furrer@unifr.ch

Mouhoub Hani is an assistant professor of strategic management at Paris 8 University, Paris, France. His research focuses on interorganizational relationships in complex structures of global networks. He has published articles on global network coopetition and on dynamic interactions between competitors. He is currently interested in more complex and emergent structures of interaction such as digital platforms and ecosystems. His work was published in international journals such as *Journal of Business and Industrial Marketing*, *Finance-Contrôle-Stratégie*, and *Management International*. Email: mouhoub.hani@univ-paris8.fr

Michael A. Hitt is Distinguished Professor of Management at Texas A&M University and holds the Joe B. Foster Chair in Business Leadership. He received his PhD from the University of Colorado. He has coauthored or co-edited 26 books and authored or coauthored many journal articles. A recent article in the *Journal of Management* listed him as one of the ten most cited authors in management over a 25-year period. Additionally, the *Times Higher Education* in 2010 listed him among the top scholars in economics, finance and management based on the number of articles with a high citation rate on the Web of Science. He has served on the editorial review boards of multiple journals and is a former editor of the *Academy of Management Journal* and the *Strategic Entrepreneurship Journal*. He is a Fellow in the Academy of Management and in the Strategic Management Society, a Research Fellow in the National Entrepreneurship Consortium and received an honorary doctorate from the Universidad Carlos III de Madrid. He is a former President of the Academy of Management, a former President of the Strategic Management Society and a member of the Academy of Management Journals' Hall of Fame. He received awards for the best article published in the *Academy of Management Executive* (1999), *Academy of Management Journal* (2000), and the *Journal of Management* (2006). He received the Irwin Outstanding Educator Award and the Distinguished Service Award from the Academy of Management and the Falcone Distinguished Entrepreneurship Scholar Award from Syracuse University. Email: mhitt@mays.tamu.edu

Ha Hoang is Professor of Management at ESSEC Business School, Paris, France. She holds a PhD from Haas School of Business, University of California, Berkeley, CA. Her work integrates strategic and relational perspectives to the study of alliance formation and subsequent performance. Her research interests include the study of competitive and cooperative dynamics, founder role identity development, and employee entrepreneurship. Her work has been published in *Academy of Management Journal*, *Administrative Science Quarterly*, *Journal of Business Venturing*, *Strategic Management Journal*, and *Strategic Organization*. Email: hoang@essec.edu.

Markus Kreutzer is a Professor of Strategic and International Management at EBS Business School at EBS Universität für Wirtschaft und Recht, Oestrich-Winkel, Germany. Earlier, he worked as Assistant Professor of Strategic Management at the Institute of Management at the University of St. Gallen, St. Gallen, Switzerland, and as Visiting Professor at the Entrepreneurship Department of IESE Business School, Barcelona, Spain. He holds a master's degree in Business Administration and a master's degree of Economics from the University of Passau, Passau, Germany, as well as a doctoral degree from the University of St. Gallen. In his doctoral thesis at the intersection of strategy and corporate entrepreneurship, he examined how multi-business firms effectively steer and coordinate different types of strategic initiatives. His research interests include interorganizational strategy making, organizational control, strategic renewal and adaptation, business model innovation, and ecosystems. He has published in journals such as the *Academy of Management Annals*, *Academy of Management Review*, *Journal of Management Studies*, *Long Range Planning*, *Strategic Management Journal*, and *Harvard Business Manager* (in German). He is an active journal reviewer and an editorial board member of the *Journal of Management*. He was Dean of EBS Business School from 2017 until 2019 and Vice Dean Research of EBS Business School from 2016 until 2017. Email: markus. kreutzer@ebs.edu

Rekha Krishnan is Associate Professor of International Business and Entrepreneurship at the Beedie School of Business, Simon Fraser University, Burnaby, Canada. She completed her PhD from Tilburg University. Her PhD dissertation won the prestigious Richard N Farmer Best Dissertation award sponsored by the Academy of International Business and was one of the finalists for the Gunnar Hedlund Best Dissertation award of the Stockholm School of Economics, and the Academy of Management's Business Policy & Strategy Division outstanding dissertation award. Her research has been published in journals such as *Administrative Science Quarterly*, *Academy of Management Journal*, *Organization Science*, *Strategic Management Journal*, *Journal of Management*, *Journal of Management Studies*, and *Resources, Conservation and Recycling*. Her research has twice received the support of SSHRC Standard Research Grant of the Government of Canada. Also, she was a visiting scholar at the Institute of Research on Social Sciences at Stanford University. Email: rekhak@sfu.ca

Steven S. Lui is Associate Professor at the Australian School of Business, University of New South Wales, Sydney, Australia. He is currently on the editorial boards of *Journal of World Business*, *Asia Pacific Journal of Management*, and the *Journal of Trust Research*. His research interests are in inter-firm cooperation, trust, and innovation. He holds a PhD from the Chinese University of Hong Kong, Hong Kong, China. Email: steven.lui@unsw. edu.au.

Natalia Martín-Cruz is Associate Professor at the Faculty of Business and Economics in the University of Valladolid, Spain, where she teaches strategic management. Currently holding the Chair of the Department of Management, she became doctor in Business Economics (2000, University of Valladolid). In her dissertation, she compared the institutional frameworks of the US and Spanish pharmaceutical industries. She has conducted research in a variety of topics (e.g., entrepreneurship, teamwork, knowledge sharing, corporate spin-offs, and strategic alliances), visiting several external institutions, such as the Institute of Business Innovation (University of California at Berkeley, CA) and Stanford Institute for Economic Policy Research (Stanford University, CA). Email: ambiela@eco.uva.es

Victor M. Martín-Pérez is Associate Professor at the Faculty of Business and Economics in the University of Valladolid, Spain, where he teaches courses of Operations Management and Strategy. An expert in the organizational architecture of non-profit organizations, he earned his PhD in Business Economics (University of Valladolid, 2006), subsequently visiting the University of Texas-Pan American (Edinburg) for postdoctoral research. Aside from studying the impact of business simulation games in students' learning skills, he has mainly investigated how the processes of delegation and motivation affect knowledge transfer and efficiency in non-profit organizations. Email: vmartin@eco.uva.es

Ángeles Montoro-Sánchez is a Full Professor of Management at the Complutense University of Madrid, Madrid, Spain, where she obtained her PhD in business administration. Her research interests include strategic alliances, mergers and acquisitions, innovation and entrepreneurship. Her research has been published in *Research Policy*, *Transport Policy*, *Journal of Organizational Change Management*, *Service Industries Journal*, *Group Decision and Negotiation*, *Canadian Journal of Administrative Science*, *International Journal of Technology Management*, and *International Journal of Manpower*, among others. Email: mangeles@ccee.ucm.es

Eva-María Mora-Valentín is an Associate Professor of Management at Rey Juan Carlos University, Madrid, Spain, where she obtained her PhD in business administration. Her research interests include strategic alliances, cooperative agreements, mergers and acquisitions, university-firm relationships, science and technology parks, open innovation, and open data. Her research has been published in *Journal of Technology Transfer*, *Research Policy*, *International Journal of Technology Management*, *Journal of Knowledge Management*, *International Business Review*, *Science and Public Policy*, *International Journal of Manpower*, *Government Information Quarterly*, and *Journal of Organizational Change Management*, among others. Email: evamaria.mora@urjc.es

Jan Mouritsen is a professor at Copenhagen Business School, Frederiksberg, Denmark. His research is oriented toward understanding the role of management technologies and management control in various organizational and social contexts. He focuses on empirical research and attempts to develop new ways of understanding the role and effects of controls and financial information in organizations and society. He is interested in translations and interpretations made of (numerical) representations (e.g., as in budgets, financial reports, non-financial indicators and profitability analysis) in the contexts they help to illuminate. His interests include intellectual capital and knowledge management, technology management, operations management, new accounting and management control. He is currently an editorial board member of a number of academic journals in the various areas of management and business research including accounting (e.g., CAR and AOS), operations management, IT and knowledge management. He has published in journals including *Accounting, Organizations and Society; Management Accounting Research; Scandinavian Journal of Management; Accounting, Auditing and Accountability Journal; Journal of Intellectual Capital and Critical Perspectives on Accounting*. Email: jm.om@cbs.dk

Gordon Müller-Seitz is Chair of Strategy, Innovation and Cooperation at the Department of Business Administration and Economics, Technische Universität Kaiserslautern, Kaiserslautern, Germany. He is a management researcher focusing in his research upon interorganizational networks, open innovation and open strategy. Currently, he is focusing on business model innovations in light of the digital transformation and artificial intelligence in particular. His work has appeared in journals such as *Journal of Public Administration, Research and Theory, Research Policy, Organization Studies, Industry & Innovation*, and *R&D Management*. His research insights have been applied at large-scale organizations and small and medium sized enterprises. Email: gms@wiwi.uni-kl.de

Pia Kerstin Neudert is a doctoral candidate and research assistant at the Chair of Strategic and International Management of EBS Business School at EBS Universität für Wirtschaft und Recht, Oestrich-Winkel, Germany. Previously, she worked in different management positions at the Lufthansa Group, Frankfurt, Germany; in her last position, she served as Senior Manager for joint venture and partner sales in the EMEA region. She holds a bachelor's degree in Aviation Management from EBS Universität für Wirtschaft und Recht and a master's degree in Management from HHL Leipzig Graduate School of Management, Leipzig, Germany. Her research focuses on ecosystems; particularly, she investigates mechanisms of orchestration, interactions among incumbents and new ventures, and technology-related governance questions. She has published her research in *Best Paper Proceedings* (Academy of Management, 2021) and *Global Focus Magazine* (EMFD Global, 2021). She also regularly presents her work at the annual conferences of the Academy of Management, the European Academy of Management, the Strategic Management Society, and the World Open Innovation Conference. The Strategic Management Division of the Academy of Management designated her twice as Outstanding Reviewer for their Annual Meetings. She received a Dean's List Award from EBS Business School in 2021, a scholarship for her master's studies from the Federal Government of Germany and Mitteldeutsche Flughafen AG in 2015, and a travel grant from the German-American Fulbright Commission in 2016. Email: pia.neudert@ebs.edu

Hang-yue Ngo is Professor at the Department of Management, the Chinese University of Hong Kong, Hong Kong, China. His research interests are in strategic HRM, gender in business, and international management. He holds a PhD in Sociology from the University of Chicago, Chicago, IL. Email: hyngo@baf.msmail.cuhk.edu.hk.

Amalya L. Oliver is George S. Wise Chair in Sociology at the Department of Sociology at the Hebrew University, Jerusalem, Israel. She is an organizational sociologist focusing on interorganizational networks, collaborations, and innovation among knowledge-creating industries and social enterprises. Currently, she is studying collaborative networks in consortia, entrepreneurship and innovation among Palestinian Arabs and innovation in the periphery. Her work has been published in journals such as *Organization Science, Organization Studies, Research Policy, Journal of Management Studies, Social Networks*, and *Social Studies of Science*. Email: amalya. oliver@mail.huji.ac.il

Marta Ortiz-de-Urbina-Criado is Associate Professor of Management at Rey Juan Carlos University, Madrid, Spain, where she obtained her PhD in business administration. Her research interests include strategic alliances, mergers and acquisitions, human resources, innovation, and open data. Her research has been published in the *Government Information Quarterly, Journal of the Association for Information Science and Technology, Journal of Technology Transfer, Cities, International Business Review, International Journal of Manpower, Journal of Knowledge Management*, and *Journal of Organizational Change Management*, among others. Email: marta.ortizdeurbina@urjc.es

Laura Poppo is the Donald and Shirley Clifton Chair in Leadership at the University of Nebraska-Lincoln, Lincoln, NE. She received her PhD from the Wharton School, University of Pennsylvania, Philadelphia, PA, and has been on the faculty of Washington University, St. Louis, MO, Virginia Tech, Blacksburg, VA, and University of Kansas, Lawrence, KS. She is a leading researcher in strategy, and her research interests include: outsourcing, alliances, vertical integration, contracting, and trust, including the context of doing business in China. Her current research examines problem solving, creativity, and innovation. Email: LPoppo2@UNL.edu

James Robins is University Professor Emeritus at Vienna University of Economics and Business, Vienna, Austria. He is a former Editor-in-Chief of *Long Range Planning* and a former Associate Editor of *Global Strategy Journal*. He holds a PhD from the University of California at Los Angeles, Los Angeles, CA (UCLA). His academic career has spanned three continents. He has been on the faculty of Stanford University and the University of California in the United States, HKUST and City University in Hong Kong, served as Associate Dean for Faculty at Lee Kong Chian School of Business, Singapore Management University, and is now at the WU Wien. His research deals with a number of basic issues in strategic management, including corporate strategy, strategy theory, international ventures, knowledge transfer, and emerging economy firms. His work has been published in such journals as *Strategic Management Journal*, *Organization Science*, *Administrative Science Quarterly*, *Organization Studies*, and *Asia Pacific Journal of Management*. Email: james.robins@wu-wien.ac.at.

Jens K. Roehrich is Professor of Supply Chain Innovation and Co-director of the HPC Supply Chain Innovation Lab at the School of Management, University of Bath, Bath, UK. Earlier, he was a researcher at Imperial College London, London, UK. He has carried out funded research, consultancy, executive education, and competence development activities with a wide range of public and private organizations. Significant strands of his research agenda explore the long-term interplay of contractual and relational governance mechanisms in complex projects and multipartner alliances, and the management of collaborative public-private relationships. More recently, he has been exploring the dark side of relationships by investigating coordination failures, conflicts, and trust breaches. His research is multidisciplinary, drawing theoretical inspiration and methodological support from operations management, economics, strategy, innovation management, healthcare, and policy management. His research has been published in journals such as the *Journal of Management Studies*, *International Journal of Operations & Production Management*, *British Journal of Management*, *Social Science & Medicine*, and *Industrial Marketing Management*. Email: j.roehrich@bath.ac.uk

Kristie M. Rogers is an Associate Professor of Management in the College of Business Administration at Marquette University, Milwaukee, WI. She received her PhD in organizational behavior from Arizona State University, Tempe, AZ. Her research focuses on identity processes at work, and the factors that potentially facilitate (e.g., respect) and challenge (e.g., ambivalence) identity growth and transformation. She has extensive experience conducting qualitative, field-based research, publishing her work in leading management journals such as *Administrative Science Quarterly*, *Academy of Management Journal*, *Academy of Management Review*, and *Organization Science*, and in practitioner outlets such as *Harvard Business Review*. Email: Kristie.Rogers@Marquette.edu

Hilary Schloemer is an Assistant Professor of Management in the Neil Griffin College of Business at Arkansas State University, Jonesboro, AR. She earned her PhD in Human Resource Management at the University of Kansas, Lawrence, KS. Her research focuses on how social and psychological group dynamics affect complex problem solving, creativity, and innovation, and can be leveraged to facilitate effective decision making in firms. Email: HSchloemer@AState.edu

Angelo M. Solarino is an Associate professor at the Durham University Business School, Durham, UK. He was Assistant professor at Leeds University Business School, Leeds, UK, and visiting Scholar at the Ross School of Business, University of Michigan, Ann Arbor, MI. He obtained his PhD at City University of Hong Kong, Kowloon, Hong Kong. His research focuses on corporate governance, the determinants of corporate performance, and methodological issues related to corporate governance studies. His research has been published in *Journal of Management*, *Journal of Management Studies*, and *Strategic Management Journal*, among others. Email: angelo.solarino@durham.ac.uk.

Brian Squire is Deputy Dean, Professor of Operations Management, and Co-director of the HPC Supply Chain Innovation Lab at the School of Management, University of Bath, Bath, UK. His research is broadly concerned with the design and management of operations and supply chains for resilience, innovation, and sustainability and has been published in outlets such as *Journal of Operations Management*, *Production and Operations Management*, *Journal of Supply Chain Management*, *British Journal of Management*, and *International Journal of Operations and Production Management*. Email: b.c.squire@bath.ac.uk

Renate Taubeneder is Doctoral Researcher at the University of Bath, School of Management, Bath, UK, and Assistant Manager at KPMG's Strategic Advisory arm for infrastructure in London, UK. Her research is broadly concerned with the formation processes of multipartner alliances in large projects. Email: renate.taubeneder@kpmg.co.uk

Sof Thrane is a professor at Copenhagen Business School, Frederiksberg, Denmark. He received his PhD from Copenhagen Business School where his thesis work provided fresh insights on the problem of managing interorganizational relationships. He has held the position of head of the PhD School in Business and Management (2008-2016) and is currently academic director of the Master in Business Development (MBD). His research is focused on the ways in which interfirm relationships and innovation networks develop and change, often taking into account the role of managerial technologies in developing and maintaining relationships and organizational networks. This research interest has led to a range of studies on the paradoxical ways in which managerial technologies shape organizational life and on innovative approaches to the use of management accounting for creating and overcoming boundaries within and between organizations. Professor Thrane has published in journals such as *Research Policy*, *Accounting Organization and Society*, *Management Accounting Research*, *Journal of Accounting and Organisational Change*, *Journal of Management Accounting Research*, and *Scandinavian Journal of Management*. Email: sth.om@cbs.dk

INDEX

A

Aaltonen, K., 2–3, 8
Aarikka-Stenroos, L., 156
Abdi, M., 92
Aben, T. A. E., 10
Abramovsky, L., 243
Absorptive capacity, 117, 227, 231, 264
Academic Health Science Networks (UK), 187
Accelerator networks, 159, 168–169, 175, 179, 182, 186–187
Accelerators, 159, 161–162, 164, 168–169, 175–176, 179, 181–183, 186
Acosta, J., 226
Acuisost Consortium, 330–331, 334–350
Adegbesan, J. A., 210
Adler, P. S., 130, 277
Adner, R., 157–160, 163, 171, 173, 184–185, 191, 249–250, 255–256, 265
Advice.net, 285–291
Afuah, A., 159, 248, 255
Agarwal, N., 167, 186

Agouridas, V., 159
Aguinis, H., 315, 318, 323
Ahlstrom, D., 316
Ahrne, G., 161, 166, 184
Ahuja, G., 264, 280, 316
Aiken, L. S., 107, 114
Airbus A380, 173
Ålandsbanken, 183
Albert, S., 47, 66, 202
Albino, V., 259
Alchian, A., 133
Alexy, O., 159, 248, 253, 255, 262–264
Allen, T. J., 64
Alliance and firm-level performance, 51
Alliance dynamics, 276, 279
Alliance management capabilities, 83–84
Alliance networks, 275–277, 280, 299–300
Alliance partner diversity (APD), 305–315, 317–318, 322–323
Alliance performance and organizational institutional differences, 95–96

Managing Interpartner Cooperation in Strategic Alliances, pp. 367–394
Copyright © 2022 by Information Age Publishing
www.infoagepub.com

Alliance performance and
　regulatory institutional
　differences, 96–100
Alliance performance and trust,
　95–100
Alliance performance, 33, 35,
　38–40, 43–46, 51, 91, 93, 95–96,
　99–100, 102–106, 108–118,
　305–312, 315, 317–318, 322
Alliance performance, measure,
　102–103, 125
Alliance process models, 37
Alliance team and parent firm,
　46–48
Alliance teams, 33–41, 43–55,
　66–68, 71, 73, 75–85
Alliances and interorganizational
　innovation networks, 255–256
Almirall, E., 159
Alston, L. J., 124
Al-Tabbaa, O., 253
Altman, E. J., 173, 175–176, 180,
　187
Alvesson, M., 281
Amabile, T. M., 43
Amazon, 165
Ambivalence and alliance
　dysfunction, 40–42
Ambivalence and alliance
　performance, 42–46
Ambivalence in the alliance
　context, 39–51
Ambivalence, 33–36, 38–55, 66–67
Ambivalence–enhancing
　mechanisms, 35, 46, 52, 54
Ambos, B., 2
American National Standards
　Institute, 165
Amesse, F., 249
Amir, Y., 205, 216
Amit, R., 160, 187
Amorphous network, 289

Anand, B. N., 334
Anand, J., 205, 217–218, 316
Andersen, B., 180
Anderson, C. P., 60
Anderson, J. C., 108, 132, 140,
　332, 347
Andresen, E., 2, 7
Andrevski, G., 203
Ang, S. H., 211
Ansari, S., 159–160
Apheris, 171
Appel-Meulenbroek, R., 159
Apple, 68, 98–99
Appropriability, 227, 230–231
Aqua-Environ Consulting, 335,
　337
Arentze, T., 159
Argote, L., 37, 46, 52
Argyres, N. S., 133, 148
Ariño, A., 36, 277, 279, 282, 315–
　316, 333, 339, 345, 347, 349
Armitage, C. J., 42, 54
Armstrong, S. J., 101
Arnaout, R. A., 255
Arregle, J. L., 92
Arrow, K. J., 253, 267
Artificial intelligence (AI), 167
Ashcraft, K. L., 49
Ashforth, B. E., 35, 38–39, 42,
　46–47, 49, 51
Asplund, F., 188
Asset specificity, measure, 141
Assimakopoulos, D., 159
Atos, 172–173
Auerswald, P. E., 170, 186
Aulakh, P. S., 91–127, 133, 138–
　139, 350
Autio, E., 137, 159, 161, 170, 186,
　277
Axelrod, R., 159–161, 165, 184,
　186

B

Bachmann, R., 120
Bacon, E., 159
Bagozzi, R. P., 108
Bai, T., 311
Bain & Company, 173–174
Bain Advisor Network, 173
Bain Alliance Ecosystem, 163, 173
Bains, W., 218
Bakker, H., 2–3
Bakker, R. M., 306, 316
Balasubramanian, S., 205
Baldwin, C. Y., 178, 188, 255
Balestrin, A., 227
Baptista, R., 262
Barboza D., 98–99
Barnard, C., 35
Barnett, C. K., 46, 50
Barney, J. B., 94, 206
Baron, R. A., 157, 174
Bartsch, V., 315
Battilana, J., 48
Battisti, S., 167, 186
Baughn, C. C., 105
Baum, J. A. C., 4, 202–203, 209–210, 277
Bayliss, B. T., 309, 311, 313
Bayus, B. L., 205
Beamish, P. W., 307, 309–316, 322
Beaty, J. C., 318
Bechky, B. A., 43, 49
Beck, S., 163, 175
Becker, W., 226
Beersma, B., 50
Belderbos, R., 227, 229–231, 235–236, 243, 255
Bell, D. W., 42, 44
Bello, D. C., 93, 132
Belussi, F., 249
Ben Jemaa-Boubaya, K., 63–90
Ben Letaifa, S., 159
Bengtsson, L., 202, 248

Bengtsson, M., 64–69, 85
Bennett, D. S., 159–161, 165, 184, 186
Bercovitz, B., 36
Bereti, M., 48
Bergh, D. D., 318
Berkowitz, H., 158, 161, 167, 186
Bernassi, M., 277, 299
Bernheim, B. D., 205
Berntson, G. G., 40
Berry, L., 266
Bessant, J. R., 156
Bessenbach, J., 178
Bettenmann, D., 175–176, 181, 185–186
Beugelsdijk, S., 316
Beyer, J. M., 254
Bhagavatula, S., 170
Bhaumik, S., 96
Bianchi, M., 160, 165, 253
Biedenbach, T., 206
BigchainDB, 172
Biggiero, L., 261
Bingham, C. B., 161, 168, 186
BioMilk, 336, 338, 340, 342–343, 345
Biosecurity subproject, 335
Bitektine, A., 4–5, 25–26
Björk, J., 188
Blau, P. M., 332
Blind, K., 165–166
Block, E. S., 94, 95, 97
Blu-ray Disc (Sony), 165
BNP Paribas Bank Polska, 183
Boeker, W., 205–206
Böger, M., 159, 163, 177–178, 180, 184, 186
Bogers, M. L., 159, 173, 248–249, 252
Boik, R. J., 318
Bolino, M. C., 277
Bonaccorsi, A., 106
Boon, W. P. C., 250

Bor, S., 161, 167, 180, 186

Borenstein, M., 318

Borgatti, S. P., 249–250, 258–260

Bortagaray, I., 92, 95

Borza, A., 92

Bosch, 171

Bosco, F. A., 315, 318

Bossink, B., 157, 159

Boudreau, K. J., 156, 172, 255

Bouncken, R. B., 68, 248, 255

Boyd, B. K., 318, 323

Boyd, N. G., 347

Boymans, C., 69

Bradshaw, M., 169

Brandenburger, A. M., 64–65

Brass, D. J., 203

Brem, A., 167, 175–176, 181, 185–186

Brenner, B., 2

Breschi, S., 260

Bresnen, M., 254

Brewer, M., 259

Breznitz, D., 176

Brickson, S., 279

Brockman, B. K., 169

Brockner, J., 102

Broerse, J. E. W., 250

Brömer, P., 44

Brown, A. D., 4

Brown, J. R., 131–132

Brown, K. W., 43

Brown, R., 169

Browning, L. D., 253–254

Brownstein, A. L., 42, 53

Bruderer, E., 159–161, 165, 184, 186

Brunsson, N., 161, 166, 184

Brunswicker, S., 159

Brush, T. H., 132, 205

Brusoni, S., 159

Bruyaka, O., 315–317

Bryant, I., 45

Buckley, P. J., 227–228, 230, 309–311, 313

Bunker, B. B., 92–94, 96, 99

Burford, N. J., 158, 180, 187

Burgers, W. P., 332

Burt, R. S., 290

Buyer-supplier MPA, 1–5, 7, 25–28

Buyer-supplier relationships, 1, 19

C

Cacioppo, J. T., 40

Calcei, D., 165

Caldwell, D. F., 103

Caldwell, N. D., 7, 27

Cameron, C. A., 212

Campbell, D. T., 107

Cannella Jr., A. A., 217

Cannon, J. P., 132, 138, 140

Cano Giner, J. L., 176

Cantner, U., 170

Cantwell, J., 118

Cao, Z., 37

Capaldo, A., 258–259, 262

Cappetta, R., 115

Capron, L., 157

Caputo, A., 170

Carayannis, E. G., 68, 159

Carree, M., 227, 229–231, 235–236, 243

Carson, S. J., 94, 104, 115, 130

Casanueva, C., 255

Cassiman, B., 227, 230, 236, 238, 243

Castro, L. M., 232

Catena–X, 163, 171–172

Cavaliere, A., 253

Cavusgil, S. T., 132–133, 138–139

Cennamo, C., 158–159, 171–172, 178–180, 184, 187

Chakkol, M., 27

Chan, C. M., 97, 309–311, 313

Chan, W., 317

Chandrasekaran, A., 2–3
Chang, S., 137
Chatman, J., 103, 279
Chemics & Proteins, 336, 338, 340
Chen, C. C., 104
Chen, H., 68
Chen, M. J., 202, 205, 207, 217
Chen, S., 227
Chen, X. P., 330, 332, 334, 347–348
Chen, X., 3, 6, 287
Cheriet, F., 63–90
Chesbrough, H. W., 173, 176, 226, 248–252, 255, 267–268
Cheung, M. W. L., 317
Chiambaretto, P., 64–67, 85, 89
Chiaroni, D., 253
Chiesa, V., 253
Child, J., 105, 248
Choi, C. J., 227
Choi, J., 104
Christoffersen, J., 314
Chu, W., 93–94, 132, 277
Chuang, Y. T., 205
Chung, C. C., 315–316
Circunomics, 171
Clark, K. B., 314
Claro, D. P., 2
Clarysse, B., 159, 168, 175, 264
Clay, K., 97, 99, 116
Clegg, S. R., 31
Clerix, A., 156–157, 184
Cliques, 259, 261–262, 293
Cloodt, M., 159
Clore, G. L., 45
Clusters, 159, 169–170, 180, 227, 249, 256, 259–262
Coff, R., 34
Cohen, S. L., 159, 161, 168–169, 175, 184, 186
Cohen, W. M., 226, 314
Coleman, J. S., 281

Collaboration, 33, 40, 42–43, 47, 52, 77, 103, 158, 161, 174–175, 201–204, 206, 208, 210–211, 214, 216–218, 226, 231–233, 236, 249–250, 253, 255–256, 259, 261–262, 264–266, 312, 332–333, 343–344
Collaborations and interorganizational networks, 256–264
Colombo, M. G., 227
Colonization, 97, 118
Common benefits, 67, 208, 210, 212
Community Innovation Survey (CIS), 233
Competition–cooperation tension, 52
Complementarities, 77–79, 85, 130, 148, 155, 158–159, 172, 175, 180, 227, 275–276, 278, 299–301
Complementary relationships, 48, 69–71, 82, 148
Complementor selection, 180, 183
Complementors, 156, 159, 163–164, 172–176, 178–183, 186
Conlon, D. E., 50
Connecting Partners program, 167
Connectivity Standard Alliance, 165
Connelly, B. L., 205–206
Conner, M., 42, 54
Conservative network, 294
Contextual factors for harnessing ambivalence, 46–50
Contracting, similarity, and cooperation, 133–134
Contracting, trust, and cooperation, 131–133
Contractor, F. J., 59, 219
Contracts, 1, 3, 7, 9–11, 13–28, 33–38, 51, 53, 97, 117, 130–135,

147–149, 155, 161, 165, 180, 258, 276–277
Contractual hazards, 93, 115–116
Contractual safeguards, 34, 36, 54, 132, 276
Cook, K. S., 121
Cooke, P., 249
Cooperation, similarity, and contracting, 133–134
Cooperation, trust, and contracting, 131–133
Cooperative agreements, 227
Cooperative behavior, 10, 49, 71, 84, 130–135, 141–148, 275–277, 279, 282, 292, 330, 334, 338, 345, 350
Cooperative behavior, measure, 140
Cooperative relationships, 230, 236
Cooperative-competitive interplay, 203, 217
Coopetition (external), 63–65, 67–77, 79–86
Coopetition (internal), 63–77, 79, 82–86
Coopetition (nested), 71–72, 76, 79, 84–86
Coopetition management team, 80–81
Coopetition situations, 329, 331, 334, 338–341, 343, 345–350
Coopetitive tensions, 63, 65–68, 70, 74, 80, 82, 84–86
Coping mechanisms, 40, 47–49, 54
Corbin, J., 10, 284
Corley, K. G., 7, 47
Corporate development mode choice framework, 157
Corsten, D., 36–37
Cost focus, measure, 141
Cozzolino, A., 182
Cramer, P., 40

Crawford, R., 133
Creativity, 34–35, 40–41, 45–46, 50–52, 55, 287–288
Creswell, J. D., 43
Cropper, S., 153, 161, 167, 180, 186, 249
Cross, R., 261
Cui, A. S., 306–307
Cullen, J. B., 138–139
Cultural diversity and firm performance, 311–312
Cultural diversity, 307–314, 316, 318–320, 322
Cummings, J. L., 210
Cunningham, J. A., 170
Currall, S. C., 34, 36, 40, 52, 130, 276–277
Czakon, W., 64, 68–69, 89

D

D'Amour, A., 208
Dacin, M. T., 4, 92, 316
Daellenbach, U. S., 206
Dagnino, G. B., 65, 306, 309, 311, 323
Dahl, J., 66–68, 85
Dahlander, L., 159, 248, 250–251, 256, 263
Dahlin, K. B., 205
Daidj, N., 165
Dalton, C. M., 315, 318
Dalton, D. R., 315, 318
Daly, J. P., 102
Damanpour, F., 104
DaMatta, R., 121
Dana, L.-P., 170, 186
Danzon, P. M., 204
Das, T. K., 2–7, 26–27, 34, 52, 64–65, 88, 130, 132, 135, 148, 217, 245, 260, 271, 277–278, 287, 324–325, 328, 330–333, 347–348, 351

Dattée, B., 159
David, R. J., 5–6
Davies, A. C., 7, 27
Davies, G., 159
Davis, G. F., 254
Davis, J. H., 94, 132
Davis, J. P., 249–250, 265
De Carolis, D. M., 316
De facto standard, 165
De Jong, J. P., 266
De jure standard, 165
de la Torre, J., 277, 279, 282
de Leeuw, T., 306
de Liver, Y., 48
De Loo, I., 228, 230
de Man, A-P, 130, 132, 157, 159,
    350
De Propris, L., 160, 187
de Rochemont, M., 266
De Silva, M., 176
de Vasconcelos Gomes, L. A., 159
DeBresson, C., 249
Decoupling, 69–70
Dedehayir, O., 157, 161, 163, 173,
    177
Deeds, D. L., 106, 316
Del Sarto, N., 323
Delcamp, H., 165
Deligonul, S., 132
Delmastro, M., 227
Demand volatility in host country
    market, measure, 106
Depeyre, C., 69
Dess, G. G., 101
Deutsch Telekom AG, 171, 174
DeVellis, R. F., 103
Dhanaraj, C., 156, 249, 253, 262
Di Minin, A., 160, 165, 323
Di Paola, N., 306, 311
Diagonal relationships, 69
Diederen, B., 227, 229–231,
    235–236, 243

Diehl, M., 44
Diestre, L., 211, 309–310, 313
Dietz, J., 226
Dikmen, L., 63–90
Dilemmas in interfirm networks,
    299–300
DiMaggio, P. J., 4, 254
Dittrich, K., 251–252
Doconomy AB, 183
Donaldson, L., 130
Doney, P. M., 132
Doolin, D. M., 208
Dorn, S., 66
Doucet, L., 42
Dougherty, D., 249
Dowling, J., 5
Doz, Y. L., 330–333, 350
Du, J., 311
Dualistic compensation, 50–51
Duarte, F., 93, 98
Duhigg C., 98–99
Dukerich, J. M., 281–282
Dumez, H., 64, 69, 158, 161, 167,
    186
Dunning, J. H., 118
Durand, R., 315–317
Dushnitsky, G., 187
Dussauge, P., 204, 315–316
Dutta, S., 306, 314
Dutton, J. E., 281–282
Duysters, G., 251–252, 306, 350
Dyer, J. H., 34, 93–94, 130, 132–
    133, 141, 156, 254, 259, 262,
    264, 276–278, 296, 349–350
Dyer, W. G., 339

E

Ebers, M., 153, 249, 254, 256, 258,
    315
Economist, 98
Ecosystem native, 183
Ecosystem orchestration, 159

Ecosystem-as-affiliation, 155, 157–160, 169, 171, 175, 184–187
Ecosystem-as-structure, 155, 157–171, 173, 175, 184, 186–187
Eden, L., 2–3, 137, 315
Edmondson, A. C., 49–50
Eggertsson, T., 124
Eisenhardt, K. M., 2, 133, 157, 159, 163, 172, 176, 182, 203, 277–278, 281, 300, 335, 337, 339–340, 349
Elec.net, 291–296
Elfring, T., 102
Ellis, S. C., 248
Embeddedness, 116
Emerging economies/markets, 91–93, 97–100, 118
Emmons, R., 42
Enders, A., 167, 186
Ener, H., 206
Enterprise Resource Planning (ERP), 71–73
Entrant–incumbent ties, 203–214, 216, 218
Entrepreneurial ecosystems, 169–170, 179, 182, 186, 188
Equity ties, 308, 317–320, 323
Eriksson, J., 330, 332–333, 348
Ertug, G., 93, 115–116
Esses, V. M. 42, 44
Estrada, I., 156, 329–353
Estrin, S., 96
European Union, 167, 232
Evans, W. N., 205
Everett, M. G., 249–250
External coopetition and internal coopetition, relationship, 68–69
External knowledge flows, 225, 227, 229, 233, 242

F

Facin, A. L. F., 159

Faems, D., 34, 38, 51, 130, 132, 134, 148–149, 252, 255, 276, 287, 336–337, 350
Fagerberg, J., 272
Falcke, C. O., 100
Fan, G. H., 38
Faulkner, D., 248
Faust, K., 249–250
Fayard P., 227
Federal Ministry of Traffic, Innovation, and Technology, Austria, 170
Federickson. J. W., 136
Fehder, D. C., 159, 161, 169, 175, 184, 186
Feiler, D., 159
Feller, J., 316
Fernandez, A. S., 65–66, 89
Fernandéz, D., 175
Fernández-de-Lucio, I., 232
Ferriani, S., 259, 262
Ferrier, W. J., 203
Ferrigno, G., 305–328
Festinger, L., 39–40, 42
Fetch.ai, 171, 172
Findeisen, H., 158, 167
Fineman, S., 59
Firfiray, S., 44
Firm similarity, 129, 134–135, 138–139, 141, 143–145
Firm similarity, measure, 139
Fish&Meals, 336, 338, 340, 344–345
Fish, A., 249, 255, 266
Fiske, D. W., 107
Fleming, L., 208
Fligstein, N., 265
Flint, D. J., 69
Flynn, F. J., 279
Folger, R., 277
Fombrun, C. J., 97
Fong, C. T., 35, 45
Fonti, F., 3, 6

Formal contract, measure, 140
Forman, C., 176
Foss, N. J., 160
Foster, P. C., 249, 260
Fox, C. R., 37, 52
Fox, P. B., 176
Fraga, A., 95
Frank, K. A., 277
Frankort, H. T., 202
Frattini, F., 160, 165, 253
Frederiksen, L., 7
Fredrich, V., 68, 248, 255
Free appropriation, 230
Free-riding, 3, 231, 283
Friedman, R., 149
Friedrich, E., 194
Fuentelsaz, L., 209
Fuller, J., 177, 180
Furr, N. R., 156–158, 175–176,
    180–181, 186
Furrer, O., 63–90

G

Gabbay, S. M., 277
Gallego, Á., 255
Galunic, C., 261
Gambardella, A., 253
Gambetta, D. G., 99, 120
Ganesan, S., 132, 138, 140
Gann, D. M., 248, 250–251, 256,
    263
Garaudel, P., 167
García-Canal, E., 316, 333, 345,
    347
García-Piqueres, G., 230, 235, 238
Gardberg, N. A., 97
Gardner, W. L., 40
Gargiulo, M., 93, 115–116, 211,
    277, 299
Garnsey, E., 174, 177, 188
Garrett, R. P., 2, 3, 315
Garrette, B., 204, 315–316

Garud, R., 159–160
Gassmann, O., 159–160, 163,
    176–178, 180, 184, 186, 248
Gast, J., 64–65
Gawer, A., 158–159, 171–172,
    178–180, 184
Gelbach, J. B., 212
Geletkanycz, M. A., 136
Gemünden, H. G., 174, 177
Generalized exchanges, 332
Geographical proximity, 204, 213,
    242
George, G., 27, 31, 253, 255,
    262–264
Gephardt, R. P. Jr., 280
Gerbing, D. W., 108, 140
Geringer, J. M., 102
German Aerospace Center, 171
Gernsheimer, O., 64–65
Gerrone, P., 227
Geyskens, I., 37, 104, 115
Ghoshal, S., 130, 277, 280
Gianiodis, P. T., 207, 217, 248
Gibbert, M., 10, 334, 349
Gibson, D. V., 120, 124
Giddens, A. G., 277–280
Gies, O., 159
Giesecke+Devrient, 183
Gillier, T., 156
Gimeno, J., 202, 205–206, 346
Gino, F., 46
Giones, F., 175–176, 181, 185–186
Giudici, A., 156
Glaister, K. W., 309–311, 313
GlassDollar UG., 157
Global supply chains, 149
Glynn, M., 95
Gneiting, P., 175–176, 181, 185–
    186
Gnyawali, D. R., 64–66, 69, 306
Goerzen, A., 307, 312–315
Gomes-Casseres, B., 158, 167, 346
Gomez, J., 209

Gomez-Mejia, L. R., 44
Goodrick, E., 93, 98
Goodstein, J., 205–206
Google, 165
Goswami, K., 170
Gouldner, A. W., 259, 265
Gove, S., 323
Governance forms and contexts for open innovation, 257–259
Governance forms and network models, 257–259
Governance mechanisms, 63, 66–68, 71, 74, 79, 84, 258, 276–277, 350
Governance models, 253
Gözübüyük, R., 249
Granovetter, M., 265
Granstrand, O., 159
Grazia, C., 165
Green Solutions, 336, 338, 340
Greenwood, R., 5–6, 25, 122
Greer, C. R., 255
Greidanus, N. S., 149
Greimas, A. J., 69
Greve, H. R., 37, 52, 277
Grewal, R., 203
Griffith, D. A., 140
Grigoroudis, E., 159
Griliches, Z., 229
Grodal, S., 254
Guarana, C. L., 40, 42–45, 48–49
Guinan, E. C., 255
Gulati, R., 34, 36, 40, 51–52, 93, 96, 105, 132, 163, 175, 180, 202, 204, 209, 211–212, 276
Gurau, C., 67
Gutiérrez-Gracia, A., 232
Güttel, W. H., 157, 176

H

Haack, P., 4–5, 25–26
Hackman, J. R., 50

Hagan, J., 121
Hagedoorn, J., 202, 306, 316
Hahn, K., 158–159, 180, 183
Haleblian, J., 306, 316
Hallen, B. L., 161, 168, 186
Halman, J. I. M., 156, 187
Hambrick, D. C., 136
Hamel, G., 64, 333, 339, 347
Hammoudi, A., 165
Han, J. S., 170
Hani, M., 63–90
Hanlon, S. C., 347
Hannah, D. P., 159, 163
Hansen, M. H., 94
Hansson, F., 227–228
Hardy, C., 31
Hargadon, A. B., 43, 49, 314
Harrison, D. A., 278, 282, 301
Harrison, J. S., 312
Harrison, R., 159, 161, 170, 186, 188
Harrison, S. H., 50
Hartmann, A., 7
Hashai, N., 205, 216
Hass, M. R., 31
Hatch, N. W., 264
Haugland, S. A., 334
Haunschild, P. R., 36, 203
Haupt, R., 179
Haveman, H. A., 5–6, 203, 211
HD DVD (NEC/Toshiba), 165
He, J., 69
Heath, L., 57
Heavey, C., 318
Hebert, L., 102
Hechter, M., 282
Heckman. J. J., 211
Hedges, L., 318
Heide, J., 137–138
Heiden, C., 163, 175
Heine, K., 166
Heitor, M. V., 120, 124
Held, D., 279

Helfat, C. E., 206, 264
Helper, S., 104
Henderson, C. R., 278
Henderson, R. M., 314
Henfridsson, O., 163, 171
Henkel, J., 248, 253, 263
Hennart, J. F., 34
Henriksson, K., 202
Hernandez, H., 43–44, 48–49
Hernandez, M., 40, 42, 44–45, 48–49
Hertogh, M., 2–3
Hess, A. M., 248
Hess, D. J., 121
Hesterly, W. S., 258–259
Heterogeneous networks, 260–261
Hettich, E., 156
Hiatt, S. R., 6
Hierarchical network, 289
Hietajärvi, A. M., 3, 8
Higgins, J., 318
Higgins, M. J., 210
Hildebrandt, L., 107
Hillebrand, B., 130, 135, 148
Hinings, C. R., 5–6, 25
Hirsch, P., 149
History, working with partner, measure, 141
Hitt, M. A., 2–3, 92, 312, 315–316
Hoang, H., 201–224
Hobday, M., 254
Hochberg, Y. V, 159, 161, 169, 175, 184, 186
Hodgson, G. M., 96
Hoetker, G., 317
Hoffmann, W., 217
Hofman, E., 156, 187
Hofstede, G., 105, 309, 312
Hogg, M. A., 55
Hohberger, J., 248–250
Holgersson, M., 159
Holism, 33, 39, 41–42, 47, 51
Hollenbeck, J. R., 50

Holmberg, S. R., 210
Holmström, J., 188
Hölzle, K., 174, 177
Homogeneous networks, 260–261
Hoover, V. L., 69
Horizontal flows, 229
Horizontal relationships, 1, 9, 26–27
Hornung, F., 316
Hoskisson, R. E., 312
Hou, H., 160
Howard, M. B., 27
Howard–Grenville, J., 2, 6, 27
Howells, J., 156
Hsieh, K. Y., 217
Huber, F., 159
Huber, G. P., 101
Huberman, A. M., 74, 337
Hubert, M., 163, 175
Huggins, R., 249
Hughes, K., 205
Huizingh, E. K., 248, 250–251, 254
Human, S. E., 5–6
Humphrey, S. E., 50
Hunt, S. D., 132
Hunter, J. E., 314
Husted, B. W., 277
Huxham, C., 153, 249, 262
Hwang, P., 332

I

Iansiti, M., 177
Ibarra-Yunez, A., 120, 124
Iberian Eels, 336, 338, 340–341
Identity bridging, 91, 93–94
Identity, 36, 39, 41, 47–48, 52–53, 92, 95–96, 117, 167, 278
IKEA, 165
Ikenami, R. K., 159
Ilgen, D. R., 50
Imbrication, 63–65, 68, 77, 84–86

Incoming spillovers, 229–231, 236
Incubators, 156, 172, 227
Incumbent firms, 155–157, 159, 160–170, 172–188
Incumbent-entrant ties, 203–214, 216, 218
Incumbent-led innovation ecosystems, 173, 179, 187
Industrial Packages Co., 340, 345
Industry diversity and firm performance, 312–313
Industry diversity, 307–314, 316, 318, 320, 322
Inexperienced partners, 329–331, 334, 345–348, 350
Information processing, 41, 43–45, 48, 52
Information selection for dissemination, 81–82
Ingram, P., 43, 97, 99, 116, 121
Inkpen, A. C. 34, 36, 40, 52, 130, 276–277, 280, 299
InnoCentive, 163, 175
Innovation ecosystems, 157, 159, 171–187
Innovation intermediary, 175, 186
Innovation networks, 156, 187, 253, 255
Innovation types, 187, 227
Institutional entrepreneur, 5
Institutional spillovers, 231, 235, 238
Institutions, 93–99, 106, 116–118
Intel, 53
Interfirm networks and dilemmas, 299–300
Interfirm networks and paradoxes, 299–300
Internal coopetition and external coopetition, relationship, 68–69
Internal coopetition, 66–67
Internal knowledge flows, 229, 233, 235–236, 238

Internet of Things technologies, 165
Interorganizational innovation networks, 255–256
Interorganizational networks and collaborations, 256–264
Interorganizational networks, 247–251, 254, 257
Interorganizational relationships, 92–93, 131, 157–158, 160, 226, 230
Interorganizational trust, 93–94, 96, 100, 102, 104–105, 109–110, 114–115
Interorganizational trust, measure, 104
Interpartner conflict, 92, 98
Interpartner cooperation, 93–94, 201–202, 305–307
Interpartner legitimacy, 2–4
Interpersonal circle, 69
Interpersonal risk, 49
Interpretive schemes, 282, 288, 299
Intraorganizational tensions, 84
Ireland, R. D., 2–3, 312, 315
Isenberg, D. J., 161, 169–170
Isidor, R., 316
Isobe, T., 97, 309–311, 313
Isomorphic relationships, 69–71, 79–82, 85

J

Jaatinen, M., 316
Jacobides, M. G., 158–159, 171–172, 177–180, 184
James, A., 156
Janssens, M., 34, 38, 51, 130, 132, 134, 148–149, 276, 287, 336–337, 350
Jap, S. D., 36, 131, 138, 140–141
Jarillo, J. C., 249

Jarrad, J., 93, 98
Jayachandran, S., 205–206
Jeitinho (Brazil), 93, 98
Jensen, M., 203
Jensen, R. J., 115
Jeppesen, L. B., 156
Jiang, R. J., 306–307, 309–310,
    312–313
John, G., 94, 104, 115, 137
Johns, T., 156
Johnson, J. C., 249–250
Johnson, J. L., 138–139
Johnson, M., 27
Johnson, S. A., 47
Joint innovation, 155
Jonas, K., 44
Jones, C., 258–259
Joo, H., 318
Jorde, T. M., 287
Joreskog, K. G., 107–108
Joshi, A. M., 306, 316
Joshi, H., 31
Judd, J., 158, 167
Juneyao Airlines, 167
Jung, J. C., 322

K

Kabst, R., 316
Kafouros, M. I., 227–228, 230
Kaiser, U., 227, 229–230, 236, 243
Kale, P., 36–37, 92
Kalish, Y., 249, 253
Kalnins, A. 217
Kamien, M. I., 229, 231
Kanbach, D. K., 64–65, 187
Kang, J., 170
Kang, S., 187
Kang, W., 205
Kanter, R. M., 50
Kaplan, R. S., 53
Kapletia, D., 27
Kapoor. R., 159, 173

Karhu, K., 174
Karlsson, C., 160
Karren, R. J., 278
Kastelle, T., 249
Katila, R., 157, 172, 176, 182
Katsikeas, C. S., 93, 132
Katsoulacos, Y., 229, 231, 236
Katz, R., 64
Kaufmann, D., 104
Keil, T., 43, 166
Kenis, P., 254, 258
Kenney, M., 170
Kerk, M., 166
Kessides, I. N., 205
Ketchen Jr, D. J., 69, 205–206, 318
Key Performance Indicator (KPI),
    23
Khan, Z., 253
Khanna, P., 36
Khanna, T., 65, 68, 202, 276, 334
Kherrazi, S., 156
Kiesler, D. J.,
Kim, J., 202, 307, 309–311, 313
Kim, S., 43
Kim, Y., 160, 187
King, G., 211, 216
King, L., 42
Kirkpatrick–Husk, K., 306, 322
Kivleniece, I., 27
Klein Woolthuis, R., 130, 135, 148
Klein, B., 133
Klein, K., 202
Kleinbaum, A. M., 212
Klijn, E., 315
Klimas, P., 68
Kloet, R. R., 250
Kloyer, M., 179
Knoben, J., 306
Knockaert, M., 264
Knoke, D., 249, 254
Knowledge creation, 51, 228
Knowledge exchange, 247, 250,
    256, 260–261, 263–264, 266

Knowledge exchanges, pecuniary versus non-pecuniary, 250, 263

Knowledge flows and R&D alliances, 228–232

Knowledge integration, 68

Knowledge leakage, 66, 202, 204, 331, 346, 348

Knowledge sharing, 33–34, 38, 227, 249, 259, 262–264, 286, 333, 349

Knowledge spillover, 51, 204, 226, 229, 231, 233, 235–236, 238, 242–243, 348

Knowledge transfer, 115, 202, 208, 226, 229, 231, 236, 261, 299, 314

Kock, S., 64–69

Koen, C. I., 316

Kogut, B., 105, 277, 311, 314

Kohler, T., 168

König, A., 167, 186

Konrad, K., 158–159, 180, 183

Koput, K. W., 249, 253–255, 264, 266

Korn, H. J., 209–210

Koschmann, M. A., 253

Kostova, T., 3, 92

Kotabe, M., 102, 104, 115

Koza, M. P., 277, 279–281, 292, 300

Kraatz, M. S., 94–95, 97

Kraay, A., 104

Kramer, A., 187

Kramer, R. M., 96, 122, 125

Kraus, S., 68, 248, 255

Kremp, E., 243

Kreutzer, M., 155–199

Kriauciunas, A., 92

Krishnan, R., 37, 91–127, 132

Kuhn, T.R., 253

Kumar, K., 279

Kumar, M. S., 208

Kumar, N., 104

Kumar, R., 2, 4–7, 26–27, 333, 349

Kumaraswamy, A., 159–160

Kutner, M., 212

Kwon, S. W., 277, 306, 316

L

Lado, A. A., 347

Lahiri, N., 204, 306, 316

Lai, R., 208

Lai, Y. C., 205

Lakemond, N., 248

Lakhani, K. R., 156, 255

Lane, P. J., 92, 96, 106, 118, 212

Lange, K., 254

Lange, M., 179

Langfred, C. W., 94, 115

Langley, A., 74, 337

Larsson, R., 202, 337, 339

Latin America, 91, 93, 95, 97–98, 115, 117

Lau, C. D., 278

Laubacher, R. J., 156

Laudien, S. M., 248

Laursen, K., 248, 251–253, 264

Lavie, D., 2–3, 34, 36, 40, 51–52, 156, 204–206, 210, 216–217, 316, 330, 332, 338

Lazzarini, S. G., 2

Le Roy, F., 64–66, 69, 87, 89

Leach, D., 253

Learning facilitation, training, and coaching, 82–83

Learning networks, 254

Lechner, C., 2, 3, 156, 330, 332, 338

Lee, B. H., 6

Lee, D., 306, 322

Lee, J. Y., 101–102, 137, 317

Lee, K., 65, 68

Lee, T., 280

Leenders, R. T. A. J., 277

Legitimacy and the process of legitimation, 4–5
Legitimacy build–up, 1, 4, 10, 28
Legitimation process, 1, 4–7, 11, 13–18, 21, 25–28
Legitimation, 1, 4–7, 9, 11, 13–18, 21, 25–28, 276, 279, 282, 288, 290–291, 293, 296, 298–299
Legitimizing, 1, 8
Lehavy, R., 43, 45
Lehmann, E. E., 170
Lei, D., 255
Lei, Z., 49–50
Leiponen, A., 165
Lejarraga, J., 160, 165
Leonard-Barton, D., 337, 339
Leong, Y. Y., 174, 177
Leten, B., 156–157, 184, 255
Level of equity, measure, 105
Levén, P., 188
Levien, R., 177
Levin, D. Z., 261
Levinthal, D. A., 226, 309, 311, 313–314
Levitas, E., 92, 316
Levy, B., 98
Lewicki, R., 92–94, 96, 99
Lewin, A. Y., 277, 279–281, 292, 300
Lewis, M. A., 7–8, 27
Lewis, M. W., 39, 42, 66
Li, D., 2–3, 315
Li, G.–C., 208
Li, J. J, 36, 188
Lieberman, M., 159
Liebeskind, J. P., 253, 259
Lindell, M. K., 102
Lingens, B., 159–160, 163, 176–178, 180, 184, 186
Lipparini, A., 262
Livengood, R. S., 47
Lloyd-Walker, B., 3
Local partner size, measure, 106

Local partner's alliance experience, measure, 106
Local partner's international experience, measure, 106
Lokshin, B., 227, 229–231, 235–236, 243, 306
Longitudinal study, 4, 25–26, 148
Lonstein, E., 255
Looy, B. van, 156, 187, 255
López, A., 226–227, 231, 235–236, 243
López-Fernández, M. C., 230, 235, 238
Lorenz, J.–T., 178
Lorenzoni, G., 262
Lounsbury, M., 6
Lovallo, D., 37, 52
Love, E., 227–228
Lubatkin, M., 212
Lufthansa German Airlines, 167
Lui, S. S., 129–154, 160, 187, 315
Lumineau, F., 37, 306, 315
Lundan, S. M., 118
Lundberg, H., 2, 7
Lundgren-Henriksson, E. L., 67–68
Lundvall, B.-Å., 249
Lunnan, R., 334
Luo, X., 67
Luo, Y., 104–105, 132, 137, 148, 309–310
Lusch, R. F., 131–132
Lüscher, L. S., 42
Lydon, M., 255
Lyles, M. A., 92, 106, 117

M

M'Chirgui, Z., 165
MacCormack, A., 2–3, 255
MacDuffie, J. P., 149
Macher, J. T., 36
MacKenzie, S. B., 101–102, 137

MacMillan, I., 259, 262
Madhavan, R., 69, 306, 322
Madhok, A., 34, 38, 40, 51, 94,
    104, 115, 130, 132, 134, 148–
    149, 276, 287, 336–337, 350
Magnusson, M., 188
Mahnke, V., 332, 334
Mahoney, J. T., 206
Maio, G. R., 44
Makadok, R. 34
Mäkinen, S. J., 157, 177
Makino, S., 97, 309–311, 313
Malerba, F., 260
Malhotra, D., 105
Malik, K., 156
Malone, T., 156
Management of objectives, 77–78
Managing competition and
    cooperation in strategic
    alliances, 36–39
Managing nested coopetition,
    79–84, 86
Mangelsdorf, A., 165–166
Mannix, E. A., 60
Maoret, M., 3, 6
Marhold, K., 170
Mariani, M., 64
Markman, G. D., 207, 217
Martin, C., 102
Martin, J. A., 203
Martin, X., 104, 115, 132
Martin-Cruz, N., 156, 329–353
Martin-Perez, V. M., 329–353
Martins, L. L., 43, 45–46
Martynov, A., 36
MASEM (Meta analytic structural
    equation model), 308, 317–320
Mass'e, D., 65–67, 85
Massa, L., 160, 187
MasterCard, 183
Mastruzzi, M., 104
Mathiassen, L., 188
Matutes, C., 251

Maurer, I., 254, 315
Mawson, S., 169
Mayer, K. J., 14, 133, 148
Mayer, R. C., 94, 132
McAdam, D., 265
McAllister, D. J., 96, 148
McCann, B. T., 204
McCann, P., 230
McCarthy, A. M., 206
McEvily, B., 92–94, 96, 98–99, 104,
    116, 137, 258, 261
McGahan, A., 31
McGill, J. P., 312, 314
McGrath, R., 348
Mechanisms for managing
    tensions, 52, 63, 65–66, 85
Mechanisms, ambivalence-
    enhancing, 35, 46, 52, 54
Mechanisms, coping, 40, 47–49, 54
Mechanisms, governance, 63,
    66–68, 71, 74, 79, 84, 258,
    276–277, 350
Mechanisms, relational, 34–38,
    51–53, 66–68, 71, 74, 79, 84–85
Mediation analysis, 310
Mediterranean Aquaculture, 340,
    343–344
Meissner, F. D., 43
Meissner, S., 248
Melwani, S., 45
Mendes, M., 254
Mennillo, G., 194
Menter, M., 170
Mercedes-Benz Group AG, 171–
    172
Merchant, H., 309–310, 322
Meschi, P. X., 315
Mesquita, L. F., 2, 205, 217–218
Messeni Petruzzelli, A., 259
Meta–analysis, 305–306, 314–315,
    317–318, 322
Meta-organizations, 166–168, 170,
    180, 183–184, 186

Meyer, J. W., 4
Meyer, K. E., 96, 118
Meyer, M., 176
Michaels, S., 149
Michaelsen, L. K., 279
Microsoft, 53, 174
Miehé, L., 160, 163, 176–177, 180, 184, 186
Milanov, H., 249
Miles, M. B., 74, 337
Miller, C. D., 160, 163, 171–173, 186
Miller, D. L., 202, 212
Miller, S. R., 316
Millington, A. I., 309, 311, 313
Mills, A., 3
Miner. A., 138
Minssen, T., 173
Mirc, N., 65–67, 85
Miron-Spektor, E., 39, 46
Mirror effect, 71
Mishra, A., 2–3
Mistrust, 309–311, 313, 333
Mitchell, J. R., 170
Mitchell, W., 157, 159–161, 165, 184, 186, 202–204, 315–316
Mitsuhashi, H., 5, 277
MngProjects, 336, 338, 340
Mobilization of social technologies, 279–280
Mode choice framework, 157, 178, 181
Model, J., 48
Modrego, A., 226
Modularity, 155, 159
Moedas, C., 248
Mohr, A., 315
Mohr, J., 93
Molinsky, A. L., 35
Monitoring, 94, 97, 99, 130–131, 133–134, 136, 139, 147, 149, 262, 276, 312
Montgomery, C. A., 326

Montoro-Sanchez, A., 225–246
Mooi, H., 2–3
Moon, H., 50
Moore, J. F., 158, 177
Moorefields Eye Hospital NHS Foundation Trust, 174
Moral and pragmatic legitimacy, 1, 4, 10–11, 19, 25–26, 28
Moral legitimacy, 6–7, 10, 13–19, 21, 23, 25–28
Moran. P., 130
Mora–Valentin, E.–M., 225–246
Mordida (Mexico), 93, 98
Morgan, R. M., 132
Morreale, A., 204
Morrison, A. J., 312
Mothe, C., 332–334, 338–339, 345, 347
Mouritsen, J., 275–304
Mowery, D. C., 211, 226, 272
MPA, see Multipartner alliance
Mu, J., 227, 228
Muller, E., 229, 231
Müller-Seitz, G., 192, 247–274
Multimarket contact (MMC) theory and R&D collaboration, 204–206
Multipartner alliance (MPA), 1–14, 16, 18–28
Multipartner innovation mode choice, framework for incumbent firms, 178–181
Multipartner innovation mode choice, framework for new ventures, 181–184
Multipartner innovation, 155–157, 159–164, 167–168, 171, 173, 177–178, 181, 183–188
Murmann, J. P., 205–206
Murnighan, J. K., 105, 278
Murray, F., 159, 161, 169, 175, 184, 186
Mustar. P., 170

Muthusamy, S. K., 259–260
Mutual identification, 91–94, 96, 99, 116
Myers. M. B., 140
Myrtle, P. B., 278, 282, 301

N

Nagle, F., 173, 175–176, 180
Nahapiet, J., 277
Nalebuff, B. J., 64–65
Nambisan, S., 157, 159, 161, 165, 170, 174, 186
Nandan, J., 178
Nandhakumar, J., 163, 171
Narus, J. A., 132, 332, 347
National cultural distance, 104–105, 109, 111, 118
National cultural distance, measure, 104–105
National Strategic Consortia for Technical Research (CENIT), 335, 342
Neale, M. A., 60
Negotiation routines, 48–50
Nelson, R. R., 272, 314
Neo-institutionalism, 116
Nerkar, A., 348
Nested identities, 34, 47–48
Neter, J., 212
Network centralization, 259, 262
Network governance, 247, 250, 257–259, 264, 266
Network identity, 278
Network models and governance forms, 257–259
Network models for open innovation, 257–259
Network structure, 261–264
Neudert, P. K., 155–199
Nevens, M. T., 165
New ventures, 155–158, 160–174, 176–183, 185–188

Newburry, W., 309, 311, 313
Newell, S., 254
Ng, W. K. B., 159
Ngo, H.–Y., 129–154, 315
Nicholson, S., 204
Nickerson, J. A. 36, 40, 133
Nielsen, B. B., 251
Nieto, M. J., 249, 306
Nigro, G. L., 204
Nobeoka, K., 254, 259, 262, 278, 349
Nohlen, H. U., 48
Nohria, N., 202, 276
Nonaka, I., 229
Nonnemaker, L., 211
Noorderhaven, N. G., 115, 132, 165–166, 316
Nooteboom, B., 130, 132, 135, 148, 254
Nord, W. R., 31
Nordgren, L. F., 48
North, D. C., 124
North, D. C., 96–97
Northcraft, G. B., 49
Northern Trouts Co., 340
Norton, D. P., 53
Novartis AG., 174
Novartis Biome, 163, 174
Nti, K. O., 333, 349
Nunnally, J., 103, 107
Nutrition subproject, 343
Nyanaponika, T., 43

O

O' Connor, G., 306–307
O'Keeffe, K., 156
O'Reilly III, C., 103
Ocasio, W., 50
Ocean Protocol Foundation, 172
Oerlemans, L. A., 306
Oetzel, J., 104
Oh, C. H., 104

Oh, W. Y., 36
Oliver, A. L., 247–274
Oliver, C., 4, 94, 122
Olk, P. M., 330–333, 345, 350
Olsen, C. P., 37, 52, 331
Open innovation and governance forms and contexts, 257–259
Open innovation and network models, 257–259
Open innovation, 250–254
Openness to alternatives, 41–52
Opportunism of partners, 3, 75, 78–81, 84, 115, 131–133, 202, 217, 330, 333
Opportunism, internal and external, 78–70
Oppositional relationships, 69–70
OptoNet Photonics Network Thuringia, 170
Orchestration modes of multipartner innovation, 184–185, 187
Organ, D. W., 102
Organizational economics, 131, 149
Organizational institutional difference, measure 103
Organizational institutional differences and alliance performance, 95–96
Organizational institutional differences and trust, 95–96
Organizational institutional differences, 91–92, 94–96, 102–103, 108–110, 114–116, 119
Oriani, R., 316
Ortiz-de-Urbina-Criado, M., 225–246
Osborn, R. N., 105
Oskam, I., 157, 159
Oswald, L. R., 69
Ouchi, W. G., 133
Oughton, C., 205

Outgoing spillovers, 229, 231
Overby, M. L., 332, 334
Overholm, H., 174
Over–identification, 116
Overton, T. S., 101
Owen-Smith, J., 249, 253–254
Oxford, 261
Oxley, J. E., 34, 52, 133, 191, 204, 211, 226, 332–333, 339

P

Pache, A-C., 48
Padula, G., 204
Pan, X., 67
Pandian, R. J., 206
Panico, C., 253
Panourgias, N., 163, 171
Paquin, R. L., 2, 6, 17
Paradoxes in interfirm networks, 299–300
Paradoxes, 39, 43, 46, 48, 54, 63, 65–69, 81–82, 119, 253, 275, 277, 290
Parasuraman, A., 266
Paredes, R., 98
Paredes-Frigolett, H., 250
Parhankangas, A., 316
Park, S. H., 53, 95–96, 104, 202–203, 345
Parkhe, A., 39, 102, 105–106, 132–133, 141, 156, 249, 253, 262, 307, 309–311, 313
Parley for the Oceans, 183
Parmigiani, A., 202
Partner asymmetry, 201, 206–207, 209–210, 217
Partner dependence, measure, 105
Partner selection, 201–202, 205, 207, 212, 216–218, 307, 322
Paruchuri, S., 264
Patch, 183
Patrick, A. J., 188

Patzelt, H., 130, 140
Paulus, P. B., 42
Pauwels, C., 159, 168, 175
paybox Bank AG, 183
Pearce, R. J., 138, 140
Pelled L. H., 277–278, 300
Pellegrin-Boucher, E., 67
Peng G., 227–228
Peng, M. W., 96
Penta [bank], 177
Pentland, B. T., 337
Pereira, N. S., 204
Pérez, T., 175
Pérez–Santana, P., 156
Performance risk, 50
Perkmann, M., 254–255
Perreault, W. D. Jr., 132, 138, 140
Perrone, V., 92–94, 96, 98–99, 104, 116, 137
Perrons, R. K., 259
Persson, S. G., 2, 7
Peters, L., 278
Pettigrew, A. M., 337
Pfarrer, M. D., 253
Pfeffer, J., 5
Phan, P. H., 207, 217
Phelps, C. C., 227, 258–259, 262, 264
Phene, A., 204
Phillips, W., 27
Photonics Austria, 170
Phyllis, A. S., 102
Physical proximity, 242
Piat, G., 156
Piccaluga A., 309, 323
Pierce, C. A., 315, 318
Piezunka, H., 157, 172, 176
Pitelis, C., 159
Pituto (Chile), 93, 98
Plambeck, N., 35, 42, 49
Plug and Play, 169
Podsakoff, N. P., 101–102, 137
Podsakoff, P. M., 101–102, 137

Polidoro Jr, F., 316
Poole, M. S., 66
PoooliPrint, 166
Poot, T., 252
Poppo, L., 33–61, 130, 132, 135, 140, 148
Porrini, P., 316
Porter, M. E., 169–170
Portes, A., 277
Posen, H. E., 43
Pothukuchi, V., 104
Powell, T. C., 37, 52
Powell, W. W., 4, 248–249, 253–255, 264, 266
Power asymmetry, 16, 23
Power, D. J., 101
Pradies, C., 35, 38–39, 42, 46–47, 51
Pragmatic legitimacy, 1, 4–7, 10–11, 13–28
Prats, M. J., 175
Pratt, M. G., 33, 35, 38–40, 42, 46–47, 50–53, 281
Prencipe, A., 159
Pretorius, M. W., 306
Prexl, K.-M., 163, 175
Price, K. H., 278, 282, 301
Prigogine, I., 300
Prior ties, 210, 212, 215–217
Private benefits, 202, 208
Private benefits, 67
Problem solving, 33–34, 38–40, 43–44, 46, 51, 131, 139–140
Propensity to cooperate, 233, 235–236
Property rights, 97, 118
Provan, K. G., 5–6, 249, 255, 258, 266
Provance, M., 159
Prügl, R., 163, 175
Psychological safety, 34, 36, 41, 48–50, 53, 119
Public spillovers, 238, 242

Puranam, P., 130, 148–149, 163, 175, 180
Purdy, J. M., 159, 161, 169–170, 185
Pure knowledge flows, 229
Putnam, L. L., 39
Pyka, A., 250

Q

Qualls, W. J., 160–161, 166, 186, 317
Quelin, B. V., 332–334, 338–339, 345, 347
Quinn, J. B., 264

R

R&D alliance formation, 208–212, 215–216, 218
R&D alliances and knowledge flows, 228–232
R&D alliances, knowledge flows effects on, 229–232
R&D collaboration and multimarket contact (MMC) theory, 204–206
R&D consortia, 329–334, 336, 344–350
R&D cooperation, 226–227, 230–231, 233, 236, 242–243
R&D intensity, 208, 210, 227
R&D partnerships, 72, 217, 231, 242
R&D spillovers, 227–228
Rabeau, Y., 159
Radnejad, A. B., 180, 186
Radziwon, A., 173
Ragin, C. C., 323, 327
Ragozzino, R., 315
Rahman, N., 217
Rajagopalan, N., 211, 309–310, 313

Rajala, A., 64, 67
Ralston, D. A., 249
Randhawa, K., 248–250
Ranft, A. L., 205–206
Rasinski, K., 101
Ravasi, D., 156
Raza-Ullah, T., 64–68, 85
Ready Meals subproject, 335
Reagans, R., 258, 261
Reciprocity, 247, 258–260, 262–263, 265, 330–332, 347–348, 350
Reepmeyer, G., 248
Rees, L., 33, 35, 38–40, 42–43, 45–46, 52–53
Reeves, M., 177, 180
Reflection and negotiation routines, 48–50
Reger, R. K., 47
Regibeau, P., 251
Reguart, C. C., 95
Regulatory institutional difference, measure, 104
Regulatory institutional differences and alliance performance, 96–100
Regulatory institutional differences and trust, 96–100
Regulatory institutional differences, 91–93, 95–96, 98, 100, 104, 108–110, 112, 114–115, 118
Reineke, P., 157, 172, 176
Reingen, P. H., 49
Reinmoeller, P., 156
Reischauer, G., 157, 176
Relational governance, 33–34, 36, 350
Relational mechanisms, 34–38, 51–53, 66–68, 71, 74, 79, 84–85
Relational risk, 332
Relationship duration, measure, 105

Relationships between external and internal coopetition, 68–69, 75

Renault-Nissan alliance, 53

Rerup, C., 48

Resource sharing, 64, 71, 75–78, 80, 84, 86

Reuer, J. J., 36, 59, 152, 204–206, 217, 219, 277, 315, 330

Ribeiro-Soriano, D., 232

Riccio, E. L., 315

Richards, M., 316

Richardson, G. B., 254

Richman, B. D., 36

Rihoux, B., 327

Rindova, V. P., 43, 45–46

Ring, P. S. 10, 37, 52, 96, 131, 153, 249, 330–333, 350

Rips, L. J., 101

Risk aversion, 278

Risk sharing, 2, 211, 227

Risk taking network, 294

Ritala, P., 156, 159, 174, 248, 255

Rivera-Santos, M., 202

Roath, A. S., 132

Robba, S., 204

Roberston, M., 254

Roberts, P. W., 43

Robins, J., 129–154

Robinson, R. B., 101

Rodan, S., 261

Rodriguez, D., 210

Roehrich, J. K., 1–32

Roelofsen, A., 250

Rogers, E. M., 179, 182

Rogers, K. M., 33–61

Rohrbeck, R., 174, 177

Roijakkers, N., 130, 132, 156–157, 184

Roland Ortt, J., 157, 177

Role of asymmetry, 206–208

Roma, P., 204

Romero–Martínez, A. M., 232, 242

Rose, J. A., 281

Rosenberger, J. D., 182

Rosenkopf, L., 204

Roth, K., 3, 92, 312

Rothaermel, F. T., 106, 182, 248, 316

Rothman, N. B., 33, 35, 38–40, 42–46, 49, 52–53

Rothstein, H., 318

Rotteveel, M., 48

Roundy, P. T., 169

Rouse, E. D., 50

Roussel, B., 156

Rowan, B., 4

Rowley, T. J., 277

Roy, J. P., 94

Ruef, M., 4

Rugelsjoen, B., 53

Ruigrok, W., 10, 334, 349

Rules of the game, 96

Russo, M. V., 345

Rutjens, B., 48

Rutte, C. G., 318

Ryan Charleton, T., 65

Ryan, R. M., 43

Ryu, W., 204–205

S

S&P Global, 183

Saebi, T., 160, 350

Safioleas, S. P., 117

Sahay, A., 104, 115

Sahlin-Andersson, K., 122

Sakano, T., 138–139

Sako, M., 94, 104

Salancik, G. R., 93, 98

Saldaña, J., 74

Salerno, M. S., 159

Salk, J. E., 92, 106, 117

Salomon, R. M., 104, 133

Salter, A., 248–249, 251–253, 255, 262–264

Salvato, C., 48
Samant, S., 202
Sammarra, A., 249, 261
Sampson, R. C., 204, 314, 316,
    330, 332–334, 339, 347
Samsung Electronics, 177–178
Samsung, 68
Sanchez–Burks, J., 43, 45
Santamaría, L., 249, 306
Santoro, M. D., 306–307, 309–310,
    312–314
Santos, J. N., 66
Sapienza, H. J., 137, 277
Sarkar, M. B., 133, 138–139, 350
Savino, T., 259
Saxton, T., 105, 133–134, 141
Scarbrough, H., 163, 171
Schendel, D., 309, 310, 322
Schepker, D. J., 36
Schilke, O., 306, 315
Schilling, M. A., 227, 258–259, 262
Schlenzig, T., 194
Schloemer, H., 33–61
Schmidt, F. L. 314
Schmidt, T., 243
Schneider, I. K., 48
Schöberl, S., 248, 263
Schoenecker, T. S., 206
Schoonhoven, C. B., 2
Schoorman, F. D., 94, 132
Schreiner, M., 36–37
Schulte, M., 167, 186
Schumpeter, J. A., 314
Schüssler, E., 157, 176, 192, 249
Schwarz, N., 45
Schweiger, B., 66
Schweiger, D. M., 312
Schwens, C., 316
Science and technology parks, 159,
    227
Scott, J. T., 205
Scott, W. R., 4, 92, 97, 254
Search behaviors, 43–45, 49

Secchi, E., 248
Sedita, S. R., 249
Self–enforcing safeguards, 276
Selviaridis, K., 10
Selznick, P., 95–96
SEMATECH, 254
Semiotic square, 69–70
Semrau, T., 202
Sengul, M., 48
Seppänen, M., 161, 163, 173
Seran, T., 67
Serrano–Bedia, A. M., 230, 235,
    238
Shah, S. K., 7
Shan, W., 277
Shapiro, C., 165
Shared values, 275–276, 278–279,
    281, 300
Sharing of resources, 64, 66–67,
    71, 75–81, 84, 86
Sharma, S., 178
Shenkar, O., 152, 309, 311, 313
Shepherd, D. A., 130, 140
Sheremata, W. A., 166
Shetler, J. C., 253–254
Shi, Y., 160
Shin, S. R., 170
Shipilov, A., 157–159, 171, 175–
    176, 180–181, 186–187, 208,
    217
Sieg, J. H., 176, 180
Siegel, D. S., 39, 159, 170
Signification, 279, 281–282, 288,
    293, 296, 298–299
Signify, 165
Signori, P., 69
Silverman, B. S., 99, 116, 121, 191,
    202–203, 211, 226
Similarity, contracting, and
    cooperation, 133–134
Simonen, J., 230
Simonin, B. L., 95, 105, 334
Simpson, A. V., 48

Simpson, H., 243
Sincoff, J., 42
Sine, W. D., 5–6
Singh, H., 2–3, 34, 36, 40, 51–52, 96, 105, 130, 141, 156, 204, 206, 276–278, 296, 330, 332, 338, 350
Singh, K., 202–203
Sinolumina Technology Ltd., Shenzhen, 170
Siota, J., 175
Sirmon, D. G., 96, 118
Size diversity and firm performance, 310–311
Size diversity, 307–312, 315, 318–320, 322
Skarmeas, D., 93, 132
Slotegraaf, R. J., 67
Smeds, R., 316
Smith, W. K., 50, 66
Smith–Doerr, L., 253, 255, 264, 266
Snijders, T. A., 249
Snow, C. C., 69
Snyder, C. M., 202
Social controls, 276
Social dilemma in R&D consortia, 332–334
Social technology as process, 296–299
Social technology mobilization and structuration theory, 279–280
Social technology of networks, 277–279
Solarino, A. M., 305–328
Solarisbank, 163, 177–178
Song, J., 65, 68
Song, M., 156, 187
Sopra Steria Scale up, 175–176
Sorbom, D., 107
Sorenson, O., 209, 212
Sources of tensions, 75–79
Southern Trouts Co., 340

Spanish National Innovation Plan, 335
Sparks, J., 202
Spekman, R., 93
Spieth, P., 248
Spigel, B., 159, 161, 170, 186, 188
Spillover measures, 233
Spithoven, A., 264
Squarespace, 158
Squire, B., 1–32
Srinivasan, R., 132, 203
Srivastava, M. K., 64, 69, 306
Stadtler, L., 39, 47–48, 52
Stam, W., 102
Standard wars, 165
Standard-based innovation ecosystems, 171–172, 179, 182, 186
Standard-developing organizations (SDO), 165
Standardization alliance networks, 159, 165–166, 171, 179, 182, 186
Standard-setting organizations (SSO), 165, 171
Stango, V., 165
Star Alliance, 158, 161, 167
Startup Autobahn, 163, 175
Startup-led innovation ecosystems, 172, 177–178, 181, 183, 187
Statistical Office of the European Union (Eurostat), 227, 232
Steen, J., 249
Steenkamp, J. B. E. M., 37, 104, 115
Stengers, I., 300
Stephan, J., 205–206
Stockholm syndrome, 82
Stone, A., 98
Strauss, A., 10, 284
Structural rigidity, 287
Structuration theory, 277, 279–281
Stuart, T. E., 209, 212

Stubner, S., 187
Studer Andersson, T., 157, 175–176, 181, 186
Su, K. H., 202, 205
Su, P., 318
Subramani, M. R., 141
Subramaniam, M., 309, 311, 313
Substitution effect, 71, 131, 148
Suchman, M. C., 2–6
Suddaby, R., 4–6, 25–26, 122
Summe, G. L., 165
Sun, Y., 208
Supplier dependence, measure, 141
Supplier spillovers, 238
Suprapto, M., 2–3
Sutcliffe, K., 45
Sutton, R. I., 314
Swan, J., 254
Swann, P., 262
Sydow, J., 66, 158, 167, 192, 249, 253–255, 260, 266, 280
Sytch, M., 105
Szulanski, G., 115

T

Takenouchi. H., 138–139
Takeuchi, H., 229
Tallman, S. B., 34, 40, 204, 248
Tam, C. M., 249
Tanguy, C., 178
Tao, Q. T., 306–307, 309–310, 312–313
Taubeneder, R., 1–32
Tavassoli, S., 160
Taylor, A., 179, 182
Taylor, M., 179, 182
Teams, separation of, 79–80
Technological diversity and firm performance, 313–314
Technological diversity, 264, 306, 311–314, 318, 320–322

Technological Innovation Panel (PITEC), 232–235
Technological Innovation Survey, 225, 227
Techstars, 161, 175
Teece, D. J., 165, 180, 287
Tell, F., 248
Teng, B., 2–3, 34, 52, 64–65, 130, 132, 135, 148, 260, 277–278, 287, 330–333, 347–348
Tensions, 63–70, 74–76, 80, 82, 84–86
Ter Wal, A. L. J., 159
Terry, D. J., 55
Tesch, R., 74
Tether, B., 227
Texas Instruments, 165
Thai Airways, 167
Thai Smiles, 167
The Biscuits Co., 336, 338, 340, 345
Thelisson, A. S., 64
Theodoraki, C., 170
Third-party-led innovation ecosystems, 174–176, 181,183, 186
Thomas, L. D. W., 159, 161, 170, 186
Thomas, R. E., 159–161, 165, 184, 186
Thompson, J. B., 279
Thompson, T. A., 159, 161, 169–170, 185
Thomson, K., 205
Thorgren, S., 130, 132, 330, 332–333, 348
Thrane, S., 275–304
Tidd, J., 156
Tidström, A., 64, 66–67
Tiffin, S., 92, 95
Tilley, A., 53
Tindale, S. R., 57
Tjemkes, B., 69

Toh, P. K., 160, 163, 171–172, 186
Tolbert, P. S., 4–5, 25
Tomkins, C., 276
Tomorrow [bank], 177
Tortoriello, M., 261
Torvik, V. I., 208
Tourangeau, R., 101
Toyoki, S., 4
Tracey, P., 31
Transaction costs, 115, 132–133, 277
Truchot, P., 156
Trust and alliance performance, 95–100
Trust and organizational institutional differences, 95–96
Trust and regulatory institutional differences, 96–100
Trust, 7–8, 24, 33–34, 36–37, 91–95, 115–119, 129–131, 147–149, 230, 254, 259–263, 275–280, 290–292, 296, 300, 331, 337
Trust, contracting, and cooperation, 131–133
Trust, contracting, similarity, and cooperative behavior, 134–135
Trust, organizational institutional differences, and alliance performance, 95–96
Trust, regulatory institutional differences, and alliance performance, 96–100
Tsai, W., 67, 202, 205, 277, 280, 346
Tsang, E. W. K., 280, 299
Tucci, C. L., 248, 255
Tung, R. L., 312–313
Turkulainen, V., 2
Tushman, M. L., 50, 163, 173, 175–176, 180, 212
Tuya, 165
Tyler, T. R., 102, 122

U

Ubachs, M., 69
Ulph, D., 229, 231, 236
Un, C. A., 232
Ungson, G. R., 53, 95–96, 202–203
United, 167
Upson, J. W., 205–206
Usher, R., 45
Uttal, B., 165
Uzzi, B., 116

V

Valdés–Llaneza, A., 316, 333, 345, 347
Value capture by partners, 204
Van de Ven, A. H., 10, 37, 52, 66, 96
Van de Vrande, V., 266
Van den Bosch, F. A. J., 130, 134–135, 315
van der Pligt, J., 48
van der Valk, W., 10
Van der Zwart, A., 97
van Harreveld, F., 48
Van Helleputte, J., 156–157, 184
Van Hove, J., 159, 168, 175
van Looy, B., 34, 38, 51, 130, 132, 134, 148–149, 276, 287, 336–337, 350
Van Mierlo, H., 318
Van Tulder, R., 97
Van Wassenhove, L. N., 39, 47–48, 52
van Witteloostuijn, A., 137
Vangen, S., 249, 262
Vanhaverbeke, W., 156–157, 165–166, 184, 249, 252, 266–268
Vanneste, B. S., 130, 148–149
Vanyushyn, V., 64, 68
Varadarajan, R. P., 205–206
Vargas, L. M., 227
Varian, H. R., 165

Varman, R., 94, 104, 115
Vassolo, R. S., 205, 217–218, 316
Vega-Jurado, J., 232
Veit, P., 187
Venkatraman, N., 141
Ventresca, M. J., 159, 161, 169–170, 185
Verbeke, A., 149
Vermeulen, F., 217
Vermunt, J. K., 318
Verspagen, B., 228–230
Vertical and horizontal relationship, 1, 9
Vertical flows, 229
Veugelers, R., 227, 229–231, 235–236, 238, 243
Visa, 177, 178
Visscher, K., 158–159, 180, 183
Vlaar, P. W. L., 130, 134–135
Vogus, T. J., 33, 35, 38–40, 42, 45–46, 52–53
Volberda, H. W., 130, 134–135, 315
von Hippel, E., 156, 188, 248, 256
von Krogh, G., 176, 180
Vonortas, N. S., 100, 117, 202, 205, 218
Vörös, A., 249
Vredenburg, H., 180, 186

W

Waldman, D. A., 39
Walker, D., 3
Walker, G., 277
Wallin, M. W., 176, 180
Walsh, K., 255
Wang, C., 315
Wang, L., 216, 218
Wang, R. D., 173
Wareham, J., 176
Waschto, A., 178
Wasserman, S., 249–250
Wasserman, W., 212

Wassmer, U., 314
WasteMng Co., 336, 338, 340
Watson, W. E., 279
Weber, J. M., 105
Weber, K., 35, 42, 49
Weber, L., 34
Weber, M., 280
Weiblen, T., 176
Weick, K., 45
Weiss, J., 100
Wen, J., 160–161, 166, 186
Wen, W., 176
West, J., 248–249, 252, 267–268
West, S. G., 107, 114
Whetten, D. A., 47
Whinston, M. D., 205
Whitbred, R., 3, 6
White, D. R., 249, 253–254
White, M. A., 259–260
White, S., 141
White-label accelerators, 175
Whitney, D. J., 102
Whittington, K. B., 254
Wicki, B., 334, 349
Wiersema, M., 276–278
Wiesenfeld, B. M., 44
Wilden, R., 248–250
Wilhelm, M., 66
Wiliamson, O., 130–131, 133, 149
Wilkins, A. L., 339
Williams, M. D., 159
Williamson, O. E., 36, 52, 115
Wincent, J., 130, 132, 330, 332–333, 348
Windeler, A., 254, 260, 280
Winter, S. G., 314, 334, 347
Wix, 158
Wohlgezogen, F., 93
Woiceshyn, J., 180, 186
Wolfe, D., 50
Woodman, R. W., 50
World Trade Organization, 167

Wright, M., 159, 161, 168, 170, 175, 186
Wu, Z., 104
Wu. T., 130
Wuyts, S., 306, 314

X

Xie, X. M., 249
Xin, K. R., 277–278, 300
Xue, J., 249, 255, 262

Y

Y Combinator, 161, 168
Yami, S., 87
Yan, A., 103
Yan, Y., 105
Yang, C. C., 205
Yang, H., 42, 202, 208
Yang, S., 249
Yao, Y., 68
Yasuda, H., 306–307
Yasumoto, J. Y., 277
Yeheskel, O., 309, 311, 313
Yin, R. K., 73, 280, 284, 335, 337
Yli-Renko, H., 137, 277
Youndt, M. A., 309, 311, 313
Young, C., 333, 345
Young-Ybarra, C., 276–278
Yu, A. Z., 208
Yu, T., 217
Yuan, F., 50

Z

Zaheer, A., 92–94, 96, 98–99, 104, 116, 120, 137, 202, 208, 249
Zajac, E. J. 37, 52, 202, 216, 218, 331
Zan, A., 68
Zander, A., 50
Zang, I., 229, 231
Zeira, Y., 309, 311, 313

Zeithaml, V., 266
Zeitz, G. J., 2, 4
Zelditch, M., 5
Zeng, D., 160–161, 166, 186
Zeng, L., 211, 216
Zeng, M., 3, 6, 287, 330, 332, 334, 347–348
Zeng, S. X., 249
Zeng, Z., 103
Zenger T. R., 34, 36, 40, 52, 130, 135, 140, 148
Zhang, C., 132
Zhelyazkov, P. I., 93, 209, 212
Zheng, J., 8
Zheng, Y., 202, 208
Zhou, D., 203
Zhou, K. Z., 36, 130, 132
Zhu, F., 187
Zhu, H., 316
Zietsma, C., 38
Zimmerman, M. A., 2, 4
Zobel, A.-K., 159
Zollo, M., 206, 277, 330, 334, 347
Zott, C., 160, 187
Zucker, L. G., 4–5, 25, 259

Printed in the United States
by Baker & Taylor Publisher Services